Human Nature and Organization Theory

NEW HORIZONS IN MANAGEMENT

Series Editor: Cary L. Cooper, *BUPA Professor of Organizational Psychology and Health, Manchester School of Management, University of Manchester Institute of Science and Technology (UMIST), UK*

This important series makes a significant contribution to the development of management thought. This field has expanded dramatically in recent years and the series provides an invaluable forum for the publication of high quality work in management science, human resource management, organizational behaviour, marketing, management information systems, operations management, business ethics, strategic management and international management.

The main emphasis of the series is on the development and application of new original ideas. International in its approach, it will include some of the best theoretical and empirical work from both well-established researchers and the new generation of scholars.

Titles in the series include:

Human Nature and Organization Theory

On the Economic Approach to Institutional Organization

Sigmund Wagner-Tsukamoto

Lecturer in Management and Organization Studies, University of Leicester, UK

NEW HORIZONS IN MANAGEMENT

Edward Elgar
Cheltenham, UK • Northampton, MA, USA

#49903252

Published by
Edward Elgar Publishing Limited
Glensanda House
Montpellier Parade
Cheltenham
Glos GL50 1UA
UK

Edward Elgar Publishing, Inc.
136 West Street
Suite 202
Northampton
Massachusetts 01060
USA

A catalogue record for this book
is available from the British Library

Library of Congress Cataloguing in Publication Data

Wagner-Tsukamoto, Sigmund
    Human nature and organization theory : on the economic approach to institutional organization / by Sigmund Wagner-Tsukamoto.
        p. cm.—(New horizons in management series)
    Includes bibliographical references and index.
    1. Organizational sociology. 2. Organizational behavior. 3. Employee motivation.
    4. Psychology, Industrial. 5. Human behavior. I. Title. II. Series.

HM786 W34 2003
302.3'5—dc21
                                                                    2002072181
ISBN 1 84064 714 0

Typeset by Cambrian Typesetters, Frimley, Surrey
Printed and bound in Great Britain by MPG Books Ltd, Bodmin, Cornwall

To the memory of my dad, Onkel Hans, Theodora Cooper and Andreas

Contents

Figures

Acknowledgments

This book is the revised outcome of a doctoral dissertation on the image of human nature in organization theory, which was submitted to the department of management studies and economics at the Catholic University of Eichstaett in Ingolstadt in June 2000. This book greatly benefited from the insight of my supervisor Karl Homann. His methodically grounded understanding of the economic approach is visible throughout. I am indebted to much direct and indirect support from colleagues and students at the University of Leicester, especially the Management Centre and the Language Centre. Special thanks to Peter Jackson and Keith Taylor. Also, many thanks to various anonymous reviewers. For enduring support and understanding, very special thanks to my family and friends. To Micki and Moritz, love and ultimate thanks.

Introduction

Human Nature and Organization Theory examines accusations that organizational economics promotes an empirically incorrect and morally questionable image of human nature. The book is grounded in a pluralistic understanding of scientific research. It attests to the relevance and usefulness of different research programs in the social sciences but questions, on methodological grounds, that social sciences were pitted against each other when it comes to the portrayal of human nature.

Conventional wisdom is that economics is an amoral and dehumanized science because, so it is claimed, of an empirically incorrect and morally questionable image of human nature. Similar accusations have been leveled against organizational economics, which the book focuses on. Accusations are brought forward on psychological, sociological and moral–behavioral grounds, early on by the human relations school and behavioral economics and more recently by post-modern organization theory, critical management theory, feminine theory or anti-organization theory. The target is 'economic man': the 'rational', self-interested maximizer of own gain (homo economicus). The book suggests that for assessing the question of human nature in organization theory (and possibly in social science research in general) issues of method and approach have to be clarified first. Here, significant differences can be expected among organizational economics, organization psychology and organization sociology. Such clarifications appear promising for constructively informing a debate of the image of human nature in organization research, moving it beyond uncritical common sense argumentation and conventional wisdom. Key questions addressed in the book are:

- Does organizational economics theorize about human nature and aim at intervention with the 'human condition' in order to solve organizational problems?
- In what respects does organizational economics methodically and theoretically abstract from human nature?
- How far does organizational economics portray human nature when it invokes the model of economic man?
- How far is criticism of the model of economic man as an unrealistic and morally questionable image of human nature justified?

- Should the image of human nature of organizational economics be assessed in a different way than critiquing the model of economic man in behavioral terms?
- In examining theoretical and practical outcomes, can a morally favorable image of human nature be suggested for organizational economics, possibly even rivaling the ones of other social sciences?

The book contends that (organizational) economics applies the model of economic man as a matter of method, but not as an empirical, positive or normative statement about human nature. As later chapters detail, the model of economic man may merely be part of economics' 'mind apparatus', as Keynes hinted, or a 'heuristic apparatus' in the more technical language of Lakatos' and Popper's philosophy of science (for literature references, see Chapters 1 and 2). In terms of a simple analogy, the methodical purpose and role of the model of economic man in economics can be compared to the instrumental role of the 'unrealistic' crash dummy in the 'dismal' accident simulation setting of the car crash test.

The book argues that economics' image of human nature is better deduced from the theoretical and practical outcomes of economic analysis than from the model of economic man as such. Specifically, it has to be examined how and with what success organizational economics, equipped with the analytical tool 'economic man', theoretically analyzes organizational behavior as capital contribution–distribution interactions that are governed by incentive structures. The key thesis here is that the model of economic man enables the generation of socially desirable outcomes, even so when pluralistic interaction contexts are encountered.

The book develops its arguments and theses by focusing on three organization theories that set the agenda for much organizational research in the 20th century: the theories of Frederick W. Taylor, Herbert A. Simon and Oliver E. Williamson. These theories were chosen because of (i) their high originality; (ii) their emergence in different periods of the same socio-economic environment (here, the USA), which is important for assessing the timeliness of organization structures in relation to environmental change; (iii) their authors' apparent interest in analyzing economic aspects of institutional organization; and (iv) their authors' calls that human nature should be portrayed in empirically 'correct', behavioral terms. The latter point is challenged by the key thesis of this book – that the portrayal of human nature in empirical–behavioral and moral–behavioral terms reflects a methodological self-misunderstanding in organizational economics. The book argues that an attempted holistic, behavioral portrayal of human nature undermines the conceptual consistency and, more importantly, the practical effectiveness of organizational economics. The book develops this argument by reconstructing and critiquing the organization theories of Taylor, Simon and Williamson in non-behavioral, institutional economic terms. For the purpose of this reconstruction, methodical, heuristic concepts of economics were distinguished from theoretical–(practical) ones. On a notational note: In this book, the notions of the 'theoretical–practical' or 'theoretical–(practical)' are used to refer to an explicit or implicit design orientation of positive, theoretical analysis, that is an orientation towards practical intervention and social engineering. Chapters 1, 2 and 8 have more details on this issue. The book proceeds as follows.

Chapter 1 distinguishes research heuristics from theoretical–(practical) concepts of organization research. It spells out that research problems of behavioral organization research and organizational economics and their respective strategies for theory-building and practical intervention fundamentally differ. The rationale of an economic reconstruction and critique of the image of human nature of organization theory is outlined.

Chapter 2 details methodical and theoretical–(practical) concepts of organizational economics, connecting to institutional economics and constitutional economics. The chapter specifies that organizational economics conceptualizes organizational behavior as interactions over capital utilization and organization structures as incentive structures. It suggests that the model of economic man and the idea of the dilemma structure are research heuristics that methodically instruct organizational economics.

Chapter 3 discusses heuristic and theoretical–(practical) concepts of behavioral organization research. It argues that in a heuristic perspective, behavioral organization theory is as little concerned with the 'correct', holistic empirical–behavioral or moral–behavioral portrayal of human nature as economics. In addition, it argues that only in theoretical and practical perspectives, behavioral sciences can – selectively – aim at human nature. The practical effectiveness of behavioral intervention is questioned, especially for 'modern', pluralistic interactions' contexts.

Chapter 4 traces key elements of the institutional economic approach in Taylor's, Simon's and Williamson's organization theories. It examines whether and, if so, why they heuristically grounded the theoretical analysis of and practical intervention with incentive structures in the idea of dilemmatic social conflict, as, for example, illustrated by the prisoner's dilemma. Their suggestions on how to resolve conflict are analyzed.

Chapter 5 critiques the relevance of a behavioral approach to skills management, as favored, in different degrees, by Taylor, Simon and Williamson. The chapter proposes that organizational economics analyzes skills management as a capital utilization problem that is handled through incentives management.

Chapter 6 details that Taylor, Simon and Williamson applied the model of economic man but that its heuristic nature and purpose was not fully understood. In different degrees, they misinterpreted the model of economic man in empirical–behavioral and moral–behavioral terms. The chapter outlines conceptual and methodical inconsistencies and practical intervention problems that resulted.

Chapter 7 relates differences among Taylor's, Simon's and Williamson's organization theories to economic change in the US firm's environment in the 20th century. Key ideas of an institutional economic, historic approach to organizational change and environmental change are outlined. Changes in environmental, 'external' incentive structures and capital contingencies are related to the way Taylor, Simon and Williamson analyzed and modeled 'internal' incentive structures and capital utilization in the firm. The chapter questions that conceptual differences among their organization theories reflect a behavioral discovery process regarding 'true' human nature.

Chapter 8 rejects the suggestion that organizational economics entertains an immoral image of human nature. It stresses that moral qualities of economics' image of human nature should not be deduced from research heuristics such as the model of 'economic man' but from theoretical and practical outcomes that are generated by applying research heuristics. If this is taken into account, a morally favorable image of human nature can be proposed for organizational economics.

1. A question of method and approach: In search of human nature in organization research?

> The nature of man in these current economic models continues . . . to reflect the particular formulation of certain general philosophical questions posed in the past. The realism of the chosen conception of man is simply not a part of this inquiry. . . . The complex psychological issues underlying choice have recently been forcefully brought out by a number of penetrating studies dealing with consumer decisions and production activities. (Sen, 1990, pp. 28, 30)

> The naivety of modern empirical economists in this respect verges on absurdity. (Buchanan, 1991, p. 18)

From the 'beginning' of economics in the days of Adam Smith, the portrayal of 'economic man' as a self-interested, calculating maximizer of own gain has incited behavioral researchers. Over time, such disputes regarding the behavioral portrayal of human nature in economic research have not abated. The F-twist debate between Simon and Friedman is an example from the 1960s, which was preceded and followed by similar arguments (see Buchanan 1991; Sen 1990; for reviews of early debate on this issue, see Scott 1995a: 2–5; Machlup 1967). Of course, this debate reaches further than the studies of Smith. Political and social philosophers, such as Hobbes, were battered by behavioral critics for said egoistic and war-like views on human nature (for example Bramhall 1995; Clarendon 1995; Filmer 1995; Lawson 1995; for reviews, see Rogers 1995; Mintz 1962). Similarly, Kant puzzled behavioral researchers by suggesting that even devils could create a decent society (Homann 1997: 14, 1990: 13; Baurmann and Kliemt 1995: 15; Vanberg 1994: 6; Pyle 1994). In certain respects, such a behavioral critique of the image of human nature in social research can even be directed at a considerable body of Greek philosophy and the Old Testament (see Wagner-Tsukamoto 2001b; Wagner 2000a) and possibly theology, too. However, this book here generally voices caution. The present study questions that economics or behavioral sciences could portray and should portray human nature in complete, empirical–behavioral and moral–behavioral terms.

When critiquing the model of economic man as an unrealistic and immoral image of human nature, behavioral researchers suggested conceptual inconsistency in Smith's research. Apparently, Smith portrayed human nature 'holistically', in empirical–behavioral and moral–behavioral terms in the *Theory of Moral Sentiments* but not so in his study of the *Wealth of Nations*, which established the conceptual foundations of economics. Coase (1994: 95–116) rebuked the suggestion of inconsistency in Smith's writings by proposing that both the *Theory of Moral Sentiments* and the *Wealth of Nations* entertained a complete, holistic, empirical–behavioral and moral–behavioral image of human nature: 'I can find no essential difference between the views on human nature in the *Theory of Moral Sentiments* and those expressed in the *Wealth of Nations*' (Coase 1994: 111; see also Coase 1977: 313–14). Hottinger (1998: 194–5) argues in the same way. Such evaluation strategies may be questionable.

Similar to Coase, this book finds no inconsistency in Smith's writings when it comes to the portrayal of human nature but acknowledges differences regarding the portrayal of human nature in Smith's behavioral research and his economic research. The book qualifies Coase's suggestion and comparable suggestions of behavioral economists and behavioral scientists. It suggests that they overlooked that the purpose and methods of economic research differ from the ones of behavioral research and that such purpose-related, methodical differences have implications regarding how to assess the image of human nature of economics. Coase (1994: 113) touched on this issue when he stated that the *Theory of Moral Sentiments* reflected a 'study in human psychology' but the *Wealth of Nations* a 'study of the organization of economic life' (Coase 1994: 113). But he did not follow up this insight by assessing a purposeful, methodical role of the model of economic man in economic research. Simon (1997: 5), too, acknowledged that Adam Smith researched in the *Wealth of Nations* 'not the internal world of the mind, but the external world of economic production and trade' – but then also suggested that Adam Smith invoked 'fundamental psychological assumptions' (Simon 1997: 6).

The cynical and at times inflammatory exchanges between organizational economists and behavioral organization researchers compare to debates between behavioral economists and 'conventional' economists. Barney (1990) offers a good review of this conflict-laden discussion in organization research. This volume deepens and clarifies previous attempts to mediate in this debate, and it does so differently as envisaged by Barney (1990), Donaldson (1996a, 1995: Chapter 6, 1990) or Rowlinson (1997: 20–21), who do not interpret 'economic man' in a methodical perspective. The present study argues that 'economic man' does not reflect economics' image of human nature. It develops this argument by comparing the methodical and theoretical approach of organizational economics with the one of behavioral organization research. Section 1.1 details that some ideas of scientific research are beyond behavioral realism, stressing the problem-dependent, heuristic status of certain concepts in a scientific research program. (Later Chapters interpret 'economic man' as such a heuristic concept, especially Chapter 2, section 2.4.) Section 1.2 briefly introduces and compares heuristic as well as theoretical–(practical) concepts of organizational economics and of behavioral organization research. Section 1.3 develops the key theses of this book. Section 1.4 concludes the chapter.

1.1 BEYOND REALISM: PROBLEM DEPENDENCE AND RESEARCH HEURISTICS

It has been suggested that science is driven by arbitrary, phenomenological or ontological traditions or just dogma and ideology. If one subscribes to this view, the implication would be that nearly 'anything goes' as science (Feyerabend 1993: 14, 151–8, 230–1; see also Kuhn 1996: 13, 34, 96; Fuller 1993: 33–8 and similarly Dahrendorf 1973: 70). Such skepticism can be qualified if patterns and principles are identified that systematically organize 'arbitrary traditions'. The subsequent discussion focuses on Gödel's, Popper's and Lakatos' suggestions on problem dependence and heuristic problem-solving for developing this qualification. The following substantiates:

1. The principle of problem-dependent, heuristic thinking explains how sciences reduce complex reality. The idea of the research heuristic is here of high importance. It suggests that a pre-empirical, sub-theoretical and quasi-tautological problem formulation and problem-solving apparatus instructs complexity reduction and selectively focuses the attention of the scientist.
2. For understanding the nature and purpose of different sciences, such as economics, sociology or psychology, their different heuristic approaches have to be clarified first (but not claimed differences regarding empirical, ontologically demarcated subject matter).
3. On the grounds of a heuristic understanding of scientific research, the analytical approach of economics, sociology or psychology can be imperialistically applied to empirical subject matter that traditionally has been claimed and researched by a certain discipline only.

Problem Dependence and the Heuristic Grounding of Scientific Research

Popper (1978: 129) argued that scientists who tried to understand reality as such are quickly lost. His discussion of the possibly infinite complexity of reality and related principles for reducing complexity, for instance, 'Occam's razor' and the 'law of parsimony', is illustrative (Popper 1978: 350, 1977: 142–3). The *modeling* of reality but not the depiction of reality in its entirety is mandatory for generating scientific knowledge. Historically, different sciences could only emerge out of philosophy and theology by increasing the differentiation and complexity reduction of thinking (Homann 1994: 7, 11; Suchanek 1992: 54–6; Homann and Suchanek 1989: 74–5; see also Schlösser 1992: 41; Machlup 1978: 75–6, 1967: 9–13).

Although much of Popper's research dealt with an 'output' problem of scientific research, that is how hypotheses should be tested through attempted falsification, he also made suggestions regarding the start-up of research. Popper (1976: 25, 85–7, 134–5) proposed that complexity reduction is conducted as a matter of problem dependence. Meyer (1995) discussed this as 'problematology'. Popper argued that at the outset of an inquiry, scientists have to formulate specific research problems: '[E]very rational theory, no matter whether scientific or philosophical, is rational in so far as it tries to *solve a certain problem*' (Popper 1978: 199; see also ibid. 1992: 62–4, 1978: 222). Popper's (1957: 28–30) distinction of 'methodological essentialism', which can be linked to the idea of problem dependence, and 'methodological nominalism', which takes a (merely) ontological, descriptive stance to researching reality, is instructive. Lawson's (1997) concept of critical realism seems to be close to what Popper refers to as 'essentialism'. In Popper's understanding, problem dependence reflects that empirical phenomenons as such play a rather insignificant role when scientific research is established (in detail, see Suchanek 1999, 1992; see also Homann 1997b: 1–3; Boland 1994: 157–9; Hands 1993: 70; Machlup 1978: 224–5). It appears unjustified to suggest that Popper had a 'mystical view' (Simon 1977: 326–7) on the organization and start-up of scientific research. The opposite may be the case.

Marshall (1925: 159–71), Friedman (1953: 36, 53), Kaldor (1978: 2) or Dugger (1984: 320) hinted at the problem-dependent nature of scientific research, too, as did Max Weber (Homann and Suchanek 1989: 72). Similarly, Klein (1994: 245) stressed that for understanding different 'types' of economic theory, such as microeconomics, macroeconomics or constitutional economics, the question of purpose of theory-building has to be addressed. Or, more ambiguously, Hahn and Hollis (1979: 11) stated that 'different applications of . . . [economic] theory call for different definitions.' These suggestions can be deepened and clarified in relation to the issue of problem dependence.

Popper did not detail how problem dependence operationally instructed complexity reduction. Lakatos' suggestions on the heuristic nature of scientific research seem to fill such a void (see also Figure 1.1; Backhouse 1994a: 7–10, 1994b: 173–4, 179–81; Blaug 1994: 110–11, 114–15, 1974: 155–7; Black 1962), especially when they are connected to Gödel's incompleteness theorem.

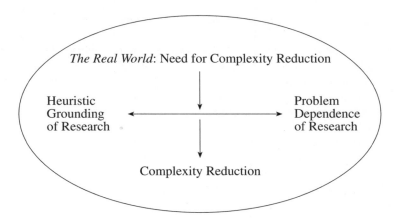

Figure 1.1   Research program

Lakatos interpreted a research heuristic as a problem formulation and problem-solving apparatus that grounds a scientific research program methodically
(but not ontologically or phenomenologically). A research heuristic reflects a
(re)search instruction for a scientific inquiry: '[It is the] . . . heuristic which
defines problems, foresees anomalies and turns them victoriously into examples according to a preconceived plan . . . It is primarily the . . . heuristic of his
program . . . which dictates the [researcher's] choice of his problems' (Lakatos
1978: 148; see also ibid. 1970: 16–17, 93, 173). Hofstadter's (1979: 183)
suggestions on a 'propositional calculus' and 'fantasy rule' seem to imply a
similar, heuristic understanding of research. Also, Kuhn's understanding of
'paradigm' compares with Lakatos' idea of the research heuristic, although
differences remain (Hausman 1994; Hands 1993). The idea of the research
heuristic relates to and details suggestions on 'heuristic fictionalism' (Black
1962) or similar suggestions of Becker (1976: 5, 13–14) on a 'way of looking'
and 'approach', Keynes's idea of a 'mind apparatus' (Heyne 1999: 3–4), Mill's
distinction of abstract, pure economic laws and concrete economic truth
(Vromen 1995: 193–4), references to 'hidden generative causes' (Boylan and
O'Gorman 1995: 3, 6), or 'ideal types' (Weber 1949; see also Machlup 1978:
271–6).

In contrast to theory, which is to be subjected to empirical scrutiny and
attempted falsifications, as Popper put it, research heuristics reside outside a
theory. They are not open to empirical scrutiny (Lakatos 1978: 4, 47–52, 1976:
144, 153, 1970: 132–7; see also Suchanek 1992: 56–7; Homann and Suchanek
1989: 74–80; Bartley 1987: 314–16; D'Amour 1976: 87–8; Black 1962). As
salient features of a research heuristic can be spelled out:

1. *Sub-theoretical*   Early on, Gödel's incompleteness theorem hinted that theory building rests on a conceptual framework that is logically different from a theory (Hofstadter 1979: 17; see also Penrose 1994: 64–5, 94, 418, 1989: 132–46, 538–41; Vollmer 1987: 167–72). Gödel examined how 'to line up intuition with formalized, axiomatized reasoning systems' (Hofstadter 1979: 20; see also Penrose 1994: 418, 1989: 135–7). He disputed that this issue could be resolved *within* a theory. The concept of the research heuristic, understood as a 'preconceived unifying idea' (Lakatos 1978: 148), acknowledges this. A research heuristic only 'under-wires', instructs and organizes theory-building but is not an element of a theory. Gödel interpreted 'axiom' as an element of a theory. Hence the suggestion that 'truth transcends axiomatic theoremhood in any given formal system' (Hofstadter 1979: 86). Possibly many scientists are ambiguous when they use terms like 'axiom', 'definitions' or 'assumption,' referring either to a theory component or to a sub-theoretical, pre-axiomatic – heuristic – idea that instructs and organizes theory-building. For instance, Homans (1976: 65) seemingly used the idea of the axiom in the sense of a heuristic construct rather than a theory component. His terminology is imprecise in this respect but not his grasp that theory-building is organized from 'outside' a theory. This distinguishes him from many scientists who do not make a distinction between the heuristic and the theoretical–(practical).

    The causality principle can be interpreted in this way as a sub-theoretical, heuristic idea, too. For example, unchallenged in (classical) theories of physics, it organizes 'all our theorizing' (Lindsay 1934: xvi; see also below). For many research problems of physics, this heuristic proved theoretically fruitful although theories of quantum physics could only emerge once certain aspects of the causality principle were modified. Such modifications happened at a sub-theoretical level and they did not abandon the physical approach as such.[1]

2. *Pre-empirical*   It goes unquestioned that the variables of a theory need to be empirically scrutinized but criticism of research heuristics as unre-alistic or empirically inaccurate is likely to be misdirected. In general, empirical research cannot be established on empirical grounds alone (Lawson 1997: 20–23, 52; Blaug 1994: 131; Mäki 1994: 253; Pies 1993: 247; Homann and Suchanek 1989: 79–80; Bhaskar 1978; Popper 1957: 80). Without pre-empirical ideas, the empirical, 'real' world remains inaccessible to science. Leibniz (1969: 199, 445) detailed that there is always an infinite number of theoretical propositions regarding empirical evidence (see also Murphy 1996: 160–61). Similarly, Marshall noted: 'Facts by themselves are silent . . . The most reckless and treacherous of all theorists is he who professes to let facts and figures speak for them-

selves, who keeps in the background the part he has played, perhaps unconsciously, in selecting and grouping them' (Marshall 1925: 159–71, quoted from Friedman 1953: 90; also Pareto as referred to by Latsis 1976: 12).[2] Similarly, Lawson's critical realism questions the project of a merely empirically grounded approach to scientific research, specifically so for economics (Lawson 1997: 282–3, 1994: 257–61; see also Vromen 1995: 198–201). Especially Lawson's (1994: 263) understanding of 'deep domains' can be examined regarding the concept of the research heuristic.

Hofstadter (1979: 18–20, 152) and similarly Popper (1976: 29) pointed out that a recursion breaker is needed to make empirical definitions.[3] Indirectly, they thus question Simon (1977: 43) who claimed that the scientific 'enterprise generally begins with empirical data' (restated by Simon 1995: 53; see also Simon and Newell 1956: 67–8). Recursion breakers can be developed as a matter of arbitrariness ('anything goes'); historicism ('a fixed destiny'); or traditionalism ('this is what we always did').[4] None of these suggestions is likely to provide methodologically more convincing advice on how to resolve the recursion problem than the concept of the research heuristic.

The pre-empirical nature of research is pervasive. Even at a very basic level, scientific research is pre-empirically grounded. As Kant outlined in the *Critique of Pure Reason*, the causality principle guides, empirically untested, 'all our theorizing *and* experiment' (Lindsay 1934: xvi, emphasis added). Scientists can only empirically discover causality in the form of 'A causes B' because it is heuristically assumed. By doing so, the potentially highly complex relationship between A and B is reduced to a causal one. Boylan and O'Gorman (1995: 160–69) seem to question a pre-empirical interpretation of causes but not necessarily of causality.

3. *Quasi-tautological* As Lakatos (1978: 148) implied, a research heuristic is a quasi-tautology but not a 'real' tautology. It provides an apparatus for raising and answering questions but leaves 'subject matter' unspecified (see also Vromen 1995: 51–6; Lawson 1989; Scriven 1959). Leibniz (1969: 199, 523, 531) hinted at this early on (see also Cassirer 1962). The idea that quasi-tautologies organize reasoning has been discussed not only for scientific thinking but also for philosophical thinking. For example, Wittgenstein (1975: 66, 77) noted: 'The meaning of a question is the method of answering it . . . A question denotes a method for searching' (see also Meyer 1995: 39). Similarly, for artistic thinking, Greeley (1993: 75a) made out a 'narrative impulse' and explicitly compared it to the way scientific research is organized.[5] Or, Penrose (1989: 538, 558) spelled out that algorithmic mathematics rests on non-algorithmic consciousness. For

everyday 'theorizing' and its manifestations as common sense, gossip, proverbs or stereotypes, tautological elements in the organization of thinking can be identified, too (Wagner 1997: 44–8, 162–71; see also Penrose 1989: 539).[6] In a crude sense, the idea of the research heuristic can be interpreted as a 'schematic stereotype' (Wagner 1997: 198, 200; Simon 1992b: 154–5), which is 'cultivated' by a philosophy of science (see also Boylan and O'Gorman 1995: 164–5).

On the basis of a problem-dependent and heuristic understanding of scientific research, key criteria for setting out a research program are not empirical correctness, the avoidance of self-reference and circularity of concepts or a potential for interdisciplinary, theoretical integration and unification. Rather, key criteria are theoretical fruitfulness and the related explanatory and predictive power, intervention power and practical relevance a research program can develop (Wagner 1997: 9–10, 197–8; Pies 1993: 247; Suchanek 1992: 97–9; Langlois 1990: 692–4; Homann and Suchanek 1989: 80–82; Lakatos 1978: 52; Stigler and Becker 1977: 76–7).

A Note on Research Programs, Disciplines and Interdisciplinary Research

Historically, it appears that subject matter was somehow empirically, phenomenologically, ontologically or ideologically 'divided up' among scientific disciplines. The idea of the scientific discipline and the related concept of interdisciplinary research reflect such a subject matter-oriented, ontological understanding of scientific research. Hodgson (1998: 190) explicitly argues along such ontological, disciplinary lines, suggesting that economics and other social sciences were 'defined . . . in terms of its object of analysis' (see also Hodgson 1998: 189). Debate on the 'boundaries' of economics and sociology (for example Swedberg 1990) reflects an ontological understanding of scientific disciplines, too. In contrast, the concept of the research heuristic and the way it sets up a scientific inquiry does not imply an ontological, 'subject matter'-related or 'object'-defined (Hodgson 1998: 189–90) understanding of scientific research. Rather, it implies that subject matter can be – imperialistically – explored by different sciences, namely by applying different heuristic apparatuses to the exploration of same aspects of reality. Lakatos's idea of the *research program* reflects this reformulated understanding of the idea of the discipline.

The concept 'discipline' can be interpreted as a special case of a research program. A discipline locks in a phenomenological, ontological or ideological manner subject matter to research heuristics. Popper (1978: 67) hinted at this when stating that most research problems ' "belong" in some sense to one or another of the traditional disciplines'. In contrast, the concept of the research program decouples subject matter and research heuristics. Popper and Lakatos implied this when they suggested that any empirical phenomenon can be 'imperialistically' explored by different research programs (Homann and Suchanek 1989: 82–4, similarly Hofstadter 1979: 609–11; see also Green and Shapiro 1996: 270). Popper noted: '*We are not students of some subject matter but students of problems.* And problems may cut right across the borders of any subject matter or discipline' (Popper 1978: 67, emphasis as in original). This should not be misread as a call for 'interdisciplinary' research which tried to examine subject matter of different disciplines at the same time, as for instance favored by Hodgson (1998: 173) or Hollis' (1994), who advocate holism in economic research. Interdisciplinary holistic research, which aims to unify disciplines for the purpose of more realistic and more complex theories, ignores complexity reduction, problem dependence and a general need for 'modeling' in scientific research. A key obstacle to unification-oriented, interdisciplinary research is the multiplicity of research questions it raises and the multiplicity of research heuristics it requires for analyzing different questions.

Hodgson (1998: 189) probably errs when he suggests that an approach-based, heuristic grounding of economics undermined 'pluralism within economics'. The opposite is probably the case. On the one hand, the idea of the research program imperialistically opens up 'real objects – the economy' (Hodgson 1998: 189) to all social sciences and their distinctively different approaches to understanding reality. Hodgson would probably not suggest that the 'economy' could only be researched by economists. On the other hand, there is ample room for pluralism within a research program, namely regarding the specification of theoretical–(practical) concepts of a research program. Also, as sketched out in this section and further discussed throughout this book, an empiricist, subject matter-oriented understanding of economics leaves various methodological questions open, at least more so than a heuristic grounding of economics.

1.2 ECONOMIC VERSUS BEHAVIORAL APPROACHES TO ORGANIZATION RESEARCH: A BRIEF INTRODUCTION

Like most social science research, organizational research does not take for granted desirable outcomes of organizational behavior. Rather, the key question of organizational analysis is how interacting agents can achieve outcomes like peaceful coexistence, prosperity for all, 'law and order', the survival of a firm and so on. Organizational analysis aims at 'securing and

directing cooperative effort in a social group' (Knight 1948: viii; similarly
North 1993a: 260). As much as both organizational economics and behavioral
organization research can be said to be interested in analyzing and generating
cooperation in organizational behavior, they theoretically conceptualize and
practically intervene in a different way. Differences in theory-building and
practical intervention can be traced to differences in heuristic approach. The
ensuing discussion briefly contrasts organizational economics and behavioral
organization research regarding the theoretical–(practical) approach and
heuristic approach (Chapters 2 and 3 provide details and more literature references). The following substantiates:

1. Organizational economics and behavioral organization research differ
   regarding their theoretical models of organizational behavior and organization structures or 'institutions'.
2. Organizational economics treats problems in organizational behavior as a
   situational condition and aims at situational intervention with incentive
   structures in order to influence organizational behavior. In contrast,
   behavioral organization research diagnoses and intervenes with the
   'human condition'.
3. Theory-building and practical intervention of organizational economics
   and of behavioral organization research are instructed by different heuristic models of human nature and by different heuristic models of social
   conflict.

Different Approaches to Organization Research

Organizational economics and behavioral organization sciences, such as organization psychology or organization sociology, specify research problems
differently. Their strategies for theory-building and practical intervention
differ regarding the conceptualization of organizational behavior, organization
structures or 'institutions' and practical, normative goals of organizational
intervention.

   Organizational economics approaches problems in organizational behavior
as a situational condition, as being caused by 'defective' incentive structures.
Problems are not approached as the human condition. Economics conceptualizes organizational behavior as interactions over capital contributions and capital distributions, institutions as incentive structures and socially desirable,
cooperative outcomes of organizational behavior as mutual gains (see Figure
1.2). Empirical and moral assessments of organizational economics have to
focus, in the first place, on its theoretical–(practical) concepts of 'incentive
structures', 'interactions over capital contributions and distributions' and

Research Heuristic I: Dilemma Structure

Figure 1.2   Economic approach

'mutual gains'. Economics may have little to fear in this respect. Possibly, economics can even make stronger claims towards a moral image of human nature than behavioral research. This suggestion is examined and returned to throughout the book.

Research Heuristic I: Role Conflict

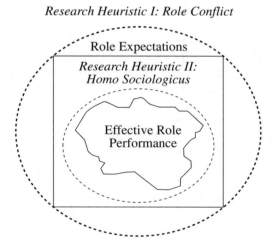

Figure 1.3   Sociological approach

Behavioral organization research approach problems in organizational behavior differently. Theoretically and practically, the human condition and human nature is directly focused on (see Figure 1.3). Behavioral organization research models organization structures or 'institutions' as value structures, role structures or organizational culture; organizational behavior as processes of self-actualization, value-sharing or role negotiation; and cooperative, socially desirable outcomes of organizational behavior, in one way or another, as social harmony, value consensus, role homogeneity or cultural homogeneity. Practical intervention tends to come as value education, role pedagogy or culture management.

Both organizational economics and behavioral organization research reflect a contracting model of organizational behavior. Schein's (1980) idea of 'psychological contracting' well illustrates a contracting approach of behavioral organization research. The concept of behavioral contracting details organizational behavior as value contracting, possibly even linking it to 'value indoctrination' and 'social conditioning', as in varying degrees suggested not only by social psychology or sociology but also by behavioral economics (Simon 1945: 102–3, see also ibid. 1993b: 159–60, 1976a: xxxv, 242). In contrast, organizational economics approaches contracting as 'economic contracting', as negotiations over incentive arrangements that are to stir social interactions over capital utilization towards mutually advantageous outcomes. Williamson's (1985: 30–5) suggestions on contracting strongly move in this direction.

Heuristic Aspects of Organizational Research

Section 1.1 suggested that research heuristics set out the methodical approach of a research program. For economic research, two important research heuristics can be identified – the model of the dilemma structure and the model of economic man. The idea 'dilemma structure' models organizational behavior as dilemmatic social conflicts over capital utilization where socially desirable outcomes (mutual gains) are threatened by the simultaneous occurrence of conflicting interests and of common interests of agents (in detail, see Homann 1994; see also section 2.3). In game theoretical terms, the prisoners' dilemma or the commons dilemma neatly illustrate the model of the dilemma structure (Hardin 1968; Luce and Raiffa 1957). The idea of the dilemma structure directs the analysis of interaction conflict in situational terms, regarding incentive structures or the 'rules of the game', and related conflict resolution is stirred towards situational intervention with incentive structures.

Economics heuristically models agents, who are thought to be caught up in dilemmatic interest conflicts, as 'economic man': a decision-maker who evaluates and chooses a course of action in relation to expectations of gains and losses as they are signaled by incentive structures (in detail Homann 1994, 1990; for further references, see Chapter 2, section 2.4). The model of economic man abstracts from a holistic, empirical–behavioral and moral–behavioral description of human nature. Like the model of the dilemma structure, it is analytically tailored to the situational analysis and situational resolution of interest conflicts but not to the analysis of behavioral questions and behavioral intervention with the human condition (see Figure 1.2).

Like economics, behavioral sciences heuristically invoke a model of social conflict and a model of human nature. Dahrendorf's discussion of the heuristic nature of 'sociological man' is illustrative (see Chapter 3, section 3.3). Behavioral organization research heuristically models social conflicts as value decay or role conflict (see Figure 1.3). Herzberg (1966: 170) speaks of a 'psychic pathology' (see also Chapter 3, section 3.2). Equally illustrative are references of behavioral organization research to an 'endemic condition of organizational misbehavior' (Ackroyd and Thompson 1999: 1–3, 25; similarly Palmer et al. 1993: 125–6), or, more abstractly, the conception of tragic, behavioral, conflict in Greek philosophy (Gosling 2002; in detail, see Nussbaum 1986). Such conflict-laden characterizations of social life are probably not meant to be depictions of empirically widespread or morally desirable outcomes of organizational behavior. This book argues that these models, like the ideas 'dilemma structure' and 'economic man', only heuristically instruct theory-building and practical intervention and hence are beyond empirical–behavioral and moral–behavioral scrutiny – but not so the theoretical propositions and practical intervention programs developed with these research heuristics.

A key thesis put forward in this book is that for the purpose of organization psychology or institutional sociology, 'economic man' and 'dilemma structure' are likely to be unfruitful and irrelevant research heuristics. On the grounds of problem dependence, they have to be rejected for behavioral research but *not* on the grounds of being unrealistic or immoral behavioral images of human nature and social life. Probably only for the research problems of behavioral organization research, behavioral scientists can rightly claim that the theoretical analysis of and practical intervention with human behavior should – selectively, but not holistically – be linked to the human condition and the behavioral portrayal of human nature. Once this is acknowledged, constructive dialogue between organizational economics and behavioral organization research, as called for by Barney (1990), has a good chance of emerging.

1.3   PORTRAYING OR NOT PORTRAYING HUMAN NATURE IN ORGANIZATION THEORY: METHODICAL ISSUES, ECONOMIC RECONSTRUCTION AND PRACTICAL RELEVANCE

From the very beginnings of industrial organization theory, organization researchers came under criticism for a claimed empirically incorrect and morally questionable image of human nature that resembled the model of economic man. The human relations school developed this type of criticism, especially regarding the model of economic man in Taylor's writings (see Burrell and Morgan 1979: 144–6; Knowles and Saxberg 1967: 22–32; see also Mayo 1990, 1949, 1933; Herzberg 1966; McGregor 1960). It critiqued 'economic man' as an unrealistic and morally questionable image of human nature, claiming that behavioral character traits such as benevolence, compassion, honesty, trust, commitment, solidarity, cooperative predispositions and so on were overlooked by classical organization theory. Simon's behavioral economic organization theory was equally influential in developing this critique. He aimed at a 'science of man' in the tradition of organization psychology and organization sociology, critiquing 'economic man' in empirical–behavioral and moral–behavioral terms (Simon 1997, 1993b, 1976a, 1957b, 1956, 1955).

On the basis of the distinction of research heuristics from theoretical–(practical) concepts, the present study re-examines behavioral criticism of 'economic man' and similar criticisms of the idea of the dilemma structure. The following substantiates:

1. Understood as research heuristics, 'economic man' and 'dilemma structure' are beyond empirical–behavioral and moral–behavioral criticism.
2. Through non-behavioral, economic reconstruction (as mapped out by Figure 1.2), (self-)criticism regarding an unrealistic and immoral image of human nature and social life is unmasked as a (self-)misunderstanding in Taylor's, Simon's and Williamson's organization theories.
3. The relevance and usefulness of organizational economics and of behavioral organization research should be assessed in relation to the practical success these research programs enjoy and the moral quality of their favored strategies for practical intervention.

Economic Reconstruction and Methodical Clarifications Regarding the Portrayal of Human Nature

Models of dilemmatic interest conflict and self-interested choice, which compare to the idea of the dilemma structure or the model of economic man, can be found in many institutional studies, for instance, Hobbes invoked in *Leviathan*, especially in Chapters 13–15, the 'war of all' (see also Mintz 1962: 135), or similarly Greek philosophy built on tragic dilemma concepts (Nussbaum 1986) as did the Old Testament (Wagner-Tsukamoto 2001b; Wagner 2000a, 2000b, 2000c). This book suggests that such 'negative' models of human nature and social life are applied as analytical tools, as research heuristics, which methodically organize and instruct theory-building and practical intervention, but which are not theoretical–(practical) concepts. Nussbaum (1986: 50–51) hints at this very issue for philosophical research that proceeds in the tradition of Greek virtue ethics. The methodical, heuristic functionality of research heuristics implies that they do not portray 'real people' or 'real life' – not even in behavioral research programs as, for instance, Dahrendorf detailed for sociology. Like Friedman, he stressed that 'models of man' should be 'intentionally unrealistic constructs' (Dahrendorf 1973: 7, 50, 58, 78; also Homann and Suchanek 1989: 79–80; see also Chapter 3, section 3.3). He referred explicitly to 'sociological man', who belongs to the same 'methodological family' as 'economic man'. Seemingly, some behavioral researchers suggested caution regarding the claim that all scientific concepts should be empirically understood. This should alert behavioral researchers to critically re-examine calls for the empirical portrayal of 'human nature as we know it', of 'real people' and 'real life'.

In line with such arguments, accusations of 'economic man' and 'dilemma structure' as empirically incorrect and morally questionable images of human nature and social life may miss their targets. Morgan's (1997: 77, 91) criticism of the model of economic man as a 'laughable caricature' and related suggestions to dispatch 'economic man' into a 'realm of fairy tales' (Heinen 1976: 395; similarly Donaldson 1995: 184, 1990: 373) are probably flawed. Indeed, understood as research heuristics, 'economic man' and 'dilemma structure' did not need to be dispatched into a realm of fairy tales since they 'already' reside in a realm of fairy tales. Differently put, they reflected sub-theoretical, pre-empirical and quasi-tautological concepts, or in Hofstadter's (1979: 183) terminology, they reflected 'fantasy rules' (see section 1.1).

The clarification of methodological issues constitutes a core problem of a philosophy of social science research. Methodological debate is likely to have manifold implications for theory-building and practical intervention (Homann and Suchanek 2000; Homann 1994; Becker 1993, 1976; Lindenberg 1990; Homann and Suchanek 1989; Buchanan 1987b; Simon 1985; Hayek 1949). The present study clarifies such issues differently than Burrell and Morgan (1979). Burrell and Morgan, similar to Donaldson (1995, 1990), tended to assess 'assumptions' in a theoretical–(practical) perspective only and predominantly so from the point of view of sociology. This book develops and applies different 'maps' of organization theory than the ones of Burrell and Morgan (1979: 22, 29–30). Thus, this book attests to methodological and theoretical differences of approach between organizational economics and organizational sociology. A comparison of Figures 1.2 and 1.3 illustrates such differences. These differences have implications for the assessment of the question of human nature for organization theory. Instead of analyzing 'side-by-side' philosophical assumptions on ontology, epistemology, human nature and methodology of organization *sociology* (Burrell and Morgan 1979: Chapter 1; see also Rowlinson 1997: 219–23), this book analyses 'assumptions' about human nature by distinguishing ontological from methodological 'assumptions' and by linking this distinction to a comparison of differences of approach between organizational economics and behavioral organization research. By making this distinction between methodological, heuristic concepts and ontologically assessable, theoretical concepts, Burrell and Morgan's (1979) analysis is deepened and revised especially regarding the nature and purpose of 'assumptions' about human nature in different research programs.

By spelling out the heuristic nature of certain research concepts, the book develops the thesis that the empirical–behavioral or moral–behavioral portrayal of human nature is not at stake when the ideas 'economic man' and 'dilemma structure' are drawn on (or when equivalent heuristic concepts are applied in other social sciences). Empirical–behavioral or moral–behavioral critique of 'economic man' and 'dilemma structure' may reflect a methodical misunderstanding, indeed a '*self*-misunderstanding' if put forward by economists (Homann 1997: 18–19). On this basis, behavioral critique of 'economic man' can be qualified. This book claims that from its beginnings organization theory has been methodologically bugged by the question of how to portray human nature.

Regarding its scope of analysis, the book focuses on the organization theories of Taylor, Simon and Williamson, reconstructing them in non-behavioral economic terms. The reconstruction clarifies the role of heuristic concepts and of theoretical–(practical) concepts in Taylor's, Simon's and Williamson's writings. Specifically, it examines whether they conceptualized institutions as incentive structures, for example, as a salary system; whether they approached organizational behavior as capital contribution–distribution interactions; whether they invoked mutual gains as interaction outcome; and whether they methodically grounded theory-building and practical intervention in the research heuristics 'economic man' and 'dilemma structure'. Figure 1.2 provides a 'road map' for the reconstruction.

As interesting as an institutional economic reconstruction of Taylor's, Simon's and Williamson's organization theories may be in itself, the purpose of reconstruction in the context of the present study is to clarify the role and relevance of portraying human nature in different research programs. The book disputes (self-)criticism of Taylor, Simon and Williamson that their models of human nature did not correspond with 'human nature as we know it' (for example, Williamson 1985: xxi–xxiii, 44, 391; see also ibid. 1975: 1–2) and reflected a morally jaundiced, dehumanized image of human nature (for example, Williamson 1993a: 453, 1985: 44, 391; Simon 1997: 42–5, 52, 1993b, 1976a: xxi; Taylor 1911: 29). Related behavioral interpretations of the idea of the dilemma structure as 'bad' (for example, Williamson 1998: 10–11) or 'unrealistic' (Simon 1976a: xxxii–xxxiii, 1957b: vii, 62–78, 99–144, 1955: 101) are rejected. The book is equally critical regarding suggestions that the model of economic man implied normative recommendations to behave in a self-interested manner (for example, Arnold et al. 1998: 457–8; Brown 1996: 91, 99, 106; similarly McGregor 1960) or that the idea of the dilemma structure implied that agents should engage in the 'war of all'. Such behavioral criticism of 'economic man' and 'dilemma structure' is probably as manifoldly flawed as accusing the unrealistic tool 'car crash dummy' of dangerous, immoral driving behavior in the accident simulation setting of the car crash test.

Practical Relevance of a Methodically Grounded, Economic Reconstruction of Organization Theory

As possibly abstract and practically removed a methodological debate about economic reconstruction and the portrayal of human nature may appear, its practical relevance is likely to be high.[7] This book suggests that practical ineffectiveness of social science consultancy is caused by the sidelining of questions of method and the prioritizing of behavioral intervention over economic intervention.[8] This book argues that organizational economics provides a viable approach for intervening with problems of institutional organization and is possibly more viable than behavioral approaches, in particular for contribution–distribution problems in modern interaction contexts.

The present study does not question that under certain circumstances behavioral organization research can solve problems in organizational behavior on its own. But such circumstances are likely to reflect anti-pluralistic, premodern interaction scenarios. Contexts, such as the city or the nation and more so the multicultural society, the multinational enterprise or the international community, are defined by pluralism or the 'condition of modernity' (Gerecke 1997: 9–20; Luhmann 1988: 102–3; see also Beck 2000: 226, 1992; Parker 1996: 483, 494; Giddens 1991; Williams 1988: 12; MacIntyre 1985: 1–5; Cochran 1972: 118, 1957: 12).[9] Scott (2000) analyzed modernization processes as the detraditionalization of society and connected in his analysis to Mannheim (1944). Or, Kymlicka (2001: 212–13, 216–17) points out that most Western democracies have become multicultural. In modern, pluralistic contexts, behavioral intervention that focuses on the human condition may be less effective, less efficient and possibly even less moral than economic intervention. Indeed, in the tradition of Mill, Hayek, or Popper, value pluralism and liberty, or liberalism in Kymlicka's (2001: 217) terms, can be argued for on ethical grounds. Max Weber also outlined that behavioral intervention at times reflects rather unfair social practices that are based on stereotyping, discrimination, traditionalism or religious fundamentalism. Hobbes and Smith already implied this and, to a degree, even the authors of the Old Testament (Wagner-Tsukamoto 2001a; Wagner 2000a, 2000b). More recent economic research (Homann 1999b, 1994; see also Gerecke 1997; Pies 1993; Suchanek 1992), sociological research (Scott 2000; Beck 1992; Giddens 1991; Luhmann 1988, 1984) and moral philosophical research (MacIntyre 1985; Williams 1988, 1985) detailed this suggestion.

Many firms encountered modern, pluralistic, detraditionalized contexts as early as the 19th century. Firms in the USA and Europe then experienced dramatic changes such as rising demand for industrially produced goods, growth of the work force, the replacement of the owner manager by professional managers, the dispersion of ownership among shareholders or the beginning of the multinational branching out of firms. Increasingly, problems of organizational behavior began to resemble social problems of modern society: 'The de-personification of possession, the objectification of the firm, the separation of property leads to the point at which the firm becomes a structural arrangement similar to a foundation or more precisely, similar to a nation state' (Rathenau 1918: 143; similarly Berle and Means 1932). Thus, the firm no longer resembled the workshop or small family business, which could be effectively run through behavioral intervention.

In industrializing and industrialized societies and the more so in a globalizing industrial world, interaction problems may be generally difficult to resolve in a behavioral manner. To a degree this is realized by behavioral researchers, some lamenting modernity and trying to hold on to behavioral intervention (for example, Küng 1999; Etzioni 1991a, 1991b, 1991c, 1991d, 1988; see also Bauman 2001; Lyotard 1984). Burrell's (1996: 657) argument for a 'pre-modern restart' of organization theory through holistic research on human nature probably falls into this category, too. The chances of behavioral research to overturn the condition of modernity and to return to a pre-modern, tribal way of life are probably small – and undesirable, as some behavioral researchers argue (for example, Cohen and Arato 2001: 186). Though, the latter insight may reflect an inherent contradiction of behavioral research, especially the post-modern project, as Sarup (1993: 145) suggests and Kymlicka (2001: 217) or Bauman (1992: xxii, 198–9) hint. Skepticism regarding the effectiveness of behavioral intervention is the more justified once the economic and political–legal institutions of the market economy are acknowledged. They enact the 'condition of modernity' for larger ethical reasons, as Adam Smith is likely to claim and as the Old Testament may have already implied. The latter tends to be overlooked by behavioral researchers (for example, Cohen and Arato 2001: 186–7).

Economics conceptually accommodates pluralism, diversity and the autonomy of the individual by theoretically analyzing and practically intervening with organizational behavior in non-behavioral terms and by heuristically grounding theory-building and practical intervention in models of self-interested choice and dilemmatic interest conflicts. Empirical evidence, both current and throughout the history of the firm, suggests that this route to solving social problems is more viable than the approach of organization psychology or organization sociology. In pluralistic contexts, behavioral sciences can probably only contribute to solving social problems *after* problems have been treated in economic terms. The present study here discusses failures of scientific management to create the 'moral manager' as an early example of failing behavioral organization research (Chapter 4, section 4.1 has details).[10]

In contrast to conventional wisdom, Taylor's organization program seemed to run into problems because of a too positive, moral–behavioral image of human nature. But still today, comparable behavioral suggestions are put forward by the human relations school, which in the 1990s experienced a revival in post-modern, empowerment paradigms. For example, in his analysis of 'soft' human resource management theory, Noon (1992: 27) projected McGregor's (1960) suggestions on managerial assumptions about human nature to the image of 'post-modern man'.[11] Similarly, Barley and Kunda (2000) assessed rhetoric and ideological components of organization theories from different periods. In the tradition of behavioral organization research, they analyzed ontological and epistemological 'content' features of claimed managerial ideology and rhetoric. But they did not analyze methodical patterns of claimed ideological, rhetoric components of organization theory. In contrast, the methodological discussion outlined in this book questions differently the nature of 'dogmatic speak' of managers (as of social scientists who talk about management). Thus, this book differently enlightens practitioners and scientists on how to 'overcome' dogmatic speak and related (self)-misunderstandings, especially in relation to the portrayal of human nature.

Taylor's misunderstanding may not be exceptional. This book argues that organization researchers, like Knight, Mayo, Coase, Simon, Herzberg, McGregor, North, Sen, Williamson, Donaldson or Etzioni, whose significant contributions to institutional and organizational research go unquestioned, may in certain respects have fallen for similar (self)-misunderstandings.

1.4   CONCLUDING REMARKS

The way a research program theoretically conceptualizes and practically intervenes with organization and organizational behavior has to be strictly understood with regard to the problem dependence and heuristic grounding of research. Of course, different social sciences can ('imperialistically') target the same research problem, for example, performance problems in organizational behavior. Still, practical success and the moral quality of practical intervention can be used as criteria for comparing economic and behavioral approaches. The important question is whether an organizational research program effectively solves its 'chosen' research problems in a morally acceptable way. If this is the case, probably little issue can be taken with the heuristic and theoretical approach of any research program.

Plato, for example, was well aware that a behavioral approach to institutional organization – he favored a virtue ethics – could only solve social problems if a value consensus was maintained (see also Popper 1962: 86–201). If Plato is interpreted in a normative way, this implied the restriction of freedom of movement, protectionism and possibly even a war for values (Plato 1999: 1317–18). Practical examples of the latter are provided by the 'crusades' of the Middle Ages in which various Churches fought out wars for values. Apparently, behavioral approaches to institutional organization come with certain moral 'costs'. They have to be considered when assessing the moral quality of behavioral research in comparison with economics. Behavioral (business) ethics has always struggled with this issue. For example, Schroeder (2001) interpreted Plato's writings much too favorably when critiquing the model of economic man. Chapter 8 follows up, discussing the moral status of economics.

The book argues the thesis that ideas like 'economic man' or 'dilemma structure' should be interpreted as analytical devices. It spells out a methodical, heuristic role of such ideas in economic theory-building and practical intervention. In their very essence, 'economic man' and 'dilemma structure' organize non-behavioral, situational analysis, but not the analysis of human nature. Research heuristics of organization sociology and organization psychology have to be similarly interpreted regarding a methodical role in behavioral theory-building and intervention. Their relevance has to be assessed with regard to how successfully they perform a heuristic, methodical function in theory-building and practical intervention. In contrast to organizational economics, behavioral research heuristics instruct, in one way or another, the analysis of the human condition and, hence, behavioral research directly intervenes with human nature in order to solve social problems. Importantly, not even behavioral organization research can portray human nature in complete, holistic, empirical–behavioral and moral–behavioral terms. A need for complexity reduction implies that behavioral sciences can only selectively portray or *model* human nature in their theories.

The subsequent chapters, especially Chapters 4–7, outline that Taylor, Simon and Williamson aimed in varying degrees at the behavioral portrayal of human nature that undermined the conceptual consistency and practical effectiveness of their organization theories. A basic misperception occurred in their research regarding the moral quality of economic research and intervention. Chapters 2 and 3 prepare the ground for this argument. They specify theoretical–(practical) and heuristic concepts of economics and behavioral organization research.

NOTES

1. Social sciences may have to question the causality principle. Research problems of social sciences considerably differ from the comparatively deterministic, ahistorical and non-experiential research problems of natural sciences (see Dahrendorf 1973: v; see also Langlois 1990: 692–4). A critical question is whether human behavior should be researched as non-random, rule-following and historical–experiential on the basis of the causality principle or whether alternative principles have to be looked for (see also Wagner 1997: 10, 13, 190, 194–6).
2. Heisenberg's *Uncertainty Relation* also qualified the role of empirical research in scientific research.
3. Possibly only in philosophical research, the recursion problem can be left open. The key purpose of a philosophical inquiry may be an explorative one, raising interesting questions rather than answering them. An explanatory or predictive purpose of research may be of secondary importance. Meyer's (1995) discussion of 'problematology' moves into this direction.
4. Moral or even aesthetic adequacy ('This is the right/pleasing thing to do') could be added as another, equally questionable recursion breakers.
5. A 'narrative impulse' can be traced in anthropological perspective (Greeley 1993) or in cognitive psychological and physiological, neurological perspectives (Wagner 1997: 169–70).
6. This statement is ironic in certain respects. It could be suggested that behavioral scientists – had they researched human nature more carefully – should have realized that the working of the human mind comprised certain 'heuristic' elements.
7. Theology and religion are probably the oldest 'bodies of thought' in which thinking about human nature was scrutinized – with significant practical consequences. In the outgoing 15th century, the Reformation was stirred by the issue of how to image God and man (see Eire 1986: 13–14, 34, 41, 316). The debate was violent and iconoclastic and had momentous practical consequences. It split the Christian Church into a Catholic wing and a Protestant wing.
8. A recent example is a behavioral organization program of British Airways. Its goal was to 'charm' employees into a better performance. The program explicitly subscribed to a claimed 'correct', empirical–behavioral and moral–behavioral images of human nature. But after four years of running the program and in the wake of rising losses, the program was abandoned, with the chief executive of British Airways resigning (see articles in the financial press from 10 and 11 March 2000).
9. The pre-eminence of war-like conflict *among* societies and tribes throughout the history of mankind reflects that, in the absence of a value consensus among groups, cooperation tends to be highly fragile.

10. Case studies of Quaker managers who tried to implement a religious image of human nature in managerial decision-making provide a similar example (see Wagner-Tsukamoto 2001a; see also Chapter 3, section 3.3).
11. Bauman (1992: Chapter 9) provides a good outline of the image of human nature of post-modern, sociological research.

2. A non-behavioral economic approach to institutional organization: Contribution–distribution interactions, interest equilibration and the incentive-compatibility of the situation

> It is surely time that rational choice theorists took stock of the immense and impressive literature of cognitive scientists that has long since reduced to an absurdity the notion of instrumental rationality (see Cherniak 1986 for a discussion of the implications of the rationality assumption as used in economic theory). (North, 1993b, p. 13)

> The irrelevance of so much criticism of economic theory does not of course imply that existing economic theory deserves any high degree of confidence. These criticisms may miss the target, yet there may be a target for criticism. (Friedman, 1953, p. 41)

Suggestions of an unrealistic and immoral image of human nature have been leveled against many institutional studies, especially economic ones. The claim is widespread that economics portrays human beings in behavioral terms as self-interested and utility-maximizing ('economic man'). This chapter questions this claim. In order to understand why and how economics applies seemingly 'unrealistic' and 'immoral' views about human nature a methodical, heuristic role of the model of economic man is spelled out. The chapter distinguishes theoretical–(practical) and heuristic concepts of economics. It reassesses findings from institutional economic research and constitutional economic research, detailing a generic, conceptual scheme of (organizational) economics. This clarification resolves problems that have hindered the application of economic ideas to organization research, as discussed by Hesterly et al. (1990). Subsequent chapters then detail the thesis that organizational economics' image of human nature should be deduced from its theoretical–(practical) concepts but not its research heuristics.

Sections 2.1 to 2.4 spell out theoretical–(practical) and heuristic concepts of organizational economics. Figure 1.2 provides a 'road map'. Section 2.1 outlines how (organizational) economics conceptualizes institutions (organization structures) as incentive structures. Section 2.2 investigates how (organizational) economics conceptualizes social exchange (organizational behavior) as interactions regarding capital contributions and capital distributions. Human capital is focused on. Section 2.3 examines how economics heuristically models social exchange as a dilemmatic interaction conflict. Section 2.4 assesses the heuristic nature and role of the model of economic man. Section 2.5 concludes the chapter.

2.1 THEORETICAL–PRACTICAL CONCEPTS (I): INCENTIVE STRUCTURES AND THE ANALYSIS OF THE INCENTIVE-COMPATIBILITY OF THE SITUATION

In paradigmatic terms, theoretical and practical–normative questions regarding whether and how social structures or 'institutions' attach certain gains or losses to choice alternatives and how institutions can be (re)designed for influencing choice behavior through a loss–gains calculus reflect economic research problems. A key concept is here the idea of incentive structures. The following substantiates:

1. Institutional economics examines 'institutions' as incentive structures. Property rights theory, principal–agent theory and transaction cost theory conceptualize incentive structures as property rights arrangements, agency structures or governance structures.
2. Institutional economics analyzes and (re)designs incentive structures with a view to the generation of socially desirable outcomes.
3. Institutional economics assesses the social desirability/undesirability of interaction outcomes in relation to the incentive-compatibility of institutions.
4. Economics does not intervene with motivational predispositions, such as altruistic or benevolent attitudes, in order to solve interaction problems and neither does economics advocate coercion as a means of solving social problems.

The Concept of Incentive Structures

A commonly chosen starting point of both behavioral and economic approaches to organizational analysis is that '[a]ll organizations are institutionalized organizations' (Scott 1995a: 136; see also Winship and Rosen 1988). Institutional *behavioral* analysis interprets institutions as cognitive psychological rules or value structures, that reflect socially shared internalized perceptions of duty (for details, see Chapter 3). In contrast, economics analyzes social problems in situational terms, interpreting the idea of the institution in relation to 'external bounds' (Buchanan 1987b: 272). As West (1976: 20) or Coase (1977: 320) remind us, from its very beginnings in the days of Adam Smith and Mandeville, economics has had such an institutional orientation when analyzing social exchange. Social arenas as diverse as markets and firm organization are conceptualized as a '*system* of social interactions characterized by a specific *institutional framework*, that is by a *set of rules* defining certain restrictions on the behavior of the market [organizational] participants' (Vanberg 1986: 75, emphasis changed).

The idea of incentive structures here plays a fundamental role. Incentive structures reflect an economic understanding of institutions, of 'system', 'situation', 'rules of the game' and so on (in detail, see Vanberg 2001, 1994; Homann and Suchanek 2000; Homann 1997: 2; Schofield 1996: 190; North 1993b: 12; von Neumann and Morgenstern 1947: 44, 49).[1] Incentive structures signal to choice-makers certain gains or losses that come with different choice alternatives (Homann and Suchanek 2000: 9, 32). Incentive structures 'are determined and guaranteed by some form of governance structure or *order* – i.e., a system of norms *plus* the instruments that *guarantee* this order' (Furubotn and Richter 1991: 2, emphasis added). Institutional economics, as it emerged from the studies of Williamson, detailed such an understanding of incentive structures as 'governance structures' (in detail, see Williamson 1985; see also Hesterly et al. 1990; Williamson 1975). Earlier, Buchanan's constitutional economics discussed how through public ordering effective incentive rules can be created. As he summed up: 'The effects of alternative sets of rules on solutions, [is] the domain of constitutional economics' (Buchanan 1994: 56; see also Vanberg 2001, 1994, 1986, 1982).

Economics from Adam Smith, Pareto to Knight, Hayek, Buchanan, North, Williamson or Vanberg have theoretically analyzed incentive structures for the purpose of advising on the intervention with incentive structures. Popper (1957: 56) noted by referring to Hayek: 'Economic analysis has never been the product of detached intellectual curiosity about the *why* of social phenomena, but of an intense urge to reconstruct a world which gives rise to profound dissatisfaction' (see also Vanberg 2001: 1–7, 21–33; Williamson 1998: 1–2, 1996c: 5; Homann 1997: 16–17, 23, 1992: 10; Brennan 1996: 256–7; Ordeshook 1996: 180, 188; Maskin 1994: 187–8; Muller 1993: 1–2; North 1993a: 253–5; Becker 1993: 402, 1976: 8; Buchanan 1987b: 16–32, 51–63; Hickerson 1987: 1117–19; Knight 1948: Preface). Positive–theoretical analysis and practical–normative analysis, and pure and applied theory are closely interrelated. The idea of the practical–normative here refers to a design orientation but not to value judgments. Practical–normative social science is concerned with what 'should be', in contrast to positive–theoretical science that examines what 'is' or 'will be'. In this sense, the economist always has been a social engineer, as many social engineers, such as managers and politicians, always have been economists (Schlösser 1992: 21; see also Shenhav 1995: 562–3; Copley 1919: 15; Taylor 1895: 54–5). In short, the notions of the 'theoretical–practical' or 'theoretical–(practical)', as used throughout this book, capture this understanding.

Early examples of a 'managerial economics' that reflect such a theoretical–practical orientation are Taylor (1911, 1903, 1895) or Gomberg (1903). A comparable interest in both positive–theoretical and practical–normative analysis can be suggested for behavioral research. Argyris (1973: 265) noted with specific reference to behavioral sciences: '[A]ll descriptive concepts, once they are used to organize reality and guide behavior, become normative.' Subsequent chapters detail differences regarding favored theoretical and practical strategies of behavioral organization research as compared with organizational economics.

Incentive structures can be created through political and judiciary processes of 'public ordering,' drawing on the sanctioning instruments of the state (Vanberg 2001; Buchanan 1991, 1987b, 1975). Incentive structures can also be established through processes of 'private ordering' (Furubotn and Richter 1991; Williamson 1996c, 1985, 1975; Alchian 1977; see Figure 2.1).

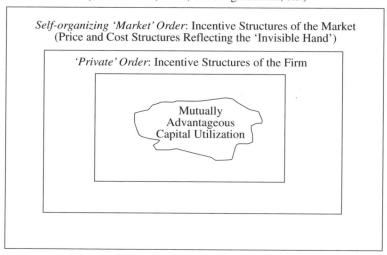

Political–legal *'Public' Order*: Incentive Structure of National/International Society (Constitutions, Laws, WTO Agreements, etc.)

Self-organizing *'Market' Order*: Incentive Structures of the Market (Price and Cost Structures Reflecting the 'Invisible Hand')

'Private' Order: Incentive Structures of the Firm

Mutually
Advantageous
Capital Utilization

Figure 2.1   Ordering through incentive structures

Regarding the latter, typical examples are hierarchical and contractual structures of the firm,[2] for example, an 'inventory of incentive and control techniques' (Williamson 1975: 81) or 'governance structures' (Williamson 1985: 30–32, 302–18), such as job ladders, grievance procedures, arbitration schemes, performance and appraisal systems, reward and retention systems, budgetary control systems or promotion systems (see also Jensen and Meckling 1996, 1976). Especially through private ordering, a firm can better utilize incomplete contracting. Since a firm cannot set out employment contracts in every detail (Williamson 1985: 71–9), non-contractual incentive structures may be useful. As Williamson detailed by connecting to Coase (1937), it is especially the capability of the firm to utilize incomplete contracting at a lower cost than the market – by means of private ordering – which enables the firm to thrive on incomplete contracting. This explains, at least in degrees, why firms exist at all.[3]

Incentive-compatible Organization Structures and Mutual Gains

In order to solve problems in organizational behavior, such as performance problems, institutional economics analyzes and engineers the 'incentive-compatibility' of organization structures (Williamson 1985: 76; for reviews, see Wolff 1999; McKenzie and Lee 1998; Cowen and Parker 1997). Milgrom and Roberts (1988: S158) point out that organization structures, such as compensation schemes, can ensure that individual and organizational goals are congruent. Incentive-compatibility implies that incentive structures ensure socially advantageous outcomes: 'The agent chooses one of a number of possible actions that influence *both* his own *and* the principal's welfare' (Furubotn and Richter 1991: 18, emphasis added). In the context of organizational behavior of the firm, socially advantages outcomes can be approached in relation to the profit goal.

Incentive-compatible organization structures ensure that gains (losses) resulting for the individual from cooperation are higher (lower) than gains (losses) resulting from non-cooperation. In this way interacting choice-makers are induced to cooperate on grounds of self-interest (see also Gerecke 1997: 130–32; North 1993b: 13; Libecap 1989: 8–13; Runge 1984: 155; also Dasgupta 1988: 50; Williams 1988: 4). Then, incentive structures provide 'correct incentives' (North 1993b: 21). Buchanan (1987b: 8, 16) speaks of the 'pareto-effectiveness' of the rules of the game. With regard to practical intervention, the concept of incentive-compatible structures strictly implies situational, non-behavioral intervention: '[T]he principal can determine a remuneration plan for the agent that depends on results ... [T]he *situation* created is one in which the agent maximizes *not only* his own *but also* the principal's utility'[4] (Furubotn and Richter 1991: 18, emphasis added). As indicated

Design criteria \ Interaction outcome	Pareto-effectiveness at the interaction level		
	Stability	**Efficiency**	
Dilemma (cooperation failure, competition)	Dilemma equilibrium: 'rational foolishness' as standard outcome (due to incentive-incompatibility of formal institutions)	Pareto-inferiority of interactions	(A): the incentive problem
Coordination Failure	Dilemma equilibrium (due to unresolved information problems, and despite incentive compatibility of formal institutions)	Pareto-inferiority of social interactions (worse than under (A) since costs for changing incentive structures occurred)	(B): the informatioɪ problem
Cooperation	Cooperation equilibrium (incentive-compatibility and information provision)	Pareto-superiority of social interactions	

Institutional Design Process

Figure 2.2   Normative institutional economics

above, institutional economics here examines institutional structures such as after-sales service agreements, guarantee schemes, inspection by an independent expert, hostage models and so on (Milgrom and Roberts 1988; Williamson 1983; see also above).

The creation of incentive-compatible institutions encompasses the resolution of information problems among interacting agents. Only after decision-makers have been informed of rule change, can cooperation and a 'coordination equilibrium' be expected (Schotter 1981: 141; see Figure 2.2). Jensen and Meckling (1996) distinguished in this respect 'control structures' and 'communication structures'. This compares to the distinction of a 'motivation problem' and a 'coordination problem' of institutional intervention (Wolff 1999: 135; see also Gerecke 1997: 134–7; Vanberg 1986: 91–3). Compared to the motivational problem, which institutional economics approaches as the problem of creating incentive-compatible organization structures, a communication and coordination problem is of a comparatively simple nature. It reflects a problem of effective information provision rather than a problem of resolving conflicts of interests. On the other hand, the attempt to solve social conflict through communication alone – Habermas is here a leading advocate – is likely to be futile. For communicative intervention to succeed, incentive-compatible institutions are needed first. This is discussed further in Chapter 4.

In many instances, the normative goal of institutional economics is to over-come interaction problems; for example managers are interested in preventing 'antagonism', 'group nonrationality' or the 'contracting dilemma' in organiza-tional behaviour, as Taylor, Simon and Williamson noted (see Chapter 4). But importantly, institutional economics is 'normatively ambivalent' (Homann 1999a: 4). Analytically, institutional economics treats cooperation and non-cooperation in the same way. And normatively, neither succeeding cooperation nor failing cooperation are viewed as inherently 'good' or 'bad'. For instance, the specific institutional arrangement of incentive structures of the prisoners' dilemma, as discussed below, make both prisoners lose as a result of their interactions. This is intended by those who installed this dilemma, namely the prosecutor and society at large. Also, the market economy deliberately institu-tionalizes a prisoners' dilemma among firms by enforcing competition, for instance through laws that ban cartels or monopolies (Homann and Pies 1991: 610; Luce and Raiffa 1957: 97).

In this regard, institutional economics makes few demands on behavioral, cooperative (pre)dispositions of the individual (for example, Homann 1997; Gambetta 1988; Becker 1976; similarly Luhmann 1988, 1984; Williams 1988). Because of this, economics may be more successful regarding conflict resolution than behavioral approaches, that rely on shared benevolent, altruis-tic predispositions among choice-makers. In particular, economics can solve social problems in the absence of a value consensus or, differently put, in the presence of value pluralism (see Chapter 3, section 3.4 and Chapter 8).

Coercion Structures: An Alternative to Incentive Structures?

Organizational structures need not necessarily be designed as incentives struc-tures. They can be developed as command and obedience structures through which 'crude force' is exerted and discretion in choice behavior is disabled. North refers to a coercive approach as an 'imperative one' (North 1993b: 13; see also Cowen and Parker 1997: 73). This reflects an essentially non-economic approach to handling social problems (see also Chapter 4, section 4.2).

A coercive approach can be effective and efficient under certain circum-stances but for many interactions it is likely to undermine performance outcomes. Long-running field experiments in communism are a good exam-ple (Buchanan 1994, 1987b; North 1993a, 1993b). Coercive structures frequently fail because they cannot entirely disable discretion. In degrees, even a slave can decide how well to perform (Buchanan 1995; see also Knight 1948). In this connection, it is a misstatement to suggest that incen-tive structures reflected coercion structures, which (ab)used power and promoted oppression and crude force. The new institutional sociology frequently argues in this way (for example, Scott 1995b). As discussed, economics does not favor command or obedience as a means of influencing social behavior. Rather, its goal is to devise incentive structures that realign self-interests so that mutual gains result. Discretion in choice behavior is not disabled.

2.2   THEORETICAL–PRACTICAL CONCEPTS (II): CAPITAL EXCHANGE AND THE ANALYSIS OF ORGANIZATIONAL BEHAVIOR AS CAPITAL CONTRIBUTION–DISTRIBUTION INTERACTIONS

In the tradition of Buchanan or Hayek, who closely follow Adam Smith's outline of economics, social behavior (including organizational behavior) is conceptualized as interactions over capital exchange. The present study focuses on capital exchange that relates to human capital. This appears particularly relevant for a debate of the image of human nature in organization theory. The following substantiates:

1. A capital utilization model of social behavior interrelates the extent and nature of capital contributions made by the agent with capital distributions received by the agent.
2. For resolving capital utilization problems, institutional economics intervenes with incentive structures. They signal to the agent what capital distributions can be expected in return for capital contributions.
3. 'Contingency features' of capital and capital utilization, such as asset specificity, specify the economic analysis of and intervention with capital exchange.
4. A capital utilization model of social behavior implies the non-behavioral analysis of and intervention with interaction problems. In this respect, it is complementary to the non-behavioral, situational analysis of incentive structures.

The Conception of Organizational Behavior as Situationally Governed Interactions over Capital Utilization

Institutional economics models organizational behavior as a capital utilization process and members of an organization – 'stakeholders' in a wider sense (Wagner-Tsukamoto 2002) – as contributors of human capital. This understanding of organizational behavior can be specified as an *interaction* process to which organization members contribute human capital and from which they expect distributions in return. The latter are signaled by incentive structures, as discussed above. Early on, Barnard's (1938) and Simon's (1945) inducement–contribution theory formulated such a model of social exchange, later extended by Olson (1971) (see also Coleman 1990; Robins 1987 and Chapter 4, section 4.2).

As Becker detailed, economics here assesses how the individual makes investment decisions regarding education, training and knowledge. Education, knowledge and skills are approached as intangible, priced assets, as 'resources in people' (Becker 1971: 9, 1962: 9–10; see also Becker 1996, 1992; Williamson 1985; Beer et al. 1984; Fama 1980; Likert and Seashore 1954). Human capital reflects physical skills, administrative skills, planning skills, decision-making skills, communication skills, interpersonal skills, problem-solving skills, engineering skills, innovation skills or craftsmanship. Problems of human capital utilization are dramatically reflected by an employee exiting from a firm. Besides exit, there are other less dramatic but equally costly problems, for example, when employees reduce human capital contributions, such as skill application and skill formation in the course of job performance. This has been widely researched in the organization theory literature as 'organizational misbehavior' (Ackroyd and Thompson 1999: 1–3, 25; see also Hikino 1997: 486–7), 'moonlighting and absenteeism' (Herzberg's 1966: 163; see Chapter 3, section 3.2), 'soldiering' (Taylor 1911: 19–20, 1903: 32; see Chapter 4, section 4.1), 'withdrawal behavior' (March and Simon 1958: 93; see Chapter 4, section 4.2) or 'perfunctory cooperation' (Williamson 1985: 262–3, 1975: 68–70, 80–81; see Chapter 4, section 4.3).

An economic resolution of problems of human capital utilization focuses on incentive structures. The basic approach can be summed up as follows:

> Entrepreneurs and members of organizations invest in the skills and knowledge which lead to revised evaluations of opportunities, which in turn induce alteration of the rules or the gradual revision of informal constraints.[5] The kind of skills and knowledge perceived to have a high payoff will, of course, reflect incentives embodied in the institutional framework. (North 1993b: 13)

Although a firm's communication structures may be implicit on this issue, references to training and organizational learning are likely to be anything than unconditional calls on organization members to indulge in learning. Rather, they express a firm's expectations regarding the formation of skills and the development of human capital. Contingency theory is in this respect close to institutional economic thought: 'The formally established educational programs, both on and off the job, that not only impart knowledge and skill but also provide another means for management to indicate how it expects organization members to behave on the job' (Lorsch 1983: 439).[6] This insight is deepened by North's explicit suggestion that incentive structures were to encourage organization members to contribute and develop human capital (see also Chapter 7, section 7.1). For the systemic governance of human capital utilization in the firm, besides employment contracts, incentive structures such as wage systems, promotion systems, pension plans or arrangements of severance payments can be considered (Becker 1965: 18, 1962: 23; see also section 2.1).

Contingency Features of Human Capital and Capital Utilization

Institutional economics analyzes and intervenes with capital utilization in relation to specific features of capital. They are discussed in the institutional economic literature as cost determinants of institutional ordering (Furubotn and Richter 1991: 21–3; Picot 1991; Williamson 1991c, 1985, 1975; Hesterly et al. 1990; Alchian 1984). Williamson (1985: 41–2, 387–8) speaks of 'transaction attributes' or Hesterly et al. (1990: 403–4) of 'inherent characteristics of the exchange'. Contingency features of (human) capital include: specificity of capital; complexity of capital; variability/uncertainty of capital inputs and outputs; strategic relevance of capital; and frequency of processes of capital utilization. In relation to the salience of these features, contractual and/or systemic incentive structures are to be designed by the firm. For example, if capital utilization in the firm involves highly specific capital, 'high-powered' incentive structures are needed to successfully safeguard incomplete contracting (Furubotn and Richter 1991: 18–21; Williamson 1985, as discussed in more detail in Chapter 4, section 4.3).

The idea of human asset specificity is of special importance. It goes beyond the conceptualization of specialization effects of human capital. It details that employees with specific skills, even if they occupy rather similar jobs in different firms, cannot be easily replaced. Firm-specific training and firm-specific learning-by-doing effects make human capital costly to substitute. It is the specification of human capital over time rather than specialization that makes human capital utilization a challenging conceptual and practical problem (Jensen and Meckling 1996: 19, 26–9; Williamson 1991c: 281, 291–2; Joskow 1988: 106–7; Alchian 1984; Klein et al. 1978; Hodgson 1991: 156–8). With asset specificity arising, potentially hazardous bargaining can occur. Then, more sophisticated high-powered incentive structures are needed (Becker 1965: 18, 1962: 23). Chapter 5 follows up.

2.3   HEURISTIC CONCEPTS (I): DILEMMA STRUCTURES AND THE SITUATIONAL ANALYSIS OF NONZERO-SUM INTERDEPENDENCE IN SOCIAL INTERACTIONS

Research heuristics play an important role in instructing theory-building and practical intervention (see Chapter 1, section 1.1). The idea of the dilemma structure is an important research heuristic of institutional economics and of economics in general. The following substantiates:

1.   The idea of the dilemma structure models unresolved interest conflict that prevents interacting agents from realizing mutual gains and leads to individual and collective loss as an interaction outcome.
2.   The idea of the dilemma structure methodically instructs institutional economic theory-building and practical intervention in a non-behavioral, situational terms: interaction outcomes are examined for the incentive-compatibility/incentive-*in*compatibility of incentive structures.
3.   The ideas of stability and efficiency provide intervention criteria for assessing the resolution of a dilemma structure.
4.   Accusations of the idea of the dilemma structure as a dark world view are misdirected. Understood as a heuristic tool, it does neither empirically nor normatively imply that social interactions always come or should come as dilemmatic interests conflict.

Instructing the Situational Analysis of Interdependence in Social Interactions

Interaction outcomes, such as cooperation, are not taken for granted in institutional analysis, not in economics or in behavioral, institutional studies. Brennan (1996: 256–7) here is explicit: 'To assume at the outset that the actor is motivated directly by a desire to promote the collective interest simply subverts the analytical exercise.' It appears that, in one way or another, most studies in economics and behavioral sciences start up analysis by modeling social conflict. Nussbaum (1986) implies this for Greek philosophy or Wagner-Tsukamoto (2001b) for Old Testament theology.

It can be suggested that institutional economics applies the idea of the dilemma structure as a heuristic analytical tool. It invokes interaction conflict in order to theoretically analyze and ultimately resolve it (if desired) by means of intervention with incentive structures (in detail, see Homann 1994; see also Goodin 1996; Hardin 1996, 1982; Maskin 1994). The idea of the dilemma structure suggests that common interests among agents, namely in mutual gains, are subverted by conflicting interests among agents, namely to improve individual gain at the expense of others (Homann 1994; see also Homann and Suchanek 2000: 32–40; Homann 1999b: 125–7, 1994; Vanberg 1994: 63, 91–3). This idea was touched upon by Williamson (1996a: 137) or Buchanan (1995: 142–7, 1987b: 42–4, 1975: 136–42) and more incompletely by many other institutional researchers, for example, Hayek (1976: 70, 1960: 270) or Popper (1957: 62, 158). Broadly speaking, the idea of the dilemma structure suggests that unresolved interest conflict undermines mutually advantageous interaction outcomes: '[P]otential *conflict* threatens to undo or upset opportunities to realize *mutual* gains' (Williamson 1996a: 137, emphasis as in original). A 'contracting dilemma' is to be investigated (Williamson 1985: 62–3; see also Chapter 4, section 4.3). This dilemmatic model of social behavior is reminiscent of Hobbes's model of the war of all (Homann and Suchanek 2000: 35; Williamson 1996a: 137; Baurmann and Kliemt 1995: 33; Furubotn and Richter 1991: 8; Homann and Suchanek 1989: 79; Buchanan 1987b: 157; Mintz 1962: 135; see also Hirschman 1970: 1). For the firm unresolved interest conflicts leads to 'organizational misbehavior', such as absenteeism, low productivity, strikes, grievance problems and other forms of 'subversive behavior' (Ackroyd and Thompson 1999: 1–2, 25; similarly, Pruijt 1997: 15).

In game-theoretical terms, institutional economics models interaction dilemmas as *nonzero*-sum interactions but not as zero-sum ones. In zero-sum interactions, it is inconceivable that all agents could be winners or losers *at the same time*. Neither mutual gains nor mutual loss are possible interaction outcomes. In contrast, in nonzero-sum interactions mutual gains but also mutual loss can be the outcome when self-interested decision-makers interact. The nonzero-sum game 'played' in the prisoners' dilemma well illustrates the idea of the dilemma structure (Homann and Suchanek 2000: 36–8; Homann 1999a: 2–3, 1997a: 5–11, 1994; Vanberg 1994: 91–3, 1986: 93–6; Homann and Pies 1991: 609–11; see also Lohmann 1996: 132; Nozick 1993: 50–9; Coleman 1990: 203–4; Buchanan 1987b: 42–7, 157; Schotter 1981; Hardin 1968: 1244–5; Luce and Raiffa 1957: 94–7). The specific incentive structures of the prisoners' dilemma instigate an interaction process that drives interacting agents, on the grounds of individually rational, self-interested choice, to violate their own best interests (see Figure 2.3). Mutual loss results for interacting individuals and the group as a whole. This could be interpreted in behavioral terms as 'rational foolishness' (Hollis 1994: 139, 255–6; Sen 1990: 43; see also Rowlinson 1997: 10–11; Elster 1989: 108; Sen 1987: 81–8).

The idea of the dilemma structure models individual agents as codetermining – unavoidably, intentionally or unintentionally – gains or losses for each agent. Game theory here is explicit. It details that economics conceptualizes social problems as interdependence problems in which 'every participant is

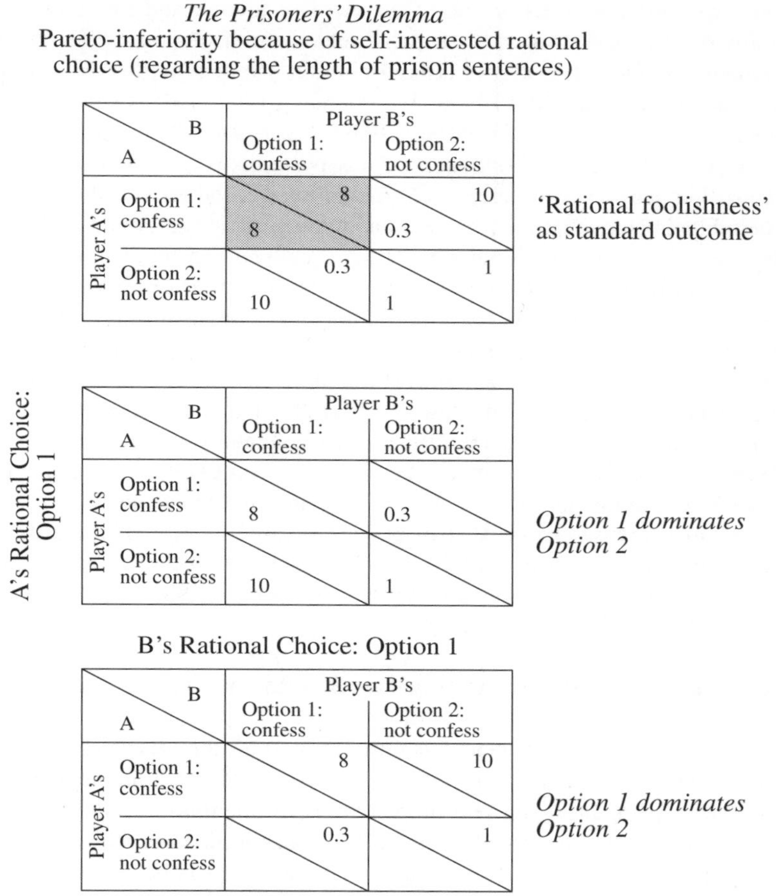

The Prisoners' Dilemma
Pareto-inferiority because of self-interested rational
choice (regarding the length of prison sentences)

	B A	Player B's	
		Option 1: confess	Option 2: not confess
Player A's	Option 1: confess	8 8	10 0.3
	Option 2: not confess	0.3 10	1 1

'Rational foolishness'
as standard outcome

**A's Rational Choice:
Option 1**

	B A	Player B's	
		Option 1: confess	Option 2: not confess
Player A's	Option 1: confess	8	0.3
	Option 2: not confess	10	1

*Option 1 dominates
Option 2*

B's Rational Choice: Option 1

	B A	Player B's	
		Option 1: confess	Option 2: not confess
Player A's	Option 1: confess	8	10
	Option 2: not confess	0.3	1

*Option 1 dominates
Option 2*

Figure 2.3   Rational fools?

influenced by the anticipated reactions of the others to his own measures'
(von Neumann and Morgenstern 1947: 13; see also Vanberg 1994: 92;
Buchanan 1987b: 155). For example, in the prisoners' dilemma, interdependence of individual choices is set up by the way the pay-out matrix is
constructed. Or, in the commons dilemma, an arrangement of shared property
rights regarding the communal asset 'meadow' sets up interdependence
among individual farmers (Hardin 1968; see also Scott 2000: 44; Coleman
1990: 20–21; Nussbaum 1986: 1–3, 47–50, Chapter 12; more generally on the

property rights issue, see Hart 1995; Barzel 1989; Alchian and Demsetz 1973). By invoking interdependence of individual choices, economic analysis is developed as *inter*action theory rather than as a theory of collective action or individual action (Homann 1999a: 3–4; Gerecke 1997: 102; Buchanan 1994: 56; see also Vanberg 2001: 1994: 92, 1986: 75; Becker 1993: 386). Etzioni's (1988: 3–4) critique that economics did not investigate codetermination has to be qualified in this regard. In general, (institutional) economics is disinterested in individual behavior *per se*. Rather, it analyzes *aggregated* outcomes of individual decisions. Although much neoclassic analysis moved beyond the idea of the single person 'Robinson Crusoe economy' (von Neumann and Morgenstern 1947: 12–13), the neoclassic model of an infinite number of choice-makers implied that decision-makers were merely structurally but not strategically interlinked. When an infinite number of agents is encountered, the individual's choices do not affect the overall outcome of social interactions (von Neumann and Morgenstern 1947: 13–15). Free-riding, outguessing and bargaining problems are no issue. In contrast, outcomes of social interactions cannot be calculated by just 'adding up' the gains and losses attached to individual choices when the number of players is finite – and when interdependence conflicts can arise (Gerecke 1997: 118–19, 137–40; Coleman 1990: 20–21; Vanberg 1986: 75; see also Williamson 1990: 2, 1985: 76; Moss 1981: 8; Jacquemin 1987: 48–9; Machlup 1967: 9, 16).

Intervening with a Dilemma Structure: Stability and Cost Effects

In practical–normative perspective, the model of the dilemma structure reflects an intervention tool for resolving interest conflicts. Normative institutional economics here suggests intervention in situational, non-behavioral terms. Its maxim is 'that the [situational] rules of certain social "games" must be changed whenever it [irrationality] is inherent in the game situation' (Luce and Raiffa 1957: 97). Whereas behavioral analysis of 'rational foolishness' suggests a weakness of character and a problem of human nature (for example, Sen 1999, 1990, 1987; Hollis 1994; to a degree, see also Rubinstein 1998: 122–4, 184–5; Binmore 1994: 18–19; Binmore and Dasgupta 1986: 6–8; Elster 1983: 42), institutional economics analyzes 'foolish' interaction outcomes as a situational condition. Interaction conflict is traced to 'defective' incentive structures, that is incentive structures that induce rational, self-interested individuals to maximize individual utility but, because of the interdependence of individual choices, yield an interaction outcome, which is not in the best interest of any individual involved (Homann and Suchanek 2000: 35–8; Homann 1997: 26, 1994, 1990; see also Lohmann 1996: 132). Hence, normative institutional economics analyzes how to change the rules of the game in order to resolve conflict.

Vanberg (1994: 63) quite clearly picks up Luce and Raiffa's suggestion when he proposes that Hobbesian anarchy can be prevented by 'deliberately changing the pay-off structure of the generalized prisoners' dilemma matrix'. Nussbaum (1986: 51) develops a comparable view regarding the conception and resolution of tragedy in Greek philosophy: that 'a political system . . . should order things so that the sincere efforts of such persons [who are caught up in tragic conflict] will regularly meet with success'. Such insights on the systemic resolution of social conflict seem to play a small role in Sen's (1990, 1987) assessment of the prisoners' dilemma. Unsurprisingly, Sen favors behavioral ethics of a communitarian tradition for discussing and resolving societal problems (also Sen 1999). In this regard, he proceeds like neo-Marxist, post-modern ethics (for example, Bauman 2001, 1992).

It is important to note that institutional economics only heuristically examines social problems as prisoners' dilemma (Homann and Suchanek 2000: 456–62; also Homann 1994). The idea of the dilemma structure provides an analytical device to examine interaction problems as a *situational* condition but not as the human condition. This reflects the classical understanding of economics, as set out by Adam Smith. Some of Elster's (1989: 107–8) suggestions can be reinterpreted in this way, reconstructing loss/loss outcomes of interactions as heuristic concepts of normative institutional economics. If desired, normative institutional economics resolves a dilemma structure to the mutual advantage of interacting agents by intervening with 'defective' incentive structures, making them incentive-compatible. It takes dilemmatic interaction outcomes as a starting point. And, in this respect, the analytical approach of economics may well compare, like the ones of most other social sciences, to Hobbesian philosophy (see also Mintz 1962: 135). Nussbaum (1986) provides an excellent discussion of the nature and relevance of a model of tragic conflict in Greek philosophy. She points out that tragic dilemmas lie at the heart of ethical theory. They are invoked in order to discuss their resolution and constraints that prevent the resolution of dilemmas (Nussbaum 1986: 50–51). Equally, Old Testament theology seems to proceed similarly (Wagner-Tsukamoto 2001b). Such a wide application of dilemma models may have implications for the moral assessment of the idea 'dilemma structure'. Chapter 8 follows up.

Institutional economics aims to resolve interaction conflict in a different way than behavioral sciences or an evolutionary economics. The former relies on behavioral intervention, intending to generate a value consensus (see Chapter 3); the latter expects that cooperation 'evolved' through the moves of the game, for example, tit-for-tat behavior (Baurmann and Kliemt 1995; Axelrod 1986; Schotter 1986; Tullock 1985; see also Rowlinson 1997: 12). Both strategies for conflict resolution have in common that the rules of the game are not intervened with but that agents somehow learn to resolve the dilemma through the moves of the game. Such conflict resolution is likely to be time consuming and costly and as long as the original dilemma structure remains in place, conflict resolution is likely to be of a temporary nature (see also Ockenfels 1999: 9–10; Schramm 1997; Vanberg 1994: 92–3, 1986: 85–96; North 1993b: 12; Gambetta 1988: 227; Williams 1988: 6; Buchanan 1987b: 157). Classic here is Hardin's (1968: 1246) argumentation, who sourly noted that, unless the incentive structures of a dilemma structure are intervened with, the moral conscience of agents who are caught up in the dilemma is 'self-eliminating' (see also Homann and Pies 1991; Chapter 3, section 3.3).[7] The success of behavioral intervention to remedy 'rationally foolish' interaction outcomes, for example through moral pedagogy, which tried to make agents less self-interested, can be questioned.

Operational intervention criteria of institutional economics can be detailed stability and efficiency features of incentive structures. Depending on what is desired, incentive structures should resolve/install interaction conflict *for some time* and *at low cost*.[8] Conventions regarding stability in social interactions are common in most studies of social order, in economic, political, sociological, socio-psychological or philosophical studies (Wagner-Tsukamoto 2001b; Gerecke 1997: 102; Scott 1995a: 49, 1995b: xiii; North 1993b: 6; Pies 1993: 159–87; Coleman 1990: 38–44; Williams 1988; Becker 1976: 5; von Neumann and Morgenstern 1947: 41). Economics conventionally conceptualizes stable interactions through the equilibrium models.[9] They reflect supplementary heuristic conventions of economic analysis. Interactions can be viewed to be in a stable state of a cooperation equilibrium if interactions yield the same mutually advantages outcome when repeated. However, an equilibrium of non-cooperation – a dilemma equilibrium – is met if the pay-out matrix of a dilemma structure is not changed (see Figure 2.2).

Besides stability assessments, normative institutional economics makes efficiency assessments. Design costs, information costs (including retraining costs), intervention costs (destabilizing and restabilizing costs[10]), as well as maintenance costs (for example, policing costs) of institutional organization have to be assessed. Such costs are paid by those involved in social interactions. If one neglected these costs, for instance, by applying an unlimited future time horizon, which would make the one-off consideration of design costs and information costs irrelevant, the redesign of incentive structures would be worthwhile as soon as some gains greater than zero could be generated through redesign. However, under a restricted time horizon, and/or the (financial) discounting of future gains, and/or the consideration of design costs, information costs as well as changes to maintenance costs, gains resulting from institutional redesign had to be higher than zero, covering these costs. For reasons of such cost considerations, institutional organization cannot be changed as soon as the effectiveness of existing incentive structures begins to deteriorate. Some of North's (1993a) suggestions can be reapproached in this respect.

Transaction cost theory, as proposed by Williamson (1985, 1975) or Hesterly et al. (1990: 404), explicitly focuses on efficiency rather than stability analysis of interactions. This has been interpreted as a comparatively low relevance of transaction cost theory for certain types of institutional analysis. Buchanan (1987b: 155–66) here is rather critical, although he may interpret the idea of transaction costs possibly too narrowly as mere search costs. But at least implicitly, it can be suggested that stability and equilibrium analysis are conducted by transaction cost theory, too, for instance when issues of 'interest equilibration' are discussed (Williamson 1985: 34). Likewise, it appears a misstatement to claim (DiMaggio and Powell 1991b: 63–4) that institutional economics *only* conducts efficiency analysis and that efficiency analysis is *irrelevant* to institutional analysis. As outlined, institutional economics analyzes the stability of interactions, although in a different way than behavioral sciences (see also Chapter 3 and Chapter 8, section 8.2). Institutional economics stresses the relevance of efficiency analysis in relation to costs of institutional ordering. Those who pay these costs are likely to have an interest to keep costs low.

2.4   HEURISTIC CONCEPTS (II): ECONOMIC MAN AND THE SITUATIONAL ANALYSIS OF SELF-INTERESTED, UTILITY-MAXIMIZING CHOICE

Conventional wisdom is that the model of economic man depicts an empirically incorrect and morally questionable image of human nature. Such suggestions can be revised if the model of economic man is interpreted as a research heuristic. The following substantiates:

1. Concepts such as 'economic man', 'sociological man' or 'psychological man' are methodical fictions whose primary function is to heuristically instruct theoretical–(practical) analysis. On holistic, empirical–behavioral grounds, they could all be dismissed as unrealistic.
2. Understood as a research heuristic, the model of economic man should not be subjected to empirical–behavioral and moral–behavioral scrutiny.
3. (Institutional) economics heuristically applies the model of economic man (and the model of the dilemma structure) as analytical devices for analyzing and intervening with incentive structures.

Behavioral Criticism of 'Economic Man'

Behavioral criticism of 'economic man' as unrealistic and immoral is common. Classic is Sen's (1990) 'rational fool' critique of the model of economic man. Representative is Morgan (1997: 77, 91), too: 'Rational economic man is essentially a caricature: there is something inherently laughable about him. . . . A caricature relies on a distortion or exaggeration of certain characteristics beyond the point of objective truth.' Machlup (1978), especially Chapters 10 and 11 on *Homo Oeconomicus and His Class Mates* and *The Universal Bogey*, provide a rich and entertaining review of similar, derisory criticism of the model of economic man in 19th-century and early 20th-century writings.

Then and now, on empirical–behavioral and moral–behavioral grounds, the model of economic man has been criticized as a 'caricature', 'rational fool', 'cold calculator', 'social moron', 'fairy tale character', 'super human being with unfaltering foresight and total knowledge', 'human being with omniscient rationality' and so on (Schroeder 2001: 65–6; Hunt 2000: 116–18; Mohammadian 2000: 11, 36; Rabin 1998: 11–13; Zey 1998: 99–103, 111; Morgan 1997: 77, 91; Brown 1996: 99; Green and Shapiro 1996: 244–5, 270–71; Murphy 1996: 172; Donaldson 1995: 169–72, 184–7; Scott 1995a: 21–2, 50–51; Hollis 1994: 116–18, 185–6, 258; England 1993: 37–47; Ferber and Nelson 1993: 4–6; Mumby and Putnam 1992; Menell 1992: 493; Woolsey Biggart and Hamilton 1992: 480–1, 488; Biervert and Held 1991: 7; Held 1991: 26–7; Lindenberg 1990: 727; Etzioni 1988: ix, 140–41; Jensen 1987: 1068–9; Zey-Ferrell 1981: 194–5; Heinen 1976: 395; Argyris 1973; Knowles and Saxberg 1967: 24–6, 32; Herzberg 1966; Storing 1962; Veblen 1898: 389). Such critique is frequently brought forward by sociological and psychological researchers. But is was also proposed by behavioral economists and behaviorally oriented economists, for example, Sen (1999: 4–5, 1990: 25, 30, 35, 37, 1987: 78–9), Hodgson (1998: 173, 1993b: 5–7, 14–16, 1988: 73–4, 147), Rubinstein (1998: 16, 22–3), Coase (1994: 111), Jensen and Meckling (1994: 5–13, 18–19), Tool (1994: 210–12), North (1993b: 13, 15), March (1978: 591) or Georcescu-Roegen (1971), to name a few. Research in the tradition of 'old' institutional economics, such as Commons (1961, 1931), is rather behaviorally orientated, too (Hodgson 1998, 1993b).

Of course, Simon is the leading protagonist of behavioral economics, followed, to a considerable extent, by new institutional economists like Williamson (see Chapter 6, section 6.3), to a lesser degree by Vanberg (1993) and, more expectedly, by economically orientated sociology (for example, Coleman 1990). See Chapter 3, section 3.1, Chapter 6 and Chapter 8, section 8.1 for further details. Such behavioral criticism of the model of economic man ignores the problem-dependent and heuristic nature of the research concept 'economic man' (see Chapter 1, section 1.1; Persky 1995: 223–4, 230; Homann 1994: 6–7, 11; Suchanek 1993; Zintl 1989; Buchanan 1987b; Becker 1976; Machlup 1978, 1967; even the early Hollis, for example Hollis 1977: 181–2). Economics neither theoretically analyzes nor practically intervenes with human nature in the way behavioral sciences do.[11] The model of economic man may just be instrumental regarding economics' non-behavioral approach to theory building and practical intervention. On the other hand, the model of economic man can probably not instruct behavioral theory-building or behavioral intervention, for example, psychological research on human motivation or sociological research on role behavior.

A Situational Model of Self-interested, Utility-maximizing Choice

The model of economic man organizes the situational analysis of decision-making. It focuses research attention on the individual's rational reaction to incentive structures and the gains or losses they signal (Homann and Suchanek 2000: 31–2, 42–3; Homann 1997a: 2–3, 1994: 7, 1990: 9–10; Abell 1995: 6–7; Buchanan 1994: 47–8, 1987b: 51–63; see also Binmore 1998: 13–14; Gerecke 1997: 120–21; Becker 1993: 385, 402; Pies 1993: 94, 141; Suchanek 1993: 6, 7, 14; Zintl 1989: 62–3; Stigler and Becker 1977: 76, 82–3; Becker 1976: 5, 9; Machlup 1967: 11; Friedman 1953).[12] As Machlup formulated: '[T]he purpose of . . . [economic] theory . . . [is] not to explain observed actions but only observable *results* of imagined (postulated) reactions to observable events' (Machlup 1967: 11, Footnote 5; see also Homann 1994: 7; Homann and Suchanek 1989: 75–80; Machlup 1978: 281, 298–9). 'Results' and 'observable events' can be conceptually detailed as capital exchange that is organized by incentive structures. In economic research, only 'incentive structures' and 'capital utilization' are to be empirically scrutinized. And in this respect it is wrong to characterize economics as a 'non-empirical discipline', as done by Mueller (1995: 1231). Only the model of economic man – the 'imagined reaction' – should not be empirically tested. It is a 'mere' research heuristic, and is thus being realism and 'objective truth'. In the first place, the model of economic man has to be understood as a '*method* of analysis, not an [empirical–behavioral] assumption about particular motivations' (Becker 1993: 385).

'Economic man' only sets out a methodically *individualistic* model of choice behavior. Economics 'uses [rational choice] theory at the micro-level as a powerful tool to derive implications at the group or macro level' (Becker 1993: 402; similarly Abell 1995: 6; Vromen 1995: 199–200; Madison 1995; Homann 1994: 5; Suchanek 1993: 3, 10; Coleman 1990: 5; Brunner 1987: 576; Buchanan 1987b: 54–5, 63; Schotter 1981; Machlup 1978: 292–9, 1967: 7; Hayek 1949; see also Ockenfels 1999: 64). Theoretically, empirically and practically, economics applies this 'individualistic' heuristic to the analysis of interaction problems over capital utilization, investigating how incentive structures can support the generation of socially desirable outcomes. Interdependence and codetermination is implied in a theoretical–practical perspective. Normative issues, like the goal of mutual gains, reflects such 'social issues', too.

The model of economic man does not instruct behavioral, psychological or sociological analysis. 'Economic man' heuristically models rational choice, that is – in a conventional economic understanding – self-interested, utility-maximizing decision-making. The idea of self-interest can be interpreted, broadly speaking, as the individual's interest in bettering his personal position (Popper 1992: vii). The idea of self-interest leaves the model of economic man motivationally undetermined. It is up to the individual to interpret the notion of the 'happy life' in terms of monetary and/or non-monetary gains (Olson 1971; see also Vanberg 2001: 110; Homann and Suchanek 2000: 30–31; Pettit 1996: 64–5; Becker 1976: 5). Many behavioral researchers wrongly suggest in this respect that economics modelled financial incentives and motives only, early on so advocates of the human relations school (Mayo 1990: 357; see also McGregor 1960 and Chapter 3, section 3.2). Similarly, the idea of utility-maximizing behavior reflects a heuristic convention of economics. It does not set out the model of economic man in empirical–behavioral, cognitive psychological terms. Chapter 6 follows up.

Economics heuristically treats cognition, motivation (preferences), roles and other behavioral constructs as 'stable' when theoretically analyzing and practically intervening with human behavior in situational terms (Becker 1976: 14, also ibid. 1976: 5; similarly Abell 1995: 7; Langlois and Csontos 1993: 114–15; Stigler and Becker 1977: 76–7, 87–9). Human nature, understood in a behavioral sense, is abstracted from: 'A theoretical scheme on such a high level of abstraction . . . makes people disappear from view and with them not only the motives and behavior of individuals but also the structure of social relations and the differentiated collectives in society' (Blau 1976a: 5, see also Suchanek 1992: 40–43; Coleman 1990). Interestingly, Blau (1976a) and similarly Coleman (1990) made such points for macro-*sociology* (see also Chapter 3). As a matter of problem dependence and the heuristic organization of research, economics, like macro-sociology, does not analyze human behavior in psychological or micro-sociological terms.

If an attempt was made to analyze human behavior both in economic terms as capital utilization in relation to incentive structures and in behavioral terms, for example, as a role performance in relation to cultural influences, this yields problems of interdisciplinary, holistic modeling, which are likely to stifle scientific research because of neglected problem dependence and neglected complexity reduction (see also Chapter 1, section 1.1 and Chapter 6).

Lindenberg (1985: 253) hinted at this: 'Either you are looking for changes in constraints or you are looking for changes in preferences' (see also Gerecke 1997: 122; Becker 1976: 11–12). Popper formulated in this respect: 'My thesis is that it is sound *methodological* policy to decide not to make the rationality principle, but the rest of the theory – that is the [situational] model – [theoretically, practically and empirically] accountable' (Popper 1995: 355, emphasis added; see also Hedström and Swedberg 1996: 133; Caldwell 1994: 141–4; Hands 1993: 70; Popper 1992: 79–80, 1972: 178–80; Coleman 1990: 5; Langlois 1990: 692–4, who refers to Max Weber; Becker 1976: 167). Persky (1995: 224) and Machlup (1978: 105–6) make a comparable point for Mill's research, detailing that Mill 'used' in the *Principles of Political Economy* the model of economic man only to theoretically and empirically research institutions but not to develop a psychology of human behavior (see also Crisp 1997: 178).

In a practical–normative perspective, institutional economics applies the model of economic man as a 'tool' to test out incentive structures (Brennan 1996: 257; Homann 1994: 8–10; Pies 1993: 94, 119, 141–2, 175, 189–91; Homann 1992: 10; Schlösser 1992: 9, 37; Suchanek 1991: 78, 81–2; Brennan and Buchanan 1986: Chapter 4, 382, 391).[13] Understood in this way, the model of economic man could not be (mis)read as a behavioral recommendation to behave in a purely self-interested way.

2.5 CONCLUDING REMARKS

Hart (1995: 166) observed some emerging convergence of theories that make up the new institutional economics. This chapter contributed to the identification of some common themes in (new institutional) economic thought by clarifying generic heuristic and theoretical–(practical) concepts. This may encourage the conceptual streamlining of institutional economic theories, such as property rights theory, principal–agent theory and transaction cost theory. Hart (1995) and similarly Williamson (1996d) pointed out that this is important for the further development of institutional economics as well as the successful transfer and application of institutional economic ideas to business history research, business ethics research or other 'sub-disciplines' of management studies and social studies.

It is likely to be little debated that economics formulates and addresses research problems and research questions in a different way than behavioral research. In a theoretical–(practical) perspective, economics is disinterested in behavioral inquiry, for example, the psychological examination of motivation or cognition. (Institutional) economics' strategy regarding theory-building and practical intervention can be detailed as: *Analyze individual decision-making regarding capital contributions to and capital distributions from an interaction in relation to incentive structures.* In a practical–normative perspective, this theory-building strategy can be specified as: *(Re)design incentive structures in order to equilibrate (self)interests of individual choice-makers so that interactions over capital contributions and distributions yield socially desirable outcomes, such as mutual gains.* Concepts of capital utilization, incentive structures and mutual gains are to be empirically scrutinized. In a methodical perspective, economic theory-building and practical intervention apply the 'action' heuristic 'economic man' and the 'interaction' heuristic 'dilemma structure'. These heuristics are tailored to the situational, non-behavioral analysis of capital utilization in relation to incentive structures but as heuristics they are beyond empirical scrutiny.

In this regard, Homans (1976: 65) rightly warned that certain 'ghosts' were waiting to haunt researchers who assessed all research concepts on empirical–behavioral grounds. Like other heuristic models of human nature and social life, 'dilemma structure' and 'economic man' are the wrong target of holistic, empirical–behavioral and moral–behavioral criticism. 'Dark images' of social life and 'dark images' of human nature are likely to be heuristically invoked by any social science research program that does not take for granted the resolution of social problems. Otherwise, even theology could be accused of an immoral image of human nature and of social life (Chapters 3 and 8 follow up). Also, in theoretical–practical terms, behavioral sciences can only handle a '*part*-image' of human nature. Simply expressed, they theoretically *model* human nature and they apply selective intervention strategies, which focus on certain aspects of human nature only.

By applying the ideas 'economic man' and 'dilemma structure', institutional economics can resolve interaction conflict even if interactions (only) involved self-interested agents, or differently, more favorably put, if pluralism characterized social interactions. Behavioral research is less successful in this respect. Indicative are the problems encountered by communism, ecotopian concepts, behavioral and religious business ethics approaches or 'soft', 'postmodern' concepts of stakeholder management. This is detailed in subsequent chapters (see also Wagner-Tsukamoto 2002, 2001a).

Although economics, like any research program, methodically applies research heuristics, it would be an overstatement to claim that economics is 'methods-driven' especially if method-driven research was understood as an opposite to problem-driven research. This is apparently done by Green and Shapiro (1996: 270) and similarly by Murphy (1996: 171). They linked the idea of problem-driven research to interdisciplinary theory-building. This leads to methodological difficulties because of 'comprehensive modeling' and neglected complexity reduction (see Chapter 1, section 1.1). The question of interdisciplinary research may have to be approached, in the first place, in a practical–normative perspective only. Collaboration of different research programs can then be negotiated regarding practical intervention, for example through a prioritizing logic (see Chapter 8, section 8.2).

NOTES

1. Levi-Strauss (1966: 32) similarly reckoned: '[A] game produces events by means of structure; and we can therefore understand why competitive games should flourish in our industrial societies.' And comparable to economics or to interactionist, social psychology in the tradition of Weick (1995, 1979; see also Chapter 3, section 3.2) or a sociological economics in the tradition of Coleman (1990), Levi-Strauss' structural anthropology aimed to 'decanter' the individual in anthropological analysis (Sarup 1993: 1).
2. Lobbying can probably be viewed as another mode of private ordering a firm can engage in. Although, lobbying is likely to raise a number of questions regarding potential conflicts of interest between a firm and those who are involved in public ordering, as a form of institutional behavior lobbying is likely to require different institutional regulation than contracting and the systemic structuring of the firm.
3. For both market transactions and organizational ones, the use of incentive structures comes with costs. Transaction costs arise (Williamson 1975; Coase 1972, 1937; Becker 1965; Stigler 1961; see also Jensen and Meckling 1996; Coase 1992; Williamson 1985), that is search costs for finding contract partners and contracting costs for contract negotiation, contract control and contract adaptation.
4. Interestingly, Furubotn and Richter (1991: 18) refer here to 'utility maximization', apparently implying a heuristic interpretation of the model of economic man. They may have to detail how this can be reconciled with a behavioral understanding of bounded rationality, as suggested by Furobotn and Richter (1991: 4). Chapters 5 and 6 aim at a 'reconciliation' by differentiating methods and theoretical–(practical) concepts of economics as far as they relate to 'bounded rationality'.
5. North relates 'informal constraints' to cultural norms, social glue, personal trust and perceptions of duty or virtue. The implied behavioral approach cannot correct problems of incentive-*in*compatible institutional structures. For the purpose of economic analysis and intervention, ideas like culture, social glue or trust are probably better reconceptualized as capital and/or as incentive structures (see also Chapters 5 and 6; and Wagner-Tsukamoto 2002).
6. Issues concerning the content of communication and training programs are likely to reflect behavioral research problems of organization psychology or institutional sociology.
7. See also the literature on adverse selection and free riding, for example, Runge (1984) or Tullock (1985).
8. A third criterion, which is not further discussed here, relates to innovation and the maintenance and creation of market opportunities, which appear necessary for ensuring the long-term survival of the firm (see also Chapter 7).
9. Empirically, the occurrence of stable states or 'equilibrium states' may be illusory (see also Wagner-Tsukamoto 2003). Empirical research may have to focus on *changes* in (dis)equilibrium processes rather than the identification of equilibrium states (for a review of key literature on equilibrium analysis, see Binmore and Dasgupta 1986). Market process theory proceeds this way, but heuristically it is still grounded in an equilibrium model of social exchange.
10. Destabilizing costs reflect costs incurred by the rational reaction of choice-makers to impending rule change. Time gaps between the issuing of new rules and their actual implementation frequently lead to 'cost bellies' since 'defects' of existing rules are widely publicized through the announcement of impending rule change. Restabilizing costs reflect costs of establishing a new interaction equilibrium.
11. The concept of capital utilization indirectly reflects a theoretical–(practical) model of human

nature – of human capital. In this regard, assessments of economics' image of human nature divert from a behavioral critique of the model of economic man. Chapter 5 follows up.

12. Economics models not only individuals but also social entities, such as a firm or a nation, as 'economic man'. For instance, in market structure economics, the firm is modeled as a single 'economic man'. This is fruitful for the theoretical–(practical) analysis of price and cost structures of markets and how they impact capital utilization on markets (see Chapter 7, section 7.1).

13. In the engineering sciences, a comparable test function is discussed in relation to design requirements (for example, Dasgupta 1991: 366; Addis 1983: 3).

3. Behavioral approaches to institutional organization: Towards a 'science of human nature'?

> Industry . . . must recognize that if it is to use human beings effectively, it must treat them in terms of their complete nature rather than in terms of those characteristics that appear to be suitable to their organization. Industry cannot progress by continuing to perpetuate a half-conceptual view of man. (Herzberg, 1966, p. 170)

> Many sociologists and other social scientists leave the equivalent of the axiomatic, that is their major premises, unstated. But if unstated they are still there, like ghosts waiting to materialize. (Homans, 1976, p. 65)

It is beyond the purpose and scope of this book to outline in depth a behavioral approach to institutional organization. The following focuses on selected issues that are important for assessing the portrayal of human nature in behavioral research. The chapter discounts behavioral criticism of the image of human nature of economics by investigating heuristic and theoretical–practical aspects of behavioral research. Section 3.1 suggests that even behavioral philosophy cannot portray human nature in solely empirical, holistic terms. Behavioral sciences that aim at empirical holism encounter further limits, namely regarding the problem-dependent nature of scientific research. Section 3.2 questions whether psychological theory and practice, which focuses on individual behavior, can solve social problems in the firm, especially performance problems. Section 3.3 stresses that behavioral research is, like economics, grounded in a pre-empirical, heuristic model of human nature. Section 3.4 discusses how contextual factors, such as value pluralism ('the condition of modernity') and the institutional structures of the market economy, undermine the effectiveness of behavioral intervention that aims at the human condition. Section 3.5 concludes the chapter.

3.1 THE QUEST FOR HOLISM AND INTERDISCIPLINARITY: BEHAVIORAL SCIENCES DRIFTING INTO PHILOSOPHY

The previous chapters stressed that a holistic portrayal of human nature is likely to conceptually overburden any scientific research program, both behavioral ones and economics. Probably only philosophy can conduct truly interdisciplinary research on human nature. The following substantiates:

1. Philosophical research on human nature is instructed by concepts that compare to the idea of the research heuristic. Even philosophy is not capable of developing a solely empirically grounded, holistic 'science of man'.
2. Social science research that aims at the holistic, empirical–behavioral and moral–behavioral portrayal of human nature overlooks the problem-dependent and heuristic nature of scientific research. If both economic variables and goals ('incentive structures', 'capital utilization', 'mutual gains') and behavioral variables and goals ('behavioral rules', 'human nature', 'social harmony') are included in institutional theory, scientific analysis suffers a complexity problem.
3. Sciences can at best research fragments of human nature. Holistic research on human nature, as advocated by behavioral economics and economic sociology, exits from science and enters philosophy.

Philosophy and the Question of Human Nature

The question of human nature is well debated in philosophy. Traditionally, philosophy has approached this question from an empirical–normative angle. For instance, the studies of Plato or Aristotle examined human nature in theoretical and empirical terms and on this basis made normative suggestions regarding 'good' behavior. In *De Anima*, *Parva Naturalia* and *De Spiritu*, Aristotle investigated spiritual, cognitive and physiological aspects of human existence. A comprehensive, empirically based description of human nature, in a sense, a 'true' image of human nature resulted, which reflected insights into human nature of the time. In a subsequent step, Greek philosophy, like most philosophy, projects an empirically developed understanding of human nature to normative questions, mostly questions regarding the role of morality in human behavior:

> Two of Plato's main interests were in science and morality. He thought if one did the first properly one's problems with the second would be solved . . . For in his view the main problem in morality is to discover how it is best for a man to live and a fully developed scientific understanding will reveal how it is best for things to be, where 'things' include humanity. (Gosling 1973: 1)

On the basis of empirical research into human nature, Greek philosophy advises on the moral life. Contemporary philosophy has continued in this tradition. Based on empirical observation, features of human nature are identified, attempting to generate a complete image of human nature, although moral advice on the good life is more sparingly given. For example, anthropological philosophy collects and 'unifies' findings on human nature generated by biology, physiology, psychology, sociology, anthropology, archaeology, economics and so on. It comprehensively portrays human nature (Betzig 1997; Rehberg 1988; Gehlen 1962; Gadamer 1943; see also Markoczy and Goldberg 1998 for further references). The 'unification' of research findings of social sciences and life sciences is anything than a trivial task in the face of rapidly advancing, scientific knowledge on human nature. Unification probably resembled a multidisciplinary kaleidoscope or a 'critical reader on human nature', as Betzig (1997) puts it, rather than 'interdisciplinary integration' of different concepts of human nature into a single 'theory'. The theoretical and practical purpose of anthropological philosophy and methodological principles that instruct it differ from the ones of scientific research programs.

Heuristic Basis of Philosophical Research into Human Nature

Empirical, philosophical research into human nature may appear straightforward. However, the arguments outlined in section Chapter 1.1 for scientific research apply, with modifications, to philosophical research too. Heuristic foundations of philosophical research into human nature can be set out in relation to the *identification question* of human beings: Human beings need to be identified before philosophical research on human nature can begin. The identification question can be attacked as of little practical relevance since our experience seems to tell us that it is unproblematic to identify human beings. Nevertheless, identification problems quickly develop if questions regarding the boundaries of human existence and human nature are raised, such as: From which age on does an embryo classify as a human being? Is a person who is in a state of coma a human being? Can the genetic engineering of human beings be reconciled with human existence? And so on. These questions refer to borderline cases of human existence. They are anything but unimportant for discussing human nature. Indeed, only through the discussion of these borderline questions can answers be developed regarding human nature.

Identification problems imply that a categorical, pre-empirical understanding of human nature underlies philosophical research into human nature: 'Only through the (at least implicit) application of a categorical understanding of human nature, individuals can be identified as elements of the group "man" and then be [empirically] examined for common, shared characteristics' (Herms 1993: 677). For example, Gehlen's anthropological philosophy drew in this respect on Nietzsche's (1903) notion of the 'human being as the not yet determined animal' (Gehlen 1962: 10). This openness of human nature implies openness towards a 'dark side'. This has been of key interest to theology, moral philosophy and the social sciences (see Adorno and Gehlen 1974: 226–8; Gehlen 1962: 10, 35–8).

A categorical, philosophical understanding of human nature can be axiomatized as follows: *Being capable of self-reflection, the human being is destined to self-determination* (or '*self-imaging*', figuratively expressed). By adding the idea of the human being as the *social* being, self-determination can be specified as self-determination in relation to others: *Self-determination implies codetermination among human beings*. This understanding of human nature can be taken as a heuristic starting point for philosophical, theological and social science research programs. Obviously, these programs conceptualize self-determination and codetermination in a rather different way, specifying different heuristic problem formulation and problem-solving apparatuses and different theoretical–(practical) approaches (for instance, see Figures 1.2, 1.3 and Figure 3.3; see also Hassard 1993: 4–6).

Behavioral Economics and Behavioral Management Studies: Drifting into Anthropological Philosophy

As discussed in Chapter 1, section 1.1, scientific analysis can only aim at selected aspects of reality. Even behavioral sciences can research human nature only in a focused, selective way. Higher complexity reduction and higher selectivity in formulating research problems distinguishes behavioral research programs like psychology or sociology from anthropological philosophy. This also implies that different, scientific research programs become compatible once differences in research problems and related differences in heuristic and theoretical approach are acknowledged (Suchanek 1992: 43; see also Homann and Suchanek 1989; Turk 1983: 199).

At times, behavioral scientists have argued for the 'comprehensive modeling' of human nature. For example:

> Human behavior is reflected by the individual making conscious or unconscious choices among recognized behavioral alternatives. Such choice is guided by: motives, goals, attitudes, social norms and role expectations, incentives and expected positive/negative sanctions and other environmental factors. (Wild 1988: 241)

Similar suggestions on 'comprehensive modeling' of human behavior are made by Hodgson (1998, 1988), Hottinger (1998), Simon (1997, 1993b, 1959, 1955), Jensen (1987), Wilber and Harrison (1978), in degrees also by North (1993b) or Williamson (1998, 1985). In management and organization studies, such attempts to reform scientific research through an all-encompassing conception of human nature were made by Markoczy and Goldberg (1998: 389), Nicholson (1998: 412–13), Burrell (1996: 657), Vargish (1994), Bernhard and Glantz (1992), Weinert (1987) or Zey-Ferrell (1981: 201–2). The promoted 'comprehensive modeling' of human nature cannot be reconciled with the problem-dependent and heuristic nature of scientific research. Machlup (1978: 267–301) here is rather outspoken, branding advocates of holistic reform projects of the model of economic man as 'anti-analysts, anti-theorists, anti-classicists, anti-liberals, and anti-economists' (Machlup 1978: 287). Though, post-modern organization theory might, in certain respects, not be unhappy with this type of criticism.

If such comprehensive characterizations were meant to refer to general, philosophical underpinnings of a research program but not to research heuristics, this should be made explicit. For instance, Dahrendorf knew that anthropological philosophy differed from behavioral sciences. When he set out the sociological research program, he grounded it in categorical, philosophical fundamentals of human nature, such as non-random, rule-following behavior that is of a historical–experiential nature (Dahrendorf 1973: v). On this axiomatic, philosophical note, he detailed research heuristics and theoretical concepts of sociology. However, if actually followed through in a scientific research program, a holistic empirical–behavioral and moral–behavioral approach leads social science research into anthropological philosophy or a 'pre-scientific' endeavor, as Popper (1957: 70, 87) may put it (see also Meyer 1995: 12–14, 303–5; Persky 1995: 229–30; Machlup 1978: 134–5; similarly Wagner-Tsukamoto forthcoming). Burrell (1996: 657) seemingly accepts this when he argues for a 'pre-modern' approach of claimed *post-modern* organization research. Post-modern organization research positions itself here as pre-modern research. Most institutional and organization researchers who argue for human nature holism are less explicit in this respect. Still, the outcome may be the same, research drifting into anthropological philosophy.

The drifting of scientific research into anthropological philosophy is frequently caused by methodological ambiguity regarding problem dependence, the distinction of heuristic elements from theoretical–(practical) ones and the start up of scientific research in an empirical, definitional way (see also Chapter 1, section 1.1 and Chapter 8, section 8.1). In scientific research, complexity reduction always encompasses human nature. Implicitly, Simon touched upon this insight when pointing out that the idea of bounded rationality reflected a cognitive need to reduce complex reality to a '*model* of reality that is *sufficiently simple* to be handled by problem-solving processes' (March and Simon 1958: 151, emphasis added; see also ibid. 1958: 7). This fundamental insight of Simon's research, as further detailed in Chapter 5, section 5.2

and Chapter 6, section 6.2, applies to any type of problem-solving, not only to everyday reasoning and its analysis by cognitive psychology, to which Simon referred to above, but also to scientific reasoning, for example, the modeling of human nature in a cognitive psychological theory. If behavioral economists projected this insight to their research approach, they had to get wary regarding ideas such as 'comprehensive modeling', 'interdisciplinarity', a 'true science of man' or the 'holistic portrayal of human nature' in social science research.

As a matter of the problem-dependent and heuristic nature of scientific research, organizational research programs can only model certain selected aspects of 'organizational reality'. For example, organization sociology or organization psychology examine institutional organization as systems of social values, cultural attitudes or motivational predispositions and analyze organizational behavior in terms of socialization processes and selected features of human nature. Alternatively, organization research can be developed as economics, which models institutional organization as incentive structures and organizational behavior as interactions over capital utilization (see Lindenberg 1985: 253; Merton 1976: 29, 34–5; Becker 1976: 5–14; see also sections 3.2 and 3.3). Economics does not, cannot and needs not entertain an empirical–behavioral model of human nature, neither in a heuristic nor in a theoretical–(practical) perspective. Behavioral concepts can play a role in economic theory-building and intervention only if they are reconstructed in theoretical–(practical) terms as 'human capital' and/or as 'incentive structures' or as a heuristic basis of economic theory and practical intervention, that is through the ideas of 'dilemma structure' and/or 'economic man'. Behavioral researchers who argue for the holistic, interdisciplinary, empirical–behavioral and moral–behavioral modeling of human nature overlook such issues. Coleman (1990, 1988) here is quite exceptional, his research shifting over the years towards sociological economics, leaving a unification-oriented economic sociology behind.

Indirectly, behavioral researchers attest to a need for complexity reduction by focusing research on certain aspects of human nature only. Despite explicit claims towards the portrayal of human nature as the 'total human being' (Herzberg 1966: 28) or 'human nature as we know it' (Williamson 1985: 44, 48, 57, 64, 387–8, 391; for more references, see Chapter 6, section 6.3), the idea of 'guiding principles' is invoked in order to narrow down research to specific features of human nature (Schanz 1977: 99; see also Wild 1988: 277, 281; Simon 1987: 25–7, 1963, 1957b: 62–78, 99–144; Turk 1983: 202; Weick 1979: 33–4, 45). Problem dependence and the heuristic nature of scientific research is in this way accepted, albeit only ambiguously and implicitly.

Economic Sociology: Drifting into Anthropological Philosophy

Possibly more so than economics, behavioral sciences show an inclination to drift into anthropological philosophy. This is probably due to a shared research interest in human nature. Comparable to the project of behavioral economics, economic sociology aims to merge sociological research with the situational, non-behavioral approach of economics (for example, Swedberg 1991a; Lindenberg 1990).[1] Integration is advocated on the basis of a claimed lacking capability of behavioral research to handle certain social problems. Lindenberg was here even critical of behavioral economics:

> In sociology, we have had a hundred years of experience with a preference-centred heuristic [the model of sociological man]. This experience is not encouraging in terms of explanatory power and it should be a warning to economists who are tempted to go in that direction. (Lindenberg 1985: 253; see also ibid. 1996, 1990)

Similarly argue Mouzelis (1995), Granovetter (1992), Brunner (1987) and Merton (1976). Coleman (1990) is rather outspoken, too. To a degree, even Hodgson (1998: 189) hinted at this issue.

Despite the suggestion that social sciences had to focus *either* on the situational context of behavior *or* on the behavioral make-up of the individual but could not focus on both at the same time (explicitly Lindenberg 1985: 253, as quoted above), economic sociology, similar to behavioral economics, aimed at integrating and unifying behavioral theory-building with economic theory-building. Economic sociology proposed a 'comprehensive model' of human nature such as the 'REMM' or the 'RREEMM'. The REMM was to reflect an empirical approximation of human nature, comprising the ideas 'resourceful', 'evaluating' and 'maximizing' behavior (Jensen and Meckling 1994; Brunner 1987). Jensen and Meckling and similarly Brunner, not dissimilar to North (1993b) and certain suggestions of Simon or Williamson (see Chapters 5 and 6), aimed to comprehensively 'model' human nature by linking to natural sciences like a sociobiology. Lindenberg (1990) added two further features, 'restricted' and 'expecting' behavior, thus arriving at RREEMM as a 'model' of human nature. However, already the REMM covers so many different aspects of human nature that it appears ill-suited as a research heuristic or as a theoretical–(practical) concept of scientific research. The application of REMM or RREEMM is likely to make scientific research drift into anthropological philosophy. Probably only anthropological philosophy can integrate (behavioral) economics and (economic) sociology – then collapsing into each other as a matter of philosophical research.[2]

The 'models' of REMM and RREEMM become the more questionable if they are understood as research heuristics rather than theoretical–(practical) concepts. There are indications that economic sociology proposed REMM and

RREEMM not so much as a theoretical–(practical) concept but as a research heuristic. Through 'bridge assumptions' a model of 'homo socio-economicus' was to be generated (Lindenberg 1996: 155, 1990: 738; see also Bürgenmeier 1992; Coughlin 1991; Etzioni 1991a, 1991c; Lawrence 1991; Preston et al. 1991; Swedberg 1991a, 1991b, 1990). In a heuristic perspective, the idea of a 'general model of human nature for the social sciences' (Lindenberg 1990: 727; similarly Lindenberg and Frey 1993) is probably a questionable concept, possibly even a contradiction in itself. Generality prevents the identification of research problems and the application of a problem-formulation and problem-solving apparatus, a 'research heuristic' (see Chapter 1, section 1.1). Jensen and Meckling (1994: 18–19) probably misread Becker in this regard, when suggesting that Becker applied the model of REMM. The opposite is likely to be the case. As Chapter 2, section 2.4 hinted and Chapters 6 and 8 follow up, Becker, like Friedman or Machlup, is one of the outspoken 'defenders' of the 'reductionist' model of economic man. His research is grounded in a non-behavioral, heuristic interpretation of the model of economic man and the theoretical reconstruction of behavioral concepts, such as tastes or preferences, in non-behavioral, economic terms (see Becker 1996, 1993, 1992, 1976).

Apart from an increase in realism, which may be irrelevant when setting out a scientific research program, economic sociology and behavioral economics did not outline what was to be gained by heuristically and/or theoretically–(practically) unifying 'sociology [and psychology] and economics into one category' (Lindenberg 1990: 740). Unification is likely to hinder the growth of scientific knowledge (see also Wagner-Tsukamoto 2003). As Simon attested to when interpreting bounded rationality in cognitive psychological terms, problem-solving requires complexity reduction (see Simon 1976a: 268, 1969: 104, 1945: 149; see also Chapter 5, section 5.2 and Chapter 6, section 6.2). As Chapter 1, section 1.1 detailed, for scientific problem solving, this may be best heuristically negotiated in relation to problem dependence.

3.2   TRADITIONAL ORGANIZATIONAL PSYCHOLOGY: THE ANALYSIS OF MOTIVATION AS A PROBLEM OF INDIVIDUAL BEHAVIOR

Conventionally, organization psychology has assessed organizational behavior in relation to motivational, cognitive or emotional aspects of individual behavior. Herzberg's motivation theory is a good example. The following substantiates:

1. Herzberg's conceptual separation of incentive structures ('incentive hygiene') and job satisfaction ('motivators') appears untenable for understanding performance problems in the firm. Some of Herzberg's own empirical findings hint, in line with an institutional economic interpretation, that both job satisfaction and job dissatisfaction reflect a systemic, incentive problem.

2. In contrast to institutional economics, Herzberg's organization psychology theoretically analyzes and practically intervenes with performance problems on an individualistic basis. The conceptualization of a systemic dimension and a social dimension of motivation is neglected. Adams' (1965) inequity theory of motivation diverts in this respect from Herzberg's approach. It moves, towards an economic analysis of motivational problems.

3. Herzberg's empirical–behavioral and moral–behavioral critique of the model of economic man reflects a methodological misunderstanding regarding the heuristic nature of 'economic man'. Implicitly, Herzberg even seemed to apply the model of economic man when he analyzed certain aspects of job performance.

Herzberg's Two-factor Theory of Motivation: Variables and Findings

Herzberg analyzed motivation and performance problems through two sets of variables. He suggested that one set determined job satisfaction, while a different set determined job *dis*satisfaction. Herzberg termed variables that he thought yielded job satisfaction 'motivators' or 'satisfiers'; variables that seemingly yielded job dissatisfaction he labeled 'hygiene factors', 'dissatisfiers' or 'maintenance factors' (see Figure 3.1).

Herzberg (1959 et al.: 44–9, 79–83) identified five hygiene factors, listed below in the order of their importance as established by Herzberg's analysis:

(1) 'Company policy and administration', that is, allocation structures of decision rights, personnel policies and communication lines.
(2) 'Supervision-technical', that is, supervision structures that organize delegation and training.
(3) 'Salary', that is, monetary compensation, changes to salary increases and expectations of salary increases.[3]
(4) 'Working conditions', that is, physical conditions of the work environment, such as lighting or ventilation.
(5) 'Interpersonal relations', that is, socio-technical exchange in the course of job performance.

'Hygiene factors' seemingly reflect situational, systemic variables, namely organization structures and the work environment of the employee. Herzberg

The Motivating Influence of the Psyche

	Unfilled 'Motivator Needs'	Filled 'Motivator Needs'
Unfilled 'Hygiene Needs'	Dissatisfaction	Dissatisfaction
Filled 'Hygiene Needs'	No Dissatisfaction, No Satisfaction	Satisfaction

The 'Hygiene' Influence of System (row label)

Figure 3.1   Systemic dominance of 'dissatisfiers' over 'satisfiers'

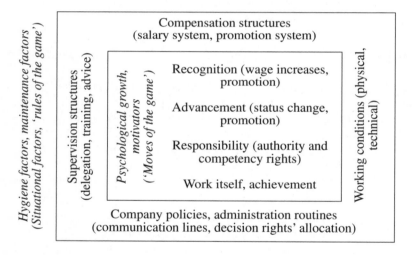

Figure 3.2   Interdependence between rules and moves

et al. (1959: 44–9, 79–83) suggested that job dissatisfaction originated in such systemic, situational – 'extrinsic' – factors (see Figure 3.2). According to his findings, if systemic factors were perceived *un*favorably by an employee, job dissatisfaction resulted; if perceived favorably, they led to the absence of job *dis*satisfaction (but not to job satisfaction).

On the other hand, job satisfaction, so Herzberg argued, was best explained through a set of 'intrinsic' behavioral factors or 'motivators'. They reflected the following variables, again listed in the order of importance as ascertained by Herzberg et al. (1959: 44–9, 79–83):

(1)   'Achievement', that is, the successful completion of a job.
(2)   'Recognition', that is, an act of praise (blame) that came with a reward (punishment), such as a wage increase or promotion.
(3)   'Work itself', that is, the actual 'doing' of a job.
(4)   'Responsibility', that is, authority rights and competency rights regarding an individual's own job and regarding others' jobs.
(5)   'Advancement', that is, changes in status or position in an organization.

Herzberg suggested that 'motivators', if perceived favorably by the individual, led to job satisfaction; if perceived unfavorably, they led to the absence of job satisfaction (but not to job *dis*satisfaction; see also Figure 3.1).

Differences between Institutional Economics and Herzberg's Theory: A Situational Dimension of the Motivation to Perform?

The previous section discussed Herzberg's theoretical–(practical) dichotomy regarding factors that caused job satisfaction and job dissatisfaction. Herzberg projected this dichotomy to the analysis of job performance problems, such as 'absenteeism, labor turnover, low morale, grievances, alcoholism and moon-lighting' (Herzberg 1966: 163; similarly Herzberg et al. 1959: 131). An interest in such performance problems compares to institutional economics, for example, Williamson's discussion of 'perfunctory cooperation' (Williamson 1985: 262–3, 1975: 68–70, 80–1). A similar research interest is expressed by post-modern organization research when it speaks of 'organizational misbehavior' (Ackroyd and Thompson 1999: 1–3, 25).

Certain conceptual parallels can be drawn between Herzberg's motivation theory and the institutional economic analysis of performance problems. His concepts of 'hygiene factors' and 'motivators' can be related to economic concepts of incentive structures and (monetary or non-monetary) gains resulting from social exchange. Herzberg's suggestion that job dissatisfaction reflected 'defective' organization structures can be linked to the institutional economic idea of incentive-*in*compatible organization structures (see Chapter 2, section 2.1). Also, Herzberg's motivators, such as 'recognition' and 'advancement', can be reconstructed in economic terms as capital gains received in the course of job performance. But then, crucial differences exist between Herzberg's organization psychology and institutional economics. In particular, Herzberg's conceptual dichotomy of 'motivators' and 'hygiene factors' split and isolated systemic 'hygiene factors' from behavioral 'motivators'. Job satisfaction, job dissatisfaction and related high- and low-job performance were explained 'separately'. In this regard, Herzberg's organization psychology and institutional economics are incompatible.

There are indications in Herzberg's own writings that a conceptual dichotomy of situational 'hygiene factors' and behavioral 'motivators' may be untenable. Herzberg et al. (1959: 47) hinted at this when stating that systemic factors encouraged the emergence of motivation: 'Responsibility' enjoyed by an employee in the course of job performance was thought to reflect the hygiene factor 'company policy and administration', that is, how decision rights were systemically allocated to the individual. Apparently, 'company policy and administration' and 'responsibility' were interrelated. Or, the systemic factor 'supervision-technical', that is, the formal organization of competency rights, seemed to relate to the motivator 'responsibility'. Herzberg suggested that in the case where 'supervision' was 'improperly' handled, dissatisfaction resulted, but if 'properly' handled, hygiene needs were not violated and satisfaction could emerge.

Herzberg observed that the variable 'salary' had shown up in his statistical analysis as frequently as 'motivator' as it had shown up as 'hygiene factor' (Herzberg 1966: 126–7; Herzberg et al. 1959: 82–3). If it is further considered that the motivators 'recognition' and 'advancement' indirectly reflect the *amount* of salary an individual could earn (as well as other non-monetary rewards that came with recognition and advancement), the sole classification and assessment of 'salary' as a hygiene factor appears questionable.[4] It had to be clarified that the amount of salary earned by an employee was a satisfying factor, as reflected by Herzberg's empirical data on the variables 'recognition', 'advancement' and indeed 'salary' (as far as it had shown up as a motivator). This can be interpreted in institutional economic terms as salary-related gains ('capital distributions') being appreciated by the individual. In contrast, a salary *system*, if improperly institutionalized, seemed to have a dissatisfying effect on performance. In this respect 'salary' reflected a situational problem, which dissatisfied the individual.

Although Herzberg explicitly questioned an interrelationship between systemic rules, job satisfaction and job performance, he seemed to imply implicitly this very thing. Using Herzberg's terminology, interrelationships between 'incentive hygiene' and 'motivators' can be proposed as follows: The hygiene factor 'supervision-technical' interrelates with the motivators 'achievement' and 'work itself'; the hygiene factor 'company policy and administration' interrelates with the motivator 'responsibility'; and the hygiene factor 'salary' interrelates with the motivators 'advancement' and 'recognition'. Possibly only the hygiene factor 'working conditions' and 'socio-technical interrelationships' may have no motivating effect (but even this can be questioned, especially regarding the motivator 'work itself'). With regard to these points, an institutional economic reconstruction of organization psychology can clarify how the emergence of motivation at the level of the individual depends on the proper institutionalization of 'incentive hygiene' in the rules of the game. The conceptualization of incentive-compatible rules here is of special interest. Selected fields of organization psychology have developed such a contextual perspective on the individual. Nord and Fox (1996) speak in this regard of the 'great disappearing act' of the individual from organizational analysis, although they noted that much organization psychology still focuses on the individual as such.

Differences between Institutional Economics and Herzberg's Theory: A Social, Interaction Dimension of Motivation?

Early on, Taylor's idea of systematic soldiering spelled out a social dimension of motivation and performance problems in the firm (see Chapter 4, section 4.1). Organization psychology in the tradition of Maslow and Mayo, to which Herzberg connected, proceeds differently. It assesses motivation and job performance by focusing on individual behavior as such. A social, interaction dimension of motivational problems remains underexplored. Herzberg only rarely touched on a social dimension of motivation problems:

> [W]hen salary occurred as factor in the lows [as a dissatisfier], it revolved around the unfairness . . . of the wage system within the company and this almost always referred to increases in salaries rather than the absolute level. It was the system of salary administration that was being described [by the employee], a system in which wage increases were obtained grudgingly or given too late or in which the differentials between newly hired employees and those with years of experience on the job were too small. (Herzberg et al. 1959: 83)

Dissatisfaction regarding 'salary' is examined as a social problem (similarly Herzberg 1966: 125–7; 1959 Herzberg et al.: 46; see also Roethlisberger and Dickson 1949: 576). Also, Herzberg et al. (1959: 46–7) argued that unfairness in training support caused dissatisfaction, for example, if provided to some employees but not to others. This hints at social dynamics that undermine organizational performance. Herzberg, however, did not conduct a systematic analysis of social effects on motivation and job satisfaction and how this in turn influenced job performance. This may reflect a considerable shortcoming of a theory of organizational behavior. Herzberg's theory can well handle organizational problems that reflect 'psychic pathologies' of individual behavior (Herzberg 1966: 170) but it is analytically ill-equipped to analyze performance problems that reflect 'social pathologies', as abstractly illustrated by the prisoners' dilemma.

A rather similar criticism can be directed at Senge (1993: 140), who seemingly models human motivation and assumptions about human nature in organization theory through Maslow's concept of the needs hierarchy (critically reviewed by Brown 1996: 97). In contrast, social psychological concepts, such as Adams (1965), examined the influence of social dynamics on individual motivation and performance. Ockenfels' (1999) research on the occurrence of altruism in social interactions is another good example. These latter studies compare with the approach of institutional economics, which analyzes performance problems through interaction analysis.

Over the years, there has been a growing realization among some psychological researchers that a focus on the individual as such may be inappropriate for understanding psychological problems in organizational behavior. Like Adams (1965), Weick (1995, 1979) and Mischel and Shoda (1995) argued for such reorientation (for a review, see Nord and Fox 1996: 155–8). Weick analyzed individual behavior as being 'constituted out of the process of interaction' (Weick 1995: 20). His research still tried to uncover issues concerning individual personality and behavioral identity but concepts like 'mutually determining processes' and the 'double interact' put the analysis of individual behavior in a social perspective (see also Nord and Fox 1996: 156–7). However, a considerable body of organization psychology has remained firmly anchored in an individualistic, behavioral approach to organization research (for example, Mount et al. 1994; Schneider 1987; see also Oswick et al. 1996).

Differences between Institutional Economics and Herzberg's Theory: Herzberg's Program of Behavioral Intervention

The previous discussion outlined that Herzberg neglected the analysis of systemic and social aspects of motivation and performance problems. His program for practical intervention reflects this, too. Herzberg favored, similar to critical management theory and post-modern empowerment paradigms (for example, Nord and Jermier 1992: 218–19), behavioral intervention with the human condition. In general, there is little issue to take with behavioral intervention that aims at the individual. However, its success can be questioned if it tries to solve systemic or social problems of organizational behavior.

Behavioral intervention cannot correct incentive-incompatible organization structures, which cause 'social pathologies' and 'rationally foolish' interaction outcomes over capital contributions and capital distributions. But then, Herzberg's program for behavioral intervention aimed at systemic and social problems in organizational behavior. He raised questions regarding performance problems, for example, when referring to the 'progress of industry' and the 'effective use of human beings' (Herzberg 1966: 170). He suggested psychological intervention at the level of the individual in order to deal with such issues. Economic intervention with incentive structures was explicitly sidelined. He recommended a flat-rate salary system: 'The worst way to pay people is on piece rate . . . Next worse way to pay people is on an hourly rate. The best way to pay them is a salary, a yearly salary. Period' (Herzberg 1982). Institutional economics and a considerable body of organization research on performance-related pay (McKenzie and Lee 1998; Flannery et al. 1996; Montemayor 1976), including social psychological research (Adams 1965; see also Ockenfels 1999; Hesterly et al. 1990: 413), disagree with this suggestion. A flat-rate salary system has a high potential to aggravate 'economic patholo-gies' and further undermine organizational performance. Classic here is Taylor's research on 'systematic soldiering' (see Chapter 4, section 4.1) and Adams' (1965: 267–8, 272–6) research on systemic and social aspects of moti-vation problems. To a degree, expectancy theory, as developed by Porter and Lawler (1968), takes account of equity considerations in the distribution of rewards, too (see also Child 1984: 181–4). Also, sociological and social psychological research, which stress a social comparison element of incen-tives, move in this direction (for example, Mueller and Wallace 1996; Peffer 1995: 73–4; Coleman 1990). Such insights can be deepened through a contri-bution–distribution interaction model and the conceptual apparatus of organi-zational economics.

Like his suggestion on the design of wage systems, Herzberg's suggestions on how to resolve cooperation problems in industrial relations may be ques-tionable. He examined interaction problems between managers and workers as 'revenge psychology': 'You see this [revenge psychology on part of the employee] often in labor relations . . . Why such grievance, such as strikes, such turmoil over such a petty event [wage levels] . . . So never deny people proper treatment with the idea that you can make it up to them later on' (Herzberg 1982). In contrast to Taylor or Williamson (see Chapter 4), he did not discuss the resolution of interaction conflict in relation to systemic struc-tures that were to ensure fairness regarding standards for contributions and distributions.

To a degree, Herzberg sensed this problem in his organization theory. For example, he was puzzled that job performance and satisfaction had in certain instances increased in the face of increasing factory automation (Herzberg et al. 1959: 132–3). This implied that – contrary to Herzberg's prediction – the motivators 'work itself' and 'responsibility' did not positively relate to job performance. Institutional economics here would suggest that interactions can succeed in any institutional setting as long as contributions and distribu-tions are 'balanced', that means organization structures are incentive-compat-ible.

Herzberg also realized that his behavioral, ethical recommendations to organize work and job enrichment as a matter of human dignity might not be successfully implemented because of 'other issues' (Herzberg et al. 1959:

131–3). To what extent such 'other issues' amounted to was not explored. Again, institutional economics can shed light on such 'other issues'. Reif and Luthans (1969: 375–6) examined 'other issues' in relation to an inner-organizational, interaction dimension and a systemic dimension of job motivation and performance. To a degree, this realization of Herzberg compares to Williamson's self-realization that dignitarian values are difficult to conceptualize and implement in organizational behavior (see Chapter 6, section 6.3).

Herzberg's Behavioral Interpretation of the Model of Economic Man

Herzberg's dichotomy of motivators and hygiene factors and his program for behavioral intervention was driven by the attempt of portraying human nature in holistic, empirical terms. In particular, he criticized the model of economic man in empirical–behavioral and moral–behavioral terms. He viewed the model of economic man as unrealistic and immoral, characterizing it as the 'Adam' model of human nature (Herzberg 1966: Chapter 3).[5] Herzberg suggested that this model of human nature needed to be supplemented by moral–behavioral character traits and that organization theory should apply an 'Abraham' model. Herzberg (1966: Chapter 3), similar to Senge (1993), Simon (1997: 42–5, 52, 1993b), Etzioni (1988), Knowles and Saxberg (1967) or McGregor (1960), advocated a holistic, complete, empirical–behavioral and moral–behavioral image of human nature – the 'total human being' (Herzberg 1966: 28) – as a conceptual basis for motivation research.[6] Sievers (1986) moves in a similar direction. In general, scientific research is likely to encounter severe methodological problems when aiming at 'comprehensive modeling', as implied by the 'Abraham' model. Previous chapters, in particular Chapter 1, section 1.1 and Chapter 2, section 2.4, detailed this (see also Chapter 3, section 3.3).

Herzberg hoped that by transforming 'Adam' into 'Abraham', performance problems could be solved:

> Industry . . . must recognize that if it is to use human beings effectively, it must treat them in terms of their complete nature rather than in terms of those characteristics that appear to be suitable to their organization. Industry cannot progress by continuing to perpetuate a half-conceptual view of man. As already suggested, its present personnel programs . . . can lead only to temporary, opiate relief and further the basic pathology. (Herzberg 1966: 170)

Like the human relation school (for example, Knowles and Saxberg 1967; McGregor 1960) and suggestions of 'soft', post-modern organization research (for reviews, see Kamoche 2001; Alvesson and Deetz 1996; Sanchez 1994; Noon 1992; Hendry and Pettigrew 1990), Herzberg approached performance problems as a matter of humanizing personnel management (Herzberg 1966: 171–7). The model of economic man was interpreted in theoretical–(practical) terms but not as an analytical device. Herzberg (1966: Chapter 3) explicitly projected the conceptual dichotomy of 'motivators' and 'hygiene factors' to a competition of images of human nature: 'Adam' versus 'Abraham', and economics versus psychology. To a degree, his approach anticipated a radical humanist, post-modern approach.

As emphasized in Chapter 2, institutional economics methodically applies the model of economic man in order to analyze and repair incentive-*in*compatible organization structures. Herzberg's behavioral critique of 'economic man' has to be adjusted for the problem-dependent, heuristic application of 'economic man'. For the purpose of economic analysis, it is counterproductive to replace 'Adam' through 'Abraham'. In certain respects, Herzberg here probably misunderstood his own research, especially when he seemingly applied the model of economic man for discussing gains/losses and the influence of salary, recognition and advancement on job performance.[7] Interesting in this connection is a study by Herzberg that he carried out with Soviet researchers. In this study, Soviet researchers suggested that workers applied a social utility calculus when deciding their performance levels. This suggestion comes close to Herzberg's portrayal of 'Abraham' as a caring and altruistic man or similar suggestions of Etzioni (1988) on an 'I and we' utility function. However, in the Russian study Herzberg explicitly questioned the relevance of a social utility calculus. (In the quote below, the Soviet scientists' interpretation of worker performance is highlighted in italics whereas Herzberg's qualification appears in plain script):

> *In the case of the unskilled manual laborer, the widening of his mental horizon and the increase of his education does not improve, but rather, worsens his attitude to work and it impels him to quit his job. In this case the appeal to the social value of labor hardly helps, since other work is more useful to society due to its greater productivity. It is not by accident that the manual labor group was found in our research to be the least stable.* Perhaps a more realistic psychological view of their conclusion would be a restatement of the next-to-last sentence in this paragraph, as follows: In this case, the appeal to the social value of labor hardly helps, since other work is more meaningful to the individual – not, as the Soviet sociologists suggest, since it is more meaningful to society. (Herzberg 1966: 167, emphasis changed)

Herzberg seems to say that the individual decides 'skills contributions' in relation to a share in productivity increases. Apparently, he drew on a calculus of self-interest in order to qualify 'sociological' proposals of Soviet colleagues.[8] This mirrors institutional economic thought.

3.3   HEURISTIC ASPECTS OF MODELING HUMAN NATURE IN BEHAVIORAL RESEARCH

Behavioral organization research conceptualizes 'institutions' as systems of social values, culture or shared perceptions of duty. For example, organizational sociology examines organizational behavior through ideas of cultural climate, role hierarchies or value structures. In practical terms, it aims to strengthen cultural assimilation among organization members, generate congruent role perceptions or maintain a value consensus within the organization. As discussed in the previous chapter, economics intervenes with behavior in situational terms, and approaches institutions as incentive structures. The following substantiates:

1.   The model of sociological man, like the model of economic man, represents a research heuristic, that is, a sub-theoretical, pre-empirical and quasi-tautological concept of human nature.
2.   The purpose of the model of sociological man differs from the one of economic man. Whereas 'economic man' instructs the analysis of capital contribution–distribution interactions in relation to incentive structures, 'sociological man' instructs the analysis of role behavior in relation to behavioral institutions, such as social values or culture. It directly instructs the analysis of human nature and the human condition.
3.   In 'modern' interaction contexts, where pluralism prevails, the effectiveness, efficiency and moral quality of sociological intervention is likely to be lower than of economic intervention.

Sociology conceptualizes 'institutionalized norms and values' (Blau 1976a: 8; similarly Scott 1995a, 1995b; Elster 1989: 100–102). Not incentive structures but behavioral constraints are discussed: 'Individuals are strongly influenced by collective norms and values that impose social obligations on them, constraining their choices . . . The terminology is one of duties and roles' (Scott 1995b: xvi, see also ibid. 1995b: xvii; Boland 1979: 963–4): Institutional processes are interpreted as behavioral processes of socialization. The stability of social behavior, of 'enduring, persistent social behavior' (Homans 1976: 3), is theoretically and practically approached as a matter of shared values, social harmony or conformity in role behavior (Dahrendorf 1973: 71). The 'sociological' effectiveness of human behavior is intervened with (Warner 1994: 1161; Kieser 1993: 113–23; Argyris 1992; Schanz 1982: 72). Sociology comes in this regard close to theology (see Cima and Schubeck 2001: 230, Note 4). Specific variables of sociological research are social position, social status, social acceptance, group pressure, opinion leadership and so on (Hollis 1994: 163–8; Burrell and Morgan 1979: 10–12; Blau 1976a: 2,

10–11, 1976b: 221; Dahrendorf 1973: 12, 19, 34–8; see also Wagner 1997: 21).

Micro-sociology connects to psychology, 'focusing on the elementary social behavior exhibited by individuals in their daily social relations, the psychological processes governing it and the social structures to which it gives rise' (Blau 1976a: 4; also Homans 1976: 64). Theoretically and practically, a micro-analytic, behavioral science of human nature is aimed at. In contrast, macro-sociology abstracts from psychological, behavioral aspects but explores norm and value systems in aggregated terms. For instance, Parsons' or Lenski's sociological theories made 'people disappear from view and with them not only the motives and behavior of individuals but also the structures of social relations' (Blau 1976a: 5; see also Layder 1994: 13–33; Coleman 1990: 13–23). As indicated in Chapter 2, section 2.4, in certain heuristic respects, macro-sociology compares to economics, abstracting to a high degree from behavioral features of human nature, though macro-sociology theoretically and practically still conducts behavioral analysis – in aggregated form. For example, it examines peer group dynamics or conceptualizes social structures as networks of roles. Micro-sociology and macro-sociology share an interest in the behavioral analysis of selected aspects of human nature (Layder 1994: 32–3; Warner 1994: 1161–2; Simon 1987: 26–7; Blau 1976a: 4–5; Homans 1976: 64; similarly Cazeneuve 1972: 24–5).

In a heuristic perspective, sociology is differently grounded than economics. Sociological debate, both of social conflict and social order, heuristically presupposes conflict. This may be implied when Burrell and Morgan (1979: 10) characterize the 'order–conflict debate' in sociology as 'spurious'. Sociology commonly draws on conflict models of role conflict or value conflict. Besides a conflict model, sociology heuristically invokes a model of human nature – 'sociological man' (see Figure 1.2 in Chapter 1):

> We may formulate the proposition that implicitly or explicitly underlies all [empirical] research and theoretical work in modern sociology: *Man behaves in accordance with his roles* . . . This abstraction [of man], the scientific unit of sociology, may be called homo sociologicus. (Dahrendorf 1973: 72–3, emphasis as in original)

The model of sociological man belongs to the same 'methodological family' as the model of economic man. Machlup's (1978: Chapter 10) review of the 'classmates of homo economicus' is instructive.

Dahrendorf explicitly stressed the heuristic nature of 'sociological man', referring to it as 'scientific construct', an 'invention', an 'artificial man' and a 'deliberately "unrealistic" fiction' (Dahrendorf 1973: 7, 50, 58, 78). He was well aware that 'the assumption that all men behave in accordance with their roles at all times is demonstrably false' (Dahrendorf 1973: 74; see also

Homann and Suchanek 1989: 79). He rejected an empirically grounded, holistic approach to sociological research:

> One might infer, therefore, that all sociological theories, in so far as they operate on this assumption[9] [the homo sociologicus], are bad theories; and in fact this point is occasionally made by laymen and even scholars, who do not understand the logic of scientific discovery[10]. In economic theory the protracted argument over whether the homo economicus . . . is a realistic image of man's economic behavior has been decided: literal realism is quite unnecessary so long as the theories based on this model provide powerful explanations and useful predictions. (Dahrendorf 1973: 74, emphasis added, similarly ibid. 1973: 7, 48, 58, 76–7)

Following Dahrendorf, in a heuristic perspective, sociology is seemingly as indifferent to empirical–behavioral accuracy when modeling human nature as economics. The model of sociological man reflects '. . . predetermined ways . . . [and] paths as they appear on the maps of sociology' (Dahrendorf 1973: 58; similarly Mouzelis 1995: 1–3; see also Dürkheim 1982), reducing complex social reality to sociological terms. Quasi-tautological elements regarding the heuristic portrayal of human nature in sociology are apparent in Dahrendorf's argument.[11] His interpretation of 'sociological man' fundamentally differs from Hollis' (1994: 159) holistic interpretation.

Competition between Economics and Sociology?

Considering methodical and theoretical differences of approach, sociological research (psychological research) and institutional economics do not directly compete with each other. They may be 'just' different regarding heuristic and theoretical approaches and favored strategies for practical intervention. This is implied by the idea of imperialistic, 'interdisciplinary' research (see Chapter 1, section 1.1). Nevertheless, competition can arise if the same practical problems, such as performance problems, are aimed at. 'Competition' is probably best resolved by looking at intervention criteria such as effectiveness, efficiency and the moral quality of intervention. In this way, competition can be resolved in a practical perspective: examining which approach to prioritize over the other (see Chapter 8, section 8.2).

Interactions in modern society seem to be defined by pluralism, which reflects value fragmentation, diversity and even the weakening of values. Modern sociology speaks of the detraditionalizing of society and the dislocation of the traditional citizen (Scott 2000; Beck 1992; Giddens 1991; Luhmann 1988, 1984; see also Cohen and Arato 2001; Kymlicka 2001; Mannheim 1944). Such processes probably began as early as in biblical times (see Wagner-Tsukamoto 2001b; Wagner 2000a), but in the multicultural society, the multi-national firm or the global community, pluralistic interaction conditions are ever present.[12] In addition, the effectiveness of behavioral institutions is actively eroded by the economic and political institutions of the market economy, such as constitutional structures, business laws or the systemic structures of the firm. They enact pluralism – for larger, moral reasons (see Chapter 8).

If value pluralism arises, is accepted or promoted as an interaction condition, behavioral intervention needs to be accompanied by, probably even be subordinated to, economic intervention. Probably, a minimum level of trust and consensus over shared social values is required for any interaction to succeed. If choice-makers have diverse socializations *and* are not aware of this, outcomes of interactions tend to be fragile and unstable. This is a particular problem in cross-cultural interactions. On the other hand, sociological researchers acknowledge that in modern contexts 'trust [understood as a behavioral category] remains vital in interpersonal relations, but participation in functional systems like the economy or politics is no longer a matter of personal relations' (Luhmann 1988: 102; see also Rippberger 1998; Gerecke 1997). Behavioral concepts like trust are then best reapproached in economic terms, for example, as social capital (Coleman 1988). Chapter 8 details a moral quality of such reconceptualization. The next section (3.4) spells out effectiveness problems for behavioral research in the face of modernity.

3.4   EFFECTIVENESS LIMITS OF MORAL–BEHAVIORAL ORGANIZATION THEORY

Regarding approach, behavioral business ethics compares to psychology or sociology. It conceptualizes institutions as behavioral rules for good social conduct. Violations of rules come with behavioral sanction, which are self-enacted by the individual through conflicts of conscience or perceptions of guilt. They are also enacted through group processes, for example, peer group pressure. Behavioral, ethical intervention comes as moral appeal, the teaching of values or religious healing. The following explores how far behavioral ethics can solve social problems in a 'modern' context, that is, generally speaking, a pluralistic context. The following substantiates:

1. The effectiveness of behavioral business ethics depends on the generation and maintenance of a value consensus, in the case of global competition a value consensus among global competitors.
2. Due to its conceptualization as a systemically *un*conditioned 'moral science of man', behavioral (business) ethics is overburdened to analytically accommodate pluralism.

3.   The institutional structures of the market economy not only tolerate but also impose pluralism – for moral reasons.
4.   If concepts of behavioral ethics are favored over economic research, economic analysis and intervention are undermined and a viable route, possibly the only one to solving social problems in a 'modern' context is disabled.

The Quaker Ethics: The Goodness of the Individual and Harmony in Social Relations

The Quaker ethics well illustrates the approach of behavioral ethics and behavioral, institutional research in general. It focuses on the moral–behavioral goodness of the individual. Ethical assessments are made independent of systemic constraints. Child's (1964) analysis of industrial relations in Quaker firms in early 20th-century UK holds important clues regarding the viability and relevance of behavioral business (ethics) research in a pluralistic context. He identified the main principles of the Quaker ethics as:

1.   a dislike of one person profiting at the expense of another;
2.   the promotion of the value of hard work;
3.   the advocacy of egalitarianism in social behavior;
4.   a dislike of conflict.

These principles prescribe what the 'good' person should do and what 'good' social relationships should look like. Principles (1), (3) and (4) refer to ideals such as unselfishness, altruism, equality, fraternity, solidarity or pacifism – which well mirror Herzberg's 'Abraham' model, comparable propositions in the behavioral literature (see Chapter 3, section 3.2) and Bauman's (2001) project of post-modern ethics, which draws in a surprisingly traditional and possibly even pre-modern manner on the concept of personal, authentic altruism. They focus on human nature in order to conceptualize morality in behavioral terms (see also, Etzioni 1988: xii, 11–13; behaviorally oriented economists, for example, Simon 1997, 1993b; Sen 1999, 1990, 1987; Margolis 1982). Such principles can be reconstructed in economic terms but not without major conceptual specifications and modifications (for a review, see Wagner-Tsukamoto 2002). Principle (2) is of a different nature. It directly links to economic thought, focusing on the idea of productivity, of making good use of one's time. Roots of a capitalist work ethic can in this respect be made out in the Judeo–Christian tradition (see also Gordon 1989: 2–5).

In their outlook, principles (1), (3) and (4) of the Quaker ethics compare to principles promoted by many behavioral approaches to business ethics. Behavior is examined by focusing on the 'goodness' of the individual:

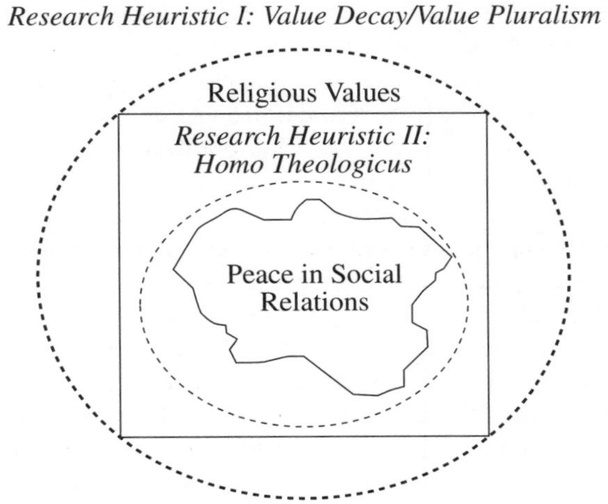
Research Heuristic I: Value Decay/Value Pluralism
Religious Values
Research Heuristic II: Homo Theologicus
Peace in Social Relations

Figure 3.3 Theological approach

> [T]he Quaker precept [was] that it is the spirit in which one individual approaches the other which determines the harmony of their relationships. Much was seen [by the Quakers] to depend on the 'goodness' of individuals; in other words on their psychology – what is in the mind. (Child 1964: 305)

Internalized behavioral precepts are expected to make the individual cooperate and live a 'good' life. Through 'correct personal spirit' (Child 1964: 296),[13] harmony in social relations is to be achieved. This reflects the theological approach to generating 'common good' (Cima and Schubeck 2001: 230, Note 4). On this basis, social problems are expected to be solved (see also Figure 3.3). Undeniably, not necessarily in heuristic terms (see also Figure 1.2) but at least regarding theory-building and practical intervention, the Quaker ethics, and theology in general, seem to cherish a noble image of human nature. They stress the goodness of the individual and the promotion of behavioral ethical ideals of caring and altruism.

Effectiveness and Efficiency Limits of the Quaker Ethics in a Business Context

In the early decades of the 20th century, there was intensive debate within the Quaker business community on how to implement the principles of the Quaker ethics. Quaker owner-managers[14] tried to reconcile their religious beliefs with their behavior as businessmen. Numerous conferences were held on this issue between 1900 and 1940 and large-scale 'field experiments' were conducted in which the implementation of the Quaker ethics in business practice was attempted. The outcome of these 'experiments' was disappointing for Quaker managers. They experienced severe conflicts of conscience when trying to implement religious principles: '[O]ne Quaker businessman . . . called the title of Quaker employer . . . a flat contradiction in terms' (Child 1964: 297).[15]

In general, the effectiveness of behavioral ethics depends on the sharing of behavioral norms among interacting individuals. Practical intervention needs to ensure a value consensus. It comes as the 'purposive investment by authorities such as the state or the church [or the firm] in propaganda with the intention of creating new sets of values in the citizens' (Eggertsson 1993: 27). If moral norms are not held by interacting individuals or if diverse moral norms are subscribed to, the 'psychological' and 'sociological' sanctioning of violations of 'good' conduct fails to work. Those who do not share in a certain moral code do not realize that they behaved as a 'bad' person. Especially the need not only to revive morals at the level of the individual, but also to ensure the *sharing* of morals among interacting agents, hints at effectiveness limits of behavioral ethics. The onset of value pluralism here poses a fundamental problem for moral–behavioral approaches. This may have been overlooked by Etzioni (1988: 8–9) or Menell (1992: 498), who advocate behavioral solutions to social problems of modern society. This problem is ever present for the multinational enterprise, the multicultural society and the international community. MacIntyre (1985: 1–5) more generally hints at this problem of modern society:

> [T]he language of morality is in the . . . state of grave disorder . . . What we possess, if this view is true, are the fragments of a conceptual scheme, parts which now lack those contexts from which their significance derived . . . We possess indeed simulacra of morality, we continue to use many of the key expressions. But we have – very largely, if not entirely – lost our comprehension, both theoretical and practical or morality . . . [W]e are all already in a state so disastrous that there are no large remedies for it. (MacIntyre 1985: 2, 5, spelling as in original)

Behavioral ethics runs into such problems especially in interaction contexts other than tribal, pre-modern ones, in which interacting choice-makers intrinsically share values and other behavioral dispositions. Such contexts may have disappeared as early as in biblical times but probably the more so in industrialized and industrializing societies (see Wagner-Tsukamoto 2001b; Wagner 2000a, 2000c). This diagnosis is shared across the social sciences, for example, Cohen and Arato (2001), Kymlicka (2001), Scott (2000), Homann (1997, 1988), Beck (1992), Giddens (1991), Williams (1988), Gambetta (1988), Luhmann (1988, 1984) and probably already Mannheim (1944) and

Rathenau (1918). Interesting in this connection is Sarup's (1993: 145) suggestion of an inherent, conceptual conflict in post-modern research – he refers to Lyotard's *The Postmodern Condition*, and post-modernists' acceptance of the 'individualistic, fragmented' society, on the one hand, and the nostalgic search for the 'premodern traditional society', on the other hand. A similar criticism can be directed at Bauman (2001: 138–9, 143, 1992: xxii, 203), who hopes that the post-modern project can restore full moral responsibility to the individual agent. Bauman realizes that value fragmentation and diversity potentially undermine this (conversion) project but wider economic constraints as, for example, encountered by Quaker managers, are not considered by him. Also, once individualization, value fragmentation, pluralism and enlightenment as defining conditions of *modernity* are considered, more serious questions can be raised regarding the post-modern project and how it differs from modern and pre-modern thinking.

Quaker managers seemingly found out that the institutions of the market economy aggravate pluralism or the 'condition of modernity': They enforce competition and profitability as survival requirements on the firm. Unless the firm engaged in non-cooperative, 'non-harmonious' behavior, it is likely to be eliminated from the market process. Also, the institutional rules of the market economy, such as cartel laws or monopoly laws, prevented Quaker firms from eliminating 'less moral' competition, for example, through taking them over. In this way, the market economy intentionally individualizes firms in market interactions. In a sense, the firm is forced into a prisoners' dilemma game – for moral reasons (Homann and Pies 1991). The important question seems to be in this connection whether behavioral ethics can be effective and efficient in a business context, whether it can generate *stable* speak: 'harmonious' interactions *at low cost*.

If value decay or value pluralism is encountered as an interaction condition, behavioral (business) ethics needs to reverse this. In the context of the market economy, this brings behavioral ethics in conflict with the institutional and constitutional structures of the market economy, which in certain respects enact pluralism. It could be argued that Quaker firms should have lobbied for tougher business laws that were more in line with their ethics. A religious toughening of business laws, however, raises ethical questions regarding the tolerance of value pluralism. And, it is likely to be ineffective on global markets unless global markets are regulated by the same religious laws (Vanberg 1994; see also Wagner-Tsukamoto 2002).

Child points at such economic reasons why Quaker managers ultimately compromised ethical beliefs: '[A]ccommodation took the form of minimizing those Quaker maxims most in opposition to entrepreneurial interest . . . with counterbalancing emphasis on other precepts not so antithetical to this interest' (Child 1964: 299). This left Quaker businessmen with conflicts of conscience and the problem of how to retreat from religious beliefs. Only the Quaker principle of the promotion of the value of hard work was fully implemented because it was apparently cost-neutral or even profitable. Other principles, like a 'better treatment' of employees, were only pursued if costs were offset by gains, such as productivity increases.

It could be argued that Quaker managers could have prevented the failure of their behavioral program in business ethics by morally re-educating their stakeholders, making them share in the principles of the Quaker ethics and thus be more willing to 'pay' for moral behavior that lived up to the ideals of the Quaker ethics. Here, Quaker managers probably inadequately considered to 'transfer' morals into ethical capital. This would have enabled them to hand down the costs of moral behavior to stakeholders who are prepared to 'pay' for moral corporate behavior (Wagner-Tsukamoto 2002). Since Quaker companies like Cadbury and Rowntree were founded for ethical reasons, namely to combat alcohol consumption through selling chocolate drinks, the economic transformation of behavioral ethics into 'ethical capital' could have been an obvious consideration. Although, in a pluralistic context, this is likely to succeed in niche markets only.

It appears that the implementation of the Quaker ethics met effectiveness limits and incurred considerable costs that put Quaker firms at disadvantages on competitive markets. Probably only under exceptional conditions, as they can be derived, for instance, from a case study of the Amish society, behavioral ethics can effectively and efficiently handle social problems in modern societies. However, under conditions of rising pluralism, partly aggravated through the institutional structures of the market economy, economic costs but also moral 'costs' for creating and maintaining a value consensus become prohibitively high.[16]

Seemingly, the situational qualification of behavioral ethics in relation to interaction effects and interaction contexts is required. The conditional qualification of behavioral ethics for the 'conditioned unconditionedness' of moral behavior (Homann 1999a: 6) is necessary (see also Wagner-Tsukamoto 2002, 2001a; Wagner 2000b). Such qualifications appear difficult to make 'within' the conceptual confines of behavioral ethics. The Quaker ethics, like behavioral ethics in general, cannot be theoretically grounded in hypothetical, qualified imperatives to do the right thing only *if* this was compatible with business requirements such as profitability or the survival of the firm.

3.5 CONCLUDING REMARKS

Probably only philosophy can research human nature in holistic, empirical–behavioral and moral–behavioral terms. Anthropological philosophy is a good example. It unifies findings on human nature that are generated by different life sciences and social sciences. In contrast, behavioral sciences research and intervene with human nature only in a selectively focused, problem-dependent way. Behavioral sciences exit from science if holistic research is aimed at. Empirical–behavioral or moral–behavioral holism is at odds with ideas like 'modeling', 'focus', 'problem dependence' and the heuristic grounding of research. These ideas appear important for understanding the nature and progress of scientific research.

Behavioral researchers frequently criticize the model of economic man on empirical–behavioral and moral–behavioral grounds. A number of misunderstandings occur in this regard. In the first place, 'economic man', like 'sociological man', has to be interpreted as an analytical device that heuristically instructs non-behavioral theory-building and practical intervention. A holistic behavioral critique of 'economic man' as, for example, put forward by Herzberg and eagerly taken up by many behavioral researchers, overlooks that behavioral sciences apply a heuristic model of human nature, too, such as the model of 'sociological man'. In one way or another, a need for a complexity reduction of 'real life' constrains the holistic portrayal of human nature in theoretical–practical terms and/or in heuristic terms in any research program.

Besides conceptual reservations, behavioral research that aims at the comprehensive, holistic portrayal of human nature is practically probably less effective and possibly even less moral than economics. Chapter 8 follows up. The failure of religious communities or communist societies to implement a claimed humane, empirically holistic image of human nature – the failure to create the 'new good man' (Buchanan 1987b: 275, Footnote 9) – should alert behavioral researchers. Behavioral sciences probably have not taken on board insights of moral philosophers like MacIntyre and much earlier Adam Smith regarding conceptual and practical problems of behavioral intervention in 'modern' contexts where, behavioral research can probably only solve an institutional 'rest-problem'; that means it can contribute to solving social problems once they have been treated in economic terms. This requires the reconceptualization and modification of behavioral ethics in economic terms.

NOTES

1. To a degree, Williamson (1998: 1–10, 1993a: 454–5, 1991a: 14, 1975: 1–2) voiced similar intentions regarding the integration of economics and sociology (see Chapter 6).
2. The same may apply for the integration project of bio-economics and the advocacy of 'homo bio-economicus' by Mohammadian (2000). For a review of this approach, see Wagner-Tsukamoto (2003).
3. The only variable in the set of dissatisfiers that showed as much dissatisfying as satisfying effects was the variable 'salary'. On the basis of the depth of satisfaction/dissatisfaction that

'salary' generated, Herzberg categorized 'salary' as a dissatisfier rather than as a satisfier (Herzberg 1966: 126–7, Herzberg et al. 1959: 82–3). It is interesting to note that 'salary' cut across both sets of satisfying and dissatisfying variables. This may hint that Herzberg's strict dichotomy of satisfying variables and dissatisfying ones may have to be further scrutinized.

4. Herzberg seemingly labeled salary-related variables as 'recognition' and 'advancement'. Possibly this was a mainly rhetoric exercise that reflected the behavioral spirit of the time. Then, the human relations school perceived itself as the 'force of light' (Perrow 1983: 90).

5. Herzberg's empirical–behavioral interpretation of Adam as 'economic man' can be heuristically reinterpreted. The resulting economic reconstruction of the Bible can freshly examine the purpose and nature of Bible stories (see Wagner-Tsukamoto 2001b; Wagner 2000a).

6. If the stories of the Old Testament are read carefully, it is apparent that Abraham was a very wealthy man. He was rewarded with riches for leading a godly life. Also, he was involved in slave trading and in warfare against neighboring tribes. In this respect, Herzberg's terminology for referring to altruistic, caring behavior as 'Abraham'-behavior may be unfortunate.

7. Besides, the model of economic man is too narrowly interpreted regarding 'monetary gains', as similarly done by organizational researchers (for example, Mullins 1999: 49–52; Arnold et al. 1998: 457–8; Buchanan and Huczynski 1997: 340–43; see also Chapter 4, section 4.1). The model of economic man covers both monetary and non-monetary gains and losses (see Chapter 2, section 2.4).

8. Herzberg's change of terms from 'useful' to 'meaningful' may be less helpful. The idea of usefulness connects to an economic understanding of choice behavior (see Chapter 2, section 2.4 and Chapter 6).

9. Dahrendorf's terminology, like Friedman's, was at times ambiguous. He frequently used the term 'assumptions' for referring to research heuristics. Such references may be better supplemented by qualifiers like 'methodical', 'pre-empirical', 'sub-theoretical' or 'heuristic' in order to avoid misunderstandings. This is important since the idea of assumptions has been traditionally used to refer to theoretical–(practical) concepts of research, which are open to empirical scrutiny (see also Chapter 2, section 1.1 and Chapter 8, section 8.1).

10. Dahrendorf could have detailed suggestions on the nature of scientific research through ideas of problem dependence and research heuristics. He was ambiguous in this respect, especially when he suggested that disciplines reflected 'arbitrary traditions' (Dahrendorf 1973: 70). In other passages, Dahrendorf (1973: 7) indicated that scientific research was not so arbitrary after all.

11. Also, behavioral research and economic research may have in common that they are heuristically grounded in methodological individualism (see Hedström and Swedberg 1996: 131–3; Homann 1994: 12; Lindenberg 1990: 736; Zintl 1989: 56–8)

12. An early example of cross-cultural conflict in a globalizing world is contracting between European settlers and native American Indians. In 19th-century USA, when European settlers started to buy land from American Indians, the two sides were unaware that they differently understood the concept of 'owning land'. For American Indians, owning land did not imply that access to land would be exclusively restricted to the owner. Such an understanding probably reflects that they had not yet encountered scarcity and resulting contribution–distribution conflicts. Sales contracts appeared clear to both sides but conflict erupted once a different understanding of 'property' became apparent (Good 1988: 45–6).

13. Similar ideas of 'spirit' and 'harmony' as guiding principles for analyzing and resolving social problems can be found in Taylor's organization theory (see Chapter 4, section 4.1). Like Quaker managers, Taylor found out that moral–behavioral intervention was ineffective and in certain respects aggravated interaction problems in the firm.

14. Apparently, a stockholder problem was not a reason why Quaker managers failed to implement behavioral business ethics.

15. The Quakers' failure to implement their religious beliefs in business behavior compares to Taylor's failure to make managers and workers 'heartily cooperate' (see Chapter 4, section 4.1) or Williamson's self-admitted failure to include moral character traits in his model of human nature (see Chapter 6, section 6.3).

16. Besides 'economic' costs, the project of a value consensus is likely to come with certain moral 'costs'. Questions regarding the quality of morality of behavioral ethics have to be raised. Regarding an anti-pluralistic orientation, it may compare unfavorably with an economic approach to ethics. The combating of value pluralism, for example, through religious crusades, hints at moral 'costs' of behavioral ethics. Questions of cultural imperialism arise, too. Modernity and related ethical ideals of enlightenment, emancipation, tolerance and pluralism here are under threat and so is the 'great society', in Hayek's (1979, 1976) terms, or the 'open society', in Popper's (1962) terms. Hobbes' concept of ethical relativism hinted at this early on (Mintz 1962).

4. Taylor's, Simon's and Williamson's search of organizational economics: Incentive structures, dilemmatic interest conflict and mutual gains

> A higher degree of . . . rationality can . . . be achieved, because the environment of choice can be . . . deliberately modified . . . One function that organization performs is to place the organization member in a psychological environment that will adapt their decisions to the organization objectives and will provide them with the information needed to make these decisions correctly . . . The rational individual is and must be, an organized and institutionalized individual. If the severe limits imposed by human psychology upon deliberation are to be relaxed, the individual must in his decisions be subject to the influence of the organized group in which he participates. (Simon, 1945, pp. 79, 102)

> Transactions, which differ in their attributes, are assigned to governance structures, which differ in their organizational costs and competencies, so as to effect a discriminating (mainly transaction cost economizing) match. (Williamson, 1985, pp. 387–8)

This chapter examines whether Taylor, Simon and Williamson analyzed institutional organization structures through a non-behavioral, economic approach or whether they favored a behavioral one, which directly focused on human nature. In particular, the application of the conflict model 'dilemma structure' and suggestions on situational analysis and intervention with incentive structures are traced. Other conceptual elements of organizational economics, especially the ideas of 'human capital' and 'economic man', are discussed in later chapters. The chapter also examines how far an institutional economic reconstruction of Taylor's, Simon's and Williamson's organization theories does not succeed. A behavioral approach to social conflict is searched for in their studies. The following suggests that, in considerable degrees, Taylor, Simon and Williamson aimed at organizational economics. But that, at times, especially Taylor and Simon, they ambiguously intertwined the 'question of human nature' and related psychological and sociological concepts with institutional economics. This led to conceptual inconsistencies in their organization theories and, more significantly, to implementation failures when behavioral intervention with human nature was prioritized over economic intervention with incentive structures.

4.1   TAYLOR'S SCIENTIFIC MANAGEMENT: BETWEEN INCENTIVE SYSTEMS AND MORAL APPEAL

Taylor's studies in scientific management are one of the starting points of modern industrial organization theory.[1] Scientific management focused on the operational level of factory organization, to which Taylor referred as 'shop' or 'shop floor'.[2] At the time, his suggestions on organizational structuring, operations management and personnel management radically challenged existing views on good management practice. Taylor termed his organization theory 'scientific management' largely in order to differentiate it from another then debated management concept: the so-called 'systematic management' approach (Nelson 1992a: 7–8). He revised ideas of this approach in various respects. The following suggests:

1. Scientific management cannot be equated with time-and-motion studies, functional foremanship or the standardization of job contents structures. These are important elements of scientific management but they tell little about the institutional economic concepts of scientific management.
2. Taylor analyzed performance problems as interaction problems that were caused by 'defective' incentive structures. To a considerable degree, his program for practical intervention focused on the (re)design of incentive structures.
3. Taylor invoked the idea of the dilemma structure through the concept of systematic soldiering, although his understanding of the heuristic nature and purpose of this concept in organizational economics was incomplete and intuitive.
4. Taylor suggested mutual prosperity among organization members as a normative goal of organization theory. If mutual prosperity did not result from organizational interactions, he reasoned that all organization members would ultimately lose.
5. Taylor exited from organizational economics and entered behavioral analysis when examining uncooperative behavior of managers as a weakness of human nature but not as a problem of defective incentive structures. The behavioral concept of hearty cooperation yielded theoretical inconsistency in his analysis. In a practical perspective, it led to implementation failures, caused by 'rationally foolish' managers.

Taylor's Idea of the Dilemma Structure: Antagonistic Interaction Conflict as a Threat to Mutual Prosperity

The idea of mutual gains plays a prominent role in Taylor's writings. Pugh and Hickson (1996: 102) and Wrege and Greenwood (1991: 255) hint at this as did Nyland's (1998, 1996) historic economic research trace in depth the idea of mutual gains in Taylor's and his followers' writings, especially regarding union–management relations. The subsequent discussion puts the idea of mutual gains into perspective with regard to a wider institutional economic logic of scientific management, by interpreting it in relation to the idea of the dilemma structure.

The idea of the dilemma structure models interactions in which choice-makers fail to realize mutual gains because of unresolved interest conflicts (see Chapter 2, section 2.3). Taylor invoked such a model of social conflict when he conceptualized two 'conditions' that in his view undermined mutual prosperity as an outcome of organizational behavior (Taylor 1911: 53, 1903: 21–3). 'Condition one' referred to the attempt of managers to make employees do more work for the same pay (or do the same amount of work for less pay); 'condition two' referred to the attempt of employees to get wages and other benefits increased while keeping performance levels constant (or lower their work performance while receiving same rewards). Taylor stated: 'Employers and workmen alike should look upon both of these conditions with apprehension, as either of them are sure, in the long run, to lead to trouble and *loss for both parties*' (Taylor 1903: 23, emphasis added; see also ibid. 1912: 38, 128, 1911: 53, 1903: 21, 63, 131, 137). Both conditions yielded 'antagonism' (Taylor 1911: 53; see also 1912: 38, 128; 1903: 63, 131, 137) in social interactions in the firm – and Taylor stressed that unresolved antagonism threatened the prosperity of all organization members.

Alternatively, Taylor suggested that organization members had a common interest in cooperating and preventing loss/loss outcomes. If 'antagonizing' conflicts were resolved, it could result in sustainable profit increases, which he argued were to be shared among organization members: '[B]y joining together and pushing into the same direction instead of pulling apart – they can so enormously *increase this surplus* [profit] that there will be ample for *both* sides to divide' (Taylor 1912: 151, emphasis added). To sustain interactions, mutual gains were required as an interaction outcome – 'permanent prosperity for both employer and men', as he put it (Taylor 1903: 20–21, similarly ibid. 1912: 40, 1911: 10, 121).

Taylor's suggestions on interest conflict mirror the idea of the dilemma structure, as illustrated by the commons dilemma or the prisoners' dilemma. Clearly, he did not advocate confiscatory strategies for conflict resolution, which characterize zero-sum games. He explicitly dismissed a zero-sum concept of organizational behavior as 'fallacy' (1911: 27). Rather, he approached organizational conflict through a model of nonzero-sum interactions. He argued that, because of the feasibility of win/win outcomes, managers and workers had a mutual interest in cooperating. The prosperity of both 'employers' and 'employees' could rise – if only cooperation succeeded (Taylor 1911: 10, 138–9). To a degree, Taylor projected the idea of mutual gains, in the tradition of Adam Smith, to wider ethical, societal welfare goals, specifically 'national efficiency' (1911: 6, 9–10, 27).

Taylor thus outlined a different route to resolving alienation and antagonism between employers and workers than envisaged by Marx (1974, 1973) or advocates of critical management theory (for example, Nord and Jermier 1992). Interpretations of scientific management, such as Braverman (1974), err in this respect when suggesting that Taylor aimed to distribute profitability gains generated by scientific management to managers and the factory owners. Equally, interpretations of scientific management by Barley and Kunda (2000: 308–12), Kanigel (1997: 533–5), Pruijt (1997: Chapter 1), Nelson (1995: 56–61, 71), Waring (1991: 12), Rowlinson (1988: 381–3, 385, 391–2), Stabile (1987), Bluedorn (1986), Merkle (1980: Chapter 1), Kelly (1982) or Aitken (1960) pay too little or no attention to Taylor's model of dilemmatic interaction conflict and how Taylor aimed to resolve it in relation to the idea of mutual gains.

Systematic Soldiering and Taylor's Situational Analysis of Antagonistic Interest Conflicts

Taylor detailed the analysis of antagonistic interaction conflict through the idea of systematic soldiering. He interpreted 'systematic soldiering' as work-avoiding, opportunistic behavior that was systemically induced by 'defective' incentive structures:

> [B]y far the greatest evil from which *both workmen and employers* are suffering is the *systematic soldiering* which is almost universal under all of the ordinary schemes of management and which results from a careful study on the part of the workmen of what they think will promote *their best interests*. (Taylor 1903: 32, emphasis changed; similarly ibid. 1912: 118–19, 1911: 19–20)

Here, Taylor did not analyze cooperation problems as behavioral conflict or as a behavioral problem of low motivation, frail morals or predispositions towards laziness. Rather, he applied the model of a defective incentive logic. This compares to the institutional economic analysis of the incentive-*in*compatibility of organization structures. They are examined as the cause of antagonizing, 'rationally foolish' interaction outcomes. Game theory can well detail the situational analysis of such interdependence effects. Luce and

Raiffa (1957: 97) is classic. They suggested that irrational outcomes in nonzero-sum interactions should be strictly analyzed as a situational condition (see Chapter 2, section 2.3). Empirical research on the relationship between performance contributions of employees and wage distributions to employees (Ockenfels 1999: 157–64) provides a game-theoretical confirmation of Taylor's suggestions (also hinted at by Adams 1965).[3] The concept of systematic soldiering directed Taylor's analysis towards the systemic, situational analysis of cooperation problems. Consequently, he arrived at rather different recommendations for institutional organization, discussed in more detail below, than the ones made by behavioral organization research, for example, the human relations school, which focused on the research of human nature.

For employee–employee interactions, Taylor discussed how systemically unresolved contribution–distribution conflicts encouraged systematic soldiering, undermined organizational performance and yielded mutual loss to all organization members. Taylor explicitly referred in this respect to the 'logic of the situation':

> The common tendency to 'take it easy' is greatly increased by bringing a number of men together on similar work and at a uniform standard rate of pay by the day. Under this *plan* the better men gradually but surely slow down their gait to that of the poorest and least efficient. When a naturally energetic man works for a few days beside a lazy one, the *logic of the situation* is unanswerable: 'Why should I work hard when that lazy fellow gets the same pay that I do and does only half as much work?' (Taylor 1903: 31, emphasis added, similarly, ibid. 1895: 36)

Taylor suggested that defective incentive structures instigated interaction dynamics that caused performance problems or 'systematic soldiering' in his terms. This left all involved in the interaction worse off. Leaving certain behavioral connotations of ideas like 'common tendency' and 'naturally energetic' aside at this stage (see Chapter 6, section 6.1),[4] he criticized incentive structures that did not link distributions received by the individual with contributions made. Defective incentive structures undermined performance contributions of 'better men' (see also Taylor 1912: 113–21, 1911: 13, 19–23, 1903: 30–34, 37, 45, 48, 1895: 33, 36). Nichols and Armstrong (1976: 125) and Ackroyd and Thompson (1999: 71) are in line with Taylor's observations that incentive-incompatible management structures can cause interaction problems:

> [T]he solidarity of the cement workers caved in whenever it came under pressure. Each time groups saw a short-run advantage for themselves they were willing to forget the consequences for their workmates. In the event, most of these short-run advantages turned out to be very short-run indeed or completely illusory. (Nichols and Armstrong 1976: 125)

Worker solidarity could not prevent the breakdown of cooperation when 'defective' incentive structures were encountered. Taylor even bluntly conceded that he himself, when working as a machinist, had not been able to escape performance-lowering interaction dynamics that were driven by 'defective' incentive structures (Taylor 1912: 113–14, see also ibid. 1911: 21, 1903: 35, 137). Despite the knowledge that gains from defection were of a short-run, unsustainable nature, defection still occurred. Apparently, when facing incentive-incompatible organization structures, it does not matter whether interactions occur among workers themselves, managers themselves, managers and workers or involve other stakeholders of the firm. For example, if unions are allocated competency rights in a way that enables them to dominate interactions, mutuality of gains is threatened (Hayek 1960: 270). Role conflict or class conflict between a ruling class of 'managers' and a ruled class of 'workers' is then not the important issue but 'incentive defects' of organization structures.

Situational Intervention with Cooperation Problems

In order to resolve interaction problems, institutional economics suggests a change in incentive structures. Rules and sanctions that set standards for contributions and distributions are to be intervened with. Taylor's analysis followed such a situational intervention logic:

> In the future it will be appreciated . . . that no great man can (with the old system of personal management) hope to compete with a number of ordinary men who have been properly organized so as efficiently to cooperate. In the past the man has been first; in the future the system must be first. (Taylor 1911: 6–7, see also ibid. 1903: 62)

Seemingly, Taylor favored the (re)design of incentive structures – 'system' – over behavioral intervention – 'man'. Equally, he rejected coercive structures; he spoke of command structures that were not coupled with incentive structures (Taylor 1911: 26).

Situational intervention had to ensure that the employer's and the employees' 'best interests are mutual' (Taylor 1903: 21). Taylor here anticipated Luce and Raiffa's (1957: 97) situational suggestions on how to prevent 'rationally foolish' interaction outcomes. For avoiding 'loss/loss' situations, it was mandatory to 'change the system of management, so that the interests of the workmen and the management should become the same, instead of antagonistic' (Taylor 1911: 53). Interests had to be made the 'same' or as Williamson (1985: 34) put it, they had to be 'equilibrated'.

Taylor advocated incentive structures for intervening with job performance:

The problem before the management, then may be briefly said to be that of obtaining the *initiative* of every workman. . . . [I]n order to have any hope of obtaining the initiative of his workmen the manager must give some *special incentive* to his men (Taylor 1911: 32–3, emphasis as in original).

He rejected organization structures suggested by earlier organization theories, such as a fixed-rate wage system,[5] a piece-rate system, the contractor system, which reflects an outsourcing concept (see also Chapter 7) and profit-sharing arrangements. In his view, these systems did not provide 'proper' incentives to the employee (Taylor 1912: 22–32, 1911: 33–4, 72–4, 121, 129–30, 1903: 23, 99–200).

Instead, Taylor favored a premium wage system. In his view, this system was best suited to yield both high quantity and a high quality of work performance. Both workers and factory managers were to be offered incentives in this way (Taylor 1911: 127, 1909: 85, 1903: 104–5, 141–2). Besides pay-related incentives, such as salary increases, promotion or fines, Taylor discussed various non-monetary incentives, such as the shortening of working hours or 'comfortable lavatories, eating rooms, lecture halls and free lectures, night schools, kindergartens, baseball and athletic grounds, village improvement societies and mutual beneficial associations' (Taylor 1903: 199, see also ibid. 1911: 33–4, 83, 95, 1903: 25, 141–2, 190). In their substance, such suggestions do not fundamentally differ from similar proposals of behavioral organization research (see also Chapter 3, sections 3.2 and 3.3). In this regard, it is an overstatement to suggest that Taylor intended to motivate organization members by 'using financial (and *only* financial) incentives' (Arnold et al. 1998: 457, brackets and emphasis as in original; similarly Casey 2002: 72–3; Waring 1991: 12; Mayo 1990: 357; Knowles and Saxberg 1967: 32; Roethlisberger and Dickson 1949: 575–6). Such critique is further flawed when grounding it in a behavioral critique of the research heuristic 'economic man', as seemingly implied by Burrell and Morgan (1979: 144) (see also Chapter 6, section 6.1). In these respects and regarding Taylor's suggestions on mutual gains, scientific management can even be reconstructed in the terms of feminist organization theory (for a review of such terms, see Hatch 1997: 291–2; Calas and Smircich 1996: 228).

Besides the intervention with incentive structures, Taylor suggested the redesigning of job contents structures and communication structures. For successfully implementing a premium wage system, he argued that traditional rules of thumb for defining and measuring job performance, job contents and communication among employees had to be given up (Taylor 1911: 41, 83, 1909: 87, 1903: 133). Only the formalization and standardization of rules enabled performance measurement and thus performance-related sanctioning. Standardized contribution rules should specify what skills contributions were expected from employees. He studied in this respect the division of labor in tedious detail in order to set out a 'fair day's work' and proper tool support, for both workers and supervisors (Taylor 1911: 36–9, 47–9, 129–30, 1903: 102–4, 124–5, 141–2, see also ibid. 1912: 6).

Taylor's suggestions on 'functional foremanship' split job responsibilities of factory managers according to functional competencies. Morgan's (1989: 51) diagnosis that 'his [Taylor's] system of management served to mechanize the worker in effect by splitting the functions of hand and brain' may be incomplete. Scientific management 'mechanized', to a considerable degree, the work of factory managers, too. An engineering department was to provide operational support to workers. It comprised the positions of 'gang boss', 'speed boss', 'inspector' and 'repair boss'. An administrative department informed workers on job scheduling, provided job-relevant information, mostly in written form, and checked performance. The administrative department comprised the positions 'order of work and route clerk', 'instruction card clerk', 'time and cost clerk' and 'shop disciplinarian' (Taylor 1903: 99–109, 123–5, see also ibid. 1912: 27, 31, 51, 86–7, 1911: 26, 36–9, 103–6, 122–3, 1903: 45, 64, 75, 87). Taylor began to conceptualize administrative behavior and corporate planning (see also Figure 4.1).

Taylor's suggestions on job contents and communication structures as well as time-and-motion studies can be criticized for individualizing and mechanizing organizational behavior of managers and workers (for example, Jones 2000: 632, 648–9; Guillen 1997: 688, 1994: 79; Warner 1994: 1158; Waring 1991: 11–12; Morgan 1986: 30–38; Burrell and Morgan 1979: 126–7; Knowles and Saxberg 1967: 32). In certain respects, this critique cuts too short. An assessment of scientific management may have to be put into perspective regarding the analytical logic and favored conflict resolution strategies of scientific management. Job structures and time-and-motion studies of individual behavior have to be viewed as elements of Taylor's wider interaction analysis of contribution–distribution conflicts. Hence, conventional perceptions of scientific management that it predominantly dealt with job description analysis, time-and-motion studies and so on, as well reviewed by Roper (1999), are incomplete. Such criticism of scientific management can be further qualified when considering social and ethical ideals that drove Taylor's program, namely the resolution of 'antagonism' in organizational behavior, the maintenance of fairness in rewarding performance and the generation of mutual prosperity. Furthermore, Taylor's suggestions on management structures reflected the specific socio-cultural context of late 19th-century USA, in which ethnic and cultural inhomogeneity on the shop floor was high (Gutman 1976: 22–3; see also Wrege and Greenwood 1991: 104; Chapter 7, section 7.3). This favored, on economic grounds, a highly formalized, standardized, instruction-oriented approach to communication and work organization.

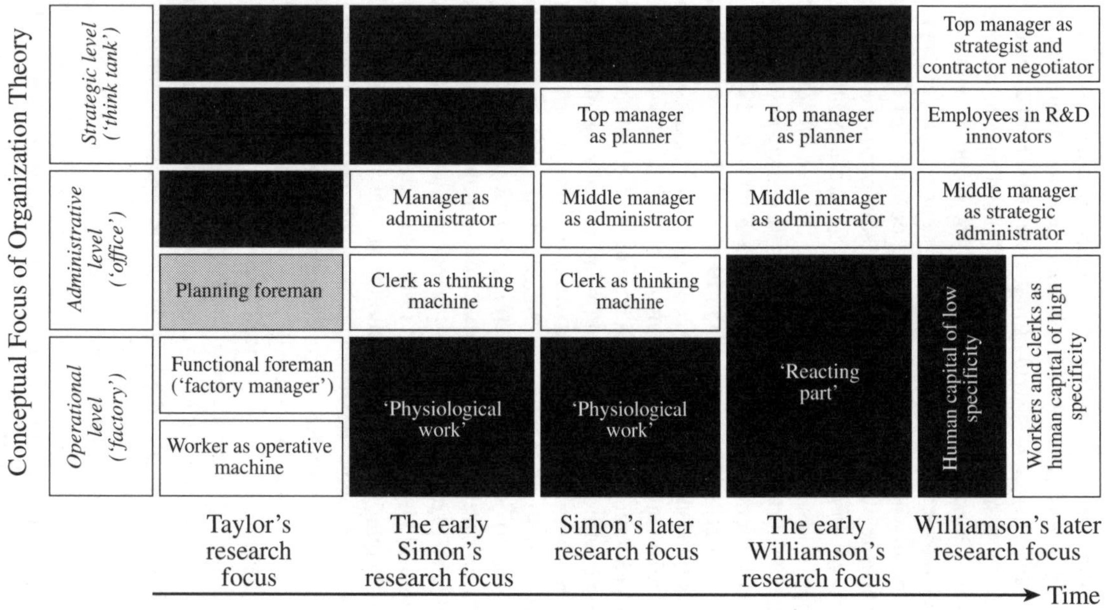

Conceptual Focus of Organization Theory

	Taylor's research focus	The early Simon's research focus	Simon's later research focus	The early Williamson's research focus	Williamson's later research focus
Strategic level ('think tank')	(black box)	(black box)	(black box)	(black box)	Top manager as strategist and contractor negotiator
	(black box)	(black box)	(black box)	(black box)	Employees in R&D innovators
Administrative level ('office')	Planning foreman	Manager as administrator	Middle manager as administrator / Top manager as planner	Middle manager as administrator / Top manager as planner	Middle manager as strategic administrator
	(black box)	Clerk as thinking machine	Clerk as thinking machine	(black box) 'Reacting part'	Workers and clerks as human capital of high specificity
Operational level ('factory')	Functional foreman ('factory manager') / Worker as operative machine	'Physiological work' (black box)	'Physiological work' (black box)	'Reacting part' (black box)	Human capital of low specificity (black box)

↑ Time →

Note: 'Black boxes' without inserts were neglected in the respective approaches; those with 'inserts' were explicitly excluded.

Figure 4.1   Evolution (of the analysis) of human capital

Taylor's Behavioral Approach to the Managerial Condition: The Moral Appeal to Heartily Cooperate

Taylor was aware that scientific management was ineffective unless both the 'employee condition' and the 'managerial condition' were resolved. As discussed above, Taylor examined the 'employee condition' and its antagonizing effects on interaction outcomes through the concept of systematic soldiering. And, he suggested resolving the 'employee condition' through systemic intervention with incentive structures. Regarding the 'managerial condition', however, Taylor did not apply the concept of systematic soldiering and he did not advocate intervening with incentive structures.

Taylor was aware that under scientific management the 'managerial condition' could easily derail social interactions in the firm, especially regarding managerialist rule change on wage levels (Taylor 1911: 125, 1903: 103–5, 107, 119): '[T]he workman must . . . be fully assured that this increase [of wages] beyond the average is to be permanent' (Taylor 1911: 121; similarly ibid. 1903: 26). Employees had to be guaranteed that promised gains for raising contributions could not be taken back. Taylor's concepts of 'fairness in profit sharing', 'justice' in distributing gains from efficiency increases or a 'fair day's work' (Taylor 1911: 49, 68, 95, 1903: 38, 174) carry this understanding, too. Taylor applied the concept of the 'heartily cooperative' manager when analyzing and intervening with interest conflicts between managers and workers (Taylor 1911: 27–9, 36–8, 114, 130; see also ibid. 1912: 27–31, 37–45, 145–53, 1903: 63–8, 96–8, 129–32). He appealed to managers to perceive it as their moral duty to be impartial, friendly and fair in their interactions with employees, especially when it came to the sharing of gains generated under scientific management. A behavioral approach to business ethics here is endorsed by Taylor. Bendix (1956: 278–81, 286) and Merkle (1980: 14–16) interpret this as Taylor's call for a new 'management ideology'. A 'complete mental revolution' was required (Taylor 1912: 26–7, similarly ibid. 1912: 7):

> The indispensable prerequisite for bringing in an era of industrial peace was a radical change of heart on the part of employers . . . Taylor could not make this too emphatic. Over and over again he said that employers must undergo a change of heart like unto that of a religious conversion. (Copley 1919: 8–9, similarly ibid. 1919: 15)

Taylor even developed a pedagogic program on how managers should be trained over a period of two to five years to make them impartial and heartily cooperative (Taylor 1912: 153; see also Goldberg 1992: 44–5, 53). Seemingly, he aimed to (re)-educate the manager as the 'new good man', an idea that later prominently resurfaced in McGregor's (1960), Argyris' (1962), Knowles and

Saxberg's (1967: 32–8, 174–6), Rothschild's (1979: 519), Donaldson's (1995: 183–7) or Tomer's (1999) research. Herzberg's (1966) suggestions on cooperative organization man 'Abraham', Simon's (1945) expectation that managers showed a 'desire for efficiency' (see section 4.2), and, in minor degrees, some of Williamson's (1991b: 95, 1985: 62–3, 241–2) behavioral suggestions (see section 4.3) move in a similar direction.[6]

Undoubtedly, Taylor's suggestions on the heartily cooperative manager are a highly interesting theory component of scientific management. They tend to be ignored by behavioral organization research, possibly because they do not easily fit conventional views of what scientific management is about. In this respect, accusations that Taylor cherished an incomplete, too mechanistic and negative image of human nature may be doubly unfortunate (for example, Casey 2002: 72–3; Mullins 1999: 49–52; Buchanan and Huczynski 1997: 340–43; Perrow 1983: 90; similarly Barley and Kunda 2000: 311; Wrege and Greenwood 1991: 257–8; Drucker 1989a: 188–9; Morgan 1986: 31–4; Knowles and Saxberg 1967: 32; Nadworny 1955). They overlook that Taylor portrayed (at least some) organization members in moral–behavioral terms – but that this led to practical implementation problems for his organization theory (discussed below). Taylor anticipated in this respect the pitfalls of behavioral business ethics and behavioral organization research that tries to solve cooperation problems by focusing on the human condition, through 'winning hearts and minds' of organization members, as Thomason (1991: 6) or, similarly, Nord and Jermier (1992: 218) put it. Elster (1990: 49–50), who analyzed this issue in general terms, advocates 'codes of honor' to restrain the potentially debilitating effects of self-interested behavior.

As far as the spirit-principle is discussed in the organization theory literature, for example, Bendix (1956), Drury (1968), Merkle (1980) or Kelly (1982), often a too uncritical view is taken. Its purpose regarding the prevention of managerialist rule change is not clearly understood. Probably only Kanigel (1997: 476–9) touches, to a degree, on this issue. Nelson (1992a: 5–6, 1992b: 240) suggested a number of reasons why Taylor invoked hearty cooperation: being a defense against humanistic criticism or being a selling and consultancy proposition of scientific management. Buchanan and Huczynski (1997: 340–3) argue similarly. Although such suggestions cannot be entirely discounted, the deeper reason why Taylor drew on the concept of hearty cooperation relate to his attempt – which proved to be unsuccessful with hindsight – to resolve cooperation problems in non-economic but behavioral terms.

The sincerity and emotive depth of Taylor's moral appeal to managers to heartily cooperate may not be questioned, but the vehemence of the appeal possibly just reflects that he sensed a severe conceptual problem, possibly even a self-contradiction in his economic analysis of organizational behavior. It goes unquestioned that behavioral intervention can strengthen cooperative attitudes and the moral–behavioral climate in the firm and this in turn can support the resolution of interaction problems. But behavioral intervention is probably only effective after incentive-compatible organization structures have been installed. As discussed above, Taylor outlined with regard to the 'employee condition' how a single 'lazy' – uncooperative – employee could undermine interactions among employees. If Taylor had examined systematic soldiering for managers, he would have discovered that moral appeal did not systemically equilibrate managerial self-interest and worker self-interest. To induce managerial cooperation on grounds of self-interested behavior may be the more necessary because competitive pressures and self-interested choice is imposed on managers, to a considerable degree, by the firm's organization structures (Fama 1980: 293–4) and by the constitutional, political–legal and economic institutions of the market economy that enact and protect competition among firms.

Where Quaker owner-managers with considerably deeper religious beliefs and more moral authority failed because of systemic economic pressures (see Chapter 3, section 3.3), Taylor's expectation that 'plain', non-owner managers could be trained as moral agents was utopian. Jones' (2000: 53) findings on workers who mistrusted managerial attempts to create 'inclusive cultures' in Taylorist work settings underlines this point. Actual implementation failures of scientific management confirm that Taylor's moral–behavioral appeal did not prevent managerialism. Nelson (1992a: 13, 1992b: 239) and Goldberg (1992: 43) reviewed a number of cases in which managers retreated on given wage promises (see also Cochran 1968: 79). Copley (1919: 8) spoke in this respect of the 'myopic greed' of managers when it came to appropriating and distributing gains generated under scientific management. Not surprisingly, worker discontent with (potential) uncooperative managerial behavior, fueled by actual occurrences of broken promises, grew strong and led to strikes against scientific management and Taylor's summoning to testify before the US Congress.[7]

When being questioned before the US Congress, Taylor (1912: 153) explicitly admitted to the failure of the concept of hearty cooperation: 'Nine tenths of the trouble comes from those on the management side in taking up and operating a new device [the scientific management program] and only one-tenth on the workmen's side. Our difficulties are almost entirely with the management.' This leads back to the question of how far behavioral concepts can resolve cooperation problems. In 'modern' interaction contexts in which family-type, sociobiological bonding and an unambiguous value consensus have been eroded and in which the institutional structures of the market economy enforce competitive, 'uncooperative' behavior (for moral reasons), the effectiveness of behavioral intervention is likely to be in doubt. Then, cooperation problems may be more successfully treated as a systemic condition but not as the human condition and even less so a class-related or role-related reflection of the human condition. Probably only in pre-modern contexts, where a culturally homogeneous work force is encountered and managers are nearly intrinsically predisposed towards cooperation – Rowlinson's (1988: 391–2) discussion of scientific management in British Quaker firms is instructive – the appeal for hearty cooperation stood a chance of succeeding. But then, successful Quaker employers also systemically self-bound themselves regarding managerialism by involving unions in the organization of employer–employee interactions (Rowlinson 1988: 386–7).

Non-behavioral Alternatives to Handling the Managerial Condition

There are numerous ways in which Taylor could have prevented the 'managerial condition' in institutional economic terms. North's 'ruler–constituent' analogy is insightful in this regard. North (1993b, 1990) hinted that as long as the ruler can change rules at will, for example, issue confiscation rules that change the distribution of gains, a dilemmatic interaction problem exists: '[T]he constituents face the dilemma that the ruler may at some point renege on his promises and confiscate the accumulated wealth of his constituents' (North 1993b: 14). In order to resolve this problem, North (1993b) suggested that promises of gains have to be safeguarded by incentive structures. Trust or fairness is thus approached in economic terms rather than in behavioral ones.[8] Fama's (1980) discussion of how to control managerialism moves in a similar direction. For instance, scientific management could have granted unions certain competency rights on behalf of workers; collective bargaining arrangements could have been advocated; or other codetermination schemes between workers and managers could have been installed. Williamson (1985: 34) and Mortensen (1978: 585) stressed such a stability-building role unions play in generating 'industrial peace' (see also section 4.3). A jointly organized process of negotiations over contributions and distributions is in this way set up, safeguarded by institutional economic structures, inside and outside a firm. Rowlinson's (1988: 386–7) review of Cadbury's success in implementing scientific management by involving unions in wage negotiations points at such an institutional economic rationale.

In his testimonial before the US Congress in 1912, Taylor's thinking seemed to move into this direction, too:

> [T]he moment it becomes the object of both sides *jointly to arrive* at what is an *equitable and just series of standards* by which they will *both* be *governed*; the moment they realize that under this new type of cooperation . . . they can so enormously increase this surplus [profit] that there will be ample for both sides to divide. (Taylor 1912: 151, emphasis added)

These suggestions come close to some of Williamson's (1985) institutional economic proposals on governance structures (see section 4.3). Unfortunately, in his studies before 1912, Taylor did not approach the 'managerial condition' in such institutional economic terms. He only later proposed 'jointly administered schemes' after implementation failures of scientific management had occurred and after he had been invited to testify before the US Congress. However, even then Taylor did not fully realize how institutional safeguards could have helped to resolve the managerial condition. His continued argumentation against unionization reflects this (Taylor 1912: 149–53, also ibid. 1903: 184). It was only after Taylor's death in 1915 that his followers began to revise the scientific management approach in this respect (see also Nyland 1998: 525–6; Nadworny 1955: 105, 111–19, 144; Hoxie 1915: 147). They introduced formal 'checks and balances' for managerial behavior by involving unions in the institutional organization of interactions between managers and workers:

> The best known of these changes was the reconciliation of Taylor's followers and union leaders that followed the engineers' formal endorsement of collective bargaining. The practical importance of this concession is unclear but it removed a major source of misunderstanding and demonstrated the appeal of scientific management among union leaders once its anti-union implications were muted. (Nelson 1992a: 15)

Similarly argues Nadworny (1955: 144–7). From an institutional economic point of view, the practical importance of bringing unions into the structural organization of employer–employee interactions is clear. The temptation of managers to appropriate gains that had been promised to workers was systemically constrained by (re)designing incentive structures here: reallocating property rights on distribution decisions. As discussed, before 1912, Taylor favored a moral–behavioral approach to resolving the managerial condition.

4.2 SIMON'S ADMINISTRATIVE BEHAVIOR APPROACH: BETWEEN COMPENSATION SCHEMES AND PSYCHOLOGICAL ENVIRONMENT

Like Taylor, Simon was very much interested in problems of organizational performance. He analyzed the individual organization member's ability to make decisions that are 'rational' from the point of view of the organization (Simon 1945: 39). He examined organizational rationality problems. The following suggests:

1. Simon modeled rationality problems in behavioral terms as conflicts between the *individual's* values and knowledge and the *organization's* values and knowledge. A methodical relevance of game theoretical concepts was not seen. Rather, they were rejected on behavioral grounds.
2. Simon conceptualized institutional organization in motivational and cognitive terms as psychological environment. Behavioral intervention focused on job contents structures and communication structures. This was to ensure organizationally rational decision-making.
3. Simon's analysis of 'inducement–contribution equilibriums' and related suggestions on 'compensation structures' hint at economic foundations of his organization theory. These ideas were methodically and theoretically vaguely integrated with his behavioral analysis.
4. Simon prioritized behavioral organization theory over organizational economics. He implied competition between behavioral organization research and organizational economics (largely by assessing 'economic man' in empirical–behavioral and moral–behavioral terms; see Chapter 6).

A Behavioral Model of Rationality Conflicts: Simon's Rejection of Game Theoretical Concepts

A key concept of Simon's analysis of performance problems was the idea of 'non-rationality' in organizational decision-making:

> [T]he term 'rational' behavior . . . refers to rationality when that behavior is evaluated in terms of the objectives of the larger organization; for . . . the difference in direction of the individual's aims from those of the larger organization is just one of those elements of nonrationality with which the theory must deal. (Simon 1945: 41)

Institutional economics conceptually specifies rationality problems as dilemmatic interest conflicts and examines their resolution in relation to the incentive-(in)compatibility of organization structures. In contrast, Simon analyzed rationality conflicts in behavioral terms. He argued that motivational and cognitive issues should be examined in order to understand the individual organization member's 'ability to make correct [rational organizational] decisions' (Simon 1945: 39, also ibid.: 40–41, 79, 243). He criticized in this respect earlier organization theories, for instance, Gulick and Urwick (1937) or Urwick (1945), for not distinguishing behavioral conditions on which 'rational' organizational decision-making depended (Simon 1945: 20–21). Simon spelled out three such behavioral conditions: physiological skills, motivation and cognition:

Two persons given the same skills, the same objectives and values, the same knowledge and information, can rationally decide only upon the same course of action. Hence administrative theory must be interested in the factors that will determine with what skills, values and knowledge the organization member undertakes his work. (Simon 1945: 39)

Regarding physiological conditions, Simon referred to the successful studies of Taylor (for example, Simon 1950: 4, 1945: 40, 138) and excluded them and related questions of factory organization from his research.[9] Although, as discussed in section 4.1 and Chapter 5, section 5.1, scientific management is likely to reflect more than 'physiological theory' (March and Simon 1958: 136–7, 139; also Simon 1945: 38). Having excluded physiological issues, Simon focused the analysis of rationality conflicts on motivational issues of unresolved goal/value conflicts and cognitive issues of lacking knowledge.

Simon was aware that he could have modeled rationality conflicts in non-behavioral terms, through economic, game-theoretical concepts. He discussed the game of matching pennies, in which two players try to outguess and outwit each other (Simon 1945: 70–73). In this connection, Simon touched on the idea that interdependence of choice behaviors of individual agents could destabilize interactions:

[E]ach individual, in order to determine uniquely the consequences of his actions, must know what will be the actions of the others. This is a factor of fundamental importance for the whole process of administrative decision-making. There is really a serious circularity involved here. Before A can rationally choose his strategy, he must know which strategy B has chosen; and before B can choose his strategy, he must know A's . . . The resulting behavior system will be of a highly indeterminate nature, for the *instability of each of the behavior choices* leads to the *instability of the other*. (Simon 1945: 71, emphasis added, similarly ibid. 1945: 105–6)

The prisoners' dilemma implies a similar, circular interdependence among decision-makers. However, Simon dismissed this dilemmatic interaction concept for modeling rationality conflicts.

With regard to the zero-sum game of matching pennies, this was a wise conceptual decision. In the game of matching pennies, each player can only gain at the expense of the other (see von Neumann and Morgenstern 1947: 143–5). No 'win/win' outcomes exist. In this respect, Simon could rightly claim that a game theoretical, dilemmatic interaction model is only useful for analyzing 'purely competitive activity', for which he gave as examples military decision-making and market interactions[10] (Simon 1945: 71–2, 1950: 3; similarly March and Simon 1958: 130–35), but not for analyzing organizational problems (Simon 1945: 40–41, 110, 119, 149, 161–3; also March and Simon 1958: 129–32). Simon here meets Taylor, who had characterized zero-sum concepts as a 'fallacy' for organization research.

In contrast to the game of matching pennies, the prisoners' dilemma or the commons dilemma model *nonzero*-sum interactions, which means that gains of one agent do not necessarily imply losses to others. In the prisoners' dilemma, mutual gains, but also mutual loss or 'rational foolishness', are feasible interaction outcomes. Initially, Simon (1952–53, 1945) did not seem to be aware of such nonzero-sum concepts. Nevertheless, Simon kept rejecting game-theoretical models of rationality conflicts even after he had become aware of nonzero-sum games, 'cooperative games', 'bargaining theory' and 'nonzero-sum theory' (Simon 1976a: xxxii; March and Simon 1958: 132; similarly Cyert and March 1992: 33–4). Simon continued to suggest that game theory was only useful for analyzing competitive interactions among firms. He spoke of 'interorganizational conflict' (March and Simon 1958: 131–5). Only at the very end of his research career, Simon (1997: 34) indirectly admitted to this shortcoming of his organization research. He then attested that his organization theory had not conceptualized win/win outcomes of social interactions. Such a 'deficit' relates to his rejection of game-theoretical, nonzero-sum concepts for modeling interaction conflict in organizational behavior.

The rejection of nonzero-sum game theory was an unfortunate theory-building decision. It left Simon's organization theory without an economic concept for assessing dilemmatic cooperation problems in organizational behavior. As detailed below, the model of nonzero-sum interactions could have helped Simon to coherently develop his suggestions on 'inducement–contribution analysis' in institutional economic terms.

In contrast, Taylor's and Williamson's theories were explicitly based on a nonzero-sum model of dilemmatic rationality conflicts: Taylor modeled 'antagonism', 'loss to both sides' and 'systematic soldiering', and Williamson invoked the 'contracting dilemma', which undermined 'mutual gains' as interaction outcome (see sections 4.1 and 4.3). Indeed, Williamson (1985: 32–4, 42, 1975: 135–6) argued that such a dilemmatic interaction concept was especially fruitful for analyzing organizational behavior rather than competitive interactions on markets. The latter was suggested by Simon. Buchanan's economic analysis of public order proceeded similarly, building on the idea of an interaction dilemma, the 'punishment dilemma', in order to analyze interactions and systemically intervene with interactions (for instance, Buchanan 1975: 130–46).

To a considerable degree, Simon justified the rejection of game-theoretical ideas on empirical–behavioral and moral–behavioral grounds. He criticized game theory because of its unrealistic 'assumptions about human motivations and behavior' (March and Simon 1958: 134; similarly Simon 1955: 101). By pitting behavioral concepts, both heuristic and theoretical–(practical) ones, against a research heuristic of (institutional) economics, he fell for a mis-understanding regarding the problem-dependent and heuristic nature of certain concepts in scientific research (see also Chapter 1, section 1.1, Chapter 2, section 2.3, Chapter 5, section 5.2 and Chapter 6, section 6.2).

The Behavioral Resolution of Rationality Conflicts: A Psychological Environment of Value Indoctrination and Knowledge Programming

Simon aimed to handle rationality problems in organizational behavior by 'defining the psychological capacity of the human organism and to program activities to make full use of that capacity' (March and Simon 1958: 47, 139; Simon 1957a: xxxv). He specified in this respect various motivational and cognitive conditions such as 'desire for efficiency', 'obedience', 'acceptance of authority', 'internalization of values', 'organization personality', 'organizational loyalty', 'group loyalty', 'identification' or 'altruism' (Simon 1993b: 159–60, 1991: 30, 38, 1976a: xxxv, 1957b: 62–78, 99–144, 1945: 71, 242). Simon (1997: 43–5, 52) explicitly interpreted organizational loyalty in relation to the idea of altruism. Thus, he advocated the comprehensive socialization of the individual (March and Simon 1958: 51–2, 65–6, 157–8; also Simon 1993b: 160, 1976a: 267–8, 1945: 14, 123, 161, 170, 198–9, 204–10). Psychological–sociological 'contracting', as Schein (1980) put it, and psychological 'governance' were aimed at. A 'science of man' was the declared goal (Simon 1945: 41; also March and Simon 1958: 1–2; Simon 1945: 130, 209). This is diametrically opposed to Williamson's approach, namely that interest equilibration and the intervention with incentive structures should harmonize social interactions. Simon's behavioral suggestions are also difficult to reconcile with his suggestions on inducement–contribution analysis (discussed below) or Simon's (1997: 34) late admission that organizational conflict should be better approached in relation to 'making interests of the firm and self-interests of the employee' coincide.

When advancing a behavioral, psychological approach to resolving organizational conflict, Simon even argued for 'value indoctrination':

> [T]he organization trains and indoctrinates its members. This might be called the 'internalization' of influence, because it injects into the very nervous systems of the organization members the criteria of decision that the organization wishes to employ. (Simon 1945: 103, also ibid. 1945: 40–1, 71–3, 106–7, 149–51, 243)

Job contents structures and communication structures should achieve this. They were to channel organizational 'goals', 'value premises', 'ends' and task-relevant 'facts', 'knowledge premises', 'means' to 'decision points'. With regard to underlying conflicts, he spoke in this respect of 'conflicting values', 'conflicting premises', 'conflicting ends' and of 'lacking facts', 'lacking means', 'lacking information', 'lacking knowledge' (March and Simon 1958: 13–15, 33, 40, 138–59, 181; Simon 1957a: xxxv; Simon 1952: 1132; Simon 1945: 3, 40–43, 72–3, 102–3, 189–90; Ridley and Simon 1943: 5, 53; see also Simon 1991: 38–40). The implied consensus-oriented communication program compared to the favored intervention strategies of organization psychology. Urwick (1967: 12–13) explicitly supported Simon's communication programs to solve organizational problems. As Bendix (1956: 313–21) detailed, a similar communication-based approach can be made out for Mayo (1949, 1933). Or Steffy and Grimes (1992: 195–9) spelled out a communication orientation for organization psychology that proceeds in the tradition of Habermas.

Related to the discussion of value indoctrination, Simon argued for the idea of the 'psychological environment' (March and Simon 1958: 26–7; Simon 1945: 79, 102, 243; similarly, McGregor 1960: 49). It reflected behavioral intervention with motivational and cognitive conditions:

> A higher degree of . . . rationality can . . . be achieved, because the environment of choice can be . . . deliberately modified. One function that organization performs is to place the organization member in a psychological environment that will adapt their decisions to the organization objectives and will provide them with the information needed to make these decisions correctly. (Simon 1945: 79)

Regarding the value prescriptive character of Simon's proposals, other organization theories spring to mind, such as Czarniawska-Joerges' (1988) and Etzioni's (1975) discussions of the 'ideological organization' or Rothschild's (1979) elaborations on the 'collectivist organization'.

Simon specified that motivational and cognitive conditions were to be 'programmed' in different degrees for different organization members (see also Figure 4.1). For low-level administrative employees, job descriptions and communication structures were to prescribe both 'value premises' and 'knowledge premises' (Simon 1945: 102–3).[11] Discretion in decision-making existed here only in a narrow procedural sense (March and Simon 1958: 90–92, 142–58, 160–68, 195; Simon 1957a: xxiv, xxv, 1945: 4, 8, 71, 133, 148, 157–62, 198, 217–18; Simon et al. 1941: 50–51). Comparisons to a 'thinking machine' may be invoked (Burrell and Morgan 1979: 151–2).

Middle managers enjoyed the freedom to decide about means. Their performance was measured against clearly defined goals (Simon 1945: 14, 123, 209; also March and Simon 1958: 55, 90, 145, 195–8). Simon suggested 'pro forma participation', later referred to by Argyris (1973) as 'pseudo participation', as a way for top managers to ensure 'correct' goals and values of middle managers (March and Simon 1958: 54, 112–17, 129, 161–8, 198–9; also Simon 1945: 129, 148, 157–67).

Simon pointed out that creative, complex tasks of top managers, such as innovation, entrepreneurship, organizational design and 'external tasks', could not be programmed, neither regarding ends nor means (March and Simon 1958: 136–50, 159, 172–9, 197–9; Simon 1945: 79, 106, 118, 123–8, 199, 217). He reasoned that job descriptions and communication structures can only successfully organize 'analytic problem solving', where means but not ends of decision-making are in question (March and Simon 1958: 130). In contrast, 'non-analytic problem solving' reflected bargaining and interest conflicts (see March and Simon 1958: 131–4). Simon realized that this latter problem arose at the top management level. Institutional economics would in this regard analyze and intervene with incentive structures and analyze dilemmatic interest conflict. In contrast, Simon favored the concept of psychological predispositions of top managers, namely a 'desire for efficiency' (Simon 1945: 123, 209, see also ibid. 1945: 14, 179, 197, 217).[12] He was convinced that '[t]he habits of mind characteristics of the administrative roles at the lower and higher levels of an organization undoubtedly show differences corresponding to these differences in function' (Simon 1945: 217, see also ibid. 1945: 209). These suggestions compare to Taylor's principle of hearty cooperation and the conceptual function this principle fulfilled regarding the prevention of managerialism.

Simon probably wisely questioned whether the market mechanism or shareholder vigilance on their own were sufficient to prevent 'organizationally non-rational' managerial behavior (Simon 1945: 52–9, 113–18, 162). But the concept of the desire for efficiency is probably theoretically and practically inadequate for analyzing and preventing this problem. Simon's organization theory here relied upon the good, virtuous person at the top management level. In a sense, top managers had to effectively value-program themselves.[13] In certain respects, Arrow (1974: 73–6) here followed Simon. Also, Simon's proposals compare to Taylor's concept of the heartily cooperative manager and similar suggestions by the human relations school.

Berle and Means' (1932) studies of managerialism underlined early on that such predispositions of top managers (as of any other organization member) may be illusive (see also Hikino 1997; Walsh and Seward 1990, Fama 1980; Williamson 1967). Quaker managers or similarly Taylor's factory managers might voice caution, too, regarding a behavioral approach to solve problems of non-rational managerial behavior (see Chapter 3, section 3.3 and section 4.1). Shortcomings of a behavioral approach, which leaves the 'top controller' only controlled by his own 'goodness', have been frequently exposed in the history of societies, profit organizations, non-profit organizations and even church organizations. Williamson (1985: 49–52) or Buchanan (1987b: 275, Footnote 9) generally reject this approach as 'utopian'. They argue that it is more viable to realign self-interest with organizational interests by means of (re)designing incentive structures, such as share option schemes, pension schemes or 'golden parachutes' (Williamson 1985: 312–22; see also Becker 1962: 23). Williamson would probably distance himself from Simon in this respect, especially with regard to the idea of value programming and the idea of the psychological environment. It appears safe to suggest that he would view them as 'tantamount to non-self interest seeking' (Williamson 1985: 49).

Questions can be raised regarding Simon's interpretation of the economic approach. The later Simon (1993b: 160) criticized Williamson for applying the model of economic man and for not drawing on behavioral concepts in order to generate organizational values, loyalty and altruism. Simon (1993b) then detailed the concept of 'bounded self-interest', which can be interpreted as a conceptual specification of his earlier concept of the 'desire for efficiency' (see also Simon 1997: 42–5, 52). Theoretically and empirically, both ideas, 'desire for efficiency' and 'bounded self-interest', are questionable in economic research but also in behavioral research, especially when formulated in a role-related way with a focus on managerial behavior only.

This book does not generally question the fruitfulness of behavioral organization research or behavioral business ethics research that draws on communication programs and other 'soft' intervention techniques, as Mayo (1990, 1949, 1933) or McGregor (1960) favored them early on. However, the present study warns of effectiveness problems of organization psychology and sociology if they aimed at organizational performance problems but having not resolved interest conflicts that result from incentive-*in*compatible organization structures. Morgan (1986: 107) and Waring (1991: 49) hinted at this possible shortcoming when assessing Simon's organization theory as an information-processing-based rationalization of organization structures rather than a discussion of how to analyze and resolve problems of organizational rationality conflicts. Similarly argues Zey-Ferrell (1981: 188–9) regarding structural approaches to organization theory. But, it should be added here that Simon and most structurally oriented organization theory was very much interested in this latter issue, too, as the previous discussion hinted (see above). Waring (1991: 62), connecting to Wolin (1960: 380–89), indeed stated that Simon's idea of rationality conflicts mirrored the Hobbesian idea of the war of all. Morgan seems to generally underestimate this, especially when he suggested that it was only the political systems view of organization that began to conceptualize organizational behavior as networks of 'people with divergent interests' (Morgan 1986: 153–4; similarly Waring 1991: 49; Zey-Ferrell 1981: 189–92). Simon, similarly to Taylor, was very much interested in interest conflicts in organizational behavior, although their analytical and practical strategies to handle this issue were not always successful.

The effectiveness of behavioral intervention is probably in doubt if a value consensus is difficult to enact on practical grounds, for instance, when a culturally diverse, ethnically inhomogeneous interaction context such as the Taylorite factory is encountered (see Chapter 7, section 7.2). Or, behavioral intervention can be questioned on moral grounds, namely in so far as it is incompatible with pluralism. In this regard, the moral quality of some of Simon's suggestions on value indoctrination can be questioned. They compare, in degrees, to some of Marx's totalitarian proposals. Thompson's (1993: 193–4) critique of post-modern, behavioral organization research and its endorsement of organizational culture programs, which move in the direction of value indoctrination, develops similar warnings.

Simon's Inducement–contribution Analysis and his Conception of Compensation Structures

In the preface to the third edition of *Administrative Behavior*, Simon admitted that his interpretation of environment as psychological environment omitted situational categories (Simon 1976a: xxii; see also Simon 1990). He made this qualification regarding the macroeconomic environment of the firm (see also Chapter 7). Such a qualification may also be needed regarding the 'economic environment' within the firm, as it manifests itself in incentive structures. To a degree, Simon's inducement–contribution analysis hinted at such an economic concept of environment, namely the idea of compensation structures (see also Robins 1987). Mainstream interpretations of Simon's research, for example, Morgan (1986) or Pugh and Hickson (1996), probably pay too little attention to these elements of Simon's organization theory.[14]

Inducement–contribution theory analyzed incentive effects on choice behavior. Methodically, it appears to be grounded in the model of economic man (see Chapter 6). Simon interpreted inducements as monetary and non-monetary gains, for example salary, promotion or 'prestige incentives' (Simon 1945: 110–21; similarly March and Simon 1958: 101–5). For clerical employees, he discussed monetary rewards. Like Taylor, he favored a premium wage system (March and Simon 1958: 50, 62–3, 84, 89; Simon 1945: 17, 115–17, 133, 209). For middle managers, Simon viewed fixed-rate salaries and promotion as appropriate incentives (March and Simon 1958: 50–51, 62–3, 74). For top managers, he examined prestige, power, friendship or status as incentives (March and Simon 1958: 67–9, 102–4, 162–4; Simon 1945: 117, 161–2, 209).

Connecting to Barnard (1938), Simon conceptualized the decision of the individual organization member to remain in, join or leave an organization in relation to inducement–contribution equilibriums (Simon 1945: Chapter 6; March and Simon 1958: 50–51, 62–3, 74, 81–111). He reasoned that as long as inducements outweighed contributions, exit or other forms of withdrawal behavior, such as absenteeism, would be prevented (March and Simon 1958:

93). Simon detailed a basic cooperation problem: Organization members were thought to be interested in 'joint cooperation' since they were 'unable to attain . . . own objectives unaided' (Simon 1945: 114). He suggested that the question had to be addressed 'whether the organization objective is sufficiently close to his personal goal to make him choose to participate in the group rather than try to attain his goal by himself or in some other group' (Simon 1945: 114–15). In certain respects, this argument is close to organizational economic thought. Williamson (1985: 34) might follow up with suggestions on 'interest equilibration'. In contrast to an otherwise behavioral approach, Simon here did not analyze 'organizational loyalty' in behavioral terms but in economic terms, that is, as the balancing of personal 'goals' with 'inducements' (Simon 1945: 115). For resolving inducement–contribution conflicts, Simon suggested that the 'consistency of the reward structure' (March and Simon 1958: 125–6), especially the manipulation of 'incentive schemes' and 'compensation structures' (Simon 1945: 115–17; also March and Simon 1958: 55–6, 62) had to be focused on. In these respects, inducement–contribution analysis is compatible with institutional economics, for example the discussion of compensation schemes for managers and employees and their role in ordering principal–agent relationships between managers and employees. (For a review of agency models and their application of incentive schemes, see Spulber 1993: 561–6; Milgrom and Roberts 1992; see also Chapter 2, section 2.1 and section 4.3.)

In 1945, Simon was at a crossroads when he embarked on the study of organization. Much depended on how he would further develop inducement–contribution analysis and how he would position it in relation to his behavioral organization research. He could have anticipated Williamson's new institutional economics, if he had addressed various issues that conceptually plagued inducement–contribution analysis. First, inducement–contribution analysis was too atomistically oriented, focusing on the individual's behavior. This was explicitly (re)stated by Simon (1976a: xi) and noted by Williamson (1985: 19). Inducement–contribution analysis neglected the modeling of interdependence in social interactions. In addition, it only analyzed individual behavior at the 'boundaries of an organization' (Simon 1976a: xxxvii–xxxviii). How decision-makers could destabilize inducement–contribution equilibriums within an organization, as for instance analyzed by Taylor, was not explored. The lacking conceptualization of interaction dynamics in organizational behavior reflected Simon's relegation of game theoretical concepts. To a degree, he assumed a resolved dilemma, speaking of a 'bilateral monopoly' regarding the exchange of contributions and distributions between organization member and organization (March and Simon 1958: 102; see also Chapter 4, section 4.3 and Chapter 5, section 5.2).

Second, because of a lacking conceptualization of interdependence effects, Simon's inducement–contribution analysis aggregated outcomes of organizational behavior by merely adding up contributions and inducements of individual organization members. In this regard, Simon did not progress beyond the aggregation logic of neoclassic economics. The idea of mutual gains, of 'win/win' outcomes of self-interested decision-making, implies a rather different aggregation logic. Simon (1997: 34) quite explicitly attested to this shortcoming (though he continued to favor the behavioral reform of the model of economic man; see Simon 1997: 38–43). A nonzero-sum model of social interactions had no place in inducement–contribution analysis as in his organization research in general. Indicative is Simon (1945: 105): '[Organizationally] rational choice, as has been explained, consists in selecting and bringing about the result that is preferred to the others' (see also Simon 1952–53: 42, 1945: 40, 72–3, 149). This hints that Simon applied a zero-sum conception of organizational behavior. Institutional economics would detail that 'organizationally rational choice' had to yield results that are also preferred by the individual decision-maker.

Third, inducement–contribution analysis conceptualized organizational goals of top managers, such as 'organizational growth' and 'conservation', as *inducements* that top managers were expected to aspire to: '[I]nducements include the organization goal itself, conservation and growth of the organization and incentives unrelated to these two' (Simon 1945: 122). Institutional economics proceeds differently. It approaches growth and survival goals and related efficiency and profitability goals as *outcomes* of social interactions. The idea of mutual gains is invoked and managerial behavior is modeled as self-interested behavior (through the model of economic man). Waring (1991: 62) and similarly Storing (1962: 89–93) hinted at this lacking conception of 'mutual advantageous exchange' in Simon's theory. On the other hand, if survival and conservation goals are modeled as inducements, rationality conflicts are partly assumed 'away' and partly they are left to behavioral intervention. The conceptualization of organizational goals as inducements is probably even less tenable than the modeling of character traits like a 'desire for efficiency' or 'bounded self-interest' (see above).

Finally, Simon (further) infused inducement–contribution analysis with behavioral concepts. He detailed, with specific reference to inducement–contribution analysis, that the 'acceptance of an authority relation' was the crucial 'participation criterion' when an organization member decided to join, remain in or leave the organization (Simon 1945: 116, see also ibid. 1945: 115, 118; March and Simon 1958: 90). As discussed above, he suggested the development of authority acceptance or organizational loyalty through a psychological environment. In his mid-1970s' review of his organizational research, which by then spanned about three decades, Simon explicitly strengthened such a behavioral interpretation of inducement–contribution analysis, namely as a motivational concept that could shed light on 'individual motives' regarding the 'decision to belong' (Simon 1976a: xi, xiii). Indeed, then he viewed inducement–contribution analysis as a 'diversion' (Simon 1976a: xi) from his behavioral approach to organizational analysis. This 'admission' reflected his project of behavioral economics and the quest for the 'true' portrayal of human nature in organization research.[15] This brought him in direct confrontation with organizational economics. Simon's (1993b) critique of Williamson, as reviewed above, is illustrative.

4.3   WILLIAMSON'S GOVERNANCE APPROACH: INCENTIVE STRUCTURES AND THE RESOLUTION OF THE CONTRACTING DILEMMA

Williamson suggested analyzing and resolving problems in organizational behavior as an economic contracting problem. He pioneered the idea of the governance structure as a means of situational intervention. His organization theory specified in detail key concepts of institutional economics. The following suggests:

1.   Williamson's idea of the contracting dilemma compares to the model of the dilemma structure, although he underestimated the heuristic rather than empirical nature of this concept.
2.   Williamson's concept of governance, understood as a systemic, situational intervention for resolving the contracting dilemma, lies at the heart of non-behavioral, organizational economics.
3.   Williamson's governance approach focused on the analysis of the incentive-compatibility of governance structures, that is a capability to generate mutual gains as an interaction outcome.

Organizational Performance and the Contracting Dilemma

The idea of the dilemma structure shines vividly through in Williamson's organization research. He invoked the model of the contracting dilemma:

> Except when . . . investments are transferable to alternative suppliers at low cost, which is rare, the benefits can be realized only so long as the relationship between the buyer and seller is maintained . . . How to effect . . . adaptations poses a serious contracting dilemma. (Williamson 1985: 62–3)

The idea of the contracting dilemma implies that common interests – in mutual gains – could only be achieved if conflicting interests, which Williamson seemingly conceptualized in relation to the idea of 'opportunism', were resolved. He specified the contracting dilemma for all organization members who held asset-specific human capital, that is, organization members who held skills that did not easily transfer from one organization to another (Williamson 1985: 24, 243, 255). Chapter 5, section 5.3 follows up (see also Chapter 2, section 2.2). The process that gave rise to asset specificity and thus the contracting dilemma reflected a 'fundamental transformation' of organizational behavior (Williamson 1988: 575, 1985: 31, 61–2), namely from simple contracting problems to complex contracting problems, where strategic interdependence and bargaining problems occurred. Williamson examined in this respect 'strategic behavior', 'mutual interdependence' and 'bilateral dependency' among interacting agents (Williamson 1985: 90, 373–4, 1975: 81, see also ibid. 1985: 62–3, 76, 85; 1975: 135–6). These suggestions are incompatible with Simon's view that dilemmatic interactions arose primarily in 'purely competitive situations', such as market interactions or military decision-making (Simon 1945: 70–73, see also section 4.2). Like Simon, Williamson was not so much interested in pure market interactions, which he interpreted as simple contracting problems or 'contracts as competition', rather, he focused on organizational behavior that involved asset-specific capital. He interpreted this as complex contracting or 'contract as governance' (Williamson 1985: 32–4, 76, 79).

Williamson detailed that the contracting dilemma arose independent of whether conflicts among interacting agents had broken out or not. Already *potential* conflict could cause the contracting dilemma: 'The object is not merely to resolve conflict in progress but also to recognize potential conflict in advance and devise governance structures that forestall or attenuate it' (Williamson 1985: 29, see also ibid. 1985: 30–35, 64). He reasoned that the mere possibility of one agent retracting from promises without 'defection' being sanctioned was going to cause problems in social interactions. This insight can be sharpened: Institutional economics applies the idea of the contracting dilemma *heuristically*. Even if conflict is not observed (now/past/future), institutional economics still analyzes interactions as dilemmatic. The conceptual relevance of the idea of a dilemma structure does not relate to empirical occurrence but to its methodical function in institutional economic theory-building and practical intervention (in detail, see Homann and Suchanek 2000: 405–9; see also Homann 1994; Homann and Suchanek 1989; Buchanan 1975; see also Crisp 1997: 179–82; Nussbaum 1986: 1–3). Implicitly, Williamson seemed to know this. His suggestion that 'moral hazard [is analyzed by institutional economics] as an *endemic* condition' (Williamson 1985: 3, emphasis added) implies that empirical occurrence or non-occurrence is irrelevant for analyzing organizational behavior as the contracting dilemma. Behavioral organization research seems to acknowledge the same when 'organizational misbehavior' is discussed as an 'endemic condition' (Ackroyd and Thompson 1999: 1–3, 25). Possibly in a generic, heuristic perspective, there are little differences among the social sciences regarding the modeling of social conflict, although considerable differences prevail when it comes to the specification of research heuristics, theoretical concepts and techniques for practical intervention.

Despite hinting at the heuristic, non-empirical nature of the idea of the dilemma structure, Williamson quite explicitly questioned the heuristic nature and purpose of this idea. For example, he critiqued the dilemmatic interaction scenarios of the prisoners' dilemma or Hobbes' 'war of all' in empirical–behavioral and moral–behavioral terms. He assessed the prisoners' dilemma as a 'bad game' (Williamson 1998: 11, see also ibid. 1998: 10; see also Chapter 2, section 2.3). Regarding the empirical occurrence of the 'war of all', Williamson (1988: 569, similarly ibid. 1985: 204–5) can rightly claim that the frequent occurrence of a 'Hobbesian war of all against all is *not* implied' by invoking the contracting dilemma. But then, this insight should be transcended in heuristic terms, examining the methodical purpose of the idea of the contracting dilemma in institutional economics. Like Simon, Williamson (1998: 7, 10) explicitly rejected game theory because of a claimed unrealistic and immoral portrayal of decision-makers, as being too self-interested and too knowledgeable. He probably underestimated that game theory only illuminated methodical foundations of institutional economics.

Similarly, despite having acknowledged that normative institutional economics aimed 'to alter the pay-off matrix' in order to resolve interaction dilemmas (Williamson 1998: 10–11, see also ibid. 1985: 204), he did not interpret the idea of the contracting dilemma as a methodical device for analyzing how to change incentive structures. On a related point, he examined opportunistic behavior in the contracting dilemma in empirical–behavioral terms: 'The concern here is with what Knight . . . has referred to as "the internal problems of the corporation, the protection . . . of members and adherents against each other's predatory propensities" ' (Williamson 1985: 243, Footnote 4, regarding his reference to Coase, see Williamson 1985: 44). This overlooks the heuristic nature of the model of economic man (Chapter 6 follows up).

Certain conceptual ambiguities exist in these respects in Williamson's research. A behavioral (mis)interpretation of the idea 'dilemma structure' reflects methodical imprecision. As Homann (1997: 18–19) indicated, Williamson apparently fell for a methodical self-misunderstanding regarding his own heuristic application of the idea of the contracting dilemma.[16] Such methodical ambiguity not only affects the coherence of theory-building but also the effectiveness of practical intervention. For example, an empirical–

behavioral assessment of the idea of the dilemma structure made Williamson apparently underestimate that normative institutional economics could aim not only at resolving a dilemma structure but also at establishing and protecting it (see also Homann and Pies 1991). As discussed in Chapter 2, the idea of the dilemma structure is normatively ambivalent. Depending on whether 'competition' (non-cooperation) or 'cooperation' is viewed as socially desirable, a dilemma structure can be promoted and protected for moral reasons. Also, certain behavioral 'rest-elements' in the governance approach, for example Williamson's endorsement of Simon's idea of a desire for efficiency of top managers (see below), can be linked to imprecision regarding a heuristic approach.

Incentive-compatible Governance Structures, Situational Intervention and Mutual Gains

Williamson's key concept for analyzing institutional organization was the idea of the governance structure. He proposed that governance structures were to 'equilibrate' potentially conflicting interests by means of (re)designing incentive structures (Williamson 1985: 34). Thus, they were to prevent and resolve the contracting dilemma. He approached the idea of harmony and continuity in social interactions as a matter of generating mutual gains as an interaction outcome (Williamson 1998: 5, 1985: 2, 72–80, 178). Governance structures that ensured this were 'incentive-compatible' (Williamson 1985: 76). They resolved conflict and induced cooperation on grounds of self-interested behavior. Williamson (re)conceptualized in this way the entity 'firm' in relation to its special capability of (re)designing governance structures, and thus went further than Alchian and Demsetz (1972). Because of this capability, Williamson reasoned that the firm could resolve certain – complex – cooperation problems more efficiently than price-based ordering on markets, especially with regard to utilizing capital of high asset specificity (Williamson 1991c: 281, 291–2, 1985: 33–5; see also Chapter 2, section 2.2).

Already in his early studies, Williamson favored a situational approach for resolving problems in organizational behavior: '[D]esign a control system that will achieve integrity of purpose by realizing effective, low-cost selection on profitability criteria' (Williamson 1970: 174). 'System', later conceptually specified and detailed as 'governance structures' (Williamson 1985), was to induce effective and efficient decision-making (Williamson 1985: 62–3). Behavioral ideas were reconceptualized as the outcome of systemic, economic ordering. Williamson argued that, by means of governance, cooperation and cooperative attitudes, commitment, trust, integrity or confidence could be ensured in social interactions – even if merely self-interested decision-makers interacted.[17] These suggestions have little in common with proposals on obedience, trust or loyalty, as put forward, in varying degrees, by Simon and Taylor. For example, Williamson would voice caution regarding Taylor's concept of hearty cooperation or Simon's concepts of value indoctrination and the psychological environment. He can be expected to suggest that the resolution of performance problems required, first and foremost, the analysis of the incentive-compatibility of governance structures.

However, Williamson tried to maintain certain minor conceptual links with Simon's behavioral economics. For instance, like Simon, he suggested that managers had a psychological obligation to behave efficiently and to show a desire for efficiency (Williamson 1991b: 95, 1985: 62–3, 241–2, 262–3, 311–13, 1975: 68–70, 80–81). If it were clarified that this idea played only a supplementary role to analyzing and solving interaction problems, *after* basic interest conflicts have been resolved by means of economic governance, probably little issue could be taken.

Williamson's suggestions on governance structures compare with Taylor's (1912: 151, 1911: 6–7) suggestions on 'system' and 'governing standards' and Simon's (1945: 115–17) suggestions on 'compensation schemes' (see above), but the extent, depth and coherence of analysis easily surpasses Taylor's and Simon's discussion of institutional organization. Williamson detailed a host of incentive structures through which interests of interacting agents could be 'equilibrated'. He examined a hostage model, reciprocity arrangements, collective bargaining schemes, different types of reward structures of the firm, special incentive structures for preventing managerialism and so on (Williamson 1985: Chapters 8–12, 1983, 1975; see also Hikino 1997, Walsh and Seward 1990).

Williamson differentiated proposals on governance structures for different 'types' of organization members.[18] In his early studies, Williamson (1967, 1970) specified incentive structures, like Simon, for three types of organization members: the operational employee, the middle manager and the top manager. In his later studies, this typological categorization was revised in relation to the idea of human asset specificity. Williamson (1985, 1975) distinguished in relation to the degree of human asset-specificity: the pre-Taylorite employee who had no asset-specific skills;[19] operational and clerical employees who had some asset-specific skills; middle managers who had comparatively high asset-specific skills; and top managers and research and development (R&D) employees who had very high asset-specific skills (see Figure 4.1). Williamson argued that for any organization member who commanded asset-specific skills in one form or another special incentive structures should be designed. In this regard, Williamson interrelated features of incentive structures and features of capital utilization: 'Transactions, which differ in their attributes, are assigned to governance structures, which differ in their organizational costs and competencies, so as to effect a discriminating (mainly transaction cost economizing) match' (Williamson 1985: 387–8, see also ibid. 1985: 41–42).

For highly skilled operational and clerical employees, Williamson suggested governance through a wage system, a promotion system and the long-term guarantee of employment. For middle managers, he examined bonus payments and status symbols as additional incentives. For top managers and R&D employees, Williamson analyzed incentive structures such as premium payment systems, share option schemes or arrangements for special compensation payments for not leaving a company (Williamson 1985: 247, 268–9, 313–15, 1975: 75–7, 99–100, 145–7, 1970: 91, 99, 151). In order to prevent managerialism, Williamson proposed governance structures such as a supervisory board or even an external supervisory authority. They should ensure that (self-)interests of top managers were realigned with organizational goals (Williamson 1985: 296–7, 305–6, 313, 316–17, 320, 323–4, 1975: 128, 135–6, 143, 225, 229–30).

With regard to the governance of manager–employee interactions, Williamson advocated that unions should play an active role in resolving interest conflicts between management and employees. Arbitration schemes should be established; employees should be granted certain information and codetermination rights; and an internal labor market should be organized in order to safeguard both managerial and employee interests (Williamson 1991a: 13, 1985: 252, 257, 303, 308, 1975: 72–4, 76, 81, 128–9). Williamson's discussion of unionization is a good example. Arbitrary, confiscatory managerial decision-making on the (re)design of incentive structures is systemically restricted, by changing rights regarding the intervention with contribution and distribution arrangements (Williamson 1985: 34).[20] Such a restriction of decision rights is in the (self-)interest of managers since it prevents 'rational foolishness'. Thus, Williamson resolved conceptual problems that had been left widely open in Taylor's and Simon's organization theories.

As part of his discussion of incentive structures, Williamson also examined job descriptions and communication structures. He analyzed how they 'empowered' employees with competency rights to engage in information search, decision selection, anticipatory behavior and proactive error recognition (Williamson 1985: 76, 231–3, 242, 254–6, 1975: 57, 62–70, 252–9). His suggestions on comparatively programmed, standardized job descriptions and communication structures for lower-ranking employees as well as comparatively unprogrammed, non-standardized job descriptions and communication structures for top managers are compatible with Simon's proposals on this issue. Top managers were to deal with the functional integration of the organization, long-term strategic planning, diversification decisions and the adaptation of the firm to changes in the external environment. In contrast to Simon, Williamson's examples of unprogrammed job and communication structures also included employees in R&D departments and any other employee with asset-specific skills (Williamson 1985: 221–2, 281–9, 1975: 73–8, 136, 146–8, 185–92, 1970: 21, 46–8,125–34).[21] Here, Williamson hinted at an essentially economic rationale for conceptualizing communication structures and job descriptions when moving, in degrees, to a property rights analysis of these organization structures. Thus, the idea of the governance structure reflects a widening interpretation of the idea of the incentive structure (see also Jensen and Meckling 1996).

4.4 CONCLUDING REMARKS

In considerable degrees, an economic approach to institutional organization can be identified in Taylor's, Simon's and Williamson's organization theories. They examined organizational behavior as interest conflicts that could be resolved through the situational intervention with incentive structures: Taylor modeled a premium wage system that 'made interests the same' and intervened with the 'unanswerable logic of the situation', as Taylor (1903: 31) exemplarily referred to. Simon discussed 'inducement-contribution equilibriums' in relation to compensation schemes; and Williamson suggested the 'equilibration' of interests through 'incentive–compatible governance structures'. Regarding the extent and coherence of institutional economic conceptualizations, Williamson clearly advanced furthest.

In terms of heuristic approach, Williamson and Taylor applied ideas which compare to the idea of the dilemma structure. Williamson analyzed the 'contracting dilemma' and Taylor invoked 'antagonism' and 'systematic soldiering'. Both stressed that dilemmatic interaction dynamics undermined mutual gains as an interaction outcome and disadvantaged both sides. A model of nonzero-sum interaction here instructed their analysis. Seemingly, they applied game-theoretical concepts that mirror the prisoners' dilemma. The purpose is to theoretically analyze and practically intervene with a defective incentive structure. Although, they did not fully realize the heuristic nature of the idea of the dilemma structure, interpreting it, in degrees, in empirical–behavioral and moral–behavioral terms.

There are economic elements in Simon's organization theory, too, especially the analysis of inducement-contribution equilibriums. However, the more Simon ventured into behavioral economics from the mid-1950s onwards, the more he sidelined such economic elements in his organization research. This happened mostly on the basis of empirical–behavioral and moral–behavioral (mis)interpretations of research heuristics of organizational economics, especially the idea of the dilemma structure and the model of economic man (regarding the latter, see Chapter 6).

Like Taylor and Williamson, Simon was very much interested in the analysis and resolution of 'rationality conflicts' in organizational behavior but, in contrast to Taylor and Williamson's models of interest conflicts, he predominantly conceptualized conflicts as behavioral conflicts, as conflicts between individual values and organizational values. He explicitly rejected a game-theoretical approach to modeling rationality conflicts and favored behavioral intervention, even 'value indoctrination' (Simon 1945: 103). To a degree, Taylor (1911: 27–9, 36–8) proceeded in a similar, behavioral tradition when he suggested the concept of the 'heartily cooperative' manager which, in certain respects, compares to Simon's (1997: 42–5, 52, 1993b, 1945: 123, 209) concepts of a 'desire for efficiency', 'bounded self-interest' and altruism of top managers. In this regard, Taylor and Simon did not handle managerialism in institutional economic terms. Then, practical failure is likely to result. Taylor, like Quaker managers (see Chapter 3, section 3.3), painfully discovered this. Williamson, not dissimilar to Dahrendorf (1967), explicitly questioned the success of such a behavioral approach as 'utopian', although, in minor degrees, he hang on to some of Simon's behavioral suggestions: the concept of a 'desire for efficiency', the empirical–behavioral and moral–behavioral critique of the idea 'dilemma structure' and the behavioral modeling of human nature in economics (regarding the latter, see Chapter 6).

NOTES

1. Some of Taylor's figurative and down-to-earth language appears unscientific under today's expectations of good scientific writing but in the late 19th century there was no established research tradition in management studies.
2. His business card read: 'Systematizing Shop and Manufacturing Costs a Speciality' (Cochran 1957: 68). This hints at a basic economic interest in studying organization.
3. Some of Taylor's experiments on the organization of performance control, for example the quality inspection of bicycle balls (see Taylor 1903: 88, similarly ibid. 1911: 83) compares regarding structural set-up and analytical intent with such game-theoretical experiments.
4. In certain respects, Taylor proceeded in behavioral terms, namely when he discussed 'hearty cooperation' (see below) and 'natural soldiering' (see Chapter 6, section 6.1).
5. A fixed-rate wage system was also suggested by Herzberg (see Chapter 3, section 3.2).
6. Taylor's concept of hearty cooperation or Simon's suggestions on the top manager's desire for efficiency may compare to Weber's idea of 'bureaucratic rationality' or Drucker's concept of 'corporatist virtue' (more generally, see Waring 1992: 221). Such similarities hint at the fruitfulness of an institutional economic reconstruction of Weber's and Drucker's organization studies.
7. The legend of the exodus of the Israelites from Egypt tells a similar story. Once the pharaoh increased contribution rates for the Israelites without changing distribution rates, rebellion occurred and the pharaoh was punished by plagues. Such interaction outcomes compare to the occurrence of strikes, as experienced by Taylor. Elements of

institutional economic thought here shine through in the legends of the Bible (see Wagner-Tsukamoto 2001b; Wagner 2000a).

8.   More generally on this issue, see Rippberger (1998).

9.   In economic terms, skills can be approached as human capital. Chapter 5 follows up.

10.   With regard to market interactions, Simon's claim regarding the problematic nature of strategic behavior may need to be qualified. In market interactions, which reflect polypolistic ('perfect') competition and the exchange of highly standardized, simple goods, 'outwitting' or 'outguessing' may hardly present a problem. If merely structural interdependence exists, as is the case in a polypolistic ('perfect') competition context, outwitting and outguessing is no issue. However, if asset specificity comes into play, strategic interaction problems arise (see also Chapter 2).

11.   March and Simon (1958: 159) grouped 'trained employees' and 'machines' together as 'specialized means' of production processes.

12.   This idea was, in degrees, also drawn on by Williamson, although conceptually it played a less significant role in Williamson's research than it did in Simon's (see section 4.3).

13.   The early Simon pointed out that managerial values could be in conflict with organizational goals *if they were too ethical.* He suggested that a lower bound to pursuing personal 'ethical' goals was set by 'conservation objectives', namely the goal to ascertain organizational survival, which for the 'firm' implies 'profits' (Simon 1945: 119, similarly March and Simon 1958: 84). Simon's analysis here meets the theoretical suggestions of Friedman (1970) as well as the practical experiences of Quaker employers (see Chapter 3, section 3.3 and Wagner-Tsukamoto 2002). This also implies that managerialism is limited by conservation goals, but this still leaves considerable room for managers to appropriate profits. And, if they behave as 'rational fools', they may even 'kill' the firm.

14.   In rudimentary form, inducement-contribution analysis hinted at a stakeholder interpretation of management. Simon (1945: Chapter 6) included external members of the firm like customers – in modern management speak, 'stakeholders' (Freeman 1984) – in the analysis of inducement-contribution equilibriums.

15.   The lack of a prioritizing logic of economics over behavioral research was reflected by Simon's suggestions on how to transform positive–theoretical knowledge into practical–normative knowledge – by means of 'semantic, tautological transformation' (see Chapter 8, section 8.2). When it comes to practical intervention, this approach may fall short of addressing the question of 'interdisciplinary' collaboration among research programs.

16.   Williamson claimed to portray organization members in an empirical–behavioral perspective, on grounds of 'human nature as we know it', when he probably only applied the research heuristic 'economic man'. This is detailed in Chapter 6, section 6.3.

17.   In contrast, North interpreted, in certain respects, ideas like commitment in behavioral terms, as a psychological input category of institutional analysis (North 1993b: 13, 15). Similarly, he drew on the idea of 'commercial morality' to discuss social problems (Eggertsson 1993: 25). Chapter 6 points out that certain misunderstandings here permeate institutional economics.

18.   Highly standardized job structures and communication structures, as discussed by Taylor and Simon for most organization members, were examined by Williamson only for employees with no asset-specific skills – the 'pre-Taylorite worker' (Williamson 1985: 302, 1975: 72).

19.   He also examined 'external' organization members, such as suppliers, who locate at the firm–market interface. As for Simon's suggestions on customers or Taylor's brief references to customers and society at large, rudiments of a stakeholder model can be made out in Williamson's research.

20.   It can be suggested that the standardized skill formation programs introduced by Taylor and Simon contributed over time to the rise of asset specificity of human capital.

21.   On this ground, it would be expected that cooperation problems, as indicated by strike frequency and the turnover of human capital, would decrease – up to a certain point – if unionization existed. Interfering factors like the extent of constitutional–legal institutionalization of unionization, long- and short-term orientation of corporate planning or owner-/manager-run governance had to be examined. For instance, low strike frequencies in Japan come with a low

labor turnover, whereas low strike frequencies in the USA come with a high labor turnover. Such differences may reflect that US legislation tends not to support unionization, thus making labor turnover ('exit') a more attractive route of resolving conflict in a firm. In Japan, traditionally long-term-oriented employment contracts favor 'internal' conflict resolution, generating stability in social interactions in the firm.

5. Organizational behavior and capital utilization: Modeling human capital as boundedly rational or as asset-specific?

> The science which underlies each workman's act is so great and amounts to so much that the workman who is best suited actually to do the work is incapable ... either through lack of education or through insufficient mental capacity. (Taylor, 1911, p. 41)

> Transaction cost economics maintains that governance structures must be crafted more carefully as the degree of human asset specificity increases. (Williamson, 1985, p. 243)

This chapter explores how Taylor, Simon and Williamson modeled skills and skills utilization in their organization theories. It suggests that organizational economics analyzes and intervenes with skills utilization in non-behavioral terms (in relation to incentive structures), skills being approached as human capital. The chapter questions whether organizational economics could conceptualize skills and skills utilization in behavioral, cognitive psychological terms, that means in relation to the question of human nature. It argues that, in certain respects, Taylor, Simon and Williamson, especially Taylor and Simon, conceptually drifted between an organizational economic and a behavioral approach to skills management. This yielded certain problems for their organization theories. Sections 5.1, 5.2 and 5.3 explore these arguments for Taylor's, Simon's and Williamson's organization theories, respectively. Section 5.4 concludes the chapter.

5.1 TAYLOR'S ANALYSIS OF HUMAN CAPITAL: BETWEEN COMPETENCE AND INSUFFICIENT MENTAL CAPACITY

Taylor suggested that certain cognitive psychological features of human nature were important for analyzing skills formation and management. This section assesses how far, with what success and for what purpose Taylor interrelated a behavioral, psychological approach with an economic approach to skilling. The following substantiates:

1. Taylor approached skills management in economic terms when making systemic suggestions on how to develop and utilize 'competence' of organization members, proposing that scarcities in 'competence' should be handled through incentive structures.
2. Taylor investigated skills utilization through the cognitive psychological concept of 'insufficient mental capacity'. This led to inconsistencies in an economic approach to organizational analysis and unnecessarily incited behavioral criticism regarding an apparently untenable, psychological 'image of human nature'.
3. Interpretations of scientific management as 'physiological organization theory' have to be revised. Both Taylor's economic suggestions on 'competence' and his behavioral suggestions on 'insufficient mental capacity' imply this.

Taylor's Economic Approach to Utilizing and Developing 'Competence'

A key thesis of Taylor regarding skills management was that limits to skillfulness could be relaxed and 'brains'[1] could 'grow' if organization structures were intervened with. A systemic approach to training was at the heart of his program:

> [A] man who under the old system of management has only sufficient brains to sweep the floor, under scientific management is trained and taught and helped so that he finally learns how to use, say, a grinding machine . . . He is taught to do a class of work which is far more interesting and requires more brains than sweeping to which he formerly was limited. (Taylor 1912: 155)

And:

> It is only when we fully realize that . . . our opportunity lies in systematically cooperating to train and make this competent man. . . . In the past the man has been first; in the future the system must be first . . . [T]he remedy for . . . inefficiency lies in systematic management, rather than in searching for some unusual or extraordinary man. (Taylor 1911: 6–7; emphasis added, similarly ibid. 1911: 27, 39, 101, 114, 1903: 45)

A systemic framework that institutionalized training programs was to be established for both factory workers and factory managers (the 'functional foremen'). He advocated the standardization and functional specialization of skills, and he favored intervention with incentive structures, such as the introduction of performance-related pay, in order to improve skills formation and utilization.

Taylor realized that 'competence' of all organization members needed to be developed: 'The search for better, for more *competent* men, from the presidents of our great companies down to our household servants, was never more rigorous than it is now' (Taylor 1911: 6). Although, he did not analyze skills development for top managers,[2] he set out a program for developing and 'upgrading' industrial skills of other organization members. Urwick (1967: 12) or Drury (1968: 242–3) argue in this direction, too.

This is contrary to the views expressed by Braverman (1974), Morgan (1986), Waring (1991: 11) or Pruijt (1997: 3–4) that scientific management did aim to raise efficiency and performance levels by *deskilling* labor. Lazonick and O'Sullivan (1997: 503) are less extreme and only diagnose the '*absence of skill formation on the shop floor of US industry*'. Casey (2002: 106–7) and Hatch (1997: 25–6) provide a good review of sociological arguments for and against the deskilling and domination thesis. Furthermore, if the historic, economic context of Taylor is considered, namely that the typical employee who entered the Taylorite factory was not a craftsman but an unskilled immigrant, former slave or farm worker (for example, Phillips 1929; Wells 1926; Chapter 7, section 7.2 has further details), scientific management is probably best interpreted as a skill formation program that was less 'ambitious' than craftsmanship. In Taylor's time, the availability and quality of operative and administrative human capital was low. Taylor's management program began to change this, contributing to a rise in industrial skills over time. This in turn necessitated more sophisticated approaches to skills utilization (see also Williamson 1985: 243). Only when comparing scientific management with craftsmanship, can scientific management be characterized as a deskilling and domination program. It could even be suggested that, to a degree, Taylor's skill formation program mirrored some of Herzberg's suggestions on job enrichment, especially regarding the intent to upgrade skills (see Chapter 3, section 3.2), although Taylor embedded skill development in an economic framework. Some of Herzberg's later critics pointed out this issue (for example, Reif and Luthans 1969).

Historical empirical evidence on the spread of craftsmanship in Taylor's time questions the deskilling hypothesis further: Coinciding with the emergence of the Taylorite factory and the build-up of a skilled industrial labor force, the earnings and numbers of craftsmen increased dramatically. For example, Outerbridge (1895: 229) found that from 1880 to 1890 the number of carpenters nearly tripled from about 50 000 to over 140 000 and average earnings rose by about 50 percent in this period.

In general, Taylor's suggestions on work specialization compare to the ones of Simon or Williamson, discussed below (or even the Old Testament; see Wagner-Tsukamoto 2000a). Likewise, Taylor's suggestions on 'competence' compare with certain ideas of Simon (1945: 39–41) and Williamson (1985: 45–6) (see sections 5.2 and 5.3). The high measurability of work performance in the Taylorite factory made output-related sanctioning of performance easy

(Taylor 1911: 47). Inputs to work performance, such as skills application in the course of job performance, did not need to be monitored. Apparently, Taylor's skills formation problem was of a comparatively simple nature, simpler than the ones discussed by later organization theories. For instance, Williamson assessed output measurement problems in relation to input monitoring and process sanctioning techniques (see Chapter 4 section 4.3 and Chapter 5, section 5.3).

Simon's claim that scientific management viewed 'personnel as a given rather than as a variable in the system' (March and Simon 1958: 29; similarly Knowles and Saxberg 1967: 32) appears difficult to uphold. Taylor's skilling program did not view 'brains' as a psychological feature of human nature and even less so as a given, invariant feature of human nature. Also, Simon's criticism that scientific management was only interested in 'muscular activity' (March and Simon 1958: 33) and reflected a 'physiological organization theory' (March and Simon 1958: 136–7, 139; Simon 1945: 38) cuts too short, as does Casey's (2002: 73) comparable critique of scientific management (see also Derickson 1994). Time-and-motion studies of physiological aspects of work performance were an important element of scientific management, but scientific management cannot be reduced to these elements. It misrepresents Taylor's interest in skill formation as well as his economic approach in analyzing and organizing skills utilization. Other elements of scientific management, although they are questionable on institutional economic grounds, make an interpretation of scientific management as a physiological theory difficult, too. For instance, Taylor's moral–behavioral concept of hearty cooperation compares in tone and intent with suggestions of the human relations school and, indeed Simon's (1945: 123, 209) proposals on the top manager's 'desire for efficiency' (see Chapter 4, section 4.2). Or, Taylor's cognitive psychological suggestions on 'insufficient mental capacity', as discussed below, well compare with Simon's and Williamson's suggestions on 'bounded rationality' (see sections 5.2 and 5.3).

Interestingly, Simon increasingly turned on Taylor only in his later studies once Simon's organization research had shifted towards behavioral economics and organization psychology. In his early studies, Simon (1945: 40, 138) was more positive about Taylor. Then, he explicitly connected to Taylor's suggestions on skill formation for administrative employees:

> When all activities to which engineering decisions are relevant are organized in a single department, then it is easy to allocate the function of decision in such a way as to secure the necessary technical competence.' (Simon 1945: 138) [referenced by Simon in a footnote on the same page with: 'Cf. Frederick W. Taylor, *The Principles of Scientific Management* (New York: Harper & Bros., 1911), pp. 99–113.']

Here Simon acknowledged that scientific management aimed to develop 'competence' and that Taylor had begun a discussion of administrative organization theory. It can be speculated that in the wake of rising behavioral criticism regarding Taylor's apparently untenable image of human nature, for example, Knowles and Saxberg (1967: 32), Herzberg (1966: 35–69) or McGregor (1960), Simon's evaluation of scientific management changed. Seemingly by the 1950s, Taylor's program had become 'politically incorrect'.

Taylor on 'Bounded Rationality': 'Insufficient Mental Capacity' as a Psychological Variable in the Economic Analysis of Skill Formation?

Taylor was convinced that psychological limitations of the human mind were important for understanding skill formation and utilization. He examined problems of skills utilization through the concept of 'insufficient mental capacity' (Taylor 1911: 26, 41, 59, 1903: 28, 141–2, similarly ibid. 1895: 75) – an idea that compares with Simon's and Williamson's cognitive psychological suggestions on 'bounded rationality' (see sections 5.2 and 5.3).

In rather blunt language, Taylor characterized abilities of organization members in behavioral terms of inborn, cognitive features: '[S]ome people are born . . . inefficient.' (Taylor 1911: 29, similarly ibid. 1903: 142). He thus linked effective skills formation and utilization to psychological features of human nature:

> Now one of the very first requirements for a man who is fit to handle pig iron as a regular occupation is that he shall be so stupid and so phlegmatic that he more nearly resembles in his mental make-up the ox than any other type. The man who is mentally alert and intelligent is for this very reason entirely unsuited to what would, for him, be the grinding monotony of work of this character. (Taylor 1911: 59, similarly ibid. 1911: 62)

This statement is difficult to reconcile with Taylor's systemic suggestions on skills management, for instance, his discussion of how sweepers could be trained to do more demanding jobs (see above).

In general, behavioral 'traits paradigms' that tried to discover inborn features of human nature in order to advise on job performance were popular in Taylor's time. For instance, leadership research in the early 20th century examined psychological and physiological features of managers, aiming to identify inborn features of the good leader. Only by the 1940s and 1950s, the conceptual inadequacy of this approach was realized. In the face of mounting contradictory empirical findings of traits research, systemic theories of leadership, based on situational contingency models, emerged and displaced psychological, individualistic traits research (Fiedler 1990; see also Quarstein et al. 1992). The new approach analyzed effective job performance (of leaders) in terms of tasks and functions rather than in terms of features of human nature. In this regard, an institutional economic reconstruction of contingency theories of leadership appears promising.

If it was the case that scientific management required 'stupid' people – 'intelligent gorillas' (Taylor 1911: 40) – for effective skill utilization, a dark image of human nature had to be suggested for Taylor's organization theory and ethical reservations could be raised. However, Taylor's view that 'insufficient mental capacity' is a behavioral prerequisite for effective skill utilization can be challenged both by psychology and by institutional economics. His suggestion on low intelligence being a necessary input feature of human capital can be rejected if it can be either shown that those whom he viewed as 'stupid and phlegmatic' and well suited for scientific management were not 'stupid and phlegmatic' – but still performed effectively under scientific management; or it could be shown that those whom he viewed as 'mentally alert and intelligent' and hence as unsuitable for scientific management performed effectively under scientific management. Both types of 'evidence' would hint that simple tasks, which were characterized, for example, by 'monotony of work' (Taylor 1911: 59), did not need to be matched with features of human nature but merely reflected a task feature of capital utilization (a 'capital contingency'), which could be systemically intervened with in order to influence behavior. For instance, if monotony characterized skills utilization, institutional economics examines how organization members can be compensated for this kind of work. 'Monotony' is handled through incentive structures and 'distribution payments' of one kind or another.[3] Interestingly, Taylor's own writings provide both types of 'evidence'.

Taylor (1911: 46, 62) claimed that some people by nature were 'mentally sluggish', 'phlegmatic' or 'born stupid'. The human relations school questioned and disproved such psychological suggestions on intrinsic, invariant features of human cognition and motivation (Knowles and Saxberg 1967; Herzberg 1966; Mayo 1949, 1933). But already Taylor's own writings, especially on the worker 'Schmidt', indicated that such characterizations were untenable. Taylor viewed 'Schmidt' as a prime example of a worker with 'insufficient mental capacity' who was well suited for scientific management: 'Schmidt' was a 'man of the mentally sluggish type' (Taylor 1911: 46). However, on the basis of the background information Taylor provided about Schmidt, an assessment of Schmidt as 'ox' (Taylor 1911: 59) can be questioned. For example, Taylor noted that Schmidt had acquired a piece of land and was building a house (Taylor 1911: 43–4). This suggests that Schmidt understood ideas like property and investment and that he must have commanded not only physical skills but also various cognitive and motivational skills that are likely to be required for building a house. Apparently, Schmidt was a successful problem-solver in everyday life.[4]

Taylor probably suffered under certain stereotypical preconceptions about worker behavior. Such stereotypes may have been widespread in late 19th-century USA, where slavery had only recently been abolished, when class-related 'master–servant' attitudes were common and when on-setting scientific research into human behavior came as 'traits research'. Merkle (1980: 25) gives a couple of examples of stereotypical perceptions of worker behavior that were held by managers in those days. In a number of passages, Taylor quite explicitly admitted that his psychological conception of worker intelligence was stereotypical and inadequate: 'I remember very distinctively the perfectly astonishing awakening at the end of six months of my apprenticeship [on the shop floor], when I discovered that the three other men who were with me in the pattern shop were all smarter than I was' (Taylor 1909: 85).

Taylor's argument that insufficient mental capacity is a behavioral prerequisite for effective skill formation and utilization on the shop floor is also undermined by his acknowledgement that he himself had highly enjoyed monotonous factory work. He described the time he spent at a lathe machine, despite its high degree of monotony, as 'the happiest year I have had since I got out of my apprenticeship' (Taylor 1912: 125). If 'insufficient mental capacity' were a psychological prerequisite for effective skills utilization, some unflattering conclusions had to be drawn regarding Taylor's 'mental make-up'. Such conclusions seem unwarranted from what we know about Taylor and his life as a worker, manager, businessman, consultant and researcher. He had an inquisitive mind and easily counts as one of the founding fathers of management studies and, in certain respects, even of organizational economics.

Taylor's psychological suggestions on insufficient mental capacity may be best interpreted as an ill-formulated reference that no special cognitive requirements were needed for training organization members under scientific management. In some passages Taylor hinted at this: '[H]e was a man so stupid that he was unfitted [sic] to do most kinds of laboring work, even. The selection of the man [for skill formation under scientific management], then, does not involve finding some extraordinary individual' (Taylor 1911: 62, similarly ibid. 1911: 7). Taylor seems to say here that basically anybody could be trained under scientific management.

Of course, Taylor's claim that workers were born stupid, similar to claims of early leadership research that leaders were 'born right', provided an easy target for behavioral researchers. Nevertheless, Taylor's behavioral suggestions have to be put into perspective regarding the research problems he addressed – and these may not have been, at least not in the first place, cognitive psychological ones. The previous discussion in this section and in Chapter 4, section 4.1 substantiated this. In view of this, the idea of insufficient mental capacity may be better reinterpreted as a reference to lacking human capital, to a constraint of skillfulness, which can be systemically relaxed through properly organized skilling programs. As Taylor outlined, scarcities in competence can be handled and relaxed through training schemes and systems of performance measurement that are coupled with incentive structures. The human relations school and much organization research that followed, for example, Pugh and Hickson (1996: 102), probably too uncritically accepted Taylor's argumentation on natural abilities.

Even if a cognitive psychological model of skillfulness was scientifically tenable, such as Williamson's or Simon's suggestions on bounded rationality (see sections 5.2. and 5.3), organizational economics may still be well advised to abstract from behavioral features of human nature when discussing skills utilization. An 'interdisciplinary' linking of behavioral concepts with economic concepts is incompatible with the problem dependence and heuristic complexity reduction in scientific research. Like the idea of insufficient mental capacity, bounded rationality, understood in cognitive psychological terms, is probably unproblematic and non-limiting for practically intervening with skills utilization *in economic terms*. As later sections of this chapter detail, Simon and Williamson here confused a (mis)claimed psychological deficit in human cognition with economic problems of human capital utilization.

The considerable upskilling of human capital in the course of the 20th century also underlines that a cognitive psychological understanding of cognition and intelligence may be irrelevant for understanding skills utilization. A rise in industrial skills over time can hardly be interpreted as a rise in human intelligence or a decrease in insufficient mental capacity or even as the biological or neurophysiological evolution of cognition. Rather, it may 'just' reflect a better utilization of human capital. Hayek (1945) implied this and Becker (1962) and Williamson (1985) analyzed this issue in depth. Given proper education and training, probably anybody, apart from truly clinical cases, can reach high levels of 'intelligence'. A positive image of human nature is in this respect implied by an economic approach to (human) capital utilization.

5.2 SIMON'S ANALYSIS OF HUMAN CAPITAL: BETWEEN BOUNDED SKILLFULNESS AND BOUNDED RATIONALITY

Simon approached skills utilization as the problem of handling bounded rationality. In certain respects, he interpreted bounded rationality in economic terms; in other respects, he discussed it as a cognitive psychological concept. The following substantiates:

1. The early Simon interpreted bounded rationality as 'bounded skillfulness'. This points towards an economic concept of human capital rather than a psychological concept of cognition and the question of human nature.
2. In later studies, Simon (re)interpreted the idea of bounded rationality in empirical–behavioral, cognitive psychological terms. On this basis, he questioned the relevance of organizational economics.
3. Simon discussed skills management through the idea of a 'resolved dilemma'. He failed to investigate how asset specificity gave rise to potentially dilemmatic contribution–distribution interactions and how such problems could be handled in economic terms.

An Economic Interpretation of Bounded Rationality as Bounded Skillfulness

Simon's organization theory analyzed limits to skills of organization members. He drew in this regard on the idea of bounded rationality, broadly interpreted by the early Simon (1945: 39–41) as 'limits to abilities' and 'limits to rationality'. He explored performance problems in relation to three limits to abilities which 'bound the area of rationality' (Simon 1945: 41): limits to physiological skills, limits to motivation and limits to cognition. As assessed in Chapter 4, section 4.2, Simon then focused his organization theory on 'motivational limits', which he analyzed as value conflicts and inducement–contribution (dis-)equilibriums, and 'cognitive limits', which he analyzed as knowledge deficits.

Regarding cognitive limits, Simon interpreted bounded rationality as deficits in 'specialized skills', 'competence', 'expertise' and the 'amount of training in specialized competencies' (March and Simon 1958: 43, 91, 159). Skills were modeled as 'resources' and 'assets' of an organization. Training programs were to raise levels of skills and competence (Simon 1945: 119–20). This approach compares to Taylor's systemic suggestions on skills development. In this regard, Simon did not analyze bounded rationality in cognitive psychological terms. Rather, his interpretation of bounded rationality mirrored a concept like bounded skillfulness, which can be linked to the economic analysis of skills utilization (see also Suchanek 1992):

> The agent's limitations may take the form of an inability to solve a complex optimization problem . . . but such a limitation makes the agent not boundedly *rational* but boundedly *skilful*. Rationality, in this alternative formulation, is a matter of doing the best one can with what one is *given*, which includes one's knowledge and information-processing abilities. At some level, these two formulations are identical, their differences a matter of definition only. But definitions have rhetorical implications and rhetoric has programmatic implications. (Langlois 1990: 691, emphasis changed)

Langlois' reinterpretation of bounded rationality appears fruitful for an economic analysis of skills management (although his references to 'definitions' could be clarified with regard to the idea of research heuristics). The early Simon (1945), possibly even Simon (1969), would probably take little issue with such an economic (re)interpretation of bounded rationality. He explicitly projected an analysis of skills to organizational goals such as effectiveness, efficiency or productivity (Simon's 1945: 10, 39, 136–8). And, he examined how bounds to skillfulness could be relaxed in situational, systemic terms, by means of organizational structuring, in particular, the intervention with job contents structures and communication structures. As discussed in Chapter 4, section 4.2, incentive structures were underutilized in this connection as they were underutilized for addressing motivational problems in organizational behavior.

Other aspects of an economic model of skills utilization are visible in Simon's early writings. He did not use the sophisticated concepts of Becker (1962) or Williamson (1985) for discussing asset specificity, but he touched on this idea: '[T]he organization acquires know-how in a particular field – really an intangible sunk cost or more properly, "sunk asset" . . . [T]he organization acquires goodwill, which is also a sunk asset that may not be readily transferable to another area of activity' (Simon 1945: 120). References to 'sunk assets' and 'not readily transferable assets' hint at asset-specific production capital.[5] In another passage, Simon seemed to refer to human asset specificity. But he suggested that human asset specificity reflected a special case in skills utilization that was *not* problematic for capital utilization in the firm. He argued that firm-specific skills held by an employee reflected reciprocal interdependence between firm and employee. He invoked the idea of a 'bilateral monopoly' (March and Simon 1958: 102):

> When an individual remains in an organization for a long time, his skills become more and more *specific* to the organization in question. Consequently, he becomes more and more indispensable to that organization but more and more dispensable to other organizations. In *specialization* we approach a theoretically very interesting limiting case where the demand and supply of a particular bundle of abilities tends to decrease until we have an organization that can find a replacement only at prohibitive cost and an employee who can find another job only at prohibitive loss. (March and Simon 1958: 102; emphasis added. Similarly ibid. 1958: 43, 145)

Simon here equated asset specification with asset specialization, restating Marshall's view on this issue (see section 5.3). The suggestion of a bilateral monopoly prevented Simon from analyzing human asset specificity as a critical contingency of (human) capital utilization. Becker and Williamson argued in this respect that the idea of a bilateral monopoly is difficult to uphold, and the more so if asset specificity comes into play (see Chapter 2, section 2.2 and

Chapter 4, sections 4.3 and 5.3). Rather than a bilateral monopoly, Williamson (1996c: 14–16) invoked 'bilateral dependency'. On this conceptual basis, institutional economics analyzes human asset specificity as a problematic issue. It treats the idea of a 'bilateral monopoly' as a practical–normative goal of institutional intervention, which can be achieved by equilibrating interests through the intervention with incentive structures.

Simon's Cognitive Psychological (Re)interpretation of Bounded Rationality

Already in his early studies, Simon touched upon organization psychology and organization sociology. In later studies, Simon deepened such a behavioral research interest. From the 1950s onwards, he reinterpreted the idea of bounded rationality and here especially cognitive skills, in terms of neurophysiological capacity bounds of the human mind, language limits and the individual's selective attention to and perception of reality (Simon 1959, 1956, 1955; March and Simon 1958: 6, 166–8). He argued that organization theory should conceptualize how decision-making occurred in real life, paying special attention to the issue of how a decision-maker reduces '*complex reality*' to a '*model of reality that is sufficiently simple to be handled by problem-solving processes*' (March and Simon 1958: 151, emphasis added). Simon here spelled out the concept of satisficing behavior. Simon (1969: 104) even detailed this issue with regard to 'rules of thumb, or heuristics, that suggest which paths should be tried first' (similarly ibid. 1969: 113). He proposed that the ideas of satisficing and bounded rationality should replace the unrealistic idea of optimizing behavior in economic analysis (Simon 1976a: xxvii–xxxi; March and Simon 1958: 139–41). The concept of satisficing would take into account that 'members of organizations . . . are limited in their knowledge and in their capacities to learn and to solve problems' (March and Simon 1958: 136). The concepts of bounded rationality and satisficing behavior drove Simon's behavioral economics, which made prominent inroads into social science research, including institutional economics, for example, the studies of North or Williamson (see sections 5.3 and 5.4).

For organization psychology, the fruitfulness of a cognitive psychological interpretation of bounded rationality cannot be questioned. Also, regarding approach and research questions, organization psychology is well placed to analyze and advise on behavioral aspects of institutional organization. But as path-breaking as Simon's cognitive psychological interpretation of bounded rationality was for behavioral organization research, as probably irrelevant and counter-productive it was for (organizational) economics and the analysis of conflicts over skills contributions and reward distributions. Barney and

Hesterly (1996: 124) and Waring (1991: 58–63) imply this when remarking that Simon's behavioral approach had little impact in economics.

Especially in his later studies, Simon invoked competition between economics and behavioral organization research. He implied that empirical–behavioral research on human nature should provide the foundation for economic research (Simon 1976a: xxviii): 'Human beings are all of these things and perhaps more. An adequate theory of human behavior in organizations will have to take account of the instrumental aspects of human behavior, of the motivational and attitudinal and of the rational' (March and Simon 1958: 6, similarly ibid. 1958: 7–9; Simon 1957a: xxxv, 1945: 119, Footnote 5; see also Cyert and March 1963). Regarding its scope, this suggestion can even be questioned for behavioral sciences. It also appears to be in contradiction with Simon's own insight that any kind of problem-solving behavior necessitated the simplification of complex reality, or differently put, it relied on 'satisficing' and 'heuristic rule-following' (Simon 1969: 104; March and Simon 1958: 151, as fully quoted above). For example, Markoczy and Goldberg (1998: 390) argue quite explicitly for a reductionism in the behavioral, psychological analysis of organization, as did Waring (1991: 60) and Urwick (1967: 12–13, see also Chapter 3, sections 3.1. and 3.3). Chapter 1, section 1.1 detailed this argument in more abstract terms. For the purpose of economic research, on the one hand, behavioral features of human nature are abstracted from. Or, as far as they are relevant for theory-building and practical intervention, they are reconceptualized in economic terms, for example, as human capital. The latter is necessary in the economic analysis of human asset specificity and of how to effectively utilize asset-specific skills through the management of incentive structures.

Similarly, from an institutional economic point of view, Simon's suggestion that a cognitive psychological understanding of bounded rationality explained the existence and stability of organization structures can be questioned:

> Organization will have [communication and coordination] structure . . . insofar as there are [cognitive] boundaries to rationality . . . If there were not boundaries to rationality or if the boundaries varied in a rapid and unpredictable manner, there could be no stable organization structure. (March and Simon 1958: 170–71)

It may be doubtful whether a cognitive psychological organization program, which focuses on the intervention with job contents and communication structures, can resolve contribution–distribution conflicts and ensure stable interactions. Like Herzberg's organization psychology or Urwick's (1967: 12–13) endorsement of communication analysis, Simon's behavioral approach could not analyze performance problems that were induced by 'defective' incentive structures. Institutional economics would explain and predict organization structure differently, suggesting that organizations have stable structure if (human) capital utilization is systemically organized by incentive-compatible institutions. The early Simon would probably agree with this assessment. But, as Simon's research shifted towards behavioral economics and psychology, he began to pit behavioral analysis and its intervention techniques against economics, both in a theoretical–practical perspective and in a methodical– heuristic perspective (the latter is detailed in the next chapter).

5.3   WILLIAMSON'S ANALYSIS OF HUMAN CAPITAL: BETWEEN HUMAN ASSET SPECIFICITY AND BOUNDED RATIONALITY

Williamson analyzed skills management in non-behavioral, economic terms, by drawing on the idea of asset specificity. But then, Williamson also suggested that institutional economics should apply a behavioral model of human nature for understanding the effective governance of human capital utilization. He directly connected to Simon's cognitive psychological interpretation of bounded rationality. The following substantiates:

1. Williamson's economic approach to skills utilization focused on the ideas of human capital and human asset specificity. He conceptually overburdened an institutional economic analysis of skills utilization when linking it to the idea of bounded rationality, understood in cognitive psychological terms.
2. Williamson underestimated that institutional economic intervention is undermined if a cognitive psychological model of bounded rationality were to substitute an economic model of human capital.
3. Institutional economics reconstructs the idea of bounded rationality as a behaviorally camouflaged reference to economic variables, such as bounded skillfulness or human asset specificity (or environmental uncertainty, as discussed in Chapter 7).

An Economic Model of Skills Management: Human Capital and Asset Specificity

Williamson is one of the leading contributors to an economic approach to skills management. He deepened Becker's 'pioneering work on human capital' (Williamson 1985: 255), analyzing human capital utilization in relation to transaction costs whereas Becker had focused on production costs (see also Williamson 1985: 314–18; Mortensen 1978: 573–4). Williamson detailed the analysis of asset specificity, which appears important for the analysis and effective intervention with human capital utilization. The idea of asset specificity is basically absent from earlier discussions of human capital in organization theory (for example, Likert 1967: Chapter 9; Likert and Seashore 1954). Asset specificity reflects that skills of an employee are, at least to some extent, unique and hence costly to replace. Human asset specificity originates in the nature of skill formation processes (Williamson 1985: 243), either in firm-specific training given to an employee or mere learning-by-doing effects over time. Since learning-by-doing unavoidably plays a role in skills development, even employees who perform comparatively simple jobs develop asset-specific human capital over time, for example, when a clerk acquires 'knowledge of a particular firm's filing system' (Williamson 1985: 24; see also Mortensen 1978: 583; Becker 1975: 26, 1962: 18). It is especially the idea of asset specificity through which Williamson (1985) revised institutional economics, replacing his earlier, more ambiguous model of 'idiosyncrasy' as a transaction feature (Williamson 1975: 80; see also Jensen and Meckling 1996: 20).

Williamson argued that certain features of human capital, especially human asset specificity, aggravated the contracting dilemma. He suggested that asset specificity yields dilemmatic interest conflicts, especially when asset specificity is high (Williamson 1985: 62–3). He reasoned that with increasing asset specificity, simple control systems, for example, a wage system coupled with some standardized job and communication structures, as favored by Taylor and Simon, was no longer effective (see also Williamson 1985: 77). Then, special contracting and/or systemic structures of the firm were required to resolve conflicts of interest. Williamson's maxim for institutional economic analysis captured this: 'Governance structures needed to be crafted more carefully once the degree of asset specificity increased' (Williamson 1985: 243). His various proposals on institutional organization, as reviewed in Chapter 4, section 4.3, matched the different degree of human asset specificity of organization members.

Considering that in the course of job transfer from one firm to another an employee has to adapt to new organization structures, it could be suggested that the loss of skills investments to the exiting employee and to the firm from which the employee exited were about the same. Hence, March and Simon (1958: 102) suggested a balanced dilemma, speaking of a 'bilateral monopoly' between firm and employee (see Chapter 4, section 4.2 and section 5.2). Williamson (1985: 242, Footnote 3) and Becker (1962: 20) discussed similar, earlier suggestions of Marshall. However, they questioned Marshall's view and thus implicitly also March and Simon's suggestions on this issue. They argued that the utilization of asset-specific human capital is staked in favor of the employee rather than the firm. A key reason is that property rights in human capital 'are automatically vested [with the employee], for a skill cannot be used without permission of the person possessing it' (Becker 1962: 17). The idea of a 'bilateral monopoly' in processes of human capital utilization is probably best viewed as an important heuristic concept of *normative* institutional economics, especially equilibrium analysis (see also Chapter 2). But positive institutional economics takes 'imbalances' in capital utilization as the starting point of theoretical and empirical analysis. Indeed, it invokes a dilemma structure, the 'contracting dilemma' in Williamson's (1985: 62–3) terminology.

Also, transaction costs for dissolving an existing employment contract, for finding a replacement and for establishing a new employment relationship, tend to be unequally distributed between the firm and the employee – to the disadvantage of the firm (Becker 1962: 17–20; see also Stigler 1961). Search costs for finding a replacement may be excessively high for a firm on a seller's market. On the other hand, a social security system reduces transaction costs for the exiting employee, compensating for temporary unemployment. This further undermines the suggestion of a 'bilateral monopoly'. Other arguments can be added. Supply–demand gaps on the labor market may favor either the employee or the firm but not both to the same degree. In a market in which certain types of human capital are in high demand, for instance, in emerging, innovation-intensive industries, asset specificity does not lock employees and a firm into a 'balanced dilemma'. In a 'sellers' market, the loss of firm-specific skills in the course of job transfer is unlikely to economically disadvantage a transferring employee. Also, under certain circumstances, high human asset specificity may not present an exit barrier to the employee but actually motivate job transfer, namely in the case of market demand for employees with firm-specific skills. By acquiring asset-specific human capital of another firm, the 'purchasing' firm can disadvantage a competitor and speed up the development of its stock of human capital. This assumes that the 'purchasing' firm adapts its job contents' structures in a way that enables the recruited employee to preserve previously acquired, asset-specific skills. This argument qualifies the proposition that firm-specific knowledge was not useful to other firms (for example, restated by Becker 1993: 393).

In general, the higher the human asset specificity is, the higher powered the incentive structures have to be in order to 'balance' interests and retain employees. Differences in how firms remunerate employees with highly specific skills, such as R&D employees or top managers, as compared with employees with lowly specific skills, hint that the potential loss of highly asset-specific human capital is strongly compensated for (Becker 1993: 394). Otherwise, incentive differentials between higher remunerated and lower remunerated employees had to be largely explained as managerialism.[6] On the other hand, with decreasing asset specificity, economic analysis (re)enters the neoclassic scenario of homogeneous capital exchange in a polypolistic setting. Then, the simple incentive structures of the market are sufficient to effectively organize capital exchange.

Bounded Rationality as a Cognitive Psychological Variable of Institutional Economics?

The key thesis put forward in this chapter is that institutional economics should reconstruct the idea of bounded rationality as a reference to bounded skillfulness and human asset specificity. As discussed in section 5.2, the early Simon (1945) was still close to such an economic interpretation of bounded rationality. To a degree, like the early Simon, Williamson (1985: 45–6) hinted at an economic interpretation of bounded rationality, too, when he linked this idea to 'limits to cognitive competence'. If 'cognitive competence' is interpreted as an economic resource, Williamson here enters an economic analysis of human capital utilization, which he detailed through the idea of human asset specificity. Once reconstructed in economic terms, the question can be raised of how the idea of bounded rationality differed from concepts like (bounded) skillfulness or (bounded) human asset specificity. On the other hand, if the relevance of an economic reconstruction of bounded rationality is questioned, behavioral economics had to clearly spell out why and how organizational economics could and should draw on a cognitive psychological model of skillfulness.

Connecting to Simon's cognitive psychological model of bounded rationality, Williamson claimed that behavioral concepts on mental abilities were important in the economic analysis of organizational performance. He rather uncritically took over Simon's cognitive psychological approach (Williamson 1967: 6–7, 10–11, 20–21, 26–9; see also ibid. 1970: 52, 125) – as did many other behaviorally oriented economists (see Chapter 2, section 2.3). The attempt to ground (institutional) economic research in behavioral economics possibly still made sense for Williamson's very early research, which was closer to economic psychology rather than organizational economics (for example, Williamson 1967). However, when he later pioneered the new institutional economics (Williamson 1985, 1975), he held on to a behavioral concept of bounded rationality. In certain respects, he then even deepened a behavioral interpretation of bounded rationality:

> Bounded rationality refers to human behavior that is '*intendedly* rational, but only *limitedly* so' (Simon, 1961, p. xxiv) . . . Bounded rationality involves neurophysiological limits on the one hand and language limits on the other. The physical limits take the form of rate and storage limits on the powers of individuals to receive, store, retrieve and process information without error . . . Language limits refer to the inability of individuals to articulate their knowledge or feelings by the use of words,

numbers or graphics in a way which permit them to be understood by others. (Williamson 1975: 21–2)

Williamson claimed that institutional economics had to make concessions to 'human nature as we know it', a 'science of man' and the 'study of man' (Williamson 1991b: 92–3, 1985: xxi–xxiii, 2–3, 44, 48, 57, 64, 387–92, 405, 1983a: ix). He continued to closely follow Simon. Williamson (1998) further strengthened a behavioral interpretation of bounded rationality, then examining, like North (1993b), biological aspects of the human mind. North explicitly aimed in this regard at behavioral economics that were 'derived from individual behavior and reflected an interaction between preferences and constraints . . . even . . . drawing on theories of brain processes' (Eggertsson 1993: 27). If this project is really followed through, possibly unwittingly but unavoidably anthropological philosophy is entered (see also Chapter 3, section 3.1 and Wagner-Tsukamoto 2003). To a degree, Williamson (1985: 46, Footnote 6) was aware of the critique that the idea of bounded rationality was an unnecessary cognitive psychological concept in institutional economics. Still, he did not question a behavioral model of bounded rationality and the conceptual 'coupling' of bounded rationality with other variables, such as uncertainty (the latter is discussed in Chapter 7, section 7.4).

A behavioral concept of bounded rationality reflects a major unresolved issue in Williamson's research. Fundamental questions can be raised regarding the relevance of a behavioral model of human nature. Behavioral economics had to clearly spell out why and how a concept of neurophysiological limits and language limits should be applied in institutional economic theory and practical intervention. In particular, the theoretical relationship of a cognitive psychological understanding of bounded rationality with economic concepts of human capital and human asset specificity had to be explained. Regarding practical intervention, behavioral economics had to outline whether and how the psychological intervention with bounded rationality should support or replace the economic intervention with human capital contingencies and incentive structures. A prioritizing, substitutive or 'unifying' relationship between behavioral intervention and economic intervention had to be specified. On grounds of problem dependence, Chapter 8, section 8.2 here argues for prioritizing. It suggests that effective, practical intervention with organizational performance is likely to be undermined if a behavioral approach were prioritized over or substituted for the economic approach.

Apparently, Williamson overestimated the conceptual relevance of neurophysiological, language limits and the Simonean project of behavioral economics for institutional economics. Simon's conceptual distancing from and explicit critique of Williamson's institutional economics, as touched upon in Chapter 4, section 4.2, strongly implies this. Furthermore, it is indicative that, despite his proposition that bounded rationality were of critical importance to understanding institutional organization, this idea rarely surfaced in Williamson's institutional economic analysis. In the opening chapters, Williamson (1985, 1975) flagged up the idea of bounded rationality as a key concept of institutional economics. He then also explicitly formulated a behavioral maxim for his organization theory: 'Organize transactions so as to economize on bounded rationality while simultaneously safeguarding them against the hazards of opportunism' (Williamson 1985: 32). In a theoretical–(practical) perspective, this maxim may be fruitful for behavioral economics but probably less so for a research program that examined the crafting of governance structures in relation to the degree of human asset specificity (see above). For this latter purpose, a cognitive model of rationality and a motivational model of opportunism may be best interpreted heuristically with regard to the model of economic man (see Chapter 6, section 6.3).

This argument is supported by the way Williamson actually used the idea of bounded rationality in his research. For instance, in Chapters 8–12 of Williamson (1985), in which issues of organizational structuring in the firm are discussed, Williamson hardly examined 'bounded rationality'. In contrast, the idea of asset specificity was explicitly and comprehensively dealt with. The few times he drew on the idea of bounded rationality, he did so in the introduction or in the concluding sections of chapters. A deeper conceptual role of 'bounded rationality' in analyzing and intervening with capital utilization in relation to governance structures remained unclear.[7] Also, other researchers, for instance Mortensen (1978) and Becker (1975, 1965, 1962), to whom Williamson (1985: 255) explicitly connected, conceptualized and analyzed human capital and asset specificity without the idea of bounded rationality (similarly Walker and Weber 1984). It is revealingly in this connection that the concept of asset specificity disappeared from Williamson's (1998) analysis once he really focused on a behavioral discussion of bounded rationality. A competitive, substitutive relationship of these concepts can be expected on grounds of the problem-dependent nature of scientific research programs. Problem dependence implies different 'ways of looking' – to use Becker's (1993) phrase – when researching the same 'subject matter' by different research programs. The important question here is whether the idea of bounded rationality or the idea of human asset specificity provides the more fruitful, conceptual route for specifying 'ways of looking' in *economic* theory-building and practical intervention.

The low prevalence and low integration of the idea of bounded rationality in Williamson's institutional economic research may reflect that this concept, understood in cognitive psychological terms, is comparatively unimportant while unproblematic for institutional economics. Key arguments were already outlined for Taylor's and Simon's organization studies, which tried to apply similar or the same behavioral concepts (see sections 5.1 and 5.2). These arguments apply for Williamson, too. Institutional economic theory-building is likely to be overdetermined if it tried to apply both the idea of bounded rationality and the idea of asset specificity. Chapter 1, section 1.1 and Chapter 3, section 3.1 set out the general argument.

5.4   CONCLUDING REMARKS

This chapter did not generally question the relevance of behavioral analysis of skill formation and skill management and the related behavioral conceptualization of bounded rationality. It only questioned whether a behavioral analysis of skills utilization could be interrelated with or substituted for an economic analysis of skills utilization. In this connection, certain ambiguities were observed in Taylor's, Simon's and Williamson's organization theories and their analysis of skills, especially regarding the conceptual role they attributed to ideas like bounded rationality and insufficient mental capacity. Multiple interpretations of the ideas of bounded rationality and insufficient mental capacity permeate Taylor's, Simon's and Williamson's organization research, bounded rationality/insufficient mental capacity being related to neurophysiological, cognitive, language limits but also to limits of skillfulness, competence and human asset specificity.

In certain respects, Taylor, Simon and Williamson modeled *both* behavioral features of human nature and features of human capital when analyzing skills utilization. They imported behavioral concepts into their analyses. A crucial question is here: Why and how should/could organizational economics theoretically (or heuristically) integrate a model of neurophysiological brain processes, cognitive, information-processing limits and language limits with the analysis of human capital and incentive structures? A critique of any scientific model as unrealistic and incomplete misses crucial points regarding the nature of scientific research, especially its heuristic grounding and related issues of complexity reduction and problem dependence. Even psychology and sociology can only examine human nature in a highly selective way. They can only 'model' human nature but do not and need not portray human nature in a comprehensive, holistic sense. If attempted this is likely to increase the complexity of research to a point at which theory-building loses focus and drifts into philosophy (see Chapter 3, section 3.1 and Chapter 3 in general). Also, it may be short-sighted to contrast on ontological, empirical–behavioral grounds theoretical–practical concepts of behavioral sciences with theoretical–practical concepts of economics. Theoretical–practical concepts of economics do not necessarily reflect a model of human nature rather than a model of human capital (and incentive structures). Comparisons of concepts across research programs only make sense if qualified for the problem dependent nature of scientific research.

For the purpose of organizational economics, behavioral concepts of bounded rationality or insufficient mental capacity are best reconstructed in economic terms, in a theoretical–practical perspective in relation to concepts of human capital and/or incentive structures or in heuristic perspective, in relation to the model of economic man (see Chapter 6). To a degree, Taylor, Simon and Williamson hinted at such an economic reconstruction of bounded rationality, namely when linking it with or substituting it for ideas like 'bounded skillfulness', 'competence' and 'human asset specificity'. Reference can also be made to the economic literature on risk aversion, limited information availability and information asymmetry as attempts to 'reclaim' the concept of bounded rationality from behavioral economics and (economic) psychology. These ideas reflect that search and information costs can be (re)approached in relation to incentive structures. North made a step in this direction by linking the idea of bounded rationality to a situational concept of information availability (North 1993b: 16), although he continued to explicitly defend the idea of bounded rationality, similar to Simon or Williamson, on behavioral, psychological grounds. Similarly, the concept 'risk aversion' of the principal–agent theory can be reconstructed in relation to the idea of (lacking) compensation payments for risk-taking (payments being signaled by incentive structures). When 'bounded rationality' is reconstructed through ideas of limited information availability or asymmetric information distribution (or environmental uncertainty), an economic discourse is entered. In general, variables such as information asymmetry or incomplete information distinguish institutional economics from neoclassical economics, which drew on the idea of 'perfect information' (see also Doucouliagos 1994; Langlois and Csontos 1993; Waring 1991: 58–63; Langlois 1990).

Besides the potentially ambiguous theoretical interpretation of bounded rationality as a reference to cognitive psychological limits of the human mind, on the one hand, and bounds to skillfulness and human asset specificity, on the other hand, the idea of bounded rationality seems to have been ambiguously interpreted by Taylor, Simon and Williamson in other respects: Chapter 4, section 4.2 and Chapter 5, section 5.2 hinted that the early Simon interpreted bounded rationality as a reference to performance problems in organizational behavior, as problems of 'organizational nonrationality'. Chapter 4, section 4.2 also outlined that Simon discussed bounded rationality in certain respects as a behavioral versus economic reference to motivational conflicts (value conflict versus inadequate inducements and incentives). Chapter 6 points out that Taylor, Simon and Williamson pitted, in varying degrees, a theoretical, behavioral interpretation of bounded rationality against the research heuristic 'economic man' and here especially the idea of utility maximizing behavior. Finally, Chapter 7, section 7.4 shows that bounded rationality was in certain respects interpreted as a behavioral versus economic reference to uncertainty (behavioral uncertainty versus environmental uncertainty). Future research has to clarify such multiple and, at least partly, incompatible interpretations of bounded rationality. The important issue here seems to be that social scientists have to clarify in what theoretical and/or heuristic sense they apply the concept 'bounded rationality' in their research programs.

NOTES

1. Taylor's terminology is ambiguous in this respect. In other passages he used the notion of 'brains' as a role-related reference to the factory manager.
2. He probably saw an urgent need for performance improvements on the shop floor. Also, in Taylor's time, skills utilization at the top management level was probably comparatively unproblematic since in many cases ownership and the top management function were still united. Hence, dilemmas regarding the utilization of managerial skills, as later identified by Berle and Means (1932), did not yet exist.
3. Ockenfels' (1999: 157–7) empirical experiments support this suggestion.
4. For a review of the concept 'practical intelligence', see Wagner (1997: 48–58).
5. Simon reasoned in this connection that production programs could not be constantly and instantly adapted in relation to changes in the external environment (Simon 1945: 120). This was a rare reference by Simon to external, environmental influences on organization structure (see also Chapter 7, section 7.2).
6. In general, in relation to a capital utilization model of social behavior, the question of 'capitalism' – what it is and how and why it should be pursued – can be addressed in a fundamental way. Such a debate may have been neglected by institutional economic research. Rowlinson (1997: 82) made this point regarding Williamson's (1985) understanding of 'capitalism' (see also Chapter 8, section 8.1).
7. In the discussion of firm size and the 'M-form hypothesis', Williamson strongly drew on the idea of bounded rationality (see Chapter 7, section 7.4). Critical questions can in this respect be raised, namely whether the idea of bounded rationality convoluted the idea of environmental uncertainty.

6. Modeling motivation and cognition in organizational economics: Research heuristics or the portrayal of 'human nature as we know it'?

> The behavioral assumptions I invoke . . . are bounded rationality and opportunism. Both are intended as concessions to 'human nature as we know it'. Admittedly, the resulting conception of human nature is stark and rather jaundiced. (Williamson, 1985, pp. xii–xiii)

> [T]he more general principles of analytic economics are simply the principles of economic behavior, of the effective achievement of ends by use of means, by individuals and groups, irrespective of social and political forms. Even under a 'pharaoh', combining absolute sovereignty with outright ownership of men themselves as well as the land and goods, much the same choices and decisions would have to be made to make activity effective rather than wasteful and futile; and the abstract principles of economy and of organization are the same regardless of who makes the choices or what means and techniques are employed or what ends are pursued. (Knight, 1948, p. li)

The key thesis explored in this chapter is that (organizational) economics only heuristically applies the model of economic man, that is, ideas on self-interested, utility-maximizing choice behavior. Understood as research heuristics, these ideas imply abstraction from behavioral complexities that characterize motivation and decision-making in 'real life'. Following this line of argument, 'economic man' is beyond empirical–behavioral and moral–behavioral scrutiny (but not so theory and practical intervention that is developed by applying the model of economic man). Sections 6.1, 6.2 and 6.3 assess how Taylor, Simon and Williamson modeled motivational and cognitive aspects of decision-making. If the argument holds up that ideas of self-interest and maximizing behavior are important research heuristics of organizational economics, an economic reconstruction of their theories should unearth explicit or implicit applications of and references to these ideas. The chapter argues that Taylor, Simon and Williamson implicitly applied the model of economic man as a research heuristic but explicitly criticized and tried to reform it in empirical–behavioral and moral–behavioral terms. The chapter suggests here a (self)misunderstanding that yielded conceptual inconsistency and practical intervention problems for their organization theories. Section 6.4 concludes the chapter.

6.1　TAYLOR'S HEURISTIC MODELS OF MOTIVATION AND COGNITION: 'SYSTEMATIC SOLDIERING', 'NATURAL SOLDIERING' AND 'OPTIMUM BEHAVIOR'

There are numerous indications in Taylor's writings that he modeled motivation and cognition in heuristic terms, reflecting the model of economic man. But then, there are also many behavioral references to self-interest and maximizing behavior. And there is the attempt to correct the model of economic man in moral–behavioral terms. The following substantiates:

1.　Taylor interpreted the idea of self-interest in the heuristic terms of the economic approach when invoking the ideas of 'systematic soldiering' and 'interest in gains'.
2.　Taylor misinterpreted the heuristic nature of the idea of self-interest when linking it to inborn natural soldiering and when amending the model of (managerial) motivation through the moral–behavioral concept of hearty, cooperative attitudes and predispositions. This undermined the practical effectiveness of his organization theory.
3.　The application of a maximization (minimization) calculus is visible in Taylor's organization theory, although he did not detail the heuristic or theoretical nature and purpose of this model of cognition.

Taylor's Model of Employee Motivation: 'Systematic Soldiering' and 'Natural Soldiering'

There are many references to self-interest in Taylor's studies, such as suggestions on an interest in higher wages, prosperity, intellectual growth or a comfortable working environment (for example, Taylor 1911: 33–4, 53, 83, 95, 1903: 21–5, 141–2, 190, 199). They directly reflect the application of the model of economic man, of interests in monetary/non-monetary gains (see Chapter 2, section 2.4). Taylor stressed that self-interested behavior should be analyzed as a systemic condition but not the human condition. The idea of 'systematic soldiering' here was his key concept. It modeled a dilemma structure in which 'economic men' were caught up (see Chapter 4, section 4.1). He analyzed organizational behavior as self-interested behavior, examining incentive effects of organization structures on outcomes of organizational behavior. He analyzed the incentive-compatibility of organization structures and made suggestions on how to remedy performance problems through the (re)design of incentive structures. In this regard, Taylor heuristically applied a model of self-interest.

Yet, Taylor also portrayed human nature in empirical–behavioral terms when discussing self-interest. There are numerous psychological references to 'natural soldiering' and a 'common tendency to take it easy' (Taylor 1903: 32, see also ibid. 1912: 118, 1911: 13, 17–19, 29, 1909: 87, 1903: 30–32, 90). He even suggested that natural soldiering reflected an inborn feature of human nature: '[S]ome people are born lazy . . . and others are born greedy' (Taylor 1911: 29). In this way, he linked the analysis of cooperation problems to the human condition. Besides being untenable in psychological terms, the concept of natural soldiering camouflaged a heuristic function of the model of self-interest in organizational economics. But, in the first place, his views on natural soldiering have to be interpreted as a mere methodological self-misunderstanding of an organizational economist.

Despite reflecting a theoretical and empirical misunderstanding from the point of view of psychology and despite reflecting a methodological misunderstanding from the point of view of economics, the model of natural soldiering still allowed Taylor to (re-)enter economic analysis. With regard to analytical and practical outcomes, it does not greatly matter whether the model of economic man is applied as a misclaimed 'image of human nature', or, methodically properly understood, as a research heuristic. But damage was done in other respects. Taylor's concept of natural soldiering incited much theoretical, empirical and moral critique of behavioral researchers regarding an apparently untenable, negative 'image of human nature' of scientific management. For instance, Herzberg (1966), Knowles and Saxberg (1967), Perrow (1983) and most textbooks on organization, for example, Mullins (1999: 49–52), Arnold et al. (1998: 457–8) or Buchanan and Huczynski (1997: 340–43) took Taylor's views on natural soldiering at face value (see also Chapter 4, section 4.1). A comparable (mis)perception is widespread among organizational economists. For example, Barney (1990) or Donaldson (1995, 1990) interpret opportunism as a behavioral assumption about human nature (see section 6.3). They did not put a model of opportunism or 'natural soldiering' into perspective regarding a methodical role in economic analysis.

Taylor's Heartily, Cooperative Model of Managerial Motivation

Taylor's apparent misunderstanding of the heuristic nature of 'economic man' showed up in another respect, too – with more serious consequences than unnecessarily inciting the criticism of behavioral researchers.

Comparable to his concept of employee motivation, Taylor modeled managerial motivation in empirical–behavioral terms, but in contrast to his model of
employee motivation, he modeled the manager as the naturally 'good' person,
as not self-interested and as heartily cooperative. Taylor applied neither ideas
of systematic soldiering nor its behaviorally disguised version of natural
soldiering when researching managerial motives and interests. Here he exited
from economics. The noble model of the heartily cooperative manager probably finds favor with behavioral organization researchers. It compares to
suggestions of the human relations school or behavioral business ethics
research, for instance, an 'Abraham-model' (Herzberg 1966), a 'theory Y'
(Knowles and Saxberg 1967; McGregor 1960; similarly Argyris 1962),
'bounded self-interest', 'benevolence' and 'altruism' (Simon 1997, 1993b; in
degrees even Williamson 1998), an 'I and we' utility function (Etzioni 1988,
similarly Sen 1990, Margolis 1982), an ethereal hand (Donaldson 1990) and,
more generally, suggestions by post-modern and critical management
research on 'radical humanism' (Alvesson and Deetz 1996: 192). Bauman's
(2001: 143) post-modern ethics also seems to be based on this 'old' concept
of altruism.

For behavioral research, a role-related modeling of cooperative attitudes of
managers, but not so of workers, is theoretically and empirically untenable.
For economic research, it is likely to be counter-effective: By invoking virtuous, cooperative character traits, the model of economic man, and here especially a model of self-interested choice is discarded. Then, Taylor could no
longer analyze how a self-interested 'ruler [manager] may be able to structure
the game so that it is both in his and his constituents' interests to abide by the
rules' (North 1993b: 14; see also Chapter 4). Or differently formulated, in
Taylor's (1903: 31) terms, he could no longer analyze cooperation problems in
relation to a defective incentive logic of the situation (see also Chapter 4,
section 4.1).

In the special hearing before the US Congress, the chairman of the inquir-
ing committee pointed out this problem to Taylor that a potentially self-interested manager might retreat from wage promises given to workers:

The Chairman: Would not your suggestion of cooperation on the part of the workman with the management (the management being the sole and arbitrary judge of
the issue) be very much like the lion and the lamb lying down together with the
lamb inside? . . . Mr. Taylor, do you believe that any system of management induced
by a desire for greater profit would revolutionize the minds of the employers to such
an extent that they would immediately, voluntarily and generally enforce the golden
rule [of hearty cooperation]? . . . Is it not true that scientific management has been
developed with a desire to cheapen the production in order that there might be
greater profits? (Taylor 1912: 152–3)

The chairman questioned the effectiveness of a behavioral approach that aimed to change 'habits of mind' or aimed at the 'great mental revolution', as Taylor put it. The chairman seemed to suggest that the manager should be modeled as 'economic man': who tried to 'cheapen production' and had a 'desire for profits'. He said that the 'promotion of own best interests', which Taylor (1903: 23) had explicitly analyzed for worker behavior, should have been examined for managerial behavior, too (indeed for any stakeholder of the firm). Otherwise, potentially dilemmatic interest conflicts among organization members remained unresolved: 'The lion and the lamb' were expected to peacefully 'lie down together', as the chairman put it.

Taylor tried to fend off such criticism by suggesting that workers could counter-defect if managers broke promises:

> [T]he workman has it in his power at any minute, under scientific management, to correct any injustice that may be done to him in relation to his ordinary day work by simply choosing his own pace and doing the work as he sees fit . . . In other words, injustice on part of the employer would kill the goose that lays the golden eggs. (Taylor 1912: 152)

Taylor raised two defenses. First, he suggested that under scientific management workers still had sufficient competency rights to counter-defect. Second, Taylor implied that managers would anticipate they behaved as 'rational fools' when breaking wage promises, realizing in time that they 'killed the goose that lays the golden eggs'. Both arguments may have to be discounted. Under scientific management, the scope of workers to (counter)-defect was limited, at least considerably more so than under previous management systems. Scientific management restricted competency rights of workers to organize work and to 'choose their own pace'. It standardized work performance and enforced strict output control. Also, competency rights of workers were no longer protected by unions since scientific management had relegated unions from the organization of industrial relations (see Chapter 4, section 4.1). In fact, such a one-sided concentration of property rights provided managers with a considerable temptation to appropriate distributions that had been promised to workers. The important question is whether, over time, managers would consistently resist this temptation and anticipate that they 'killed the goose that lays the golden eggs' if they defected. Taylor banked here on the 'great mental revolution' of managerial attitudes (see Chapter 4, section 4.1). Historical evidence indicates that this was unsuccessful in early 20th-century USA (see Chapter 4, section 4.1), as it may have been generally rare in the history of mankind. It probably was already evasive as far back as in biblical times, when – in a 'pluralistic', multicultural interaction context – problems over industrial interactions escalated between Egypt and Israel (see Wagner 2000a).

Thus, the protocols of Taylor's testimonial suggest that the main reason why the US Congress summoned Taylor was the inconsistent application of the model of economic man in his organization theory. In other words the US Congress reprimanded Taylor for his too favorable image of human nature, for portraying (certain) organization members as hearty and cooperative. This criticism of the US Congress can be directed to similar suggestions of behavioral organization research, for example, Simon's (1997, 1993b, 1945) proposals on value indoctrination and his concept of altruistic, boundedly self-interested choice behavior (see section 6.2), and comparable suggestions of McGregor (1960), Argyris (1962), Herzberg (1966), Knowles and Saxberg (1967), Fletcher (1973), Etzioni (1988), Sen (1990), Bernhard and Glantz (1992), Vargish (1994), Donaldson (1995, 1990), Alvesson and Deetz (1996), Tomer (1999) or Bauman (2001).

Taylor's Model of Decision-making: 'Maximization' and Comparative Utility Assessments

In contrast to Simon and Williamson, Taylor did not discuss in detail cognitive aspects of decision-making. There are some references to maximizing behavior that hint at a utility-maximizing calculus. He spoke of optimization goals of the firm and society, for example, referring to 'maximum prosperity' (Taylor 1911: 9–10, 12). Also, his suggestions on 'national efficiency' (Taylor 1911: 6) fall into this category, too (see also Chapter 4, section 4.1). When discussing organizational performance at the shop floor, Taylor (1911: 9, 12, 1903: 18, 21) invoked the goals of the maximization of efficiency and productivity ('maximum productivity', 'maximum efficiency') and the minimization of cost and waste ('cheapest way', 'least waste'). And with regard to individual behavior, he invoked optimization goals for work performance, such as 'maximum speed', 'maximum work load' and 'maximum output' (Taylor 1911: 27, 1903: 25–6; see also Person 1964: xiii).

Taylor's suggestions on maximizing and minimizing behavior imply that he was not too concerned with a 'correct' empirical–behavioral, cognitive psychological model of decision-making. For the purpose of organizational economics, which theoretically and practically focuses on capital utilization in relation to incentive structures, such a model of optimizing behavior is a useful heuristic. The general argument was outlined in Chapter 2, section 2.4. As far as cognitive issues enter economic analysis, they are probably best theoretically treated and empirically researched as skills limitations that constrain capital utilization but not as cognitive limitations of the model of economic man (see also Chapter 5, section 5.4). As discussed in Chapter 5, some of Taylor's interpretations of insufficient mental capacity related to a systemic constraint of skills utilization rather than a view about human nature (for example, Taylor 1912: 155).

On the other hand, Chapter 5, section 5.1 also critiqued Taylor's inclination to behaviorally model organization members in claimed cognitive psychological terms. Seemingly, he did not fully realize the heuristic nature of ideas like optimizing behavior. Still, Taylor drew a line regarding how and when he abstractly referred to maximizing and minimizing behavior and how and when he talked about decision-making behavior in the real world. He seemed to follow up the latter through a comparative calculus, speaking of decision-making that aimed at *better* outcomes but not best outcomes. This hints that Taylor did not apply a maximization and optimization calculus for analyzing decision-making behavior in 'real life' but for heuristic purposes of organizational economics. For example, a model of comparative decision-making is apparent when Taylor discussed the individual's decision to soldier or not to soldier; when he analyzed the outcomes of skills formation and training programs of scientific management; when he examined the generation of profit and efficiency increases in the 'real world'; or when he investigated organizational survival in relation to competitor behavior (Taylor 1911: 6–7, 11–13, 1903: 19, see also ibid. 1909: 87). Simon and Williamson might interpret such a comparative decision-making calculus as a model of satisficing behavior.

6.2 SIMON'S HEURISTIC MODELS OF MOTIVATION AND COGNITION: 'INDIVIDUAL AIMS' AND 'OPTIMIZING BEHAVIOR'

Simon's behavioral economics modified the model of economic man in empirical–behavioral and moral–behavioral terms. If the argument has some substance that (organizational) economics applies 'economic man' heuristically and if Simon's research explicitly or implicitly connected to organizational economics, references to self-interested and maximizing behavior in his organization theory could still be expected. The subsequent discussion suggests that his behavioral critique of 'economic man' may be difficult to reconcile with considerable parts of his organization theory. The following substantiates:

1. Simon applied a model of self-interest but also a value-based model of motivation. The former seemed to methodically instruct his economic research, the latter his behavioral research.
2. The later Simon (mis)interpreted the idea of self-interest in empirical–behavioral and moral–behavioral terms, and suggested replacing it with a behavioral model of 'altruism' and 'bounded self-interest'.
3. Simon (mis)interpreted a model of optimizing behavior as an unrealistic model of human cognition and suggested reforming it through a more

'realistic' concept, such as the model of satisficing behavior and bounded rationality.

4. Simon applied an optimization calculus in his organization theory, both in his early organization research and in his later writings, even after he had developed a behavioral qualification of a maximization calculus.

Simon's Model of Motivation: 'Individual Aims' and 'Value Preferences'

Simon initially put forward a goal-oriented theory of motivation. He modeled motivation through the concepts of 'aims' and 'goals' of organization members and the related concept of 'goal conflict' between individual goals and organizational goals. Simon's related discussion of 'non-rational' organizational behavior that resulted from conflicts between individual goals and organizational goals reflects an economic rationale: '[T]he difference in direction of the individual's aims from those of the larger organization is just one of those elements of non-rationality with which the theory must deal' (Simon 1945: 41). His discussion of 'differences in direction' can be detailed as interest conflicts which, unless resolved, would lead to 'organizational non-rationality' (see Chapter 4, section 4.2). The early Simon had no problem to propose that ' "administrative man" takes his place alongside "economic man" ' (Simon 1945: 39, also ibid. 1945: 123, 179, 197, 199; Ridley and Simon 1943: 3).

In Simon's inducement–contribution analysis, a calculus of self-interest is clearly visible, too, specifically so when he analyzed inducements in relation to compensation payments made by the organization to its members (see Chapter 4, section 4.2). When discussing inducement–contribution decisions, Simon explicitly suggested that organization theory should abstract from a behavioral psychological concept of motivation (Simon 1976a: 248, 1945: 248). Organizational economics would follow up this proposal by spelling out the heuristic role of the model of economic man in analyzing and resolving goal conflicts and interest conflicts. Simon quite explicitly indicated such a heuristic purpose of modeling human nature:

> It is important to note that propositions about human behavior, *in so far as it is rational*, do not ordinarily involve propositions about the psychology of the person who is behaving . . . Psychological propositions, other than descriptions of an individual's value system, are needed only to explain why his behavior, in any given instance, *departs* from the norm of [group] rationality. (Simon 1945: 149, emphasis as in original)

The statement touched on the problem-dependent nature of scientific research and related issues of complexity reduction and 'modeling'. Simon seemingly acknowledged that scientific research is in need of abstraction. And in other passages he justified abstraction on grounds of usefulness and heuristic necessity rather than empirical adequacy (Simon 1976a: 268, 1969: 104, 113, see also section 5.2).[1] If Simon had omitted in the above quote the qualifier 'other than descriptions of an individual's value system', it could be inferred that he abstracted from the behavioral make-up of organization members and applied the model of economic man (although clarifications regarding Simon's understanding of 'group rationality' may be needed). But, of course, in the above quote Simon did not propose abstraction from certain motivational, psychological concepts in order to enter organizational economics but to sharpen a *cognitive psychological* analysis of goals and rationality conflicts. This is an interesting and legitimate behavioral research project. However, a critical comment has to be made on the way Simon pitted behavioral research against economics, both in theoretical–practical perspective, as discussed in Chapter 4, section 4.2 and Chapter 5, section 5.2 and in heuristic perspective.

With regard to the model of self-interest, Simon (1997: 42–5, 52, 1993b: 159–60) detailed the behavioral correction of 'economic man' through concepts of bounded self-interest, altruism and group loyalty (similarly Cyert and March 1992: 9; see also Sen 1999, 1987; Etzioni 1988; Margolis 1982). He suggested that a calculus of self-interest, as favored by organizational economics, is empirically wrong and 'dehumanised' organizational behavior (Simon 1976a: xxi–xxiii). Marsden and Townley (1996: 671) also related the model of economic man to the dehumanization of organizational behavior. In this connection, Simon (1997: 38–9, 1993b) also explicitly criticized Williamson's (1985) model of opportunism. Simon (1997, 1993b) then completed the behavioral reform of 'economic man', which he had began in the 1950s with the psychological analysis of bounded rationality (see also below).

In degrees, already the early Simon made moves towards a value-based model of motivation when analyzing organizational behavior. He claimed that organization theory would remain 'utopian' unless it analyzed and generated a value consensus or 'sameness of preferences', as he put it:

> In the practical world, plans are characterized as 'utopian' whose success depends upon wished-for behavior on the part of many individuals, but which fail to explain how this wished-for behavior will or can, be brought about. Now a very special situation arises when all the members of the group exhibit a *preference for the same values* and for the same outcomes out of all those possible of realization by the group. (Simon 1945: 105–6, emphasis added)

For top managers, he specified value-based, preference-centered analysis through the concept of the 'desire for efficiency' (see Chapter 4, section 4.2). This proposal and further similar suggestions of him left the resolution of certain interaction problems in the firm as widely open as Taylor's proposals on the hearty, cooperative manager.[2] Taylor, like Quaker firms or experiments in communism or behavioral job enrichment and empowerment programs, made in this respect frustrating experiences, when attempting to create the new 'good' man/woman who would be (pre)disposed towards a value consensus, same preferences, bounded self-interest or altruism (for example, Wagner-Tsukamoto 2001a; Buchanan 1987b; Reif and Luthans 1969).

Here Williamson (1985: 51–2) explicitly took a different view than Simon. He suggested that organizational analysis and intervention remained utopian unless grounded in the model of economic man. Especially if pluralism is encountered as an unavoidable or desired interaction condition, the success of behavioral research, which models motivation through a value-based calculus, is likely to depend on the prior establishment of incentive-compatible organization structures. For that purpose, a model of self-interested choice behavior is heuristically required. Furthermore, this has implications regarding the prioritizing of economic versus behavioral strategies for practical intervention. Chapter 8, section 8.2 provides an outlook on this issue.

Simon's Model of Decision-making: 'Maximization' and 'Satisficing'

The early Simon nearly exclusively modeled decision-making behavior as maximization behavior. He approached 'administrative man' as 'economic man' (Simon 1945: 38–9, also ibid. 1945: 73, 102, 121–3, 179, 197–9; Ridley and Simon 1943: 3). He even modeled the firm as a single 'economic man' which, for certain purposes of organizational analysis, he viewed as a fruitful heuristic fiction: 'In example after example, we can find individuals behaving as though the institutions to which they belong were "economic men", always calculating the "institutional utility", in both of service and conservation goals, in each decision' (Simon 1945: 202). Here, Simon applied the unrealistic model of maximizing and optimizing behavior, which probably only makes sense if heuristically interpreted with regard to economic theory-building and practical intervention. The early Simon quite explicitly hinted at such a non-empirical, non-behavioral but heuristic understanding of a model of maximizing behavior. When examining household behavior, he stated: 'Empirical limitations upon choice are introduced into the economist's scheme by the individual's stock of goods and by the price structure' (Simon 1945: 74). Similarly: '[T]he administrator must be guided by the criterion of efficiency. This criterion requires that results be maximized with limited resources' (Simon 1945: 197). These statements stress an understanding of economic research in which questions of realism only arise in relation to theory on *incentive structures* – 'the price structure' – and on *capital utilization* – 'the stocking of goods' or 'limited resources', but not in relation to human nature. Other comments of Simon, for example, that psychological aspects of decision-making could be abstracted from on grounds of usefulness for certain types of organizational analysis (Simon 1997: 62–3, 1976a: 268, 1945: 149, 1969: 104, 113; see also above and Chapter 4, section 4.2 and Chapter 5, section 5.2) imply this, too.

Cognitive bounds of rationality can be theoretically and empirically handled by economics by reapproaching them as limited resources of or capital constraints on the individual. Doucouliagos (1994: 879) specified in this connection that bounded rationality, once reconceptualized in this way, does not imply the abandonment of the notion of maximizing behavior (see also Langlois and Csontos 1993; Waring 1991: 58–63 and Langlois 1990 for further references). And, as discussed, the early Simon's interpretation of bounded rationality seemed to reflect this. A behavioral correction of economic man is then not necessary.

As much as Simon sensed that for certain purposes of organization research a model of optimizing behavior was useful, he did not spell out the heuristic nature and relevance of an optimization model (and neither did he for the model of self-interested behavior, as discussed above). Over time, this led to increasing misunderstandings in Simon's research, especially when he began to examine a maximization model in relation to the formulation of definitions (but not research heuristics):

> [The] 'principle of efficiency' is characteristic of any activity that attempts ratio-nally to maximize the attainment of certain ends with the use of scarce means, it is as characteristic of economic theory as it is of administrative theory. Actually, the 'principle' of efficiency should be considered as a definition rather than a principle: it is a definition of what is meant by 'good' or 'correct' administrative behavior. It does not tell *how* accomplishments are to be maximized, but merely states that maximization is the aim of administrative activity and that administrative theory must disclose under what conditions the maximization takes place. (Simon 1945: 39, emphasis as in original)

This statement is still fully compatible with a conventional understanding of the economic approach. Yet, Simon's suggestions on 'conditions', 'man' and 'principle versus definition' needed to be further specified. This can be done in methodological terms and/or in empirical, theoretical–(practical) terms. For the purpose of economic research, the former would imply a heuristic inter-pretation of maximizing behavior; the latter would imply the spelling out of capital constraints. For the purpose of behavioral research, however, different heuristic and/or theoretical qualifications are necessary. From the 1950s onwards, the 'psychologist' Simon began to interpret and amend the 'defini-tion' of maximizing behavior in empirical–behavioral terms. And many behav-ioral researchers followed (see also Chapter 2, section 2.3). Simon overlooked in this regard the problem-dependent and heuristic nature of the 'definition' of maximizing behavior in economic research (Persky 1995; Suchanek 1992; Waring 1991: 59–61; see also Chapter 1, section 1.1 and Chapter 8, section 8.1).[3] Simon then 'discovered' that the model of economic man reflected definitions, assumptions, premises and so on that could be easily falsified by cognitive psychology. On this basis, he felt compelled to refocus his organization research on behavioral issues and the portrayal of 'true' human nature in economics. Such critique was not new at the time.

Earlier, in (the Preface of) the 1933 edition of *Risk, Uncertainty and Profit* Knight had similarly taken issue with a non-behavioral, abstract economics, especially its apparently incomplete, behavioral image of human nature. He called for the '[r]ecognition of other elements in motivation, social-symbolic, ethical, etc' (Knight 1948: xvii). Like Simon, he suggested that economics needed a psychological and physiological model of human nature in order to make economics 'more realistic and true in a human sense' (Knight 1948: xvii, see also ibid. 1948: xxix, xvi).

On the basis of the behavioral interpretation of 'economic man', Simon's organization research shifted towards behavioral economics, organization psychology and organization sociology. He now modeled and scrutinized decision-making in empirical–behavioral terms, aiming to reform the claimed unrealistic model of maximizing behavior. He pitted maximizing 'economic man' against the ideas of satisficing and bounded rationality:[4]

> Administrative theory is peculiarly the theory of intended and bounded rationality – of the behavior of human beings who *satisfice* because they have not the wits to *maximize*. (Simon 1976a: xxviii, emphasis as in original)

or:

> [E]conomists attribute to economic man a preposterously omniscient rationality. Economic man has a complete and consistent system of preferences that allows him always to choose among the alternatives open to him; he is always completely aware of what these alternatives are; there are no limits to the complexity of the computations he can perform in order to determine which alternatives are the best. (Simon 1976a: xxvi–xxvii)

or:

> The classical organization theory . . . like classical economic theory, failed to make explicit . . . [the] subjective and relative character of rationality and in doing so, failed to examine some of its own crucial premises. (March and Simon 1958: 139; similarly Simon 1997: 90–1, 1995: 47–50, 1993a: 395–6, 1993b: 156–7, 1985: 303, 1976b: 129–30, 1956: 130–31, 1955: 99)

Simon substantiated the empirical–behavioral critique of maximizing behavior through a behavioral reinterpretation of the concept of bounded rationality, thus diverting from his earlier, comparatively economic interpretation of bounded rationality (see Chapter 4, section 4.2 and Chapter 5, section 5.2). He constructed a false conflict between economics and behavioral sciences, outplaying a research heuristic of economics with empirically testable, theoretical–(practical) concepts of psychology. Some four decades later, Rabin (1998: 11, 13) or Scott (1995a: 21–2, 51) and nearly the entire body of (economic) psychology and (economic) sociology continue to argue in the Simonean tradition. Ultimately, Simon (1997, 1993b) followed up this misunderstanding with regard to the idea of self-interest, putting forward the idea of 'bounded self-interest', thus completing the behavioral reform of 'economic man' – but also, probably unwittingly, completing his exit from economics.

That Simon may have fallen in these respects for a misunderstanding is underlined by his application of a model of optimizing behavior in his later studies, long after he had proposed an 'empirically correct', psychological model of bounded rationality and satisficing behavior. Simon (1976a: 261–2) returned to concepts of 'pareto optimality' and 'optimization' when discussing the operations research algorithm. The operations research algorithm comprises a goal function, which reflects a maximization or minimization problem, and a system of constraints. The purpose of operations research is to analyze resource utilization under situational constraints. In its generic outlook, operations research mirrors the economic approach, not only in theoretical perspective but also and above all regarding the heuristic application of the model of economic man, and here in particular the idea of optimizing behavior. Simon and other behavioral economists, for example, Cyert and March (1992: 8–9), can rightly claim that the concept of optimization is untenable on empirical–behavioral, cognitive psychological grounds. The question then arises why he applied an optimization calculus in his discussion of operations research, or similarly, an unrealistic 'equilibrium model' in his discussion of the *Architecture of Complexity* (Simon 1969: 106). Possibly Simon was just inconsistent – but, after all, he was the pre-eminent researcher and leading advocate of the realistic modeling of decision-making as satisficing. It is difficult to believe that he made a mistake. Also, a suggested 'empirical approximation function' (Schanz 1988: 80; similarly Simon 1963: 231) can probably justify the application of an optimization model or an equilibrium model only if the specific purpose of empirical approximation is spelled out. And this is likely to lead back to considerations of problem dependence and the heuristic grounding of scientific research.

A more convincing and plausible explanation of why Simon resorted to an optimization calculus, even in his later research, may be that the empirical–behavioral 'correctness' of a decision-making calculus did not matter or was even counter-productive for certain research problems, namely the ones of economics.[5] The heuristic fiction of optimizing behavior, as applied in operations research and in economic research is useful for empirically exploring problems of capital utilization ('resource utilization') in relation to incentive structures. The early Simon quite explicitly touched on this insight when discussing economic research on household behavior (see above). In these instances, Simon applied an optimization calculus probably for the reasons suggested by Friedman (1953), who defended the application of the idea of maximizing behavior in economics. The concept of 'causal holism' (Boylan and O'Gorman 1995: 195–6) and the empirical way it interprets maximizing behavior in Friedman's analysis may need certain qualifications in this respect, too.

Probably only for the research problems of organization psychology or organization sociology, Simon's claim towards the empirically correct modeling of human nature can be accepted (see also Scott 1995a: 50–52).[6] To some extent, the later Simon tried to claim this very thing, that even his research prior to 1950 reflected organization psychology and organization sociology (Simon 1976a: xvii, xxxiv–xxxv). He stated that issues of organization structure, which he linked to economic research, had not been of interest to him (Simon 1976a: xxi) and that inducement–contribution analysis, which clearly reflected an economic element in his early organization research, was a 'digression' from his behavioral research (Simon 1976a: xi). If these claims are accepted that the early Simon was not interested in organizational economics, 'only' critical comments could be made on his methodologically misunderstood assessment of the economic approach, especially in relation to the behavioral reform of 'economic man'. However, Simon's claim that he was disinterested in organizational economics appears difficult to uphold. Chapter 4, section 4.2 and Chapter 5, section 5.2 outlined that his organization theory aimed, to a considerable extent, at organizational economics, as did his later research, for example, on the operations research algorithm.

Also, in later studies Simon continued to voice interest in research problems related to organization structures – but then suggested that a behavioral approach was appropriate for analyzing and resolving the 'big questions' of 'organization structure' (Simon 1976a: xxi–xxii). Simon (1976a: xxii) stated: 'Organization design is not unlike architectural design. It involves creating large, complex systems'. But instead of calling on the economist for analyzing and solving 'large-scale' architectural problems, by means of creating incentive-compatible structures, Simon called on the interior designer, the 'organization psychologist' and 'organization sociologist'. Drucker's (1989b: 189) critical assessment of organization theory and high failure rates of organizational intervention (for example, reviewed by Wolff 1999: 1–5, 29–31, 227) confirm this (see also Chapter 8, section 8.2). Organization theorists are likely to do managers and politicians a disservice if they advised on the 'big questions' through behavioral research – since behavioral research cannot deal with issues of incentive-*in*compatible organization structures. This is the more applicable when modern interactions condition, such as pluralism and multi-culturalism, are encountered.

6.3   WILLIAMSON'S HEURISTIC MODELS OF MOTIVATION AND COGNITION: 'OPPORTUNISM', 'MAXIMIZING BEHAVIOR' AND 'ECONOMIZING BEHAVIOR'

Williamson interpreted the model of economic man as the 'twin assumptions of self-interest seeking and rationality . . . in economic theory' (Williamson 1967: 163, similarly ibid. 1998: 2). He connected in certain respects to Simon's behavioral economics when applying ideas on self-interest and deci-sion-making behavior. The following substantiates:

1. Williamson tried to reform 'economic man' behaviorally, especially with regard to the idea of bounded rationality but, somewhat surprisingly, not with regard to his model of motivation, which was solely focused on the idea of opportunism.
2. Williamson implicitly sensed that his behaviorally incomplete, motiva-tional model of opportunism reflected a research heuristic of organiza-tional economics. But, he explicitly (mis)interpreted the idea of opportunism in empirical–behavioral and moral–behavioral terms and critiqued on this basis economics as an unrealistic and amoral science.
3. Williamson applied an optimization calculus in his organization theory, despite his explicit claim that economics should model cognition in empirical–behavioral, psychological terms as bounded rationality.
4. Williamson seemingly underlined the heuristic nature of a model of cognition in economics when invoking an 'economizing' calculus. This concept is more tautological than a model of optimizing behavior.

Heuristic Aspects of Williamson's Motivational Model of Opportunism

The idea of self-interest plays a prominent role in Williamson's research. Already the early Williamson (1967: 3) attested that 'where discretion exists, it is apt to be exercised and that merely to charge someone to be a good and faithful servant is not adequate to secure his performance.' Especially detri-mental effects of self-interested choice caught his attention, such as 'free-riding', 'on-the-job-leisure', 'arbitrary behavior', 'dysfunctional behavior', 'pursuit of own goals', 'pursuit of personal goals', 'theft' or 'end games' (Williamson 1985: 47–9, 319–20, 1975: 30, 48, 64–6, 99, 202, 1970: 24–5, 46–54, 1967: 53–60). He modeled self-interested choice through the idea of 'opportunism', which he specified as 'self-seeking with guile' and 'subtle self-interest seeking' (Williamson 1998: 1, 1985: 64–7, 1975: 26–30).

There are indications in Williamson's writings that he interpreted the idea of opportunism in heuristic terms. He quite explicitly stated that a model of opportunism did not reflect 'human nature as we know it' but only empirically rare behavior:

> I do not insist that every individual is continuously or even largely given to opportunism. To the contrary, I merely assume that some individuals are opportunistic some of the time . . . Otherwise, those who are least principled (most opportunistic) will be able to exploit egregiously those who are more principled. (Williamson 1985: 64)

The methodological significance of this statement is high. Williamson implied here, referring to Hart (1961: 193), that opportunism reflected human nature as we generally do *not* know it. Only 'some individuals' behaved as opportunists and he further narrowed this down to the 'least principled ones'.[7] Barney and Hesterley (1996: 118) and Donaldson (1990: 373) sense the same when questioning the actual frequency at which organization members behaved as opportunists.

In general, research that could rightly claim to portray 'human nature as we know it' had to reflect widely observable and empirically testable patterns of human behavior. If the idea of opportunism was really meant to depict 'human nature as we know it', empirical research on opportunism should be able to observe opportunism for *all* human behavior, for *most* human behavior or at least, for *'on average'* human behavior. Otherwise, if opportunism is empirically found only in rare instances, claims towards the empirical–behavioral portrayal of human nature are untenable. As discussed above, Williamson hinted in this respect at a heuristic rather than empirical–behavioral interpretation of opportunism, referring to opportunism as empirically rare behavior. In certain respects, Williamson meets here Buchanan (1987b: 271) who proposed 'to allow homo economics to exist only as one among many men', namely for heuristic reasons of economic theory-building and intervention.

Milgrom and Roberts (1988: 160), too, seemed to imply such a heuristic role of behavioral assumptions in economic research when justifying unrealistic assumptions on grounds of usefulness. Although, their suggestion that more realistic behavioral assumptions could be introduced at later stages of research overlook that (institutional) economics applies 'economic man' as an analytical tool and would reapproach behavioral concepts, such as tastes, social norms or status, as capital, for instance, as social capital (Becker 1996; Coleman 1988; also Kreps 1990), or human capital (Becker 1976, 1975, 1962) or ethical capital (Wagner-Tsukamoto 2002). At times, behaviorally oriented economists, for instance, Hodgson (1993b: 5) or Knight (1948: xvii), also hinted at a heuristic purpose of the idea of self-interest in economics: 'The *instrumentalism* of [economic] science would conceive of each individual as pitted against each other in an endeavor to manipulate them to his private ends' (Knight 1948: xvii). Comparable statements of Simon, regarding bounded rationality, were referred to in section 6.2.

To a degree, Williamson even seemed to sharpen a non-empirical, heuristic interpretation of opportunism when discussing opportunistic behavior as *hypothetical* behavior:

> One of the implications of opportunism is that 'ideal' cooperative modes of economic organization, by which I mean those where trust and good intentions are generously imputed to the membership,[8] are very fragile. Such organizations are easily invaded and exploited by agents who do not possess those qualities ... Accordingly, those who would have cooperatives succeed must, of necessity, make organizational concessions to the debilitating effects of opportunism. *Viable cooperatives will attempt to screen against, socially recondition and otherwise penalize opportunistic invaders.* (Williamson 1985: 64–5, emphasis added, similarly ibid. 1998: 15–17, 1985: 244)

Even if an organization had not yet been 'invaded' by opportunists, still, so Williamson argued, it should take preventive measures. Furthermore, he proposed to analyze *potential* conflict: '[G]overnance is viewed as the farsighted means by which order is accomplished, thereby to mitigate *potential* conflict and realize mutual gains' (Williamson 1998: 2, emphasis added; see also Chapter 4, section 4.3, which discussed the heuristic nature of the idea of the dilemma structure). These suggestions contain the important insight that economics only heuristically applies the concept of 'opportunism' in order to analyze and detect *potential* defection and prevent *potential* conflict. The purpose of such an analysis would be, as Williamson clearly indicated, to prevent debilitating effects of self-interest in social interactions. The idea of opportunism is used here as an analytical device for investigating and advising on the resolution of interest conflict.

To a degree, Donaldson (1990: 373) sensed this, too, when he interpreted the model of economic man in a Gödelean manner (see Chapter 1, section 1.1) as a fundamental axiom outside economic theory – but then he did not inquire about the purpose of this 'outside' axiom. Rather, he spoke of 'guilt by axiom' and explicitly reconnected to McGregor's (1960) behavioral 'theory X' interpretations of the model of economic man (Donaldson 1990: 377). This reflects certain self-contradictions and overlooks that 'theory X' views may reside outside empirically accessible theorizing of economics. As discussed below,

Williamson proceeded similarly when critiquing the idea of opportunism in empirical–behavioral and moral–behavioral terms.

Williamson's Empirical–behavioral Interpretation of Opportunism

Williamson explicitly suggested that institutional economics required realistic behavioral assumptions: '[T]he principal problem in understanding the actions of men is to understand how they think – how their minds work' (Williamson 1985: 2–3, see also ibid. 1998: 2, 7–11, 1991b: 92, 1985: 391–2). He endorsed Simon's project of a 'science of man' and the research of 'human nature as we know it' in economics (Williamson 1998: 1, 6, 1991b: 93, 1985: xii–xiii, 44, 48, 57, 64, 387–8, 391, 405, 1983a: ix, 1970: 52, 125, 1967: 6–7, 10–11, 20–1, 26–9). He favored the 'interdisciplinary modeling' of human behavior, aiming to connect behavioral economics to psychology, sociology, physiology and biology (Williamson 1998: 7–17, also Williamson 1985: xii, 1975: 1–2). Similar claims are made by North (1993b) or Brunner (1987). Such behavioral interpretations of the assumption of opportunism, and also of the assumption of bounded rationality have uncritically been taken at face value by supporters and critics of organizational economics alike (for example, Rowlinson 1997: 60–61; Barney and Hesterly 1996: 117–18, 129–30; Donaldson 1995: 169–187, 1990; Mueller 1995: 1226; Scott and Christensen 1995: 303).

Williamson claimed to portray organization members as opportunistic on empirical–behavioral grounds, opportunism reflecting a feature of human nature (Williamson 1998: 2, 1985: 47–51, 63–7, 1975: 26–8, 39–40). He distinguished in this connection different behavioral types of self-interest: 'simple', 'integer' self-interest and 'subtle' self-interest (Williamson 1985: 65–6). This compares with Binmore's (1994: 19) conception of 'narrowly conceived self-interest' and 'broadly conceived self-interest'. Even if such a behavioral distinction of different types of self-interest-seeking can be substantiated by psychology, this may not greatly matter to institutional economics. In the context of incentive-*in*compatible organization structures, already 'simple' self-interest leads to the breakdown of cooperation, to 'rational foolishness' and the self-elimination of conscience, values and morals in social interactions. A behavioral distinction of 'simple' and 'subtle' self-interest encourages the (mis)understanding that only subtle self-interest could undermine cooperation while simple self-interest yielded cooperation. Evolutionary economics seems to suggest this, for example, Axelrod (1986), Schotter (1986) or Baurmann and Kliemt (1995).

Another indication that Williamson underestimated the heuristic role of the idea 'opportunism' in economic analysis is his only indirect reference to incentive-compatible governance structures as a means of preventing opportunism, namely when he detailed his understanding of 'opportunism' in a special appendix of Williamson (1985). Here, Williamson (1985: 64–7) only implicitly referred to economic governance ('otherwise penalizing opportunistic invaders') but explicitly referred to behavioral intervention ('screening', 'social reconditioning') in order to prevent opportunism (Williamson 1985: 64–5, as quoted above in italics). Such suggestions undervalue and possibly even misrepresent the key contribution of Williamson's research (see Chapter 4, section 4.3). It appears that an explicit, empirical–behavioral interpretation of opportunism got in the way of institutional economic theory-building. The behavioral interpretation of opportunism is probably as unhelpful as Taylor's views on natural soldiering. Although, a behavioral model of opportunism still allowed Williamson, like Taylor, a methodologically misunderstood re-entry into economics. But, it unnecessarily incited behavioral criticism. For example, Hunt (2000: 117) or Donaldson (1995: 169–72 183–6, 1990: 372–3), to name a few, criticized Williamson's apparently negative image of human nature, not questioning Williamson's behavioral self-claims regarding the model of opportunism.

A Behavioral 'Correction' of Opportunism: Relevance of Moral–behavioral Concepts in Institutional Economics?

Behavioral economics conceptualizes integrity, trust or benevolence in moral–behavioral terms. Simon (1997, 1993b) here was most outspoken. Other researchers in organizational economics have taken up this project. For example, Donaldson (1995: 183–7, 1990: 379) suggested integrating moral–behavioral character traits into the model of economic man. Williamson explicitly rejected a model of 'humanism', 'cooperative predispositions' and 'communitarian values'. He criticized, like Buchanan (1987b: 275), behavioral programs that built on these ideas as utopian (Williamson 1985: 51–2). In this respect, there exists a clear gulf between Williamson and Simon or Donaldson. Yet, on the basis of his empirical–behavioral interpretation of opportunism and a quest for realistic assumptions on human nature in economics, Williamson, comparable to Simon (1997: 42–5, 52, 1993b, 1976a: xxi), felt compelled to qualify.[9] Williamson argued that moral–behavioral character traits should be modeled by economics. Otherwise, economics' image of human nature reflected a 'stark and jaundiced image of man' (Williamson 1985: xii–xiii) that did not correspond to 'human nature as we know it':

> As with economic models generally, the human agents who populate transaction cost economics are highly calculative. That is plainly not an attractive or even accurate view of human nature. Economics is thought to be a dismal science partly for that reason. (Williamson 1985: 391, see also ibid. 1993a: 453, 475–6, 1985: xii–xiii, 64, 391)

Behavior assessments of organizational economics have taken over this view (Barney 1990: 384–5; Donaldson 1990: 373, 379). This assessment of economics as the dismal science, because of a claimed negative image of human nature, is widely shared by behavioral scientists (for example, Simon 1993b; Sen 1990, 1987; Etzioni 1988; see also Chapter 2, section 2.3). Arrow (1974: 17) here is less extreme, merely characterizing economics as an 'unpleasant' science. Williamson (1985: 44) aimed in this connection to amend the model of economic man, the idea of self-interest, through ideas on human dignity and individual integrity (Williamson 1985: 44, as quoted below). Also, he connected to proposals of the human relations school (Williamson 1975: 41), he favored behavioral techniques of 'social re-conditioning' (Williamson 1985: 64–5, as quoted above), and, not dissimilar to Simon (1997: 42–5, 52, 1993b), he began to flirt with the idea of bounded self-interest (Williamson 1998: 2, 15–17; see also Barney 1990: 384–5; Donaldson 1990). These moves towards the moral–behavioral reform of the model of self-interest are at odds with Williamson's extensive modeling of 'unbounded' self-interest as 'opportunism' and his assessment that the idea of opportunism only implied rare or even just hypothetical behavior in his analysis.

Williamson, and behavioral economics in general, had to clarify in this regard why and how ideas like bounded self-interest, benevolence, altruism or dignity should and could be reconciled with the model of opportunism. A behavioral interpretation of opportunism, or similarly of bounded rationality (see below), raises a number of conceptual and methodological questions. It is difficult to see how behavioral economics, which replaced a model of self-interest with moral–behavioral concepts of bounded self-interest, could yield anything other than an entry into anthropological philosophy and moral–behavioral philosophy. Indeed, Williamson seemed to realize the conceptual futility of reforming economic man in moral–behavioral terms, though reasons for this failure puzzled him:

> I originally intended also to include a discussion of dignitarian values and how these influence economic organization. The effort was not successful, however. I regard this as a regrettable shortfall and hope that it will be remedied . . . A more complete and systematic treatment of the ramifications of dignity for economic organization is surely needed. (Williamson 1985: 44, Footnote 3)

Williamson's apologetic stance hints at a self-misunderstanding in his research regarding the methodical nature and heuristic purpose of the idea of opportunism in economics, as hinted at by Homann (1997: 18–19) and also Pies (1993: 247).

If a model of self-interest is supplemented by concepts such as bounded self-interest, its heuristic role in analyzing and preventing potential interest conflicts is undermined. Taylor and Quaker managers painstakingly experienced this. Then, not a 'new economics' is entered, as suggested by Etzioni (1988) or implied by Sen (1990), Donaldson (1995, 1990) and Simon (1997, 1993b) and earlier by Commons (1961, 1931) and Veblen (1898). Rather an 'old (institutional) economics', 'part-economics' or 'old moral philosophy' is revisited, from which Adam Smith and, in degrees, already the authors of the Bible exited – probably *for moral reasons* (see Wagner-Tsukamoto 2001b; Wagner 2000a). A 'new moral economics' is likely to build on the very methodical and theoretical–practical concepts that set out the economic approach, morality being conceptualized in relation to 'incentive structures', 'capital utilization' and 'mutual gains' and analysis being heuristically grounded in the ideas 'economic man' and 'dilemma structure' (Wagner-Tsukamoto 2002; Wagner 2000b: Chapter 8, section 8.2). As Chapter 8 details, economics can, equipped with this conceptual apparatus, make considerable moral claims.

Prevalence of the Concept of Opportunism in Institutional Studies before 1970?

It is to the merit of Williamson that the idea of self-interest, formulated through the concept of opportunism, received explicit attention in institutional economics. His claim, however, that the idea of opportunism played little role in the analysis of economic organization before 1970 may have to be put into perspective:

> I seriously dispute that opportunism has been the *operative behavioral* assumption. Public goods, insurance and oligopoly aside, there was little or no provision for opportunism in most textual and other treatments of *economic organization* as recently as 1970. (Williamson 1985: 65, emphasis added)

In order to identify the idea of opportunism in early research on economic organization, it is necessary to look for operative *heuristic* conceptualizations of opportunism but not 'operative behavioral' ones. If this is considered, a model of opportunism can be diagnosed in the studies of Adam Smith or Hobbes and already in the Bible. They seem to heuristically apply concepts of opportunism when analyzing social problems (see Chapter 2, section 2.4; also Wagner-Tsukamoto 2001b; Wagner 2000a). Similarly, early economic (organization) theory of the firm already researched self-interest and opportunism. For instance, Becker's (1962: 24) discussion of sabotage hinted at this, as did the studies of Berle and Means (1932) on managerialism or Knight's (1948) references to 'predatory propensities' of organization members, as quoted by Williamson (1985: 243, Footnote 4).

Possibly, Williamson subscribed to a discipline-oriented understanding of 'economic' organization theory when he suggested that opportunism had not been conceptualized prior to his research. However, as Popper and Lakatos implied, it is not disciplines or university departments that define the scientific research process but research problems. A discipline-oriented understanding of economic organization misses out on more than a century of organizational research in the engineering sciences, in social psychology (for example, Adams 1965), in sociology and in management studies. They may have implicitly and possibly unwittingly connected to the economic approach, applying the model of economic man and 'assumptions on opportunism'. Taylor here is an early example (see Chapter 4, section 4.1 and Chapter 5, section 5.1). He conceptualized opportunism through the concepts of systematic soldiering and natural soldiering, and claimed that the engineer '. . . by the nature of his profession is an economist' (Copley 1919: 15). Or, the early Simon (1945: 39) explicitly suggested that organizational analysis built on the model of economic man. It can be speculated that implicit or explicit conceptualizations of self-interest are applied in any organization theory that aimed to analyze and resolve interaction problems in a non-utopian way. Other early organization theories, for example, Weber's bureaucracy approach, the 'systematic management' approach, which preceded Taylor's scientific management, Fayol's studies in industrial management, or the studies of Gulick and Urwick on industrial administration, which preceded Simon's research, can be further examined in this respect.[10]

Williamson's Model of Decision-making: Maximization, Satisficing and Economizing

Regarding the modeling of a decision-making calculus, Williamson closely followed Simon's suggestion that an empirically accurate, cognitive psychological model was required. Like other behaviorally oriented economists, he shared Simon's vision to integrate economics with psychology and sociology. Possibly for Williamson's (1967) early research, which moved into economic psychology rather than institutional economics, an empirical–behavioral, cognitive psychological model of decision-making was fruitful and relevant. From the 1970s onwards, however, Williamson's research shifted towards economic questions of organization. He pioneered the concept of governance structures and explored organizational behavior, with great success, in terms of asset specificity, incentive compatibility, equilibration of interests, mutual interdependence and mutual gains (see Chapter 4, section 4.3). But this conceptual switch was not fully accompanied by a modification and switch of research heuristics. Williamson continued to argue that decision-making should be modeled through a cognitive psychological concept of bounded rationality. As for the modeling of opportunism, he proposed that a behavioral model of decision-making was required as a concession to 'human nature as we know it' (Williamson 1998: 2, 1996c: 6, 1985: 12, 17, 44–6, 49, 387, 391, 402–3, 1981: 1545, 1975: 1–2, 21–2, 1967: 6–7, 14–15). He rejected the model of maximizing behavior because of claimed unrealistic assumptions on human cognition, especially on complete information availability and unbounded rationality (which he associated with neoclassic economics).

Undeniably, the conceptualization of incomplete, asymmetrically distributed information opened up a new avenue for (institutional) economic research. Behavioral economics can criticize classical and neoclassical economics in this respect but such a critique has to be put into perspective with regard to the purpose of neoclassic theory.[11] It does not necessarily imply an empirical–behavioral modification of the economic approach *in a heuristic perspective*. Williamson, and similarly Simon and other behavioral economists, here probably mixed up heuristic and theoretical–(practical) concepts within economics but also across research programs. Rather than a heuristic perspective, economics is well advised to conceptualize incomplete, asymmetric information or limited skillfulness by focusing on theoretical–(practical) concepts of capital utilization and incentive structures. Information availability or availability of skills are thus examined as capital constraints or critical 'transaction attributes' and 'incomplete contracting', as Williamson (1996c: 10, 14–16, 1985: 387–8) put it. Costs of information search and contract negotiation are discussed in relation to capital utilization and incentive structures (see also Chapter 5, section 5.4). To a degree, Williamson (1996c: 10) here began to distance himself from Simon's understanding of bounded rationality. Chapter 5 examined this issue in more detail.

It is difficult to see why and how institutional economics required and could accommodate, in a heuristic perspective, a neurophysiological, cognitive psychological concept of decision-making (Williamson was fully quoted in this respect in Chapter 5, section 5.3, when a possible theoretical–practical role of bounded rationality in institutional economics was examined).[12] Seemingly, he did not clearly reckon that the 'unrealistic' model of maximizing behavior provided a useful heuristic for institutional economics. To a degree, Williamson (1985: 44) quite explicitly rejected suggestions, similar to Murphy (1966: 168–9), North (1993b: 13, 16) or Hodgson (1988: 73–8, 104–14), that certain research concepts had to be assessed on grounds of heuristic usefulness rather than empirical correctness. The latter was implied by Friedman, Buchanan or Becker, and more recently by Homann or Persky (see Chapter 2, section 2.4).

On the other hand, Williamson hinted at a methodical, heuristic role of a maximization calculus in economics, when referring, similar to North (1993b: 13, 15–16), to the instrumental usefulness of this idea (Williamson 1967: 19) or, more ambiguously, when speaking of focus of research (Williamson 1985: xii). Indeed, Simon (1992a: 1504, 1991: 27) and Hodgson (1993b: 11–12) here criticized Williamson for not taking over more of Simon's behavioral suggestions on the modeling of bounded rationality. And, Williamson, like Simon, continued to apply a maximization and optimization calculus in his organization theory long after he had argued for realistic behavioral assumptions on bounded rationality and satisficing. For instance, when discussing the multidivisional hierarchy, he invoked optimization concepts such as 'optimum divisionalization', 'least-cost behavior', 'profit-maximizing behavior' and even 'utility-maximizing behavior' (Williamson 1975: 148–51, 1970: 134–5, 141, 162–6, 171, 177, 1967: 19). Other institutional economists, for example, Wiggins (1991: 657) proceeded similarly, invoking an optimization calculus (see also Langlois and Csontos 1993). Simon (1992a: 1503) justifiably characterized in this respect Williamson as a 'neoclassical economist'.

In later studies, Williamson replaced the idea of maximizing behavior with the idea of economizing behavior. He interpreted 'economizing' as choice behavior that aimed to improve the welfare position of the decision-maker (Williamson 1998: 3, 6, 8, 10, 33, 1985: 46, 387–8, see also ibid.: 1996d, 1991d). Indirectly, these suggestions on an economizing calculus support the proposition that a 'correct' empirical–behavioral portrayal of human cognition is irrelevant in economics. When discussing the model of economizing, Williamson made no specific suggestions on the nature of cognitive operations, complete or incomplete information and levels of improvements to a person's welfare position, for example acceptable minimum levels, satisfactory levels or optimum levels. Even more so than a maximization or optimization model, the idea of economizing reflects a conceptually 'empty', highly abstract, tautological concept.

Possibly wisely, the idea of economizing leaves nearly everything open regarding the cognitive psychological complexities of decision-making. By tautologically strengthening the model of economic man, Williamson seemed to underline the heuristic purpose of behavioral assumptions in economic research. His suggestions on economizing, probably unwittingly, stressed the heuristic role 'economic man' plays in economic theory-building and practical intervention. Also, a tautological reformulation of a model of decision-making hints that, above all, it is the motivational idea of self-interest rather than cognitive aspects of decision-making that set out the model of economic man and the economic approach in general. Possibly, an economizing calculus may be preferable to the model of utility-maximizing behavior, especially since a maximization calculus has been prone to being (mis)interpreted in empirical–behavioral, cognitive psychological terms.

In this regard, Williamson's intellectual journey compares to the one of Knight, who, over the years, increasingly seemed to accept a non-behavioral, heuristic interpretation of 'economic man'. In the added preface of the 1948 edition of *Risk, Uncertainty and Profit*, Knight modified an earlier behavioral stance. Then, he rather 'imperialistically' outlined that the economic approach and the model of economic man could be applied to the analysis of any kind of choice problem (Knight 1948: li, as quoted in the opening section of this chapter). His references to 'analytic economics' and 'abstract economic principles' that organize economic theory-building appear difficult to reconcile with behavioral economics. They are probably best linked to a heuristic interpretation of the model of economic man and the idea of the dilemma structure and the way these ideas organize economic theory-building and practical intervention.

6.4   CONCLUDING REMARKS

There are indications that Taylor, Simon and Williamson modeled motivational and cognitive aspects of choice behavior in conventional, heuristic terms of economic research, namely as self-interested, utility-maximizing behavior. Concepts of self-interest, natural soldiering, opportunism, maximization, minimization, optimization and economizing were drawn upon despite being empirically incorrect when compared with the psychological, behavioral portrayal of human nature. Taylor, Simon and Williamson seemingly applied such concepts not in order to theoretically analyze and practically intervene with human nature but to conduct economic theory-building and intervention, which aimed at incentive structures, capital utilization and mutual gains. On the basis of such a heuristic understanding of economic man, chances increase to resolve in a constructive manner 'intergroup conflict' between organizational economists and behavioral organization researchers (Barney 1990), at least more so than by interpreting all assumptions of (organizational) economics in empirical–behavioral and moral–behavioral terms. Like Simon's behavioral economics and Williamson's institutional economics, Donaldson's (1995: 90) discussion of assumptions and methods of organizational economics needs to be clarified in this regard.

To a considerable degree, Taylor, Simon and Williamson quite explicitly aimed at the empirical–behavioral and moral–behavioral portrayal of human nature. In certain respects, this reflects 'merely' methodological imprecision that has minor implications for economic theory-building and practical intervention. A behavioral interpretation of self-interest as natural soldiering and opportunism or the behavioral qualification of maximizing behavior in relation to the idea of bounded rationality still allows for a re-entry into economic analysis, albeit based on methodological misunderstandings. But then, such imprecision has a high potential to incite unwarranted criticism that economics entertained an untenable image of human nature. Williamson's moral– behavioral self-criticism regarding his model of opportunism is exemplary.

In other respects, a behavioral (mis)interpretation of the model of economic man has more serious consequences. It can severely undermine economic theory-building and practical intervention. A moral–behavioral correction of 'economic man' does not even allow for a methodologically misunderstood re-entry into economics. This became apparent when Taylor, Simon and Williamson aimed to amend the model of self-interest for moral–behavioral character traits, such as hearty, cooperative attitudes, bounded self-interest, altruism or dignitarian values. And related hereto, they advocated behavioral intervention, such as moral appeal, value indoctrination or social reconditioning. The practical effectiveness of this approach is likely to be in doubt, as Taylor and Quaker managers found out, and as long-running field experiments in communism demonstrated. It is to the merit of Williamson that he realized that his attempt to integrate moral concepts, such as dignitarian values, with the model of opportunism had failed. But the deeper, methodological reasons behind this failure were not fully understood. Over the years, he continued to characterize the model of economic man as an unrealistic, stark, jaundiced or dismal image of humanity.

Also, the project of the moral–behavioral correction of 'economic man' overlooks that economics can make strong moral claims both regarding a favorable image of human nature and a favorable image of social life. Such claims can be made once the economic approach and its research heuristics, 'economic man' and 'dilemma structure', are transcended with regard to outcomes of economic theory-building and practical intervention. Chapter 8 has further details. Not dissimilar to Williamson, Elster (1989: 99, 108) quite explicitly underestimated economics in this respect. Indeed, if the model of economic man is corrected in moral–behavioral terms, social problems can no longer be analyzed for potentially destructive effects of self-interest. Then, a viable route to solving social problems, possibly the only one under the condition of modernity, is blocked.

Economists, such as Friedman, Buchanan or Becker, and behavioral scientists, like Dahrendorf or Lindenberg, warned behavioral economics of modifying the model of economic man, that is, simply put, a decision calculus of self-interested, utility-maximizing choice behavior. If behavioral concepts are realigned with the model of economic man, issues of complexity reduction and the problem-dependent nature of scientific research are ignored. Especially in a heuristic perspective, one probably has to agree with Becker (1971: viii) that 'there is only one kind of economic theory' (see also Becker 1993: 403). In this respect, behavioral economics has to clearly outline what, if any, theoretical–(practical) and/or heuristic role it attributes to 'economic man'. It can be speculated that behavioral corrections of economic man through concepts of 'opportunism', 'bounded self-interest', 'satisficing' or 'bounded rationality' are better reconstructed in conventional economic terms, with regard to a heuristic understanding of the model of economic man (or, as Chapters 4 and 5 detailed, with regard to the heuristic idea of the dilemma structure and the theoretical–practical concepts of incentive structures and capital utilization).

NOTES

1. This insight remained underdeveloped in Simon's studies. He tended to approach scientific research as the 'definitional problem' of a 'science of man'. This reflects a misunderstanding of the heuristic nature of certain ideas in economics and of the purpose of scientific research in general. Chapter 8, section 8.1 returns to this issue in more detail.
2. As alternatives to informal institutional change, Knight discussed in this connection 'coercion' and 'deception' but rejected them on moral and effectiveness grounds.
3. The F-twist debate between Simon and Friedman was considerably marred in this respect, too.
4. Interestingly, the 'other' of the 'twin assumptions' of economics, the idea of self-interested choice, did not catch Simon's attention for a long time, despite being as untenable on empirical–behavioral grounds as the idea of maximization. But then, as discussed, Simon (1997, 1993b) modified the model of self-interest in the same behavioral way as the model of maximizing behavior.
5. As the previous discussion outlined, the economic approach here is interpreted in methodical but not in ontological or phenomenological terms.
6. But for organization psychology or institutional sociology research heuristics had to be spelled out, too (see Chapter 1, section 1.1 and Chapter 3, section 3.3).
7. This compares to Taylor's (1911: 72–3, 1903: 31) idea that a single, lowly productive organization member could exploit more productive ones and thus undermine the productivity of the entire group (see Chapter 4, section 4.1).
8. In this respect, Taylor's program of moral appeal and Simon's program of value indoctrination reflect 'psychological contracting', as Schein (1980) might put it.
9. Eggertsson (1993: 27) hints that North attempted the same.
10. Similarly proceeds contingency theory, which made prominent inroads into management studies from the 1950s onwards (see Chapter 7, section 7.1).
11. Neoclassic economic analysis probably played an important role in the historic development of economic research. Its approach prpbably well mirrored the specific market environment of the early industrial society (see Chapter 7, section 7.2, especially when Taylor's contemporary context is discussed). Neoclassic economics tended to model a scenario of complete information, thus implying structural interdependence among decision-makers but not strategic one (Gerecke 1997; see also Chapter 2, section 2.3). Under the assumptions of complete information availability and symmetric information distribution, institutional questions of how to organize interactions are greatly simplified. If institutional structures here are necessary at all for organizing interactions, their function is likely to be a mere informational, coordination-related one but not one of equilibrating conflicting interests.
12. Even more questionable is the suggestion that ideas on utility maximization and on bounded rationality could be applied in institutional economics *at the same time* (Furubotn and Richter 1991: 4, 21–2). Questions of why and how this should and could be done have to be answered.

7. The evolution of institutional organization: Economics of environmental change or a behavioral discovery process of 'true' human nature?

> From the beginning, the forces of light and the forces of darkness have polarized the field of organizational analysis and the struggle has been protracted and inconclusive. The forces of darkness have been represented by the mechanical school of organizational theory . . . The forces of light . . . came to be characterized as the human relations school. (Perrow, 1983, p. 90)

> [A] theory which illumines the right things now may illumine the wrong things another time . . . [T]here is . . . no economic theory which will do for us everything we want all the time . . . We may . . . reject our present theories not because they are wrong, but because they are inappropriate. (Hicks, 1976, p. 208)

The development of organization theory has been linked to a discovery process of 'true' human nature. Behavioral organization research, for example, the human relations school or behavioral economics, support this suggestion. The previous chapters hinted that Taylor, Simon and Williamson made certain claims in this respect, too. This chapter discounts such suggestions that organization theory and how it developed over time directly reflected on the portrayal of human nature. Chapters 4 and 5 outlined that Taylor, Simon and Williamson specified theoretical–(practical) concepts of institutional organization and skills utilization in different ways. This chapter here connects to Hicks' (1976: 208) thesis on the timeliness of organization theory. It analyzes changes in business organization over time and their conceptualization in relation to environmental change.

Section 7.1 outlines an institutional economic conceptualization of interdependence between organizational change and environmental change. It projects the institutional economic approach to the analysis of organizational and environmental change. The idea of the environment is approached in the same economic terms, theoretically and methodically, as previously outlined for the 'internal' analysis of business organization. Sections 7.2, 7.3 and 7.4

review empirical 'evidence' on changes in incentive structures and in capital contingencies in the environment of the US firm from 1850 to 2000. Conceptual differences among Taylor's, Simon's and Williamson's organization theories are related to a changing economic environment of the US firm. The discussion does not attempt to identify causal relationships between business organization and economic environment. The 'softer' approach of business history research is taken. Environmental influence is examined for changes in incentive structures, such as price and cost structures on a firm's supply and demand markets, and changes in capital contingencies of goods, such as asset specificity.

The periodization undertaken for investigating a relationship between economic environment and business organization was crude. Only three periods were distinguished, each spanning some 50 years (1850–1900, 1900–1950, 1950–2000). For issues of institutional economic theory-building, especially in relation to the question of how to portray human nature in organizational economics, this seemed sufficient (but there is room for refinements and the business history literature provides refinements). On the basis of this periodization, sections 7.2, 7.3 and 7.4 examine how far Taylor, Simon and Williamson assessed the timeliness of business organization and organization theory in relation to economic developments in the firm's environment. Section 7.5 concludes the chapter.

7.1 INSTITUTIONAL ECONOMICS, ORGANIZATIONAL CHANGE AND ENVIRONMENTAL CHANGE: MODELING INTERDEPENDENCE BETWEEN 'EXTERNAL' AND 'INTERNAL' INCENTIVE STRUCTURES AND CAPITAL CONTINGENCIES

North (1993a: 260) hinted that there may be more to understanding institutional change than a behavioral discovery process regarding 'true' human nature: 'It is institutions that provide the key constraints and therefore shape incentives and it is the interaction between the institutional framework and the organizations that are a response to that framework that shapes the evolution of economies.' North's macroeconomic analysis of how economies change over time can be applied to the analysis of organizational change. A firm's institutional, market environment can be assessed for influence on business organization (and vice versa). The following substantiates:

1. Institutional economics analyzes both 'firm' ('market participant') and its environment ('markets', 'political–legal institutions' that govern markets)

through concepts of incentive structures and capital utilization. This analysis of business organization and business environment is methodically grounded in the research heuristics 'dilemma structure' and 'economic man'.

2. By interrelating changes in 'internal' and 'external' incentive structures and capital contingencies, organizational change (and environmental change) can be analyzed in institutional economic terms. Thus, organization theories that differently specify institutional organization and capital utilization become compatible.

3. A general answer to whether interdependence between organizational change and environmental change is of a deterministic or an indeterministic nature is infeasible. Rather, conditions have to be spelled out that influence the direction of interdependence. The 'soft' methodology of (business) history research here is more fruitful than causality-based analysis.

4. Because of ongoing environmental change, organization theory is only ultimately specified regarding research heuristics ('dilemma structure', economic man') and regarding *categories* of variables ('incentive structures', 'capital structures', 'capital contribution–distribution interactions') but not regarding variables.

Antecedents of Economics of Organizational Change: Market Structure Economics, Business History Research, Contingency Theory, Organization Ecology

Contributions from market structure economics, business history research and management studies are important for the institutional economic analysis of organizational change, especially an interrelationship between organizational change and environmental change. Early on, Alchian (1950) identified economic variables of environmental change. He examined why and how markets and market structure changed over time and how this affected the survival prospects of the firm. Alchian suggested that a firm's environment reflected a changing 'cost and demand situation' and 'environmental uncertainty' (Alchian 1950: 221). He pointed out that those firms who survived over time should be analyzed as survivors of environmental uncertainty, having effectively and efficiently 'adapted through planning' to a changing 'cost and demand situation' on markets. Penrose (1952: 809–11) specified this through the idea of 'viability'. On the other hand, Alchian argued that those firms that did not survive should be analyzed as having not made adaptations to changing markets.[1] Alchian heuristically modeled in this regard the firm as a 'black box', as a single 'economic man'.

Alchian's suggestions can instruct an institutional economic approach to organizational change. They spell out the idea of 'external' incentive structures, which Alchian referred to as a 'cost (and price) situation', and the idea of 'external' capital contingencies, which he referred to as a 'demand situation'. Once such clarifications are made, organizational economics can assess how incentive effects and capital contingency effects of markets and their institutional regulation affect business organization and capital utilization in the firm. The idea of 'external capital contingencies' can be detailed in relation to features of capital utilization on markets, for example, market volume, specificity of capital, diversity of capital, substitution propensities of capital across markets and so on.[2] Alchian hinted at such capital contingencies, although initially he did not discuss a key feature of capital utilization, namely asset specificity (Williamson 1985). On the basis of a capital utilization model, markets (supply markets, demand markets, finance market, consumer market, labor market and so on) and their institutional political–legal and cultural regulation are examined in economic terms (as 'capital markets').[3] These suggestions advance institutional economic theorizing on 'environment'. Jones (1997: 24) identified in this regard various gaps that hindered the application of institutional economics to business history research.

Chandler's business history research is another valuable source for assessing the economic interrelationship between organizational and environmental change. His thesis that 'structure follows strategy' (Chandler 1962) suggests an economic model of organizational change. He opened Alchian's black box of the firm by examining economic aspects of 'planning of a firm' or 'strategy of a firm' and, importantly, he linked them to market developments (Chandler 1965, 1962):

> Clearly *the market was of overwhelming importance* to the changing structure and strategy of American industrial enterprise. The changing American market shaped strategic initial growth, integration and diversification. The coordination of the enterprise's resources, old and new, to *the changing market* called for the building of the centralized departmentalized structure. Further expansion on a wide regional scale or into new lines of business led to the construction of different autonomous divisions so that the enlarged functional activities of the enterprise could be closely integrated with *differing market demands*. An understanding of this *intimate relation between the market and the administration* of the firm . . . makes possible a more general explanation of how a large American industrial enterprise grew, and, in growing, shaped and reshaped its administrative structure. (Chandler 1962: 382, emphasis added; similarly ibid. 1962: 41)

Chandler here referred to organizational change as the 'reshaping of administrative structure', that reflected centralization or changes in capital utilization in the firm ('enterprise's resources, old and new', 'diversification'). He specified environmental change as changes in market volume ('regional expansion') and increasing diversity of capital exchange on markets ('differing market demands', 'new lines of business'). The latter hints at fragmentation and differentiation of consumer needs, and implies rising asset specificity in exchange interactions between a firm and consumers. Seemingly, Chandler approached market interactions between a firm and consumers in terms which Williamson (1985) later referred to as the 'contracting dilemma' (see Chapter 4, section 4.3).[4] These suggestions of Chandler on interrelations of market and organizational factors can be deepened through the ideas of 'internal' and 'external' capital contingencies and incentive structures. His key thesis can then be reformulated as: The structure of institutional organization follows a firm's capital utilization strategy.

Besides market structure economics and business history research, researchers in management studies examined interdependence between business organization and market environment. Pragmatic management concepts like SWOT-analysis or PESTLE-analysis[5] discussed this issue. But more interesting for an institutional economic reconstruction of organizational change are the suggestions of 'contingency theory' ('situational theory'). Contingency theory analyzes variations in organization structures of firms, which operate on different markets. It explains differences in contingency factors, predominantly 'internal' contingencies, for example technology or firm size (Donaldson 1996b, 1995: Chapter 2; Burns 1990; Lawrence and Lorsch 1990; Burns and Stalker 1961; Woodward 1958). Contingency theory links organizational change to a changing 'internal situation'.

> To be conscious of the history of an institution like the industrial concern is to become alive to two essential considerations. First, that like any other institution . . . industry has undergone substantial change in its organizational form as well as in the activity or task or objectives it performs. Secondly and in consequence, unless we realize that industrial organization is still in the process of development, we are liable to be trapped into trying to use out-of-date organizational systems for coping with entirely new situations. (Burns 1990: 43, first published in 1963)

Ideas of 'changes in organizational form', 'performance of activities and tasks' and 'new situations' can be reconstructed in institutional economic terms as the redesigning of 'internal' incentive structures and capital contingencies – and they can then be linked to environmental change. The latter can be analyzed as changes in 'external' incentive structures and capital contingencies (see above).[6]

An institutional economic reconstruction of contingency theory alleviates some of the methodical and theoretical problems of contingency theory. It can deepen theoretical concepts and practical intervention strategies suggested by contingency theorists. Initially, patience was called for regarding certain conceptual inadequacies of contingency theory:

Situational theory ... provides managers with a way to think about organization design issues in relation to the environmental and human characteristics of their situation. Since situational theory is a relatively new development, it has many of the problems of any young body of knowledge. It is not well integrated. There are still disputes about the relevant variables and the meaning of certain terminology. (Lorsch 1983: 439–40, first published in 1977)

Still, by the 1980s and 1990s, accusations were upheld that contingency theory was a 'loosely' developed concept (Kieser and Kubicek 1983: 59, 229–39, 352–4; similarly Picot 1991: 157, Schneider 1987: 211–13). Contingency theory had remained 'atheoretical' (Lorsch 1983: 439–40), and 'ahistorical' (Zey-Ferrell 1981: 189–91).

In general, behavioral proposals of contingency theory on 'human psychological characteristics' and the 'personality of organization members' (Lorsch 1983: 439–41) can be reconstructed in institutional economic terms as human capital and its features, such as human asset specificity.[7] Besides a clarification of variables, an institutional reconstruction can help to spell out a prioritizing logic for contingency theory, how different social sciences can be drawn upon for the purpose of practical intervention. At times, contingency theorists suggested that with regard to practical intervention, non-behavioral, economic intervention with organization structures should precede behavioral intervention (Lorsch 1983: 440–41, 447). Despite such references to a prioritizing logic, an integrative, holistic, interdisciplinary approach was put forward (Lorsch 1983: 440–42; similarly Donaldson 1995: Chapter 8). However, a practical–normative orientation of contingency theory should not be taken as an 'excuse' for ambiguity in theory-building and practical intervention.

In relation to a prioritizing logic that attested to problem dependence, a systematic approach to practical intervention can be developed. Contingency theory faces in this respect unresolved questions regarding how to handle 'interdisciplinarity' in theoretical perspective and/or in practical perspective. This probably considerably hampered the development of contingency theory. For example, Donaldson (1995: Chapters 7–8) suggested a unification-based approach to organization theory and the merging of various economic and behavioral organization concepts with contingency theory. This book here voices caution. Chapter 1, section 1.1 outlined the basic arguments and Chapter 8, section 8.2 proposes that the question of 'interdisciplinarity' and 'unification' is better handled in practical perspective only, through a prioritizing logic.

Critical Issues for the Economic Analysis of Organizational Change and Environmental Change

Market structure economists, business historians and contingency theorists initiated research on the interdependence between organizational change and environmental change. There are various issues that future research has to address for developing an institutional economic approach to organizational and environmental change.

A purely deterministic situational approach may have to be qualified for situational indeterminism and vice versa. The findings of evolutionary economics are of special interest, for instance, the studies of Nelson and Winter, Kirzner, or Hayek (for reviews, see Dosi and Nelson 1998; Dosi 1997; Vromen 1995; Nelson 1991; Langlois 1988). They conceptualized in different ways deterministic and indeterministic relationships between 'market' and 'firm'. Penrose (1952: 813) and Schumpeter (1947: 150) hinted at these issues early on. Williamson's apparently deterministic approach to organization form and technological change (Langlois 1988: 636) needs to be further scrutinized. Also, Sutton's (1998) discussion of the 'survivor principle' and its interrelationship with an 'arbitrage/profitability principle' considerably deepened market structure economics as it emerged from Alchian's studies, especially in relation to technological market developments. The studies of Chandler (1965, 1962), Miles and Snow (1986, 1981), Langlois (1988), Pugh (1990) or Palmer et al. (1993) can be re-examined regarding how they conceptualized incentive effects and capital contingency effects on markets as drivers of and/or are as being driven by incentive effects and capital contingency effects generated by the firm. Figure 7.1 provides an overview of different explanations of interdependence between organization structures and environment.

Donaldson (1995: Chapter 8) addressed certain unresolved issues for contingency theory, aiming to reform contingency theory by incorporating ideas from organizational economics, institutional sociology and other behavioral organization concepts. He concentrated on internal contingency factors, such as strategy, size, task, technology and so on (Donaldson 1996b: 57, 61). Also, to a degree, Donaldson's 'growth-focused' analysis of organizational change – in relation to the variable 'firm size' (Donaldson 1996b: 62) – compares to Williamson's approach, which section 7.4 critically reviews. Especially 'misfits' between organization structures and internal contingencies (Donaldson 1996b: 62) may require the examination for external contingencies. The contributions of Donaldson can be deepened by illuminating them through institutional economic concepts that interrelate internal and external incentive structures and capital contingencies. Rather than using contingency theory as an integrative paradigm, this implies proceeding 'the other way round', applying institutional economics as the lead paradigm for organization analysis, aligning ideas of contingency research with organizational economics.

Organizational ecology, as comprehensively reviewed by Baum (1996), developed the conception of 'external contingency factors' and modified in

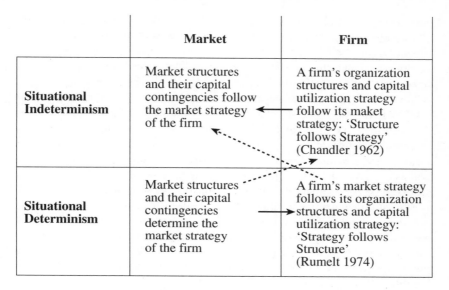

	Market	**Firm**
Situational Indeterminism	Market structures and their capital contingencies follow the market strategy of the firm	A firm's organization structures and capital utilization strategy follow its maket strategy: 'Structure follows Strategy' (Chandler 1962)
Situational Determinism	Market structures and their capital contingencies determine the market strategy of the firm	A firm's market strategy follows its organization structures and capital utilization strategy: 'Strategy follows Structure' (Rumelt 1974)

Note: Both Chandler's and Rumelt's theses can be examined in terms of situational determinism and situational indeterminism.

Figure 7.1   Organization structures, capital contingencies and market structures

this regard the comparatively deterministic and inward-looking approach of contingency theory. This approach needs to be detailed by spelling out which conditions favor 'situational (market) determinism' or 'situational (market) indeterminism'. Such conditions are the time frame of strategic planning of a firm, market volume, number of competitors, market position of a firm or costs of organizational (re)design. Once such conditions are scrutinized, deterministic versus indeterministic interdependence between business organization (and its change over time) and market environment (and its change over time) may not necessarily exclude each other. In this respect, Chandler's (1962) thesis that '[organization] structure follows [capital utilization] strategy' and Rumelt's (1974) thesis that '[capital utilization] strategy follows [organization] structure' can be reconciled. Rowlinson (1997: 206) seems to imply this for Chandler's strategy-structure thesis. Pugh (1990) raised in this connection important questions for organization research. The interesting issue here is probably not an ontological, phenomenological one but a methodical one of problem-dependent research and how to selectively analyze interdependence between 'internal' and 'external' incentive structures and capital contingencies.

Interrelationships between organizational change and environmental change are difficult to conceptualize through a nomothetic methodology. One probably has to agree with Lorsch that organization research and the research of organizational change should not theoretically and empirically focus on 'cause-and-effect relationships' (Lorsch 1983: 439). The complexity of inter-relating environmental and organizational factors may forbid this (Hoffmann 1985: 31; Lorsch 1983: 439; see also Lawson 1997: Chapter 12; Hodgson 1993a; Hahn 1991; Langlois 1988: 635–6). Nevertheless, this does not imply that research had to remain 'atheoretical'. The methodology of business history research hints how theory-building and empirical research can be conducted without causality-based inferences. The studies of Chandler or North and other business historians are illustrative. An economic conceptual-ization of organizational change here has to discuss interrelationships among double and even multiple layers of incentive structures and capital contingen-cies, which are set up by private ordering, market ordering and public order-ing (see also Chapter 2, Figure 2.2). Subsequent sections of this chapter provide an overview of the complexity of factors that had to be considered (see sections 7.2, 7.3 and 7.4).

The idea of the market and the market environment needs to be critically examined. The idea of the market environment has to be specified regarding different markets, such as the finance market, consumer market, labor market and so on. Arena and Longhi (1990: 349–484) provide a good review. Also, in the face of globalization, markets can no longer be geographically or polit-ically demarcated as 'national markets'. Neither can the idea of the market be approached in substantive terms of capital exchange, for example, with regard to a certain industry, since capital substitution and thus 'market' substitution can occur. On the basis of a problem-dependent understanding of scientific research, the idea of the market and market influence on the firm can be specified.

The complexity of the above issues implies that theory-building on the interdependence of organizational and environmental change needs to focus on certain variables only while others are abstracted from ('locked away' in black boxes). Theorizing has to be selective, with a view to the problem dependence of scientific research. Implicitly, this is reflected by the different analytical focus taken by market structure economics, business history research, contingency theory, or organizational ecology. At one extreme, analysis comes as 'pure' market analysis. Changes in incentive structures and capital contingencies on markets are focused on. Questions of market struc-ture developments, such as market concentration tendencies or the develop-ment of market entry barriers, are investigated. Business organization as such is largely treated as a black box, the firm being *heuristically* reduced to a single 'economic man'. At the other extreme, analysis focuses on business organization the market being largely abstracted from. 'Internal' incentive structures and capital utilization processes are explored, for example promotion systems or human capital contingencies (see Chapters 4 and 5). Another extreme is reflected by the approach of constitutional economics. It analyzes the influence of public ordering on markets and/or organizational change (for example, Vanberg 2001, 1982; Buchanan 1991, 1975). For economics of organizational change, these extreme scenarios set out demarcation posts for exploring 'in-between' scenarios of interrelationships between organizational change and environmental change.

The role of organization theory as a driver of organizational change and related environmental change needs to be assessed in more detail. On economic grounds, one would expect that 'new' organization theories can only drive organizational change and possibly yield environmental change if they increased survival prospects of the firm, for example, a better incentive compatibility of organization structures or a better utilization of capital in the firm. Knowledge of how to organize a firm can be interpreted as special human capital that is internally created by the firm or bought in from markets, for example consultancy markets.

Once further developed, the initial ideas sketched out in this section on the institutional economic analysis of organizational and environmental change can help to answer calls that economic models should include a 'management perspective' on organizational design and analyze interactions of a firm with 'external market forces' (Spulber 1993: 536). Also, the ideas proposed in this section may prove fruitful for specifying and broadening the conceptual basis of an institutional economic approach to business history research. For instance, an information cost-based approach to business history research (Casson 1997) can be further developed by spelling out how information costs and other costs are influenced by changes in incentive structures and capital contingencies. In general, an institutional economic reconstruction of organizational and environmental change is well capable of refuting skepticism, such as Hodgson's (1993b: 21), that the analysis of economic change over time and how it interrelates with (changes to) business organization is a weakness of institutional economic theory, especially institutional economic theory that applied 'neoclassical' concepts such as the model of economic man.

7.2 TAYLOR'S SPORADIC ANALYSIS OF ORGANIZATIONAL CHANGE IN RELATION TO ENVIRONMENTAL CHANGE

Taylor argued for functional foremanship, a premium wage system and a program for skills formation that aimed at the standardization of simple, operational and administrative skills. Regarding its structural set-up, it compared to a flat, nearly matrix-like organization structure. It was more centralized and formalized than a predecessor system such as the contractor system, but it was still structurally less hierarchical and less centralized than the functional hierarchy. This section examines how far the organization structures and capital utilization processes advocated by scientific management mirror economic developments in Taylor's contemporary environment, and, if so, how Taylor's organization theory took account of this. The following substantiates:

1. Changes in incentive structures and in capital contingencies in Taylor's market environment hint at why and how scientific management could displace the contractor system from the 1850s onwards.
2. Taylor's organization theory becomes largely compatible with earlier (and later) organization theories once changes in 'external' incentive structures and capital contingencies are examined for interrelationships with 'internal' ones.
3. Taylor undervalued economic aspects of environmental change. He only made few references to a possible interrelationship of changing incentive structures and capital contingencies on markets and organizational change.

Empirical 'Evidence' on Changing Incentive Structures and Capital Contingencies in Taylor's Contemporary Environment (1850–1900)

Taylor researched business organization in the iron-and-steel industry, which in late 19th-century USA was an emerging, rapidly growing high-tech industry. This industry then underwent dramatic changes in the organization of production and transaction activities. By the 1850s, as in most other industries, the contractor system had been the common form of business organization in the iron-and-steel industry. The contractor system reflected a comparatively loosely coupled organization structure. A so-called 'contractor' worked together with a so-called 'capitalist' (Buttrick 1952: 207–18; see also Cochran 1977, 1968 and Williamson, as discussed in section 7.3). The capitalist provided contractors with a production site, machines and raw materials and organized the distribution and selling of goods. The capitalist paid the contractor on a piece-rate basis, supplemented by a small fixed wage. Contractors produced goods on their own accounts and hired and remunerated employees.

It can be suggested that a number of developments in the late 19th century affected incentive structures and capital contingencies on most markets in a way that favored the demise of the contractor system and the coming of more

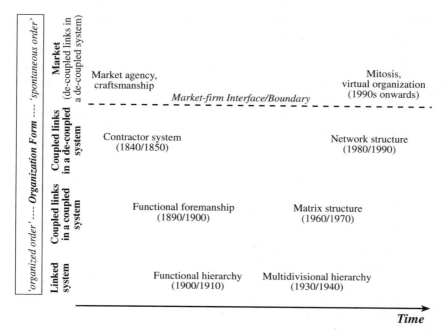

Note: Year numbers in brackets refer to the innovation period of an organization form (that means the beginning of its 'life cycle' and not necessarily its biggest spread).

Figure 7.2   Evolution of business organization

hierarchical and more formalized organization structures, as promoted by scientific management (see Figure 7.2):[8]

1. *Incentive effects and capital contingency effects of changes in production and transaction technologies: Electrification, transportation innovations and mechanization of work*   Infrastructure innovations, such as the build-up of a national electricity grid, a railway system and the invention of a new means for the transportation and storage of goods, lowered sourcing costs of capital inputs of the firm and distribution costs of capital outputs (see also point (2) below). Infrastructure innovations contributed to the emergence of a national market: Market volume increased and mass production became feasible because of economies of scale. The innovation of production technologies, as for instance suggested by Taylor regarding tool handling, further lowered production costs per unit. This in turn further incented mass production (Chandler et al. 1997: 8; Lazonick

and O'Sullivan 1997: 497–9; Cochran 1957: 14; Fabricant 1942: 3; see also Leijonhufvud 1986: 207–209; Taylor 1912: 13, 1903: 125).

2. *Incentive effects and capital contingency effects of quantitative changes in demand (market volume): The rise of demand for industrial goods* Societal, demographic, technological and political developments contributed to a rise in demand in many industries. In Taylor's industry, the iron-and-steel industry, demand expanded with the development of a military industry; increases in population; a rise in urbanization; and the progressing of industrialization, such as the build-up of a national railway system and a national electricity system. From 1850 to 1900, the population of the USA tripled from about 23 million to 76 million. And, from 1840 to 1900, the share of the urban population of the total population quadrupled from about 11 percent to 40 percent. As a result, market volume increased and economies of scale improved, mass production becoming more lucrative (Clague 1966: 45–6; Chandler 1965: 281; Gilboy and Hoover 1961: 248, 265–6; Warner and Low 1946: 28).

3. *Incentive effects and capital contingency effects of qualitative changes in demand (consumer needs): Simple, standardized, undifferentiated consumption* In the outgoing 19th century, demand patterns both for industrial and consumer goods were of a fairly uniform, lowly specific, simple character. Mass-produced, highly standardized products matched this kind of consumer demand (Habakkuk 1968: 15; Clague 1966: 47; Rothbarth 1946: 386; see also Fullerton 1988; Leijonhufvud 1986: 209–10). Market research of consumer needs, product branding or consumer-oriented marketing played a little role for a firm to survive. If pursued, it probably would have been counter-productive at the time.

4. *Incentive effects and capital contingency effects of changes in the degree of competition: Price administration* On the emerging national markets, the nature of competition changed, from regional competition to nation-wide competition. During the economic recessions of the 1870s and 1880s, it became apparent that considerable overcapacities had built up in many industries. After a phase of intense price competition, national markets consolidated and oligopolistic market structures developed in most markets. This was also the case for the iron-and-steel industry, in which, from the 1880s onwards, prices were 'administered'. Competition changed from price competition to cost competition. Cost-saving programs, as for instance promoted by scientific management, became important for the firm to stay profitable and to survive (Chandler 1997: 68; Sklar 1988: 21, 44–5, 54–6; Cochran 1957: 62; Buttrick 1952: 208–10; similarly Taylor 1903: 83).

5. *Incentive effects and capital contingency effects of changes on labor markets: Ethnically inhomogeneous, lowly skilled human capital*

Parallel to the emergence of a national market for industrial and consumer goods, a national labor market developed. From 1820 to 1910, the number of industrial employees increased from about 3 million to about 40 million (Lebergott 1961: 282; see also Phillips 1929; Outerbridge 1895: 229). The early factory managers, such as Taylor's functional foreman, had to deal with employees who frequently exhibited 'pre-industrial work habits' (Gutman 1976: 22–3). Certain features of human capital complicated skills management and skills development. Former farm workers, immigrants from Europe, and, after the abolition of slavery, former slaves entered the industrial work force as unskilled, poorly qualified labor. Immigration accounted for a substantial share of population growth in 19th-century USA. It yielded ethnic inhomogeneity and a wide mix of languages in the Taylorite factory. Diverse cultural and religious habits on the shop floor caused frequent interruptions of work. Also, most new factory workers were only accustomed to work under a fixed-wage system but not a piece-rate system, as then implemented by many firms (see Nelson 1995: 84; Gutman 1976: 19–23, 25, 36–9, 47; Clague 1966: 48; Lebergott 1965: 365, 1961: 290–92; Gilboy and Hoover 1961: 248, 265–9; Stigler 1956: 19; Wells 1926; see also the studies of Taylor, as reviewed in Chapter 4, section 4.1 and Chapter 5, section 5.1).

Incentive effects, exerted by the level of wage rates on the labor market, influenced the management of human capital, too. In comparison to Europe, land in 19th-century USA was comparatively abundant and hence inexpensive. Workers had to be paid relatively high wages in order to prevent them from becoming self-employed farmers (Habakkuk 1967: 12–17, Rothbarth 1946: 385).[9]

6. *Incentive effects and capital contingency effects of changes in public ordering (law-making, jurisdiction): Negligible socio-political forces in the early industrial society* Life in 19th-century USA was dominated by strive for economic prosperity. Societal legitimacy came inexpensively to firms. The generation of economic wealth legitimized corporate activity. Political–legal, institutional regulation of business hardly existed and governmental economic policy was oriented towards '*laissez faire*'. Incentive effects and capital contingency effects of public ordering on firms were low. First attempts were made to legally control concentration tendencies on markets, but often the early anti-merger and anti-monopoly laws proved ineffective (Chandler et al. 1997: 6; Sklar 1988; Gantt 1919: 4–5; Levasseur 1897).

Developments on consumer, industrial and labor markets after 1850 hint why the contractor system's decoupled approach to business organization became ineffective and inefficient. It could not deal with the quantitative and qualitative demand patterns of the industrializing and urbanizing society. Scientific management's more hierarchical and formalized organization structures and its standardized skilling programs better matched these developments.[10] In terms of economies of scale, scientific management enjoyed considerable production cost advantages over the contractor system. It avoided the high training costs incurred by the craftsman-like training schemes of the contractor system. In the face of ethnical inhomogeneity, costs of craftsman-like training and costs of related, intensive communication during skills development were probably prohibitively high. (The same argument applies for participatory, communicative management, as later proposed by the human relations school.)

Scientific management enjoyed transaction cost savings over the contractor system in other respects, too: In order to deal with rising market volumes, the contractor system would have had to significantly increase the number of contractors. This, however, would have dramatically increased transaction costs regarding the hiring of contractors, the sharing of production capital among contractors and the maintenance of communication and work coordination among contractors and capitalists. To a degree, Taylor (1903: 35) hinted at such a production and transaction cost rationale but much was left unsaid and implicit (see below).

The outlined economic propositions on the disappearance of the contractor system compete with suggestions that the contractor system disappeared because of a lacking capability to induce product innovation, as put forward by Williamson (see section 7.4).

Conceptual Hints at Market Influence on Organizational Change

Taylor did not explicitly discuss the question of organizational change. Neither did he say much about the role of environmental change and how it possibly affected business organization over time. Still, by examining how he conceptually positioned his organization theory in relation to earlier organization theories, it can be indirectly assessed whether he was aware of the timely appropriateness of his proposals on business organization, and, if so, whether he discussed timely appropriateness in economic terms or in behavioral terms.

As far as Taylor demarcated scientific management from other organization concepts, such as the contractor system or the systematic management approach, he seemed to imply a relative but not absolute superiority of scientific management. Taylor (1903: 35, 74–6, 98) argued that factors such as the 'number of contractors', 'volume of work' and 'variety/uniformity of work' favored, on grounds of cost considerations, the demise of the contractor system and the coming of scientific management. Taylor also suggested that functional foremanship, coupled with a premium wage system, were only superior to a strict hierarchy, which centralized production and applied a piece-rate wage system, because certain factors, especially the uniformity and volume of production output, were not high enough (Taylor 1903: 74–6, see also ibid. 1903: 98).[11] This implies that Taylor sensed a relative superiority of scientific management and the decentralized, coordination intensive, matrix-like organization structures it advocated. An economic rationale shines through in his thinking. He pointed at certain transaction and production cost considerations and related issues of economies of scale and scope. In this regard, he touched on an institutional economic conceptualization of organizational change, although much was left implicit. In particular, a conceptual linkage between organizational change and 'external' change in incentive structures and capital contingencies was not discussed. Taylor did not spell out how incentive effects and capital contingency of the market and the political–legal environment affected business organization. He did not discuss with regard to environmental change why scientific management replaced the contractor system or systematic management from the 1850s onwards. And he did not analyze and predict why and how, ultimately, the organization structures favored by scientific management would be replaced by other organization forms.

7.3 SIMON'S NEGLECTED ANALYSIS OF ORGANIZATIONAL CHANGE IN RELATION TO ENVIRONMENTAL CHANGE

Simon's organization theory favored the functional hierarchy. He suggested strictly centralized, hierarchical organization of work. In this respect, his suggestions on business organization diverted from the ones of Taylor. On the other hand, Simon's skilling program for low-level administrative employees and middle managers compared to Taylor's suggestions on job contents and communication structures for operative employees and their supervisors. Such differences and similarities can be related to the specific economic environment in which the functional hierarchy spread. The following substantiates:

1. Changes in incentive structures and in capital contingencies in Simon's market environment hint why and how functional hierarchies displaced organization structures like functional foremanship from 1900 onwards.
2. Simon's and Taylor's organization theories become compatible once economic change in the firm's environment is acknowledged.
3. Probably more than Taylor, Simon neglected environmental analysis in his organization research and increasingly so as his research shifted towards behavioral economics.

Empirical 'Evidence' on Changing Incentive Structures and Capital Contingencies in Simon's Contemporary Environment (1900–1950)

Throughout the first half of the 20th century, firms built up large hierarchies of clerical and managerial employees. By 1950, administrative employees began to outnumber operational employees, both in the industrial sector and in an emerging service sector (Scheiber et al. 1976: 448–9; Porter 1973: 18–19; Chandler 1965: 300–2; Bancroft 1958: 2, 37, 43, 209; Stigler 1956: 6, 159; Stigler 1947: 37, 41). Organizational analysis was then dominated by organization theories that discussed the functional, administrative hierarchy, for example Simon's administrative behavior approach or Weber's bureaucracy approach, which in the 1940s and 1950s was (re)discovered by US managers and management researchers.

In the Taylorite factory, the functional foremen had still been in charge of administrative functions. Scientific management split planning functions from production functions (see Chapter 4, Figure 4.1) but still located both at the shop floor, organized in a comparatively decentralized, matrix-like way. Some decades later, clerical and planning functions had been transferred into the administrative hierarchy: 'The foreman ... had become a small czar in the nineteenth-century shop, hiring, firing, promoting and planning work. By 1920 in advanced companies he had lost these functions to personnel, training, engineering and planning departments' (Cochran 1968: 79; see also Nelson 1995: 43; Cochran 1968: 78–80, 1957: 39–41; Warner and Low 1946: 31).

Changes in incentive structures and capital contingencies in the environment of the US firm illuminate such changes in business organization:

1. *Incentive effects and capital contingency effects of changes in production and transaction technologies: Spread of the assembly line, motorization and the build-up of a telephone network*   Ford's innovation of the assembly line lowered production costs per unit, motivating mass production by improving economics of scale. Distribution technologies advanced, with the railway system being extended and a national road system being built up. The motorization of US society began. Distribution innovations made the transportation of goods more flexible and enlarged market potentials by lowering transportation costs. Also, the build-up of a national telephone network enabled firms to fast communicate over long distances at lower costs (Chandler 1997: 76–9, 1977; Chandler et al. 1997: 9–10; Chandler and Hikino 1997: 26; Cochran 1972: 118, 1968: 80, 1957: 19, 31, 39–41, 51; Stigler 1956: 21, 23; Warner and Low 1946: 36, 43).

2. *Incentive effects and capital contingency effects of quantitative changes in demand (market volume): Increasing demand in the maturing industrial society*   In most industries, market volumes kept expanding.

Infrastructure innovations, as discussed under point (1), as well as large-town urbanization, contributed to rising demand for industrial goods and consumer goods. The US population doubled from about 76 million to 150 million from 1900 to 1950 (Clague 1966: 46, Gilboy and Hoover 1961: 248, 265–6). Also, the government became an important corporate customer, whose spending, by 1930, accounted for about 15 percent of the national income (Cochran 1972: 104, 1968: 88, 1957: 69, 78–9, 150–69, 194, 200). US firms began to access foreign market potentials, with overseas markets providing new business opportunities (Chandler 1977: 368–9).

3. *Incentive effects and capital contingency effects of qualitative changes in demand (consumer needs): Increasing complexity of consumption and the onset of product-oriented 'marketing'* In the early 20th century, consumer demand was still of a simple, uniform nature. The standardization of products was high and mass production the norm. This was the case up to the 1930s: '[A] producer in the United States made an article as cheaply as possible, using all methods of machine mass-production known to him and expected that if his price was low jobbers and wholesalers would dispose of the product.' (Cochran 1977: 115, see also ibid. 1977: 126, 192; Porter 1973: 17; Chandler 1965: 281, 285, 290; Buttrick 1952: 214). 'Marketing' came as product-oriented selling, even as aggressive product propaganda. However, from the 1920s and 1930s onwards and increasingly so from the prosperous 1940s onwards, consumption patterns shifted from the satisfaction of basic needs to more sophisticated needs. Capital contingencies on consumer markets differentiated and became more specific. This coincided with intensifying competition, consumer markets developing from 'seller markets' to 'buyer markets'. In response, many firms began to set up R&D departments in order to deal with consumer demand for more sophisticated, differentiated products. Product innovation became an important issue (Cochran 1968: 89, 1957: 104–5; see also Saviotti 1998: 487–92). This is reflected by an increase in spending on advertising from around $70 million in 1890 to about $880 million in 1930 and about $2800 million by 1950 (Cochran 1957: 15, 52, 62–3, 77, 157; Stigler 1956: 23).

4. *Incentive effects and capital contingency effects of changes in the degree of competition: Increases in market concentration* Practices of 'price administration', as they emerged in Taylor's time, continued on most markets. Chambers of commerce even actively organized price fixing. The share of markets that were classified as oligopolistic or monopolistic increased in the period 1909–29 from 16 percent to 21 percent. By 1939, this ratio had risen to about 30 percent, at which time it stabilized up to the 1960s (Chandler 1977: 366–8; Cochran 1972: 99, 141–2, 1968: 78, 90,

1957: 64, 67, 72, 78, 181). Price competition was low. Product-innovation-based competition slowly gained in importance (see also point (3) above).

5. *Incentive effects and capital contingency effects of changes on labor markets: Upskilling of human capital* From 1900 to 1930, immigration slowed down. But still, about one-fifth to one-third of the annual population growth was due to immigration (Nelson 1995: 81, 84–5; Lebergott 1961: 292, Gilboy and Hoover 1961: 248, 270; Stigler 1956: 19). Immigration continued to contribute to ethnic inhomogeneity of the work force. Also, the majority of immigrants was unskilled labor (Lebergott 1961: 292; Gilboy and Hoover 1961: 248, 270; Stigler 1956: 19). After the Great Depression, immigration patterns changed. The total number of immigrants per year decreased while the share of qualified immigrants rose. Because of changes in immigration policy, by the mid-1940s, less than 20 percent of immigrants were classified as unskilled. At the same time, the share of 'commercial immigrants', mostly Jewish immigrants who fled from Europe, reached in the late 1930s 25 percent of the total number of immigrants per year (Gilboy and Hoover 1961: 248, 270).

Unionization of the work force remained at a low level. Where unionization occurred, this was closely monitored and negotiated with management (Ulman 1961: 421; Cochran 1968: 86–8; Buttrick 1952: 218). In the wake of the New Deal legislation, the National Labor Relations Act banned firms from 1935 to 1947 from interfering in union–worker relationships. But rising living standards and full employment left unionization at low levels and unions in a comparatively weak position.

Human capital generally remained expensive. This was due to full employment in the 1930s, war-time booms and a still comparatively high land–wage ratio (see above). Also, the share of unskilled workers of the total work force fell in the years 1910–40 from 36 percent to 26 percent whereas the share of semi-skilled workers increased from 15 percent to 21 per cent. By 1950, the 'typical' worker was classified as skilled or at least semi-skilled. The ratio of professionally skilled employees, such as an engineer, per unskilled employee rose from 1/400 in 1900 to 1/130 in 1940 (Chandler and Hikino 1997: 26; Clague 1966: 27; Lebergott 1965: 367; Bancroft 1958: 38; Stigler 1956: 109–10). In line with increases in skillfulness, human capital became more asset-specific. This also explains, at least in part, high levels of wages (see also Williamson 1985: 245). Related, search costs, contracting costs and retainment costs for skilled employees increased. Then, many firms set up personnel departments. This seemingly yielded transaction cost savings regarding the sourcing and utilization of human capital.

6. *Incentive effects and capital contingency effects of changes in public ordering (law-making, jurisdiction): Growing affluence and the New Deal*

legislation Up to 1930, belief into the self-healing and self-regulating forces of the market had been strong. After the Great Depression, politics took a more active interest in economic policy and the making of business laws. The laws of the New Deal area encouraged the development of the 'welfare cooperation'. An increase in industrial democracy was observed. This was partly enforced by the New Deal legislation and partly it was due to scarcities on labor markets and the build-up of slack resources in the face of low price competition (Chandler et al. 1997: 6; Cochran 1972: 149, 182, 1968: 86–7, 1957: 139–40, 150–64; Clague 1966: 47, 51; Lampman 1966: 62; Starr 1946: 149; Warner and Low 1946: 31, 45; see also Simon 1945: 70).

In the period 1900–50, developments in labor and consumer markets and changes in public ordering led to the dramatic expansion of administrative functions of the firm. New administrative departments were established, such as a personnel department, a marketing department, an R&D department or a lobbying group. The procurement of human capital was no longer a mere quantitative problem, as Taylor had still encountered recruitment problems. Qualitative contingencies of human capital became more important. On consumer markets, demand rose but, more importantly, consumer needs began to fragment and differentiate. This yielded qualitative changes to capital contingencies of consumer demand. Societal legitimacy of corporate activity no longer came at a low cost. Firms began to take an active interest in those who regulated corporate behavior. In the face of increasing public ordering, many firms institutionalized lobbying as an administrative function.

These developments overburdened the Taylorite concept of a simple planning department and its 'anti-hierarchical', matrix-like, coordination-intensive organization structures, such as functional foremanship. The functionally specialized, administrative hierarchy, as discussed by Simon, then seemingly became more effective and efficient for organizing production and transaction activities of the firm.

Simon's Neglected Analysis of Environmental Change

Possibly more than Taylor, Simon underestimated that his theory reflected a timely answer to questions of institutional organization. In a few passages, Simon touched on environmental change and the timely appropriateness of organization theory. For example, he suggested that scientific management addressed 'specific problems they [Taylor and his followers then] faced in industry' (March and Simon 1958: 13, 18). Section 7.2 outlined how certain economic developments in Taylor's contemporary environment matched the organization proposals made by scientific management. Simon, however, did not analyze 'specific problems' in relation to incentive effects and capital contingency effects exerted by the market environment. Rather, he interpreted Taylor's 'specific problems' as internal, organizational problems, namely the utilization of 'physiological' skills. Similarly, he characterized the research problems addressed by his organization theory as 'psychological' ones (March and Simon 1958: 13). Chapter 4, sections 4.1 and 4.2 and Chapter 5, sections 5.1 and 5.2 substantiated that these interpretations do not do full justice to Taylor's studies nor to Simon's.

Simon's organization theory progressed over earlier theories by identifying internal contingencies for organizational performance. He analyzed 'behavioral conditions', such as bounds to motivation and bounds to cognition. His key proposal was to relax such behavioral conditions through the creation of a 'psychological environment' within the firm (see Chapter 4, section 4.2). In this connection, Simon criticized earlier organization theories, such as the studies of Gulwick and Urwin, on behavioral, phenomenological and ontological grounds. He rejected their organization theories because, so Simon claimed, of their simplistic and empirically incorrect portrayal of human nature (Simon 1976a: 288; March and Simon 1958: 13, 138, 210; see also Chapter 5, section 5.2). Simon did not analyze behavioral conditions in economic terms with regard to incentive structures and capital contingencies. His critique of earlier organization theories can be qualified in this respect.

Also, he interpreted complexity and uncertainty predominantly in psychological, behavioral terms. He did not explore interrelationships between 'internal' and 'external' incentive structures and capital contingencies in order to project complexity and uncertainty to environmental influence on institutional organization (March and Simon 1958: 55, 59, 150–51, 139, 159; Simon 1957a: xxv, 1957b: 198, 200, 204). Increasingly in his later studies, Simon explicitly aimed to reconstruct the 'theory of formal organization' through social psychology (March and Simon 1958: 1–2, 12) and sociology (Simon 1976a: xxxiv–xxxviii). This made him lose sight of the firm's environment. Interestingly, in his discussion of the *Architecture of Complexity* (Simon 1969), Simon developed in more abstract, philosophical terms the idea that hierarchical structures enjoyed certain efficiency and survival advantages over non-hierarchical structures. But he did project this insight to his organization theory and environmental conditions that could explain why efficiency and survival advantages arose.

As a consequence of a mainly behavioral approach to organization research, Simon did not and could not conceptualize economic influences of the environment and environmental change on business organization. In the mid-1970s, Simon (1976a: xxii, 294, 307) explicitly admitted to having neglected the analysis of environmental influence and change (see also Simon 1993c). But even at this point, he did not fully realize the methodical, theoretical and practical significance of this admission. Simon kept reiterating that economic organization theory competed with behavioral organization theory regarding the portrayal of human nature. Chapter 5, section 5.2 reviewed various suggestions of Simon (1976a). An economic analysis of environmental change, as presented in this chapter, suggests other than behavioral reasons why organization concepts such as scientific management were over time displaced by organization theories that favored the functional hierarchy.

Simon's behavioral approach to organizational change is shared by sociological organization theory, especially the new institutional sociology (for example, DiMaggio and Powell 1991a, 1991b; Meyer and Rowan 1991). It suggests that organizational change is driven by a libratory, humane process of cultural evolution, which is thought to reflect a better accommodation of 'true' human nature in organizational behavior. Or, political sociologists suggested that organizational change largely reflected power games played by dominant coalitions that run a firm (for a review, see Zey-Ferrell 1981). Issues concerning economic performance of the firm and environmental developments that affect the economic performance of the firm are explicitly rejected for analyzing and explaining business organization and its change over time. DiMaggio and Powell (1991b: 63–4) and Meyer and Rowan (1991: 41) largely proceed in this way. Thompson (1993:190–92) is rather critical of such approaches, especially interpretations of post-modern, sociological organization research. Some sociological organization research even questioned the very occurrence of organizational change, for example a trend towards debureaucratization and decentralization in the second half of the 20th century (DiMaggio and Powell 1991a: 13, 1991b: 63). The empirical research of Palmer et al. (1993) here is insightful. They found that economic and institutional (economic) factors rather than non-economic, political factors explained the spread of the multi-divisional hierarchy in 1960s USA (Palmer et al. 1993: 117–24; similarly Donaldson 1995: 90–91). Other literature sources quoted in this chapter on the emergence of organization structures, such as networks, matrix organization and so on, support this argumentation.

7.4 WILLIAMSON'S FIRM-SIZE-BASED ANALYSIS OF ORGANIZATIONAL CHANGE AND THE ASSUMPTION OF ENVIRONMENTAL INVARIANCE/INSIGNIFICANCE

Williamson's organization research focused on the decentralized, multi-divisional hierarchy. His analysis of skills formation and utilization moved beyond elementary, operational or administrative skills, as they were analyzed by Taylor and Simon. Rather, he dealt with complex, sophisticated, even unique skills of employees. The organization structures discussed by him included remuneration and wage systems, as similarly discussed by Taylor and Simon, but then he made numerous new proposals on organizational arrangements, contractual and systemic ones (see Chapter 2, section 2.1 and Chapter 4, section 4.3). This conceptual shift in organization theory can be linked to environmental change. The following substantiates:

1. Changes in incentive structures and in capital contingencies in the US environment hint why and how functional hierarchies were increasingly replaced by multidivisional hierarchies from the 1950s onwards.
2. Williamson wrongly implied an absolute rather than timely superiority of his organization theory when he compiled absolute efficiency ratings of organization structures from different periods and when he explicitly questioned the relevance of environmental change for understanding organizational change.
3. Williamson's behavioral explanation of organizational change in relation to a discovery process regarding human nature, especially bounded rationality, should be theoretically subsumed and/or methodically realigned with an economic analysis of organizational change.

Empirical 'Evidence' on Changing Incentive Structures and Capital Contingencies in Williamson's Contemporary Environment (1950–2000)

During the second half of the 20th century, functional hierarchies were increasingly replaced by less hierarchical, more decentralized structures (for example, Palmer et al. 1993; Miles and Snow 1986; see below for further references). Williamson (1985, 1975) suggested in this regard the 'M-form hypothesis': The functional, unitary hierarchy ('U-form') was suggested to have replaced the multidivisional hierarchy ('M-form') because the U-form did no longer cope with behavioral problems of bounded rationality and opportunism when firm size increased. The following develops a different view on the spread of the multidivisional hierarchy, suggesting that changes in 'external' incentive structures and capital contingencies drove this development:

1. *Incentive effects and capital contingency effects of changes in production and transaction technologies: Air transport and computerization* Transportation innovations, such as advances in the airline industry, lowered costs of long-distance travel. This supported the development of the multinational company. The innovation of low-cost computer technology

dramatically changed production and transaction costs. Advances in computer technology enabled product differentiation, even product customization on a mass market scale (Chandler 1997: 89–98; Thompson 1993: 190–91; Hillard 1991: 74–7; see also point (3) below). In the outgoing 20th century, globally networked computer systems, satellite-based telephone systems, mobile telephone networks or the internet lowered production and transaction costs, further favoring debureaucratization and decentralization on economic grounds.

2. *Incentive effects and capital contingency effects of quantitative changes in demand (market volume): Globalization of markets* Up to the 1970s, the globalization of US firms focused on Europe. From the 1970s onwards, it spread to other parts of the world. Globalization yielded various economic advantages: It enabled firms to enlarge market volumes, diversify risks and avoid intensifying competition in their home markets (Parker 1996: 486–92; Hillard 1991: 74; Puth 1982: 433; Chandler 1977: 476–80; Scheiber et al. 1976: 437–8; Cochran 1972: 99, 1968: 89, 1957: 127–39; Warner 1962: 8, 40).

3. *Incentive effects and capital contingency effects of qualitative changes in demand (consumer needs): Customization and product branding* In the second half of the 20th century and increasingly so by the end of the 20th century, the fragmentation of consumer needs increased and the specificity of consumer demand rose. Then, consumer markets had little in common with the seller markets of highly standardized, mass-produced products at the beginning of the 20th century. Good product engineering and low-cost manufacturing were often no longer sufficient to ensure profitability and firm survival. From the 1960s onwards, the marketing orientation of firms changed towards customer needs satisfaction (Levitt 1975: 180; see also Saviotti 1998: 494–501; Fullerton 1988; Puth 1982: 429). Product innovation, product differentiation and even product customization, and hereto-related concepts of target marketing and market segmentation became an issue. The products were now produced and offered in a wide variety of types.[12]

Through branding, product differentiation moved beyond substantive differentiation. Increasingly, intangible, psychological 'image' benefits, reflecting social reassurance, social status, esteem, feelings of well-being and so on, were added to products. In view of these developments on consumer markets, the marketing function expanded and other corporate functions, such as procurement or production, were aligned with the marketing function. This is also reflected by the increasing institutionalization of R&D in many firms. In the 1920s, only about 300 US firms had R&D departments; by the 1960s, this number had increased to about 15 500 (Warner 1962: 43). And from 1965 to 1989, the number of R&D

scientists employed by firms doubled from less than 350 000 to more than 700 000 (Chandler and Hikino 1997: 38–9, 54–6).

4. *Incentive effects and capital contingency effects of changes in the degree of competition: Globalizing competition*   Once European and Asian firms began to globalize, competition intensified on many – now global – markets (Chandler 1997 et al: 10–12; Parker 1996). Concepts of contesting markets through 'strategic management' and 'strategic marketing' spread (Porter 1985, 1980; see also Hikino 1997: 482–3). The fragmentation and differentiation of markets (see point (3) above) yielded economic advantages. It enabled firms to avoid head-on price competition and cost competition. Through differentiation, firms could mark out 'own' territory and establish 'quasi-property rights' to market share.

5. *Incentive effects and capital contingency effects of changes on labor markets: Further upskilling of human capital and the coming of the knowledge worker*   The upskilling of human capital continued in the period 1950–2000. School and university education played an increasing role in the structural transformation of human capital. Skillfulness and asset specificity rose at all levels of the firm. This coincided with the coming of knowledge-intensive production and transaction technologies (Cortada 1998; Chandler and Hikino 1997: 26–7; Lazonick 1993: 21–2; see also Argyris and Schön 1996). The capital intensity of production rose dramatically throughout the 20th century (Chandler and Hikino 1997: 41–6).

   In comparison with earlier periods, immigration no longer yielded problems for human capital utilization in the firm. Immigration rates stabilized at a low level and, because of a tightening immigration policy, immigrants of this period tended to be highly skilled (Poulson 1981: 422; Warner 1962: 5, 17–21, 41, 58).

   Unions remained a weak influence in organizing and mediating in interactions between firm and employees (Warner 1962: 11–12; see also Scheiber et al. 1976: 477).

6. *Incentive effects and capital contingency effects of changes in public ordering (law-making, jurisdiction): Changes in socio-political forces in the mature industrial society*   After the Second World War, full employment and social welfare became goals of industrial policy (Puth 1982: 408; Chandler 1977: 476, 495–6). Living standards increased steadily and the USA developed into a mature and affluent industrial society (Chandler et al. 1997: 6; Puth 1982: 421; Levitt 1975: 28; Clague 1966: 51; Lampman 1966: 5). The institutionalization of governmental activity, the judicial process, 'special interest groups' or corporate lobbying continued (Warner 1962: 10–11, 19, 25, 29, 39). Pluralism and diversity in values emerged as ever more important societal issues (in detail, see Beck 1992).

In the second half of 20th-century USA, the economic environment changed dramatically. Human capital and consumer demand further differentiated and became more asset-specific. New technologies, such as computerization, considerably lowered production costs and transaction costs. New incentive effects and capital contingency effects were exerted by the consumer market, labor market or technology market on the firm. These developments favored the demise of functional hierarchies and the coming of more flexible, decentralized, market-oriented organization structures, such as the multidivisional hierarchy, the matrix organization, network structures, outsourcing arrangements, the platform organization or structural spin-offs (Rubery et al. 2002; Child and Faulkner 1998; Baker 1996, 1992; Boddy and Gunson 1996; Ciborra 1996; Parker 1996; Hakansson and Johanson 1993; Antonelli 1992; Ghosal and Bartlett 1990; Kanter 1989; Jarillo 1988; Miles and Snow 1986). In degrees, boundaries between the firm and the market began to disappear. It became increasingly difficult to distinguish what constituted 'market' and what 'firm' (Dosi and Teece 1998; Picot et al. 1996; Williamson 1996b; Hirschhorn and Gilmore 1992; Langlois 1988; see Figure 7.2).

An Invariant Environment and/or an Insignificant Environmental Influence on Business Organization?

Williamson knew that different forms of business organization had emerged, spread and disappeared during the 19th and 20th centuries (Williamson 1985: 215–37, 1975: 152–4). He explicitly restated Hick's view that economic theories could only provide timely answers (Williamson 1985: 386 quoted Hicks 1976: 208). And, selectively, he touched on certain environmental influences on organizational behavior (Williamson 1985: 232, 249). In view of this, it could be expected that Williamson analyzed organizational change in relation to economic aspects of environmental change. To a very considerable degree, however, this does not appear to be the case.

In the footsteps of Simon's behavioral economics, Williamson predominantly examined organizational change in relation to behavioral issues. He discussed the change from the contractor system to the functional hierarchy and from the functional hierarchy to the multidivisional hierarchy in relation to behavioral factors of bounded rationality and opportunism. He detailed that, because of expanding firm size, problems of opportunism and cognitive psychological limits of organization members were encountered, which made the contractor system and later the functional hierarchy obsolete. In his view, such behavioral issues drove organizational change:

> The proposition that the management factor is responsible for a limitation to firm size has appeared recurrently in the literature ... The fundamental importance of

bounded rationality to the argument cannot be too greatly emphasized . . .
Ultimately . . . bounded rationality will operate to impose a size limit on the multi-
divisionalization process as well. (Williamson 1970: 35, similarly ibid. 1985: 296)

Similarly argue Jensen and Meckling (1996: 19). The relevance of behavioral
analysis of organizational change cannot be generally questioned. Abstraction
from environmental factors is necessary and unavoidable for behavioral analysis (Staudt 1981: 114; see also Simon 1987: 27). Otherwise, if organization
theory tried to examine both behavioral and environmental issues, it is likely
to be overburdened by too many variables (see also section 7.1). A critical
issue here for the behavioral analysis of organizational change is how intervening, non-behavioral factors are theoretically and/or methodically aligned
with behavioral analysis. Eggertsson (1993: 26) suggested: 'Mental models . . .
are not of independent interest [to institutional analysis] if they simply reflect
broad economic pressures and rapidly adjust to changes in the economic environment' (see also Palmer et al. 1993; Puth 1982, Miles and Snow 1986 who
interpret 'environment' more widely than 'economic environment'). Only if it
was disputed that environmental change affected the economic performance of
business organization, could behavioral analysis stand on its own ground.
Williamson's argumentation moved in this direction. He explicitly questioned
proposals of market structure economics and business history research, rejecting Alchian's (1950) and Friedman's (1953: 22) views on environmental
change (Williamson 1967: 19–21). Similarly, he reinterpreted in behavioral
terms Chandler's suggestions on the economics of environmental change (as
he similarly reinterpreted Hayek in behavioral terms, as discussed below). He
ontologically discounted Chandler's proposition that the market environment
affected business organization, Williamson claiming that environmental
change reflected negligible 'transitory market factors' (Williamson 1970:
113–14, Chandler's quote is in italics):

> The basic reason why the innovation [of the multidivisional hierarchy] became
> necessary . . . is traceable to more fundamental reasons than transitory market
> factors. Chandler summarizes the defects of the unitary form [functional hierarchy]
> and consequently the needs for the multidivision structure in the following way . . .
> *'The inherent weakness in the centralized, functionally departmentalized operating
> company . . . became critical only when the administrative load on the senior exec-
> utive increased to such an extent that they were unable to handle their entrepre-
> neurial responsibilities efficiently.'* . . . *'The manufacturing personnel and
> marketers tended to lose contact with each other and so failed to work out product
> improvements and modifications to meet changing demands and competitive devel-
> opments'.* (Williamson 1970: 113–14)

Even this quote indicates that Chandler would not necessarily support a behavioral explanation of the emergence of the multidivisional hierarchy. Rowlinson

(1997: 206–7) hinted at this, too, and Lazonick (1991: 200–201, 249–61) detailed this with regard to 'path-dependent innovation'. As discussed in section 7.1, Chandler and similarly market structure economics or organizational ecology explicitly focused on changes in 'external' incentive structures and capital contingencies, such as 'changing demand', 'competitive developments' or 'entrepreneurship', when analyzing organizational change.

In the analysis of the emergence and disappearance of organization forms of different periods, such as the contractor system, scientific management or the functional hierarchy (Williamson 1991b: 94, 1967: 21, 36, 55, see also ibid. 1970: 155–6), Williamson hardly investigated the influence of environmental change on organizational change. He tried to justify the fruitfulness of a merely firm-size related, behavioral analysis of organizational change by invoking the assumption of an invariant, 'given' environment (see also Rowlinson 1997: 206). Lazonick (1991: 195) spoke in this respect of a 'static methodology' of Williamson. Methodically, the assumption of an invariant environment can be interpreted as a heuristic abstraction of behavioral analysis. The assumption of an invariant environment is conceptually more sophisticated than ignoring or disputing environmental influence on organizational change altogether. Still, the fruitfulness of this abstraction depends on the explanatory power, predictive power and/or practical–normative design power it yields.

Assuming an invariant environment, Williamson (1985: 229–31) compiled 'overall efficiency ratings' for different organization structures (see also Williamson 1985: 94–5, 228–32, 285, 295, 320, 404, 1975: 96–7, 172, 1970: 130, 166). Rowlinson (1997: 149), Marginson (1993: 149) or Kay (1993: 253) criticized Williamson for not explaining why different organization forms appeared at all. Similarly, Sen (1998: 6) noted that Williamson's analysis of organization structures neglected external factors. Such criticisms can be detailed and sharpened in institutional economic terms. Williamson's compilation of efficiency ratings of different organization forms overlooked changes in 'external' incentive structures and capital contingencies. Possibly unaware of it, he projected 'his' contemporary economic environment to the analysis of organization structures that had emerged and disappeared 50 years and 100 years earlier. Unsurprisingly, in the efficiency ratings, the organization structures of the early industrial society came out worst. On the other hand, had Williamson chosen a different historic reference point, for example, the economic environment of the 19th century, results would have been rather different. Sections 7.2 and 7.3 detailed that organization forms analyzed by Taylor or Simon were well adapted to the specific economic environments of their time. Otherwise it could be asked why these organization structures could have evolved and spread at all.[13]

Williamson's review of the demise of the contractor system also reflected the assumption of an invariant environment. Again, he seemingly used the environment of the 1960s and 1970s as a reference point for assessing organizational change in the 19th century:

> [W]hatever the immediate explanation for the abandonment of inside contracting might be, it is evident that the inside contractor system possessed serious defects and that, to the extent that a more comprehensive system of hierarchical controls served to mitigate these defects . . . The defective incentives for product innovation are due, probably, to appropriability problems. (Williamson 1975: 97–8, see also ibid. 1975: 129)

Williamson's suggestion that the contractor system was not the best system to stimulate product innovation and that it suffered under an appropriability problem is difficult to question. But these 'defects' only became critical and salient in an environment in which innovation, R&D or customer-oriented marketing significantly influenced firm survival. In the early industrial society, in which the contractor system had spread, product innovation was not the most crucial factor for maintaining profitability and ensuring firm survival. Section 7.2 suggested various changes in the market environment illumine why the contractor system was abandoned in the late 19th century. Competitive pressures to innovate and a need for 'innovation-friendly' organization structures did not seem to be an important factor. Buttrick, to whom Williamson referred for supporting the suggestion of innovation defects of the contractor system, similarly stated that the contractor system was well adapted to the economic environment of the 1850s to 1880s (Buttrick 1952: 207, 210, 215–18). This is also in line with the observation that, only from the 1950s onwards, the number of R&D departments of firms increased dramatically and marketing changed from 'product propaganda' and 'product engineering' to 'customer needs satisfaction' and 'customer relationship management' (see above; see also Dougherty 1996; Burns and Stalker 1961). Indirectly, Williamson seemed to acknowledge this when pointing out that the multidivisional hierarchy had spread in force only after the 1950s, despite having been innovated decades earlier (Williamson 1985: 279, 1975: 140–42, 1970: 117).

Because of assumed environmental insignificance/environmental invariance, Williamson wrongly predicted that further decentralization of organization structures and thus the possible disappearance of the multidivisional hierarchy was unlikely: 'Mitosis of the giant M-form structure [multi-divisional hierarchy] could also be expected to have anti-bureaucratic enabling qualities . . . [E]xtrapolating the experience of the first two thirds of the 20th century does not seem to spell capitalism's early bureaucratic demise' (Williamson 1970: 176). Contrary to this prediction, in the last decades of the 20th century, many firms implemented organization structures that reflected further decentralization, debureaucratization and even 'mitosis', that is, a break-up of the large organization. Organization structures emerged such as the matrix organization, the network organization, spin-offs, strategic alliances, joint ventures or outsourcing structures (see above; see also Figure 7.2). But, even in later studies, once mitosis or spin-offs could be observed, Williamson continued to analyze these developments in the tradition of Simon's behavioral economics: as the firm's 'bounded rationality' response and 'opportunism' response to overexpansion. He did not adjust behavioral analysis for environmental change (Williamson 1991b: 105–7; 1985: 131, 166–7, 207, 280–81, 295, 402, 1975: 97–8, 133–5, 149–50, 172, 193–5). Similarly, some of Donaldson's (1996b: 61, 65) suggestions, namely that contingency theory should analyze internal factors in order to understand 'misfit stages' in processes of organizational design, can be critically examined. His focus on 'growth' (Donaldson 1996b: 62) compares to Williamson's firm size-based approach.

The successful prediction of organizational change may require the forecasting of environmental change in the first place. Seemingly, the behavioral analysis of organizational change that abstracts from environmental change fails to develop explanatory and predictive power and probably also lacks design/intervention power. The assumptions of environmental invariance or environmental insignificance implies that explanatory and predictive power of the behavioral analysis is constrained to behavioral micro-phenomena that accompany organizational change. Behavioral organization research here has to be careful how it conceptually handles environmental variance and accommodates the insight that any form of business organization is likely to develop 'defects' *when circumstances change*. As Hicks (1976: 208) hinted, timely appropriateness and environmental change have to be conceptualized. Section 7.1 provided an outline for an institutional economic approach to environmental change and organizational change. Otherwise, as Rathenau (1918: 123) pointed out early on, a fundamental mistake occurs: 'Characteristics of changing contexts (environmental contexts) are confused with characteristics of human beings who embody those contexts' (brackets and contents of brackets as in original quote).[14]

Coupling Bounded Rationality with Uncertainty and the Behavioral Reconceptualization of Uncertainty

In an analytical scheme that he called the 'organizational failures framework' (Williamson 1975: 21–6, 40; see also ibid. 1985: 30–31, 56–8), Williamson related the analysis of uncertainty with the idea of bounded rationality (see also Barney and Hesterly 1996: 118–19). In general, a coupling of variables can be questioned from a theory-building point of view. Coupling easily overdetermines theory-building. Or, if one variable just reflected a 'shadow' variable, there is little need to include both in the same model (see also Eggertsson 1993: 26; similarly Lazonick 1991: 210–11). Besides theoretical issues, a coupling of variables can be questioned from an empirical research point of view. Measurement problems are likely to result. For empirical research, a decoupling of variables seems unavoidable. Walker and Weber (1984: 374–7, 388) proceeded this way, interpreting uncertainty as environmental uncertainty, ignoring the idea of bounded rationality as well as a behavioral interpretation of uncertainty.[15] The idea of environmental uncertainty reflects that future events, such as market changes, technological innovations or political developments, cannot be fully predicted (see also Becker 1971: 57–60; Hayek 1945: 524, as referenced by Williamson 1985: 57). Conceptually, this can be further detailed through ideas on changes in incentive structures and capital contingencies in the firm's environment (see section 7.1).

Williamson hinted at the decoupling of variables when he noted that bounded rationality, like opportunism, was of interest to economic analysis only *in the face* of environmental uncertainty: of 'exogenous disturbances' (Williamson 1985: 59, similarly ibid. 1985: 30, 56–7, 243; see also Barney and Hesterly 1996: 119; March 1978: 587). But then Williamson explicitly interpreted the idea of uncertainty as 'behavioral uncertainty' (Williamson 1985: 57–9):

> As Hayek maintained, interesting problems of economic organization arise only in conjunction with uncertainty: The 'economic problem of society is mainly one of adaptation to changes in particular circumstances of time and place' (Hayek, 1945, p. 524). Disturbances, moreover, are not all of a kind. Different origins are usefully distinguished. Behavioral uncertainty is of special importance to an understanding of transaction cost economics. (Williamson 1985: 57, similarly ibid. 1991c: 277.)

Hayek probably would distance himself from a behavioral interpretation of uncertainty. He specifically discussed environmental change as 'changes in particular circumstances of time and place' (Hayek 1945: 524) and linked this to the timely appropriateness of economic organization. Regarding the distinction of 'different origins' of uncertainty, as suggested by Williamson (1985: 57), the critical question is to what *purposes* different conceptualizations of uncertainty could be put in institutional economics. The problem-dependent and heuristic grounding of scientific research may have to be paid attention. Phenomenological, typological, definitional or ontological approaches to distinguishing 'different origins' of uncertainty are probably less fruitful. The general argument was outlined in Chapter 1, section 1.1. This suggestion does not question that for a behavioral analysis of organizational change economic aspects of environmental influence have to be abstracted from and a behavioral concept of uncertainty may be instructive. But, as a matter of problem dependence, in the economic analysis of organizational change, uncertainty is better approached in relation to incentive effects and capital contingency effects that are exerted by a firm's environment. If at all, the idea of behavioral uncertainty can probably play a role in (institutional) economics only in a heuristic perspective, reflecting that a decision-maker enjoys discretion in choosing a decision alternative. Heuristically understood, 'behavioral uncertainty' can be interpreted in this regard as a reference to the model of economic man (see also Chapter 6).

7.5 CONCLUDING REMARKS

An ultimate specification of 'good' institutional organization is unlikely to exist. Each generation of organizational researchers discovers anew that 'at present' institutional organization undergoes dramatic changes (for example, Parker 1996: 483–92; Palmer et al. 1993: 100–101; Galbraith 1977: 7; Miles and Snow 1986: 62–66; Berle and Means 1932: 1). Chapters 4 and 5 implied this, too, when discussing differences among the organization theories of Taylor, Simon and Williamson.

In the 19th and 20th centuries business organization in the USA dramatically changed. The contractor system was replaced by structures like functional foremanship; functional hierarchies later displaced the coordination-intensive structures of functional foremanship; from the 1950s onwards, functional hierarchies were transformed into multidivisional hierarchies; and in the outgoing decades of the 20th century, hierarchical structures were frequently substituted by market-oriented structures, such as the matrix structure, network structures, outsourcing arrangements; then, even the structural break-up of firms could be observed. A comparison of Taylor's, Simon's and Williamson's organization theories underlined such a trend towards centralization and bureaucratization of business organization in the late 19th and in the first half of the 20th century and a trend towards decentralization and debureaucratization in the second half of the 20th century (see Figure 7.2).

These historic, economic developments can be explored in institutional economic terms by modeling interdependence between 'external' incentive structures and capital contingencies and 'internal' incentive structures and capital contingencies. Empirical research on economic developments in Taylor's, Simon's and Williamson's contemporary environments suggested that business organization and its conceptualization by organization theory mirrored environmental contexts. Future research has to further deepen ideas of an institutional economic approach to business history research as outlined in this chapter. This approach is likely to yield new institutional economic insights into organizational change, into the economic relationship between organizational change and environmental change and why in the face of environmental change no organization theory can provide a timeless answer to the question of business organization. Hicks' (1976: 208) suggestion on the temporary appropriateness of economic theory is taken seriously.

It goes unquestioned that organizational change can be explained in behavioral terms, the evolution of business organization being analyzed through behavioral variables, for example bounded rationality. Organizational analysis then researches a discovery process of 'true' human nature, providing a microscopic behavioral view on organizational change. Still, unless environmental insignificance or invariance were claimed, behavioral analysis has to outline how it heuristically and/or theoretically accommodates 'environmental assumptions'. Only if environmental change had no influence on business organization, an inward-looking behavioral analysis, which focused on firm size and behavioral attributes of organization members, could stand on its own ground. In this respect, the economic role of a changing environment remained underexplored and underconceptualized and, in degrees, misunderstood in Taylor's, Simon's and Williamson's studies.

In contrast to Taylor and Simon, who largely ignored the analysis of environmental influence on organizational change, it is to the merit of Williamson that he discussed organizational change in relation to environmental change. However, this discussion could have been methodically and theoretically sharpened through a non-behavioral, economic modeling of environmental change. Williamson seemed to undervalue economic aspects of environmental change, especially when he questioned and reformulated Chandler's, Hayek's, Alchian's and Buttrick's suggestions on this issue; when he compiled absolute efficiency ratings of organization structures, apparently assuming environmental insignificance and invariance; or when he made wrong predictions on the future development of business organization. Such shortcomings can be linked to a behavioral approach to organizational change, which originated in Simon's behavioral economics and which aimed at the holistic, 'true' portrayal of human nature in economic research. Insights generated by market structure economics, evolutionary economics, business history research, contingency theory and organizational ecology on the interrelationship of organizational change and environmental change were sidelined.

NOTES

1. Of course, 'adaptations through planning' can also be explored by organization psychology or institutional sociology.
2. For instance, Williamson's (1985: 52, 60–61) transaction attribute 'frequency' can be interpreted with regard to the variables 'market volume' or 'market potential'.

3.   A capital utilization model of markets can be developed into a stakeholder model that selectively interrelates an economic model of the firm with an economic model of the market (see Wagner-Tsukamoto 2002; Wagner 2000b: section 8.2).
4.   This hints that developments in marketing management, such as the onset of 'customer-oriented marketing' from the 1960s and 1970s onwards and 'relationship marketing' from the 1990s onwards, can be reconstructed in institutional economic terms.
5.   PESTLE analysis examines 'political', 'economic', 'social', 'technological', 'legal' and 'environmental' (ecological) factors when assessing questions of strategic management. 'Economic' factors are narrowly interpreted by PESTLE analysis in terms of macroeconomic developments, such as business cycles. An institutional economic reconstruction would treat all elements of PESTLE analysis as 'economic factors', approaching them in relation to concepts of incentive structures and capital contingencies. SWOT analysis identifies 'strengths' and 'weaknesses' of a firm and tries to match them with 'opportunities' and 'threats' in a firm's environment. Institutional economics can reconstruct strengths, weaknesses, opportunities and threats in relation to 'internal' and 'external' incentive structures and capital contingencies.
6.   Management research on organizational change, for example, the studies of Miles and Snow (1986), Palmer et al. (1993) or Senior (1997: 28–9), can be illuminated in economic terms, too.
7.   Also, clarifications on the problem-dependent nature of practical intervention, as discussed in Chapter 8, section 8.2, may be promising for contingency theory.
8.   Interestingly, the contractor system is not too dissimilar to matrix structures or network structures that (re)emerged about a century later (see below).
9.   Besides a high land–work ratio, a low capital–work ratio has been suggested as an explanation for comparatively high wages in the USA in the 19th century (see Temin 1973a: 120–21, 1973b: 166; Lebergott 1961: 290; Ulman 1961: 367–8). High wages may also partly explain an insignificant role of unions in the organization of industrial relations in the USA, as may strong ethnic inhomogeneity of the labor force have hindered unionization. Weak unionization in the USA can also be linked to lacking support of unions by a political party, as it is common in many other countries (Ulman 1961: 366–7, 381–91; Bendix 1956: 265).
10. Even at the turn of the 21st century, many organizations built on the ideas suggested by scientific management. For instance, in 1998, UK governmental authorities issued a minute-by-minute guide for primary schoolteachers. The guide specified how to teach elementary reading and writing skills, even detailing which words students had to be capable of reading and writing at certain stages of their learning process. Both the teacher and the student were brought under a program reminiscent of Taylor's and Simon's 'mechanizing' approaches. Competency rights of teachers were severely restricted. This program was not meant to 'dehumanize' teaching in the classroom but to ensure the uniform development of basic reading and writing skills.
11. A couple of decades later, the innovation of a production technology like the assembly line and the introduction of large, functional hierarchies reflected such a change in 'internal' incentive structures and capital contingencies, which was driven by changing 'external' incentive structures and capital contingencies.
12. In certain respects, output requirements began to resemble, once again, the more varied demands encountered in Taylor's time and even more so before Taylor's time when the organization of capital utilization mainly involved contractors and craftsmen.
13. One could fall back on sociological, Marxist-type explanations, invoking worker exploitation through ruling class 'managers' and 'employers', but it is doubtful whether Williamson would like to go down this route.
14. Rathenau (1918: 123): 'Es findet eine Verwechslung statt: zwischen den Eigenschaften von Entwicklungskontexten (Umweltkontexten) und den Eigenschaften von Menschen, in denen sie sich verkörpern.'
15. They also ignored the idea of opportunism, understood as a behavioral assumption. For conducting empirical measurements, such 'ignorance' appears necessary and fruitful and increasingly so when the heuristic nature of ideas like 'bounded rationality' and 'opportunism' in economic research is acknowledged (see Chapter 6).

8. Concluding discussion: The end of ethics *or* is economics the better moral science?

> At issue is human nature: How wise are we and what is the role of morality, emotions and social bonds in our individual and collective behavior? (Etzioni, 1988, p. xii)

> We can aim to promote as much cooperation as possible by deploying some reasonable degree of coercion and by supporting arrangements which encourage cooperation through self-interest, thereby making small demands on trust . . . This is not just *a* solution: it is possibly the *standard* solution, which, filtered through Machiavelli, Hobbes, Hume and Smith, has been handed down to the present day as the more realistic, economical and viable. (Gambetta, 1988, p. 224, emphasis as in original)

Behavioral researchers often suggest that economics perpetrated a morally questionable image of human nature because of the application of the model of economic man. The previous chapters here voiced caution. They argued that the model of economic man and, similarly, the idea of the dilemma structure are the wrong targets for discussing the image of human nature of economics. Section 8.1 follows up. It outlines how the image of human nature of organizational economics and its moral status as a social science can be differently assessed than by critiquing 'economic man' and 'dilemma structure'. Section 8.2 has an outlook on the question of interdisciplinary organizational intervention. It proposes that for certain problems, especially ones which reflect pluralistic interaction contexts, economic intervention may have to be prioritized over behavioral intervention – not only for effectiveness and efficiency reasons but also for moral reasons. Section 8.3 suggests directions for future research.

8.1 ON THE MORAL STATUS OF ORGANIZATIONAL ECONOMICS AND ITS IMAGE OF HUMAN NATURE

The book identified a generic pattern of economic analysis in Taylor's, Simon's and Williamson's organization theories, namely the heuristic ideas of the dilemma structure and economic man and the theoretical–(practical) concepts of incentive structures, capital utilization and mutual gains (see Chapter 1, Figure 1.2). By distinguishing heuristic concepts of economics from theoretical–(practical) ones, this book puts the question of the image of human nature into a larger than empirical–behavioral perspective. The subsequent discussion reviews whether Taylor, Simon and Williamson realized a methodical function of 'economic man' and 'dilemma structure' and that this had implications for a moral critique of organizational economics. The following substantiates:

1. In varying degrees, Taylor, Simon and Williamson assessed the image of human nature and the moral status of economics by critiquing the model of economic man and the idea of the dilemma structure in empirical–behavioral and moral–behavioral terms.
2. A behavioral assessment of 'economic man' and 'dilemma structure' is misdirected since it aims at heuristic concepts and overlooks moral outcomes of economic theory-building and practical intervention.
3. Like economics, behavioral sciences, moral philosophy and theology apply certain concepts that easily compare to the model of economic man and the model of the dilemma structure.
4. A favorable, liberatory, emancipatory and enlightened image of human nature emerges for economics once the methodological why and how of the research heuristics 'economic man' and 'dilemma structure' is transcended regarding outcomes of economic theory-building and practical intervention.

A Heuristic Interpretation of 'Definitions'?

Simon advocated that the start-up of scientific research should be approached as the 'definitional problem' (Simon 1977: xviii; see also Shen and Simon 1993: 649). Other behaviorally oriented researchers argued similarly, for example, Sen (1990: 29, 43) or Hollis and Nell (1979: 55). Although Simon realized that issues regarding the start-up of scientific research had been neglected in a methodology of social science (Simon 1977: xvi, 5–6, 326–7) – for example, Taylor or Williamson hardly elaborated on this issue – his suggestions on this problem are unconvincing. He found 'methodological inquiry interesting and instructive to the extent to which it addresses itself to concrete problems of empirical science' (Simon 1963: 229). In this respect, he ignored Popper, Lakatos and Gödel and their suggestions that certain ideas of scientific research are of a sub-theoretical, pre-empirical and quasi-tautological – heuristic – nature (see Chapter 1, section 1.1). He did not distinguish mere research heuristics from theoretical–(practical) concepts. On a related point, he implied that the definitional problem could be resolved in empirical–behavioral and moral–behavioral terms. Simon (1997, 1993b, 1976a, 1955) specifically developed this argument for the portrayal of human nature in economic research.

The F-twist debate well illustrates Simon's lacking distinction between heuristic concepts and empirically testable, theoretical–(practical) ones. In general, the F-twist debate was marred by Simon and Friedman differently interpreting the idea of assumptions. Friedman seemed to interpret 'assumptions' at times as *heuristic* concepts and at times as *theoretical–(practical)* concepts of *economic* research. When he interpreted assumptions in heuristic terms, he got close to justifying assumptions as a matter of problem dependence (Friedman 1953: 5, 23, 26, 35–6, 38–9, 41; see also Suchanek 1992; Machlup 1967: 11). In contrast, Simon (1963) merely interpreted assumptions as *theoretical–(practical)* concepts of *behavioral* research. He could rightly link them to empirical–behavioral observation (Simon 1977: 43). Supporters of Simon similarly argue, for example, Friedman (1996: 9–10), Boylan and O'Gorman (1995: 195–6), Nagel (1963: 211–14) or Samuelson (1963: 232–3). Musgrave's (1981) discussion began to clarify such ambiguities in Friedman's and Simon's reasoning. His suggestions can be detailed by explicating the heuristic, methodical status of certain 'assumptions' in scientific research. Lawson's (1992) and Mäki's (1994, 1992) critique of Friedman can be clarified in this respect, by interpreting Friedman as a 'heuristic fictionalist' (Black 1962: 228; see also Boylan and O'Gorman 1995: 109). Interestingly, Black made this suggestion before the F-twist debate erupted.

As Gödel's incompleteness theorem implied, an unresolvable issue in making assumptions or definitions or axioms is that they ultimately build on some undefined or unassumed or unaxiomatized concepts. A recursion problem exists that cannot be resolved from within a theory, neither logically nor empirically (see Chapter 1, section 1.1). The related attempt at *realistic* modeling is likely to be a contradiction in itself. It ignores the problem-dependent and heuristic organization of scientific research. In this respect, the present study shared Becker's (1976: 5) skepticism regarding definitions that are merely empirically set out: 'Let us turn away from definitions . . . because I believe that what most distinguishes a discipline from other disciplines in the social sciences is not its subject matter but its approach.' Popper's and Lakatos' suggestions on problem dependence and research heuristics detailed how to handle the recursion problem: If definitions reflect research heuristics, empirical accuracy is not an important issue but analytical fruitfulness, explanatory power, predictive power or design power are. However, if definitions reflect variables of a theory, they need to be scrutinized for logical consistency and coherence, empirical accuracy and, ultimately, practical effectiveness. Chapter 1, section 1.1 provided some more background information on this debate and section 8.2 follows up regarding practical intervention and design power.

A distinction between the heuristic and the theoretical–practical is frequently not made or not made explicit when researchers define or assume or axiomatize certain ideas. This has caused considerable misunderstandings among social scientists, especially regarding the portrayal of human nature in different research programs. Some minor imprecision may even exist in the works of Stigler and Becker (1977: 81–2), Becker (1976: 6–8, 283) or Friedman (1953: 41), who quite strongly hinted at the heuristic nature of research concepts such as economic man. For instance, if the idea of assumptions is used to refer to heuristic conventions, which Becker (1976: 206, 232) seemingly does, this may be better qualified by notions like 'pre-empirical', 'heuristic' or 'quasi-tautological' in order to prevent misunderstandings.

Economic Man and Dilemma Structure and an Unrealistic and Immoral Image of Human Nature?

Empirical–behavioral and moral–behavioral criticism of the model of economic man is widespread. The idea of self-interest is interpreted as an immoral character trait (for example, Schroeder 2001; Zey 1998; Morgan 1997; Sen 1999, 1990, 1987; Etzioni 1991b, 1991d, 1988).[1] Rowlinson (1997: 7–13) reviews comparable, behavioral criticism of the idea of the dilemma structure. If this criticism is accepted, the model of economic man may have to be replaced by a model of altruism and bounded self-interest, as Simon (1997, 1993b) suggested. And consequently, moral–behavioral intervention for solving social problems may have to be favored (for example, Zey 1998: 111; Herzberg 1966: 171–7).

Taylor, Simon and Williamson took over, in varying degrees, such suggestions of behavioral research. They did not clearly outline the heuristic purpose and nature of the model of economic man, in particular how it 'only' methodically instructs economic theory-building and practical intervention. In considerable degrees, they interpreted 'economic man' and 'dilemma structure' in empirical–behavioral and moral–behavioral terms and tried to modify these ideas on behavioral grounds. For example, Taylor modeled in claimed theoretical–(practical) terms workers as 'naturally lazy' and 'mentally insufficient' and managers as 'naturally cooperative'. Simon tried to behaviorally reform the model of economic man through psychological concepts of satisficing, bounded rationality and bounded self-interest. In similar behavioral economic tradition, Williamson aimed at the portrayal of 'human nature as we know it' and 'real people' (Williamson 1998: 2; for further references, see Chapter 6). He examined opportunism as a feature of human nature, which compares to Taylor's suggestions on natural soldiering.

He suggested modifying the model of economic man in moral–behavioral terms. On the other hand, Williamson indicated that the idea of opportunism reflected 'human nature as we generally do *not* know it' – an insight that hinted at the heuristic rather than empirical–behavioral relevance of this idea in his organization theory.

The idea of the dilemma structure was in certain respects also (mis)interpreted in behavioral terms. Taylor invoked antagonism in organizational behavior and analyzed it through the idea of systematic soldiering. This mirrored the application of the idea of the dilemma structure. But when encountering the problem of managerialism, Taylor gave up this approach and favored instead moral–behavioral theory and practical intervention. Simon criticized dilemmatic interaction concepts as unrealistic and explicitly rejected, on grounds of claimed analytical irrelevance, game theoretical concepts, both zero-sum and nonzero-sum models. Williamson implied that the idea of a dilemma structure, as illustrated by the prisoners' dilemma, reflected a dark world view, a 'bad game' (Williamson 1998: 2, 10–11), but then comprehensively analyzed contracting dilemmas for all kinds of social interactions, inside and outside a firm. Interesting in this connection are also views from outside economics. Nussbaum's (1986) discussion of the modeling of tragic dilemmas in Greek virtue ethics here is especially fascinating, in particular when she hints at a heuristic role of dilemmas in ethical theory (Nussbaum 1986: 1–2, 50–1).

Despite explicit empirical–behavioral criticism, many behavioral economists and organization researchers implicitly apply the model of economic man. For example, connecting to Simon, North (1993b: 13) claimed to reject the model of economic man on empirical–behavioral grounds. But he formulated as a research question of institutional economics: 'How to bind the players to agreements across space and time?' (North 1993b: 11) – and answered: 'Players can be bound when the gains from living up to agreements exceed the gains from defecting' (North 1993b: 11). Like Williamson, despite overt behavioral criticism of the model of economic man, North seemingly proceeded in conventional economic terms when drawing on a gains–loss calculus to examine the possible breakdown of cooperation. Similarly, Binmore (1998, 1994) basically applied the model of economic man and the idea of the prisoners' dilemma in heuristic terms but quite explicitly endorsed them in empiricist behavioral terms (for instance, Binmore 1998: 6, 13–14, 263–4, 286, 290–92, 1994: 18–19). Especially regarding the heuristic application of the model of economic man, the claim can be upheld that 'there is only one economic theory' (Becker 1971: viii).

To a degree, behavioral researchers sense a heuristic purpose of the model of economic man:

[R]ational economic man . . . is also the reason economists cite for their analytical success compared to the other social sciences . . . Economic man modeled in such a way becomes analytically tractable, whereas paradoxically, if he were a more reasonable person, he would be less tractable (Morgan 1997: 91; similarly Marsden and Townley 1996: 665).

If these insights are linked to a problem-dependent and heuristic understanding of scientific research, a claimed paradox regarding the model of economic man dissolves. Similarly, the claim that organizational economics applied a model of 'antisocial behavior' and that the model of economic man reflected 'guilt by axiom' (Donaldson 1990: 373) needs in this respect to be qualified.

However, behavioral researchers explicitly aim to replace the model of economic man through an empirically 'true', holistic, interdisciplinary portrayal of human nature. They suggested the portrayal of the 'whole man' (Morgan 1997: 78–9; similarly Marsden and Townley 1996: 671–2) or the 'total human being' (Herzberg 1966: 28) or a holistically reformed 'economic man' (Hollis 1994: 159). Taylor, Simon and Williamson followed this call in varying degrees.

Claims that Adam Smith or Mandeville dealt with 'whole man' (Morgan 1997: 78–9; Hottinger 1998 or Coase 1977, 1994 as indicated in Chapter 1) can probably not be upheld. Smith or Mandeville may still have been caught up between behavioral ethics, from which they exited, and economics, which they understood as an alternative ethics. The diagnosis of 'cynicism' (Morgan 1997: 78) in Mandeville's studies hints that he applied the model of economic man.[2] But even if the heuristic nature of the model of economic man was not clearly elaborated on by Mandeville and Smith, the defining aspect of their studies was that they gave up 'whole man'. This makes their studies stand out as the starting point of social science research and this is probably one of the reasons why we remember their research today.

In degrees, behavioral economists sense the conceptual infeasibility and practical ineffectiveness of a behavioral reform project that targets economic man. For instance, Williamson (1985: 44) admitted his own 'failure' to include moral–behavioral character traits when modeling economic agency. And he explicitly questioned the usefulness of cooperative attitudes in economic research (Williamson 1985: 51–52). Such theoretical skepticism was early confirmed by practical experiences of Taylorite factory managers or Quaker managers. They met practical ineffectiveness when applying a model of human nature that included moral–behavioral character traits (see Chapter 3, section 3.3; Chapter 4, section 4.1 and section 8.2). Reasons of such theoretical and practical failures in relation to a behavioral reform of 'economic man' are frequently not understood. Hollis (1994) and Sen (1990, 1987) here fell for certain misunderstandings. On the other hand, Persky (1995), Homann and

Suchanek (2000, 1989) and Machlup (1978: Chapters 10–11) clearly questioned the feasibility of a 'wholesale revision of the psychology' of economic
man (Persky 1995: 229–30).

   If the model of economic man is modified in moral–behavioral terms,
the analysis and resolution of interaction problems shifts towards psychology, sociology or behavioral ethics. But then, the authentically altruistic
decision-maker is required for resolving social problems. Kreps et al.
(1982) speak in this respect of an irrational choice-maker, who acted
against own rational interests (see also Ockenfels 1999: 166–71).
Institutional research here has a basic choice regarding the methodical
grounding of theory-building and practical intervention: It can heuristically invoke either 'rational fools' or 'compassionate fools', and in a
related, theoretical–(practical) perspective it can focus on 'uncompassion-
ate fools' or on 'irrational fools' (see Figure 8.1). These slightly inflammatory notions of foolishness may not be helpful for identifying the basic
heuristic and theoretical-(practical) concepts of economic research and
behavioral research, but, such provocation can bring out more clearly
misunderstandings regarding the nature of economic research versus
behavioral research.

	Economics	**Behavioral Research**
Heuristic 'conflict model' of human nature	'Economic man' in a 'dilemma structure' ['rational fool']	'Behavioral man' in a pluralistic context ['compassionate fool']
Theoretical–(practical) 'conflict resolution model' of human nature	Economic contractor in a pluralistic context ['incompassionate fool']	Behavioral contractor in a value-homogenous context ['irrational fool']

Figure 8.1   Different kinds of fools

Dark Images of Human Nature and Social Life in Behavioral Research?

The question can be raised why, apart from economists, many other thinkers on institutional issues favored 'dark' images of human nature and social life that compare to the model of economic man and the idea of the dilemma structure. For instance, Hobbes modeled the war of all and portrayed human nature as 'arch-egoistic' (Mintz 1962: 135, 143–6); Kant referred to devils who could create a decent society (Homann 1997: 14); Mill spoke of human nature as potentially evil; psychology invokes 'neurotic man' and 'psychic pathologies', to use Herzberg's (1966) terms; sociology draws on a model of social conflict in order to analyze the capability of 'behavioral institutions', such as value systems or role perceptions to create stability in social interactions (see also Chapter 3, section 3.3); post-modern behavioral organization research invokes 'organizational misbehavior' as an 'endemic' condition (Ackroyd and Thompson 1999: 1–3, 25);[3] and early on, the authors of the Old Testament modeled Adam and Eve as thieves and Cain as a motiveless killer of his brother.[4] Supposedly biblical theology, like other bodies of thought, invoked the model of 'sinful man', the dilemma scenario of the original sin and the break-out of 'war in paradise' for heuristic reasons (Wagner-Tsukamoto 2001b; Wagner 2000a).[5] It may well be the case that in a generic, heuristic perspective there is little difference among alternative approaches to institutional organization, each invoking a dark image of human nature and social life.

Despite such similarities between behavioral research and economics, few researchers have suggested that theology and behavioral sciences entertained an immoral image of human nature. To some extent, it appears astounding that behavioral researchers criticize the model of economic man and similarly the idea of the dilemma structure on empirical–behavioral and moral–behavioral grounds. Such a critique misses out on the heuristic function of economic man and the dilemma structure (and the morally desirable outcomes their application enables) and it overlooks that behavioral sciences heuristically invoke comparable 'dark' models of human nature and social life. To a degree, Cima and Schubeck (2001), two Catholic theological researchers, may sense this.

In an anthropological philosophical sense, the modeling of 'dark' images of human nature and social life can be interpreted as a reference to self-determination, namely openness towards a 'dark' side of human nature (see Chapter 3, section 3.1). If such openness did not exist, if agents consistently behaved in an authentically altruistic way, social problems would only show up as mere information problems. Then, most economic research but also most sociological, social psychological, philosophical and theological research could be shelved.

Economic Man, Dilemma Structure and the Car Crash Analogy

The model of economic man and the idea of the dilemma structure do not imply a practical-normative statement about human nature and organizational behavior. Still, the question can be raised whether and how tools could and should be assessed against certain standards of humane technology. It goes unquestioned that any tool, if misapplied, can yield immoral outcomes. In the hands of a thief, a driller may serve objectionable purposes, but not so in the hands of a dentist. Behavioral scientists frequently complain about negative moral–behavioral influences of economic thinking on actual behavior. For example, empirical research seems to suggest that students of economics behave less altruistic and more self-interested than students of other disciplines (Zey 1998; Hollis 1994: 126; see also Rowlinson 1997: 10–11). A comparable point is made by McGregor (1960) regarding managerial behavior and similarly by Donaldson (1990: 373, 379) or Mitchell Stewart (1994: 67–70), who connects to McGregor. Economics is then claimed to undermine behavioral ethics (Zey 1998; Hollis 1994; Etzioni 1988). This claim can be qualified.

If the model of economic man is perceived by students or managers or researchers as a prescription to act as 'economic man', this clearly has to be corrected. Equally, if the model of the dilemma structure is perceived as a call to engage in war-like, 'rationally foolish' behavior, this needs correcting, too. The remedy is to explain the purposive, heuristic role of 'economic man' and 'dilemma structure' in analyzing and intervening with organizational behavior and to point out socially desirable outcomes that are generated by applying these ideas. For example, Persky's (1995) metaphor of the 'guinea pig' is illustrative for outlining a methodical role of economic man. The remedy should not be to ridicule these analytical devices on behavioral or aesthetic grounds or on grounds of claimed political incorrectness. If the model of economic man is behaviorally corrected through a holistic image of human nature, this is likely to prevent the resolution of interaction problems, especially in a modern, pluralistic interaction context. Section 8.2 follows up regarding practical intervention.

It goes unquestioned that behavioral economics and economic psychology can empirically examine the occurrence of self-interested behavior in 'real life'. There is little issue to take with Rabin (1998), Donaldson (1990), Etzioni (1988) or Sen (1999, 1990, 1987) who, like Simon in the 1950s, reported that behavior resembling 'economic man' could be observed or predicted only to a limited extent in real life. But this insight may be of little relevance for understanding the methodical purpose of 'economic man' and 'dilemma structure' in economic analysis. Understood as heuristic tools, they are beyond empirical–behavioral and moral–behavioral scrutiny.

The purposeful, heuristic nature of economic man and dilemma structure can be illustrated through a simple analogy: the accident simulation setting of the car crash test and the use of crash dummies. Like economic man, the crash dummy compares badly with human nature as we know it. Made of wood, plastic, metal and wires the crash dummy reflects human nature as we never observe it in real life. And, aesthetically, the crash dummy leaves questions open, too. Also, accidents as simulated in the setting of the car crash test are empirically rather rare. In the real world, we are hardly ever involved in accidents. Still, crash dummies and crash test simulations are highly valuable for certain purposes of car design, namely the improvement of car safety. The application of these tools cannot prevent accidents, but, if accidents happen, this helps to reduce personal injury and material damage. The idea of the dilemma structure performs a similar function as the accident simulation in the car crash test. The application of the models of economic man and dilemma structure can ensure that mutual advantages result from social interactions and rational foolishness is prevented when even self-interested agents interact. From here, economics can make considerable moral claims (see below). Regarding their functional nature, accusations of 'economic man' and 'dilemma structure' as unrealistic and immoral images of human nature and social life are probably as manifoldly flawed as criticizing the crash dummy of immoral and reckless driving behavior in the simulation setting of the crash test.

The purpose of the car crash test and the use of crash dummies is to better protect 'real people' in 'real life', by advising and improving on the structural design of cars. Similarly, the application of the ideas 'dilemma structure' and 'economic man' viewed with respect to the resolution of interaction problems, by means of situational intervention with incentive structures, but *not* by means of intervening with the human condition. Of course, it is probably also a good idea to train car drivers better in order to reduce the occurrence of accidents but this reflects a different research program and requires different – pedagogic – strategies for practical intervention.

From an ethical, deontological perspective, one can criticize the car crash test for simulating the killing of people. A comparable moral–behavioral critique might be brought forward by behavioral critics against the application of 'economic man' and 'dilemma structure' and the examination of effects of self-interested choice on social interactions. Consequentialists probably have less of a problem with car crash tests in this respect since positive and negative outcomes of crash tests can be 'added up'. If positive outcomes of car crash tests, such as improved car safety, outweigh negative outcomes, such as a rise in speeding, because car drivers take higher risks due to perceived increases in car safety, no moral objections would be raised against car crash tests. In this way, ethical judgments can be made on the permissibility of car crash tests. Such considerations strongly hint that ideas like the dilemma structure and economic man have to be ethically scrutinized for socially desirable outcomes they generate. As the next section details, the ideas of the dilemma structure and economic man have little to fear in this regard.

Moral Qualities of Economics' Image of Human Nature

The critique of 'economic man' and 'dilemma structure' as reflections of an empirically incorrect and morally questionable image of human nature misunderstands the problem-dependent and heuristic nature of economic research and probably behavioral research, too. In a theoretical–practical perspective, this type of critique underestimates the extent to which economics can generate morally desirable outcomes by applying 'dilemma structure' and 'economic man'.

Economics analyzes self-interest and dilemmatic interest conflicts not in order to promote images of human nature and social life in an empirical–behavioral or moral–behavioral sense and even less so in order to normatively endorse self-interested behavior and the 'war of all'. Rather, it invokes these ideas in order to analyze and prevent disastrous social outcomes of the (potential) occurrence of self-interested choice. Regarding prevention techniques, economics favors the (re)design of incentive structures. This approach of economics implies a morally favorable image of human nature:

1. *Socially desirable outcomes* Economic intervention, in the tradition of Smith, aims at the creation of wealth for all. Chandler et al. (1997) and Chandler and Hikino (1997) review historical evidence. In general, economics approaches social interactions as nonzero-sum interactions. This is a normative dictum. Economics aims to design incentive structures that channel self-interested choice towards socially desirable outcomes: 'the wealth of nations', in Adam Smith words (see also Persky 1995: 225–6; Novak 1991; Stigler 1982: 6–7); 'mutual gains' (Williamson 1998: 5, 1985: 2, 72–80, 178); 'institutional utility' (Simon 1945: 202), 'national efficiency' and 'permanent prosperity for workers and employers' (Taylor 1911: 6–10, 27, 121, 1903: 20–21); or 'distributive justice' (Acton 1993: 125–32; Stigler 1982: 17–19; Hayek 1976). References to 'commonwealth' by Cicero and Locke (Knowles and Saxberg 1967: 32–4) or 'the wealth of a community of nations' by the Bible (Wagner-Tsukamoto 2001b) come close to Smith's ideal of the wealth of nations.

   Questions concerning mutual gains and the wealth of nations are unlikely to reflect questions of the past, as possibly implied by Sen (1990: 28) or Etzioni (1988: 1–3). It appears safe to predict that this issue and the related analysis of dilemmatic interest conflict or 'systematic soldiering', a 'contracting dilemma', 'group non-rationality', 'organizational misbehavior', 'rational foolishness', to use the terms of organization researchers discussed in this book, is going to remain a burning issue for the firm, the nation, the international community and any other social arena. This applies even more when modern, pluralistic, multicultural interaction conditions arise.

2. *Self-organization and democratic ordering* Adam Smith's idea of the invisible hand implies a liberatory, emancipatory vision of ordering social life. It does not imply unconstrained, 'unbounded' choice behavior. In order to generate outcomes like mutual gains, (institutional) economics relies on the 'invisible hand'. It does not intervene with the 'moves of the game', that is, individual choice behavior. And neither does it rely on a coercive, authoritarian ruler or a benevolent, virtuous tyrant or gracious philosopher king to solve social problems. Once incentive-compatible rules are set up, the 'invisible hand' is expected to coordinate interactions (Hayek 1996: 12–15, 1973: 41–6). In this respect, social interactions are expected to self-organize in the 'moves of the game'. Bauman's (1992: 55, 191, 193–4, 202–3) idea of 'self-constituting processes', which he identified as a defining feature of post-modern sociological research, appears compatible with this idea of self-organization of economics.

As much as institutional economics questions (behavioral) intervention with the 'moves of the game', it equally rejects a *laissez-faire*, libertarian approach that relied on the self-healing forces of the market process (Vanberg 2001, 1982; see also Gray 1992; Kukathas 1992; Minford 1992; Plant 1992; Stigler 1982). This tends to be misunderstood by behavioral researchers (for example, Cohen and Arato 2001: 186–7). Institutional economics advocates that the 'visible hand' of politicians (or managers, as far as 'private ordering' is concerned) intervened with the 'rules of the game', installing incentive-compatible institutional structures. Also, when comparing different types of constitutional ordering, such as democracy, 'Leviathan' or anarchy, democracy is likely to outperform – on economic grounds – alternative systems (Vanberg 2001, 1994; North 1990; Buchanan 1987a, 1975; see also Hayek 1979, 1976, 1973, 1960; Popper 1962). The economic approach implies in this respect codetermination regarding self-organizing social interactions and the democratic, institutional ordering of social interactions. Etzioni (1988: 3) errs in this respect when disputing that economics conceptualized codetermination. Economics' approach to codetermination may just differ from the approaches of moral philosophy, institutional sociology or social psychology.

3. *Pluralism, motivational autonomy and the economic enactment of moral-*
    ity Institutional economics does not advocate or imply that behavioral
    ethics are to be eliminated from social life. Morals, behaviorally under-
    stood, are 'tolerated' by economic interactions and rule-oriented
    economic intervention, mainly because they are unproblematic in
    economic theory-building and practical intervention. Pluralism is not a
    conceptual or practical obstacle in solving interaction problems in
    economic terms. This directly reflects economics' 'incomplete', motiva-
    tionally and cognitively undetermined model of human nature (see also
    Crisp 1997: 196–7; Coleman 1990: 4; Stigler 1982: 22).

    Bauman's (1992: xiv) suggestion that the project of modernity
    promoted 'reason-founded human order' *at the expense* of tolerance and
    autonomy – and of pluralism, one could detail – can possibly be only
    upheld for modern sociological approaches, such as Marxism, possibly
    even for Parson's structuralism (Kymlicka 2001: 217; Bauman 1992:
    35–6, 199) but not for the economic approach.[6] Similarly, Casey (2002:
    4–5) apparently criticized a *sociological* conception of the 'modern ideal
    of the social' rather than an economic one when she related modernity to
    a 'central system of institutional and behavioral regulation'.

    Behavioral, sociological and psychological approaches are potentially
    more anti-pluralistic in their orientation than economics, especially when
    they aim at 'religious conversion', 'value indoctrination' or 'social recon-
    ditioning', as Taylor, Simon and Williamson referred to behavioral inter-
    vention. Plato's (1999: 1254, 1317–18) discussion of the virtuous tyranny,
    protectionism, the restriction of freedom of movement and even a war for
    values can here be critically reviewed, too, especially if normatively inter-
    preted (Popper 1962; see also Binmore 1998: ix, 6, 272–3, 278–9;
    Fukuyama 1992; Hayek 1976: 144–7; Gosling 1973). In this regard, ques-
    tions regarding the quality of morality of behavioral ethics can be raised
    (see also Wagner-Tsukamoto 2001a).

    It may be short-sighted by behavioral researchers to claim a humane
    image of human nature, if the creation of 'virtuous man/woman' comes
    with considerable moral costs (besides rising 'economic' costs for main-
    taining a value consensus in modern interaction contexts). To a degree,
    economic intervention may even encourage the (re)-emergence of values
    and virtues – by resolving interest conflicts in economic terms and thus
    removing a source of conflict that can undermine moral–behavioral regu-
    lation. But there is also likely to be tension between economics and
    behavioral approaches. The institutional structures of the market econ-
    omy are designed to foster competition or 'non-cooperation' among
    firms (for larger moral goals, such as the wealth of nations). This poten-
    tially brings economics into conflict with behavioral ethics. Also, the

economic transformation of morals, behaviorally understood, into incentive structures and/or capital may be difficult to reconcile with a behavioral approach to ethics (see Wagner-Tsukamoto 2002).

4. *Learning and the cognitive autonomy of the individual* The idea of human capital, as discussed in Chapter 5, reflects a skills-based view of human nature. It attributes scarce, contingent and in degrees even unique skills to organization members. As simple as industrial skills may have been in the Taylorite factory, they were as complex and sophisticated at the end of the 20th century. Organization members were then conceptualized as knowledge workers (for example, Cortada 1998; Myers 1996) and firms as learning organizations and intelligence networks (for example, Child and Faulkner 1998; Argyris and Schön 1996; Baker 1996; Oswick et al. 1996; Pearn et al. 1995). Implicit to such conceptualizations are ideas like intellectual growth and self-actualization.

It can be speculated that the disappearance of undemocratic and feudal systems for organizing capital utilization was driven by economic developments (Buchanan 1995; see also Fukuyama 1992a, 1989; Knight 1948). Industrialization and here especially the need to upskill human capital in competitive interactions in a market economy probably speeded up the demise of inhumane and undemocratic institutions (Buchanan 1995: 142–7; Knight 1948: li).

Bauman's (1992: xxv) suggestion that the collapse of communism left the world without a 'collective utopia' overlooks that a utopia can be developed in different terms than in *collectivist* sociological, modern, post-modern or pre-modern ones. The points discussed above hint that the market economy or 'capitalism' may be more humanistic than behavioral ethics that directly focused on the human condition. Economics and the related market economy it advises on implies a social utopia but one that is heuristically based on *individualistic* but not collectivist behavior. Economics here marks out a 'way out of [collectivist] utopia', to use Dahrendorf's (1967) phrase. This way may even imply the 'end of history' – 'history' being understood in the Hegelian sense of societal development reaching a democratic, enlightened state (Fukuyama 1989a: 5, 1989b: 23, 28). This way out of utopia was sensed early on by Smith but, to a degree, probably already by the authors of the Old Testament. Indeed, if Smith's economics were not a moral science and did not promote a utopia, it would be difficult to comprehend why Smith, after decades of research on behavioral ethics and on the basis of a profound understanding of behavioral ethics, ultimately should have favored economics to address moral questions of society (see also Homann 1990: 4–5).

Calls for a moral–behavioral 'new economics' (Etzioni 1988; see also ibid: 1991a, 1991b, 1991c, 1991d, 1988; similarly Sen 1999, 1990; Prelec 1991;

Swedberg 1991b; Wilson 1991), as in degrees implied by Taylor, Simon and Williamson, may need to be qualified. The envisaged 'new economics' and similar, ethical aspirations of post-modern social science (for example, Bauman 1992: 203) are likely to merely re-enter an 'old' moral philosophy, from which Adam Smith and probably already the authors of the Bible exited – for moral reasons (Wagner-Tsukamoto 2001b; Wagner 2000a).

As Parker (1996: 486, 494) noted, in a globalizing world, diversity in organizational behavior increases greatly and with it the potential for interest conflicts. If this view is correct, a moral–behavioral 'new economics', like a behavioral ethics, is likely to face not only rising 'economic' costs but also rising moral 'costs', especially when a value consensus is advocated to overcome value pluralism. Regarding the quality of morality in modern interaction contexts, economics here probably outperforms behavioral ethics. To a degree, Baumann (1992: xxii) sensed this when he identified the 'ethical paradox of postmodernity'.[7] This influence of the interaction context on the moral quality of behavioral ethics and of economics is assessed in more detail in section 8.2 (see also Chapter 3, section 3.4).

8.2 'INTERDISCIPLINARY' COLLABORATION BETWEEN ECONOMICS AND BEHAVIORAL SCIENCES

The previous chapters touched on the question of interdisciplinary research, for example, when Taylor, Simon and Williamson tried to align psychological concepts of insufficient mental capacity and bounded rationality with economic research. This section has an outlook on this issue. It argues that the principle of the problem-dependent and heuristic nature of research forbids 'interdisciplinary' theory-building. The question of 'interdisciplinarity' may predominantly arise for practical intervention only. Casey (2002: 86) seems to agree on this point. The subsequent discussion complements a moral assessment of organizational economics, as begun in section 8.1. It stresses that economic intervention can resolve certain organizational problems more effectively and in a morally more acceptable way than behavioral intervention. The following substantiates:

1. The question of interdisciplinary organization research can be narrowed down to the question of how different research programs on organization can 'collaborate' for the purpose of practical intervention.
2. Interdisciplinary collaboration is best approached through a prioritizing logic, grounded in the idea of problem dependence.

3. If organizational intervention aims at performance problems, economic intervention has to be prioritized over behavioral one, increasingly so in pluralistic, 'modern' interaction contexts. Efficiency and effectiveness reasons but also moral reasons support this argument.

Problem Dependence and a Prioritizing Logic for Practical Intervention

Practical intervention nearly always faces the question of 'interdisciplinarity' either at the outset of intervention or as a result of it (Ordeshook 1996: 180–1, 188; Kappler 1992: 1326–7; Biervert and Held 1991: 7; Schanz 1982: 72–4). There has been no lack of disputes regarding how to handle questions of organizational intervention, especially regarding interdisciplinary intervention: '[O]rganization theory is the main subject taught under the heading of 'management' in many of our business schools ... [but] the practising manager did not as a rule understand the organization theorist and vice versa' (Drucker 1989b: 189). High failure rates of organizational intervention confirm such skepticism (Casey 2002: 11–12; Wolff 1999: 1–5, 29–31, 227; Uttal 1983: 66–72). A methodological void has been identified: 'Regarding the developmental stage of normative social research, the thesis of Wild (1988)[8] still applies today that a sophisticated methodology for social studies does not exist, neither in the field of management studies nor in other social science disciplines' (Wunderer 1988: 141; see also Casey 2002: 85–6; Wolff 1999: 30–31; Shenhav 1995: 557; Warner 1994: 1161; Noon 1992: 28; Wild 1988: 266–7, 288). This is the more puzzling since most social science research is initiated by practical problems.

In order to fill such a void, issues of method and subject matter have to be addressed: 'In discussing organization structure, we have to ask both *what* kind of structure is needed and *how* it should be built' (Drucker 1989b: 190, emphasis added). Noon (1992) makes comparable suggestions for human resource management. With regard to the issue of interdisciplinary intervention, these suggestions can be detailed by asking two questions: What theoretical suggestions about organization and organizational behavior should be selected, for example, economic ones and/or behavioral ones. And how should theoretical concepts of different research programs be interrelated for purposes of practical intervention. These questions can be addressed in relation to problem dependence, drawing on the same methodological principles as for 'disciplinary', theoretical research (see Chapter 1, section 1.1). This should facilitate knowledge transfer from 'theory' into 'practice'. In contrast, the unqualified advocacy of a 'prescriptive, interdisciplinary science of man' (Casey 2002: 86; similarly Pugh 1966) for solving problems in organizational behavior overlooks problem dependence. At least, certain problems in organizational behavior may be better addressed by prioritizing non-behavioral, economic intervention over behavioral intervention.

A problem-dependent approach to 'interdisciplinary' intervention can be set out by discussing 'from which direction' integration should be pursued. Basically two options exist: Behavioral knowledge is imported into an economic program. Alternatively, economic insights are imported into a behavioral program, for example, an organization development (OD) program. The former requires the reconceptualization of behavioral knowledge in economic terms; the latter requires the reconceptualization of economic knowledge in behavioral terms (see Suchanek 1992: 43; similarly Lindenberg 1990: 738–9). A methodology for interdisciplinary intervention here had to spell out two issues: how to decide the integration direction and what does the *reconceptualizing* of findings of one research program in the terms of another mean.

Problem-dependent prioritizing implies that the specific nature of a design problem has to be examined. If organizational problems reflect behavioral issues, for instance, personality clashes that are unrelated to performance issues, behavioral intervention has to take the lead role. On the other hand, if questions of contributions and distributions, broadly speaking 'performance issues', arise, economic intervention has to be prioritized over behavioral intervention. Also, interaction conditions deserve special attention: If pluralistic, 'modern' interaction contexts are viewed as unavoidable or desirable, economic intervention may have to be favored over behavioral intervention. The early Simon (1945: 253) seemingly realized such a need for prioritizing economics over behavioral sciences for intervening with performance problems. He suggested that management studies – he spoke of 'business theory' – is the practical science that built on the theoretical science of 'economics'. Contingency theory applies a similar prioritizing logic for practical intervention, which 'begins' with economics (Lorsch 1983). This is likely to reflect its interest in performance issues.[9]

The question of how to reconceptualize findings of one research program in the conceptual terms of another has to be approached in relation to problem dependence too (Homann and Suchanek 1989: 80). It can be suggested that knowledge transfer across research programs should be approached as a matter of 'pragmatic transformation': accounting for a chance of problem dependence when moving from one research program to another (see also Hoover 1994). For example, for knowledge transfer from behavioral research programs to economics, behavioral concepts have to be reconceptualized in economic terms: with regard to ideas such as 'incentive structures', 'capital contributions', 'capital distributions' or 'mutual gains'. Behavioral factors, such as fear of change or resistance to organizational redesign, can be reapproached in economic terms as expectations of loss of human capital in the course of organizational change. Institutional economics develops economic routes of how to handle fear of resistance, for instance, by compensating organization members for lost human capital (for example, Wolff 1999: 39–43). Or, organizational culture can be reapproached as 'social capital' (Coleman 1988) that is utilized – generated, transformed, consumed – in organizational behavior. The utilization of social capital can reduce production costs, lower transaction costs and/or yield certain capital gains (see also Wagner-Tsukamoto 2002). Behavioral problems of cultural inhomogeneity or distrust are thus examined as a costly deficit in behavioral capital. Suggestions of Hunt (2000: 186–90), Williamson (1993a, 1993b), Denison (1991) or Hesterly et al. (1990: 410) can be detailed in this direction.

The degree to which behavioral concepts like culture, trust or morals can be analyzed and reapproached in economic terms, heuristically grounded in a calculus of self-interest and the idea of dilemmatic interest conflict, is probably underestimated by behavioral research (for example, Scott and Christensen 1995: 310–13). For successfully intervening with performance problems in organizational behavior, such pragmatic reconceptualizations that attest to a change in problem dependence when using knowledge from different research programs appear mandatory.

It is to the credit of Simon (1945: 248–53) that he distinguished 'theoretical science' from 'practical science' by spelling out three types of propositions: theoretical ones, practical ones and ethical ones (Simon 1945: 248–9). He began to discuss important methodological considerations regarding how to bridge a theory–practice gap. This sets him apart from many social scientists who leave this issue open. For instance, Taylor and Williamson, despite their apparent interest in organizational intervention, hardly touched on a methodology for practical intervention. In this connection, Simon put forward the concept of tautological transformation. It suggests the 'semantic reformulation' of theoretical propositions into practical ones when moving from theory-building to practical intervention (Simon 1945: 248–50, 253; see also Schanz 1988: 39; Schneider 1978). Such semantic transformation can be accepted as intervention methodology for *intra*disciplinary transfer of theoretical knowledge into practical knowledge. In this respect, Simon's suggestions on semantic transformation cover a special case of pragmatic transformation.

However, for *inter*disciplinary intervention, the concept of semantic reformulation may be inadequate. It leaves all interesting questions open regarding how to transfer knowledge methodically from one research program to another and how to interrelate findings from different research programs. Of course, to Simon, semantic transformation had to appear as the general case since he had accommodated interdisciplinarity at the level of 'theoretical science' – when he outlined a unification-oriented, holistic approach to theory-building, especially regarding the portrayal of human nature. As previously discussed, especially in Chapter 1, section 1.1, Chapter 3, section 3.1 and Chapters 5 and 6, interdisciplinary theory-building encounters a complexity problem when attempts are made to unify theoretical concepts from different research programs in a single theory. Ambiguity regarding the formulation of research problems and questions is likely to result.

Other approaches to practical intervention remedy some of the shortcomings of Simon's concept of semantic transformation and the implied unification approach to theory-building. For example, the concept of 'theory pluralism' questions holistic, interdisciplinary theory-building. Theory pluralism suggests that theoretical knowledge of different sciences should be drawn on for the purpose of practical intervention but not for the purpose of theory-building (Kirsch 1988: 156, 1979: 118). Although, 'theory pluralism' does not outline how to interrelate findings from different research programs.

The concept of 'theory-free pragmatism' (Ulrich 1988: 177) probably comes closest to the concept of prioritizing and pragmatic transformation outlined above. It argues for purpose-oriented practical intervention – but rejects taking over the methodological principles of theoretical science for practical intervention. This may be wise if principles were ontologically or phenomenologically set out. However, the previous discussion suggested that such skepticism regarding the sameness of methodological principles of theoretical and practical science is probably unfounded. A problem-dependent, heuristic understanding of scientific research provides a sound methodological grounding for both theory-building and practical intervention.

It appears that intervention methodologies such as semantic transformation, theory pluralism and theory-free pragmatism are inferior to the discussed concept of pragmatic transformation and the way pragmatic transformation implies problem-dependent, prioritizing of knowledge for the purpose of interdisciplinary intervention. The implied sameness in methodological principles of theoretical–positive and practical–normative science helps bridge a theory–practice gap.

Is Economic Intervention more Effective and Morally more Acceptable than Behavioral Intervention?

Decisions on whether to prioritize economics over behavioral sciences or vice versa can be further specified by examining intervention criteria. For economics, 'pareto-effectiveness' is the meta-criterion for intervention. It reflects that a design proposal should yield stable, mutually advantageous outcomes in a cost efficient way (see Chapter 2). In contrast, behavioral intervention criteria focus on the psychological and sociological 'welfare' of the individual organization member. Herzberg, for example, advocated job enrichment that was to satisfy the complex behavioral needs of the 'total human being' (Herzberg 1966: 28; see also Chapter 3, sections 3.2 and 3.3). Similar criteria were proposed by the human relations school, behavioral business ethics approaches or post-modern, feminist and critical management approaches (for example, Vargish 1994; Alvesson and Willmott 1992: 16; Bernhard and Glantz 1992; Nord and Jermier 1992: 204–6, 218–19; Weinert 1987; Schanz 1982: 72, 84–5, 362; Kirsch 1981: 41; Fletcher 1973; Knowles and Saxberg 1967; McGregor 1960; see also Bauman 2001). Alvesson and Willmott (1992: 16) here explicitly argued for 'unashamedly utopian [post-modern] thinking in management'. On the other hand, Dahrendorf (1967) reminded behavioral researchers, in a modern manner, to search for 'ways out of utopia'.

The practical success of behavioral intervention is in doubt when it aims to integrate 'humane' intervention criteria with economic ones. The book here reviewed various examples, such as Herzberg's program to solve organizational performance problems though psychological intervention, the failing attempts of Quaker managers to reconcile religious ideals with economic ones or Taylor's unsuccessful moral–behavioral appeal to managers. Equally illustrative is the debate in the human resource management literature on whether 'soft' behavioral techniques and 'hard' structural ones were substitutive or complementary (Kamoche 2001: 16–18; Wajcman 2000: 266–71; see also Sanchez 1994; Noon 1992; Hendry and Pettigrew 1990; Schanz 1988, 1982). The present study proposed that only *after* organization structures have been made incentive-compatible, can behavioral intervention succeed. Problems of 'organizational misbehavior' (Ackroyd and Thompson 1999: 1–3), 'striking without quitting (Pruijt 1997: 15), 'theory X-type' behavior (McGregor 1960: 33–43) or 'incentive hygiene' (Herzberg et al. 1959; see Chapter 3, section 3.2) are in this respect often too narrowly approached in behavioral terms.

Only intuitively behavioral researchers sense that behavioral intervention is undermined because of a negligence of economic criteria and because of a lacking compatibility of economic criteria with 'humane' behavioral criteria. For example, behavioral researchers have been puzzled that practitioners use economic theories that have been falsified by behavioral sciences:

> The dominance of efficiency criteria [instead of humane criteria] implies that the practicing manager frequently applies theories – and they do so rightly – that have been proven wrong in the course of the growth of behavioral knowledge ... Theories that have been falsified still can be used for practical purposes since they are commonly good approximations. (Schanz 1988: 80)

Similarly argues Simon (1963). But possibly better than an empirical approximation function, a heuristic function and related issues of problem dependence can explain why managers (and scientists) 'still' apply certain unrealistic, behaviorally falsified concepts:

Organizational OD-techniques reflect a kind of normative activism whose success in its attempt to increase the efficiency of organizational change as well as to encourage the self-creation of organizational members remains questionable since, because of lacking methodological knowledge, the effects of problem dependence are overlooked.[10] (Staudt 1981: 117; see also ibid. 1981: 115–16)

Similarly argue Pruijt (1997: 103–6, 140–2), Shenhav (1995: 557, 579), Suchanek (1992: 41), Neuberger (1991: 258) or Drucker (1989b: 189–90). In general, the choice of intervention criteria is constrained by survival consider-ations. For the firm, this tends to lead back, in one form or another, to prof-itability considerations (Sutton 1998; Vromen 1995; Nelson and Winter 1982; see also Homann 1993: 38; Drucker 1989b: 189–93, 199; Porter 1985, 1980; Williamson 1967: 35–6; Friedman 1953: 22; see also Chapter 7, section 7.1). This implies that the application of behavioral intervention criteria is constrained by survival-related, economic considerations. This constraint is a formidable one since survival requirements are enacted on the firm through the market process and the way market processes are institutionally organized, through business laws and constitutional structures.[11]

As discussed, economic intervention provides a viable and morally accept-able route to solving social problems, and increasingly so in pluralistic, 'modern' contexts. On the other hand, the effectiveness of behavioral inter-vention depends on its capability to revise the condition of modernity.

Behavioral ethics, such as virtue ethics, duty ethics or religious ethics, handle social problems by locating moral responsibility and moral competence at the level of the individual. The aim is to create the 'good and true City and State [and Firm!]' through behavioral intervention, focusing on the 'regulation of the individual soul', as Plato (1999: 174) put it. The moral philosopher MacIntyre (1985) warned here, not dissimilar to Adam Smith two centuries earlier, that the effectiveness of behavioral ethics may be in doubt: modern society may have to ask what comes 'after virtue' (MacIntyre 1985). He seem-ingly implied that in interaction contexts in which pluralism is present and (pre)dispositions towards cooperative, altruistic behavior are fragile, morality, behaviorally understood, has little chance to flourish (see also Chapter 3, section 3.4). Such skepticism regarding a behavioral approach to social prob-lems is shared by many institutional researchers, by the early economists like Smith and Mandeville, probably already by the authors of the Bible (Wagner-Tsukamoto 2001b; Wagner 2000a) and Greek philosophers (Gosling 2002; Nussbaum 1986), and more recently by economic philosophers (Homann 1997, 1994, 1988; Gerecke 1997; Buchanan 1991, 1987b, 1975), sociologists (Cohen and Arato 2001; Coleman 1990; Luhmann 1988, 1984) and economic psychological researchers (Ockenfels 1999; Adams 1965).

In this regard, both cost considerations and moral objections can be raised for behavioral intervention. Lacking practical success should alert behavioral researchers to critically reassess a behavioral critique of economic man and an assessment of economics as an 'amoral', 'dismal' or 'dehumanized' science (for example, Etzioni 1988: 1–2; Williamson 1985: 391; Simon 1976a: xxi; see also Sen 1990: 30–31).

8.3   DIRECTIONS FOR FUTURE RESEARCH

Future research has to deepen issues and questions that emerged from the previous discussion:

1.   *Clarifying generic elements of the economic approach*   The book identified a generic pattern of economic theory-building – the heuristic concepts 'economic man' and 'dilemma structure' and the theoretical–(practical) concepts 'incentive structures', 'capital utilization' and 'mutual gains' (see Chapter 1, Figure 1.1). This scheme helps to clarify the basic nature of different 'types' of economic analysis, such as classical welfare economics, neoclassical economics, game theory, market structure economics, evolutionary economics, institutional economics or constitutional economics. Differences in their specifications of 'economic man', 'dilemma structure', 'incentive structures', 'capital utilization' and 'mutual gains' reflect differences in research problems. Under consideration of problem dependence, different 'types' of economic theory become compatible. In generic heuristic and theoretical terms, they probably can be reconstructed through the scheme presented by Figure 1.1 in Chapter 1.

2.   *Broadening institutional economic research on organization theory and management theory*   Economic reconstruction focused in this book on the organization theories of Taylor, Simon and Williamson. Other organization theories, such as the systematic management approach, the contractor system, Fayol's studies of industrial organization, Weber's bureaucracy approach or the studies of the human relations school, in particular Mayo's, McGregor's and Herzberg's works, await a more comprehensive assessment. For Herzberg's research, the book made some initial suggestions. Concepts of social psychology, especially Adams' (1965) inequity theory of motivation, deserves special attention, too.

      Also, if the argument has some substance that institutional economics provides a theoretically fruitful and practically effective route to handling social problems, an economic reconstruction of management theory other than organization theory may be promising. Economic reconstruction, as summarized by Figure 1.1 (Chapter 1), offers a route for management and organization theorizing to 'rediscover and renew connections with its own past' and demonstrate its relevance and usefulness, as called for by Warner (1994: 1163) or similarly Hesterly et al. (1990: 410, 415–16). Institutional economics may provide a conceptual blueprint of management studies, grounding it in managerial economics. Contingency theory, motivation theory and human resource management theory were touched on in this book. Concepts of marketing management, operations management or strategic management can be re-examined through economic reconstruction.

3. *'Interdisciplinary' research and application-oriented science*   The book argued that in theoretical and heuristic perspectives there is little room and need for interdisciplinary research. Owing to differences in research questions and approaches, economic and behavioral theory are unlikely to compete head on. Possibly unwittingly, behavioral researchers frequently raise economic questions when examining 'performance' issues. As much as economics has to remain silent regarding the micro-analytic, behavioral exploration of human nature, behavioral research has to acknow-ledge the fruitfulness and necessity of the economic analysis of 'performance' issues or the 'big questions', as Simon (1976a: xxi) put it.

   The book argued that the idea of 'interdisciplinarity' is best restricted to issues of practical intervention rather than theory-building. A frequently identified theory–practice gap for scientific research is probably caused by the attempt to negotiate 'interdisciplinarity' in a theoretical perspective (or worse, in a heuristic perspective). For application-oriented sciences like management studies or public policy studies, this debate of how to organize interdisciplinary collaboration appears highly necessary.

4. *Economics of ethical capital*   The book hinted at an economic theory of business ethics and stakeholder management. Such a theory appears fruitful for assessing whether and how markets and here especially the 'moves of the game' can take on a moral role. Once an idea like 'ethical capital' is aligned with the concept of stakeholder management, a coherent economic approach to business ethics can be proposed (Wagner-Tsukamoto 2002). This may imply that Friedman's (1970) suggestions on business ethics can be qualified: that market interactions (the 'moves of the game'), which involved the economic men 'firms', need not necessarily reflect moral-free zones but could develop into moral zones.

5. *Capitalist ethic of moral philosophy and biblical economics*   In addition to theories of business organization and management, economic reconstruction can aim at theories of society, such as Plato's *Res Publica*, Hobbes' *Leviathan*, Aesop's fables or the Bible. The interesting question here is how far the early writers on institutional issues discussed social problems in economic terms, for example, whether biblical proposals on metaphysical ordering were linked to economic cooperation principles and economic

concepts such as 'economic man' and 'dilemma structure' (for details, see Wagner-Tsukamoto 2001b; Wagner 2000a). Roots of a capitalist ethic in moral philosophical and theological thought can be searched for. The identification of a generic economic pattern in early philosophical and theological thought and the persistence of such a pattern in social analysis through time implies that the 'end of history' and the coming of 'the last man' was marked out much earlier than Fukuyama (1992, 1989a) suggests.

NOTES

1. But then, Etzioni (1988: 53), or similarly Markoczy and Goldberg (1998: 393), subscribe to a surprisingly 'egoistic' conception of altruism, namely offspring-related altruism. Bauman's (2001: 143) interpretation of the moral stance as 'attitude before relations; one-sidedness, not reciprocity, non-symmetrical' reflects a purer, more authentic concept of altruism – which Bauman claims to lie at the heart of post-modern ethics.
2. Morgan could claim the same for the legends of the Bible.
3. Post-modern, sociological research examines behavioral self-organization of interactions, recommending changes to structural imbalances of power in order to resolve problems of organizational misbehavior (Ackroyd and Thompson 1999: 150, 164).
4. Shakespeare's *The Merchant of Venice*, Act 1, Scene 3 here offers a poignant reading, too: 'Antonio is a good man . . . my meaning in saying he is a good man, is to have you understand me that he is sufficient. Yet his means are in supposition. He hath an argosy bound to Tripolis, another to the Indies – I understand moreover upon the Rialto, he hath a third at Mexico, a fourth for England and other ventures he hath squandered abroad. But ships are but boards, sailors but men – there be land-rats and water-rats, land-thieves and water-thieves – I mean pirates – and then there is the peril of waters, winds and rocks. The man is, notwithstanding, sufficient. Three thousand ducats – I think I may take this bond.'
5. Also, it could be suggested that Christian theology draws in a theoretical–practical perspective on certain quasi-economic concepts. For example, it offers incentives for good social conduct through promises of rewards or punishment in an after-world. Already Mandeville and Smith hinted at this interpretation. Such promises regarding an after-world can be interpreted as theology's program of incentive management, for encouraging cooperation in 'this' world.
6. Bauman's (1992: 199) suggestions on the 'politics of desire' can be reconstructed in economic terms: Ideas like 'heteronomy of choice' and 'autonomy of the choosing agent' may reflect, to a degree, the model of economic man.
7. For further critique of the post-modern project, see Thompson (1993) and O'Neill (1995).
8. Reprinted as Wild (1988), which is listed in the bibliography of this book.
9. Although, contingency theory (and similarly, concepts of 'soft' human resource management and behavioral business ethics) do not clearly elaborate on the distinction between the practica–normative and the positive–theoretical (see also Chapter 7, section 7.1). To a degree, it aims at 'interdisciplinary', 'unified' and 'general' theories of management. Social sciences then drift into anthropological philosophy (see Chapter 3, section 3.1). This also curtails 'interdisciplinary' collaboration among research programs when it comes to practical intervention.
10. Staudt used the terms 'Sachkenntnis' and 'Sachverwendung', which were translated as 'problem orientation' and 'problem dependence'.
11. If the survival criterion and the related profitability criterion are questioned, an ideological debate on the market economy and the organization of economic activity through different political systems is entered. This may be the case when the human relations school, behavioral business ethics or behavioral organization research recommend the application of 'humane, social welfare' criteria – independent of survival and profitability considerations.

Bibliography

Abell, P. (1995), 'The New Institutionalism and Rational Choice Theory', in W. R. Scott and S. Christensen (eds), *The Institutional Construction of Organizations: International and Longitudinal Studies*, London: Sage, 3–14.

Ackroyd, S. and Thompson, P. (1999), *Organizational Misbehaviour*, London: Sage.

Acton, H. B. (1993), *The Morals of Markets and Related Essays*, Indianapolis: Liberty Fund.

Adams, J. S. (1965), 'Inequity in Social Exchange', *Advances in Social Psychology* 2, 267–99.

Addis, W. (1983), 'A New Approach to the History of Structural Engineering', *History of Technology* 8, 1–14.

Adorno, T. W. and Gehlen, A. (1974), 'Ist die Soziologie eine Wissenschaft vom Menschen? Ein Streitgespräch', supplement to F. Grenz, *Adornos Philosophie in Grundbegriffen*, Frankfurt: Suhrkamp, 225–51.

Aitken, H. J. (1960), *Taylorism at Watertown Arsenal*, Cambridge, MA: Harvard University Press.

Alchian, A. A. (1950), 'Uncertainty, Evolution, and Economic Theory', *Journal of Political Economy* 58, 211–21.

Alchian, A. A. (1977), *Economic Forces at Work*, Indianapolis: Liberty Press.

Alchian, A. A. (1984), 'Specificity, Specialization and Coalitions', *Zeitschrift für die gesamte Staatswissenschaft* 140, 34–49.

Alchian, A. A. and Demsetz, H. (1972), 'Production, Information Costs and Economic Organization', *American Economic Review* 62, 777–95.

Alchian, A. A. and Demsetz, H. (1973), 'The Property Rights Paradigm', *Journal of Economic History* 33, 16–27.

Alvesson, M. and Deetz, S. (1996), 'Critical Theory and Postmodernism Approaches to Organizational Studies', in S. R. Clegg, C. Hardy and W. R. Nord (eds), *Handbook of Organization Studies*, London: Sage, 191–217.

Alvesson, M. and Willmott, H. (1992), 'Critical Theory and Management Studies: An Introduction', in M. Alvesson and H. Willmott (eds), *Critical Management Studies*, London: Sage, 1–20.

Antonelli, C. (1992), 'The Economic Theory of Information Networks', in C. Antonelli (ed.), *The Economics of Information Networks*, Amsterdam: Elsevier/North-Holland, 5–27.

Arena, R. and Longhi, C. (eds) (1998), *Markets and Organization*, Berlin: Springer.

Argyris, C. (1962), *Interpersonal Competence and Organizational Effectiveness*, Homewood, IL: Irwin.

Argyris, C. (1973), 'Some Limits of Rational Man Organizational Theory', *Public Administration Review* May/June, 253–67.

Argyris, C. (1992), *On Organizational Learning*, Oxford: Blackwell.

Argyris, C. and Schön, D. (1996), *Organizational Learning II: Theory, Method and Practice*, Reading, MA: Addison-Wesley.

Arnold, J., Cooper, C. L. and Robertson, I. T. (1998), *Work Psychology: Understanding Human Behaviour in the Workplace*, London: Pitman.

Arrow, K. J. (1974), *The Limits of Organization*, New York: W. W. Norton.

Axelrod, R. (1986), 'An Evolutionary Approach to Norms', *American Political Science Review* 80, 4, 1095–111.

Backhouse, R. E. (1994a), 'Introduction: New Directions in Economic Methodology', in R. E. Backhouse (ed.), *New Directions in Economic Methodology*, London: Routledge, 1–24.

Backhouse, R. E. (1994b), 'The Lakatosian Legacy in Economic Methodology', in R. E. Backhouse (ed.), *New Directions in Economic Methodology*, London: Routledge, 173–91.

Baker, W. E. (1992), 'The Network Organization in Theory and Practice', in N. Nohria and R. G. Eccles (eds), *Networks and Organizations*, Boston, MA: Harvard Business Scholl Press, 397–429.

Baker, W. E. (1996), 'Building Intelligence Networks', in P. S. Myers (ed.), *Knowledge Management and Organizational Design*, Oxford: Butterworth-Heinemann, 209–28.

Bancroft, G. (1958), *The American Labor Force: Its Growth and Changing Composition*, New York: John Wiley.

Barley, S. R. and Kunda, G. (1992), 'Design and Devotion: Surges of Rational and Normative Ideologies of Control in Managerial Discourse', *Administrative Science Quarterly* 37, 3, 363–99.

Barley, S. R. and Kunda, G. (2000), 'Design and Devotion: Surges of Rational and Normative Ideologies of Control in Managerial Discourse', in K. Grint (ed.), *Work and Society: A Reader*, Cambridge: Polity Press, 303–42.

Barnard, C. (1938), *The Functions of the Chief Executive*, Cambridge, MA: Harvard University Press.

Barney, J. B. (1990), 'The Debate between Traditional Management Theory and Organizational Economics: Substantive Difference or Intergroup Conflict?', *Academy of Management Review* 15, 382–93.

Barney, J. B. and Hesterly, W. (1996), 'Organizational Economics: Understanding the Relationship Between Organizations and Economic Analysis', in S. R. Clegg, C. Hardy and W. R. Nord (eds), *Handbook of Organization Studies*, London: Sage, 115–47.

Bartley, W. W. (1987), 'A Refutation of the Alleged Refutation of

Comprehensively Critical Rationalism', in G. Radnitzky and W. W. Bartley (eds), *Evolutionary Epistemology, Rationality, and the Sociology of Knowledge*, La Salle, IL: Open Court, 313–41.

Barzel, Y. (1989), *Economic Analysis of Property Rights*, Cambridge: Cambridge University Press.

Baum, J. A. (1996), 'Organizational Ecology', in S. R. Clegg, C. Hardy and W. R. Nord (eds), *Handbook of Organization Studies*, London: Sage, 77–114.

Bauman, Z. (1992), *Intimations of Postmodernity*, London: Routledge.

Bauman, Z. (2001), 'Postmodern Ethics', in S. Seidman and J. C. Alexander (eds), *The New Social Theory Reader: Contemporary Debates*, London: Routledge, 138–45.

Baurmann, M. and Kliemt, H. (1995), 'Zur Ökonomie der Tugend', *Jahrbuch für Ökonomie und Gesellschaft: Markt, Norm und Moral* 11, 13–44.

Beck, U. (1992), *Risk Society: Towards a New Modernity*, London: Sage.

Beck, U. (2000), 'Risk Society Revisited: Theory, Politics and Research Programmes', in B. Adam, U. Beck and J. Van Loon (eds), *The Risk Society and Beyond: Critical Issues for Social Theory*, London: Sage, 211–29.

Becker, G. (1962), 'Investment in Human Capital: A Theoretical Analysis', *Journal of Political Economy* 70, October, 9–49.

Becker, G. (1965), 'A Theory of the Allocation of Time', *The Economic Journal* 75, September, 493–517.

Becker, G. (1971), *Economic Theory*, New York: Alfred A. Knopf.

Becker, G. (1975), *Human Capital: A Theoretical and Empirical Analysis, with Special Reference to Education*, 2nd edn, New York: Columbia University Press.

Becker, G. (1976), *The Economic Approach to Human Behavior*, Chicago, IL: University of Chicago Press.

Becker, G. (1992), 'Habits, Addictions and Traditions', *Kyklos* 45, 327–45.

Becker, G. (1993), 'Nobel Lecture: The Economic Way of Looking at Behavior', *Journal of Political Economy* 101, 385–409.

Becker, G. (1996), *Accounting for Tastes*, Cambridge, MA: Harvard University Press.

Beer, M., Spector, B., Lawrence, P. R., Mills, Q. N. and Walton, R. N. (1984), *Managing Human Assets*, New York: The Free Press.

Bendix, R. (1956), *Work and Authority in Industry*, New York: J. Wiley.

Berle, A. A., Jr. and Means, G. C. (1932), *The Modern Corporation and Private Property*, New York: Macmillan.

Bernhard, J. G. and Glantz, K. (1992), *Staying Human in the Organization: Our Biological Heritage and the Workplace*, Westport, CT: Praeger.

Betzig, L. (ed.) (1997), *Human Nature: A Critical Reader*, Oxford: Oxford University Press.

Bhaskar, R. (1978), *A Realist Theory of Science*, Hemel Hempstead: Harvester.

Biervert, B. and Held, M. (1991), 'Vorwort', in B. Biervert and M. Held (eds), *Das Menschenbild in der ökonomischen Theorie*, Frankfurt: Campus, 7–9.

Binmore, K. (1994), *Game Theory and the Social Contract, Volume I: Playing Fair*, Cambridge, MA: The MIT Press.

Binmore, K. (1998), *Game Theory and the Social Contract, Volume II: Just Playing*, Cambridge, MA: The MIT Press.

Binmore, K. and Dasgupta, P. (1986), 'Game Theory: A Survey', in K. Binmore and P. Dasgupta (eds), *Economic Organizations as Games*, Oxford: Blackwell, 1–45.

Black, M. (1962), *Models and Metaphors*, Ithaca: Cornell University Press.

Blau, P. M. (1976a), 'Introduction: Parallels and Contrasts in Structural Inquiries', in P. M. Blau (ed.), *Approaches to the Study of Social Structure*, London: Open Books, 1–20.

Blau, P. M. (1976b), 'Parameters of Social Structure', in P. M. Blau (ed.), *Approaches to the Study of Social Structure*, London: Open Books, 220–53.

Blaug, M. (1974), 'Kuhn vs. Lakatos or Paradigms vs. Research Programmes in the History of Economics', in S. J. Latsis (ed.), *Method and Appraisal in Economics*, Cambridge: Cambridge University Press, 149–80.

Blaug, M. (1994), 'Why I am not a Constructivist: Confessions of an Unrepentant Popperian', in R. E. Backhouse (ed.), *New Directions in Economic Methodology*, London: Routledge, 109–36.

Bluedorn, A. C. (1986), 'Book Review: "Scientific Management by F. W. Taylor" ', *The Academy of Management Review* 11, 2, 443–7.

Boddy, D. and Gunson, N. (1996), *Organizations in the Network Age*, London: Routledge.

Boland, L. A. (1979), 'Knowledge and the Role of Institutions in Economic Theory', *Journal of Economic Issues* 13, 4, 957–72.

Boland, L. A. (1994), 'Scientific Thinking without Scientific Method: Two Views of Popper', in R. E. Backhouse (ed.), *New Directions in Economic Methodology*, London: Routledge, 154–72.

Boylan, T. A. and O'Gorman, P. F. (1995), *Beyond Rhetoric and Realism in Economics*, London: Routledge.

Bramhall, J. (1995), 'The Catching of Leviathan, or the Great Whale', in G. A. Rogers (ed.), *Leviathan: Contemporary Responses to the Political Theory of Thomas Hobbes*, Bristol: Thoemmes Press, 115–79.

Braverman, H. (1974), *Labor and Monopoly Capital: The Degradation of Work in the 20th Century*, London: Monthly Review Press.

Brennan, G. (1996), 'Selection and the Currency of Reward', in R. E. Goodin (ed.), *The Theory of Institutional Design*, Cambridge: Cambridge University Press, 256–75.

Brennan, G. and Buchanan, J. M. (1986), *The Reason of Rules: Constitutional Political Economy*, Cambridge: Cambridge University Press.

Brown, D. (1996), 'The "Essences" of the Fifth Discipline: Or Where Does Senge Stand to View the World', *Systems Research* 13, 2, 91–107.

Brunner, K. (1987), 'The Perception of Man and the Conception of Society: Two Approaches to Understanding Society', *Economic Inquiry* 25, 367–88.

Buchanan, D. and Huczynski, A. (1997), *Organizational Behaviour*, London: Prentice Hall.

Buchanan, J. M. (1975), *The Limits of Liberty: Between Anarchy and Leviathan*, Chicago, IL: University of Chicago Press.

Buchanan, J. M. (1987a), 'The Constitution of Economic Policy', *American Economic Review* 77, 243–50.

Buchanan, J. M. (1987b), *Economics between Predictive Science and Moral Philosophy*, College Station, Texas: A&M University Press.

Buchanan, J. M. (1991), *The Economics and the Ethics of Constitutional Order*, Ann Arbor, MI: University of Michigan Press.

Buchanan, J. M. (1994), 'Economic Theory in the Postrevolutionary Moment of the 1990s', in P. A. Klein (ed.), *The Role of Economic Theory*, Boston, MA: Kluwer, 47–60.

Buchanan, J. M. (1995), 'Individual Rights, Emergent Social States, and Behaviorial Feasibility', *Rationality and Society* 7, 2, 141–50.

Bürgenmeier, B. (1992), *Socio-economics: An Interdisciplinary Approach*, Boston, MA: Kluwer.

Burns, T. (1990), 'Mechanistic and Organismic Structures', in D. S. Pugh (ed.), *Organization Theory: Selected Readings*, London: Penguin, 64–75.

Burns, T. and Stalker, G. M. (1961), *The Management of Innovation*, London: Tavistock Publications.

Burrell, G. (1996), 'Normal Science, Paradigms, Metaphors, Discourses and Genealogies of Analysis', in S. R. Clegg, C. Hardy and W. R. Nord (eds), *Handbook of Organization Studies*, London: Sage, 642–58.

Burrell, G. and Morgan, G. (1979), *Sociological Paradigms and Organisational Analysis*, London: Heinemann.

Buttrick, J. (1952), 'The Inside Contract System', *The Journal of Economic History* 12, 3, 205–21.

Calas, M. B. and Smircich, L. (1996), 'From "The Woman's" Point of View: Feminist Approaches to Organization Studies', in S. R. Clegg, C. Hardy and W. R. Nord (eds), *Handbook of Organization Studies*, London: Sage, 218–58.

Caldwell, B. J. (1994), 'Two Proposals for the Recovery of Economic Practice', in R. E. Backhouse (ed.), *New Directions in Economic Methodology*, London: Routledge, 137–53.

Casey, C. (2002), *Critical Analysis of Organizations*, London: Sage.

Cassirer, E. (1962), *Leibniz' System: In Seinen Grundlagen*, Hildesheim, Germany: Georg Olms.

Casson, M. (1997), 'Institutional Economics and Business History: A Way Forward?', *Business History* 39, 4, 151–71.

Cazeneuve, J. (1972), *Lucien Levy-Bruhl*, Oxford: Blackwell.

Chandler, A. D., Jr. (1962), *Strategy and Structure: Chapters in the History of the American Industrial Enterprise*, Cambridge, MA: The MIT Press.

Chandler, A. D., Jr. (1965), 'The Beginning of "Big Business" in American Industry', in R. L. Adreano (ed.), *New Views on American Economic Development*, Cambridge, MA: Schenkman, 277–306.

Chandler, A. D., Jr. (1977), *The Visible Hand: The Managerial Revolution in American Business*, Cambridge, MA: Bellknap Press/Harvard University Press.

Chandler, A. D. (1997), 'The United States: Engines of Economic Growth in the Capital-intensive and Knowledge-intensive Industries', in A. D. Chandler, F. Amatori and T. Hikino (eds), *Big Business and the Wealth of Nations*, Cambridge: Cambridge University Press, 63-101.

Chandler, A. D., Amatori, F. and Hikino, T. (1997), 'Historical and Comparative Contours of Big Business', in A. D. Chandler, F. Amatori and T. Hikino (eds), *Big Business and the Wealth of Nations*, Cambridge: Cambridge University Press, 3–23.

Chandler, A. D. and Hikino, T. (1997), 'The Large Industrial Enterprise and the Dynamics of Modern Economic Growth', in A. D. Chandler, F. Amatori and T. Hikino (eds), *Big Business and the Wealth of Nations*, Cambridge: Cambridge University Press, 24–57.

Cherniak, C. (1986), *Minimal Rationality*, Cambridge, MA: The MIT Press.

Child, J. (1964), 'Quaker Employers and Industrial Relations', *Sociological Review* 12, 3, 293–313.

Child, J. (1984), *Organization: A Guide to Problems and Practice*, London: Harper & Row.

Child, J. and Faulkner, D. (1998), *Strategies of Cooperation: Managing Alliances, Networks, and Joint Ventures*, Oxford: Oxford University Press.

Ciborra, C. U. (1996), 'The Platform Organization: Recombining Strategies, Structures, and Surprises', *Organization Science* 7, 2, 103–18.

Cima, L. R. and Schubeck, T. L. (2001), 'Self-interest, Love, and Economic Justice: A Dialogue between Classical Economic Liberalism and Catholic Social Teaching', *Journal of Business Ethics* 30, 213–31.

Clague, E. (1966), 'Changing Living Standards of American Labor', in W. Haber (ed.), *Labor in a Changing America*, New York: Basic Books, 45–57.

Clarendon, Earl of, E. (1995), 'A Survey of Mr Hobbes His Leviathan' [spelling as in original], in G. A. Rogers (ed.), *Leviathan: Contemporary Responses to the Political Theory of Thomas Hobbes*, Bristol: Thoemmes Press, 180–300.

Coase, R. H. (1937), 'The Nature of the Firm', *Economica* 4, November, 386–405.

Coase, R. H. (1972), 'Industrial Organization: A Proposal for Research', in V. R. Fuchs (ed.), *Policy Issues and Research Opportunities in Industrial Organization*, New York: National Bureau of Economic Research, 59–73.

Coase, R. H. (1977), 'The Wealth of Nations', *Economic Inquiry* 15, 309–25.

Coase, R. H. (1992), 'Nobel Lecture: The Institutional Structure of Production', *American Economic Review* 82, 713–19.

Coase, R. H. (1994), *Essays on Economics and Economists*, Chicago, IL: University of Chicago Press.

Cochran, T. C. (1957), *The American Business System: A Historical Perspective 1900–1955*, Cambridge, MA: Harvard University Press.

Cochran, T. C. (1968), *Basic History of American Business*, Princeton, NJ: Nostrand.

Cochran, T. C. (1972), *Social Change in Industrial Society*, London: George Allen & Unwin.

Cochran, T. C. (1977), *200 Years of American Business*, New York: Basic Books.

Cohen, J. L. and Arato, A. (2001), 'The Utopia of Civil Society', in S. Seidman and J. C. Alexander (eds), *The New Social Theory Reader: Contemporary Debates*, London: Routledge, 185–92.

Coleman, J. S. (1988), 'Social Capital in the Creation of Human Capital', in C. Winship and S. Rosen (eds), *Organizations and Institutions: Sociological and Economic Approaches to the Analysis of Social Structure*, supplement to the *American Journal of Sociology* 94, Chicago, IL: University of Chicago Press, 95–120.

Coleman, J. S. (1990), *Foundations of Social Theory*, Cambridge, MA: Harvard University Press.

Commons, J. R. (1931), 'Institutional Economics', *American Economic Review* 21, 648–57.

Commons, J. R. (1961), *Institutional Economics: Its Place in Political Economy*, Madison, WI: University of Wisconsin Press.

Copley, F. B. (1919), 'Frederick W. Taylor: Revolutionist', in F. W. Taylor (ed.), *Two Papers on Scientific Management*, London: Routledge & Sons, 1–30.

Cortada, J. W. (1998), *Rise of the Knowledge Worker*, Boston, MA: Butterworth-Heinemann.

Coughlin, R. M. (1991), 'The Economic Person in Sociological Context: Case Studies in the Mediation of Self-interest', in A. Etzioni and P. R. Lawrence (eds), *Socio-economics: Toward a New Synthesis*, Armonk, NY: M. E. Sharpe, 35–57.

Cowen, T. and Parker, D. (1997), *Markets in the Firm: A Market-process Approach to Management*, London: Institute of Economic Affairs.

Crisp, R. (1997), *Mill on Utilitarianism*, London: Routledge.

Cyert, R. M. and March, J. G. (1963), *A Behavioral Theory of the Firm*, Englewood Cliffs, NJ: Prentice-Hall.

Cyert, R. M. and March, J. G. (1992), *A Behavioral Theory of the Firm*, 2nd edn., Cambridge, MA: Blackwell.

Czarniawska-Joerges, B. (1988), *Ideological Control in Nonideological Organizations*, New York: Praeger.

Dahrendorf, R. (1967), *Pfade aus Utopia*, Munich: R. Piper.

Dahrendorf, R. (1973), *Homo Sociologicus*, London: Routledge & Kegan Paul.

D'Amour, G. (1976), 'Research Programs, Rationality, and Ethics', in R. S. Cohen, P. Feyerabend and M. W. Wartofsky (eds), *Essays in Memory of Imre Lakatos*, Dordrecht: D. Reidel, 87–98.

Dasgupta, P. (1988), 'Trust as Commodity', in D. Gambetta (ed.), *Trust: Making and Breaking Cooperative Relations*, Oxford: Blackwell, 49–72.

Dasgupta, S. (1991), *Design Theory and Computer Science*, Cambridge: Cambridge University Press.

Denison, D. R. (1991), 'Organizational Culture and "Collective" Human Capital', in A. Etzioni and P. R. Lawrence (eds), *Socio-economics: Toward a New Synthesis*, Armonk, NY: M. E. Sharpe, 263–73.

Derickson, A. (1994), 'Physiological Science and Scientific Management in the Progressive Era: Frederic S. Lee and the Committee on Industrial Fatigue', *Business History Review* 68, 4, 483–514.

DiMaggio, P. J. and Powell, W. W. (1991a), 'Introduction', in W. W. Powell and P. J. DiMaggio (eds), *The New Institutionalism in Organizational Analysis*, Chicago, IL: University of Chicago Press, 1–40.

DiMaggio, P. J. and Powell, W. W. (1991b), 'The Iron Cage Revisited: Institutional Isomorphism and Collective Rationality in Organization Fields', in W. W. Powell and P. J. DiMaggio (eds), *The New Institutionalism in Organizational Analysis*, Chicago, IL: University of Chicago Press, 63–82.

Donaldson, L. (1990), 'The Ethereal Hand: Organizational Economics and Management Theory', *Academy of Management Review* 15, 369–81.

Donaldson, L. (1995), *American Anti-management Theories of Organization: A Critique of Paradigm Proliferation*, Cambridge: Cambridge University Press.

Donaldson, L. (1996a), *For Positivist Organization Theory: Proving the Hard Core*, London: Sage.

Donaldson, L. (1996b), 'The Normal Science of Structural Contingency Theory', in S. R. Clegg, C. Hardy and W. R. Nord (eds), *Handbook of Organization Studies*, London: Sage, 57–76.

Dosi, G. (1997), 'Organizational Competences, Firm Size, and the Wealth of

Nations: Some Comments from a Comparative Perspective', in A. D. Chandler, F. Amatori and T. Hikino (eds), *Big Business and the Wealth of Nations*, Cambridge: Cambridge University Press, 465–79.

Dosi, G. and Nelson, R. R. (1998), 'Evolutionary Theories', in R. Arena and C. Longhi (eds), *Markets and Organization*, Berlin: Springer, 205–34.

Dosi, G. and Teece, D. J. (1998), 'Organizational Competences and the Boundaries of the Firm', in R. Arena and C. Longhi (eds), *Markets and Organization*, Berlin: Springer, 281–302.

Doucouliagos, C. (1994), 'A Note on the Evolution of Homo Economicus', *Journal of Economic Issues* 3, 877–83.

Dougherty, D. (1996), 'Organizing for Innovation', in S. R. Clegg, C. Hardy and W. R. Nord (eds), *Handbook of Organization Studies*, London: Sage, 424–39.

Drucker, P. F. (1989a), *The New Realities*, New York: Harper & Row.

Drucker, P. F. (1989b), *The Practice of Management*, revised paperback edition, Oxford: Heinemann.

Drury, H. B. (1968), *Scientific Management: A History and Criticism*, New York: AMS Press (University of Columbia Press).

Dugger, W. M. (1984), 'Methodology Differences between Institutional and Neoclassical Economics', in D. M. Hausman (ed.), *The Philosophy of Economics: An Anthology,* Cambridge: Cambridge University Press, 312–22.

Dürkheim, D. E. (1982), *The Rules of Sociological Method*, London: Macmillan.

Eggertsson, T. (1993), 'Comment: "Mental Models and Social Values: North's Institutions and Credible Commitment" ', *Journal of Institutional and Theoretical Economics* 149, 1, 24–8.

Eire, C. M. N. (1986), *War Against the Idols: The Reformation of Worship from Erasmus to Calvin*, Cambridge: Cambridge University Press.

Elster, J. (1983), *Sour Grapes: Studies in the Subversion of Rationality*, Cambridge: Cambridge University Press.

Elster, J. (1989), 'Social Norms and Economic Theory', *Journal of Economic Perspectives* 3, 4, 99–117.

Elster, J. (1990), 'Selfishness and Altruism', in J. J. Mansbridge (ed.), *Beyond Self-interest*, Chicago, IL: University of Chicago Press, 44–52.

England, P. (1993), 'The Separative Self: Androcentric Bias in Neoclassical Assumptions', in M. A. Ferber and J. A. Nelson (eds), *Beyond Economic Man: Feminist Theory and Economics*, Chicago, IL: University of Chicago Press, 37–53.

Etzioni, A. (1975), *A Comparative Analysis of Complex Organizations*, New York: The Free Press.

Etzioni, A. (1988), *The Moral Dimension: Towards a New Economics*, New York: The Free Press.

Etzioni, A. (1991a), 'Socio-economics: A Budding Challenge', in A. Etzioni and P. R. Lawrence (eds), *Socio-economics: Toward a New Synthesis*, Armonk, NY: M. E. Sharpe, 3–7.

Etzioni, A. (1991b), 'Contemporary Liberals, Communitarians, and Individual Choices', in A. Etzioni and P. R. Lawrence (eds), *Socio-economics: Toward a New Synthesis*, Armonk, NY: M. E. Sharpe, 59–73.

Etzioni, A. (1991c), 'Socio-economics: The Next Steps', in A. Etzioni and P. R. Lawrence (eds), *Socio-economics: Toward a New Synthesis*, Armonk, NY: M. E. Sharpe, 347–52.

Etzioni, A. (1991d), *The Spirit of Community: Rights, Responsibilities and the Communitarian Agenda*, London: Fontana.

Fabricant, S. (1942), *Employment in Manufacturing 1899–1939*, New York: National Bureau of Economic Research Inc.

Fama, E. (1980), 'Agency Problems and the Theory of the Firm', *Journal of Political Economy* 88, 2, 288–307.

Ferber, M. A. and Nelson, J. A. (1993), 'Preface', in M. A. Ferber and J. A. Nelson (eds), *Beyond Economic Man: Feminist Theory and Economics*, Chicago, IL: University of Chicago Press, vii.

Feyerabend, P. K. (1993), *Against Method*, London: Verso.

Fiedler, F. E. (1990), 'Situational Control and a Dynamic Theory of Leadership', in D. S. Pugh (ed.), *Organization Theory: Selected Readings*, London: Penguin, 417–38.

Filmer, R. (1995), 'Observations on Mr Hobbes's Leviathan', in G. A. Rogers (ed.), *Leviathan: Contemporary Responses to the Political Theory of Thomas Hobbes*, Bristol: Thoemmes Press, 1–14.

Flannery, T. P., Hofrichter, D. A. and Platten, P. E. (1996), *People, Performance, and Pay*, New York: The Free Press.

Fletcher, C. (1973), 'The End of Management', in J. Child (ed.), *Man and Organization: The Search for Explanation and Social Relevance*, London: George Allen & Unwin, 135–57.

Freeman, R. E. (1984), *Strategic Management: A Stakeholder Approach*, Boston, MA: Pitman.

Friedman, J. (1996), 'Introduction: Economic Approaches to Politics', in J. Friedman (ed.), *The Rational Choice Controversy: Economic Models of Politics Reconsidered*, New Haven, CT: Yale University Press, 1–24.

Friedman, M. (1953), *Essays in Positive Economics*, Chicago, IL: University of Chicago Press.

Friedman, M. (1970), 'The Social Responsibility of Business is to Increase its Profits', *New York Times Magazine*, 13 September 1970.

Fukuyama, F. (1989a), 'The End of History', *The National Interest* 16, Summer, 3–18.

Fukuyama, F. (1989b), 'A Reply to My Critics', *The National Interest* 18, Winter, 21–8.

Fukuyama, F. (1992), *The End of History and the Last Man*, London: Penguin.

Fuller, S. (1993), *Philosophy, Rhetoric and the End of Knowledge*, Madison, WI: University of Wisconsin Press.

Fullerton, R. A. (1988), 'How Modern is Modern Marketing? Marketing's Evolution and the Myth of the "Production Era" ', *Journal of Marketing* 52, 108–25.

Furubotn, E. G. and Richter, R. (1991), 'The New Institutional Economics: An Assessment', in E. G. Furubotn and R. Richter (eds), *The New Institutional Economics*, College Station, Texas: A&M Press, 1–32.

Gadamer, H. G. (1943), 'Was ist der Mensch?', *Illustrierte Zeitung*, Kultursonderausgabe 100, 31–4.

Galbraith, J. K. (1977), *The Age of Uncertainty*, London: BBC/Andre Deutsch.

Gambetta, D. (1988), 'Can We Trust Trust?', in D. Gambetta (ed.), *Trust: Making and Breaking Cooperative Relations*, Oxford: Blackwell, 213–37.

Gantt, H. L. (1919), *Organizing for Work*, New York: Harcourt, Brace & Company.

Gehlen, A. (1962), *Der Mensch: Seine Natur und Stellung in der Welt*, Frankfurt: Anthenaion.

Georcescu-Roegen, N. (1971), *The Entropy Law and Economic Progress*, Cambridge, MA: Harvard University Press.

Gerecke, U. (1997), *Soziale Ordnung in der modernen Gesellschaft: Zum Diskurs von Ökonomik, Systemtheorie und Ethik,* Doctoral Dissertation, Wirtschaftswissenschaftliche Fakultät Ingolstadt, Katholische Universität Eichstätt.

Ghosal, S. and Bartlett, C. A. (1990), 'The Multinational Corporation as an Interorganizational Network', *Academy of Management Review* 15, 4, 603–25.

Giddens, A. (1991), *Modernity and Self-identity in the Late Modern Age*, Cambridge: Polity Press.

Gilboy, E. W. and Hoover, E. M. (1961), 'Population and Immigration', in S. E. Harris (ed.), *American Economic History*, New York: McGraw-Hill, 247–80.

Goldberg, D. J. (1992), 'Richard A. Feiss, Mary Barnett Gilson, and Scientific Management at Joseph & Feiss, 1909–1925', in D. Nelson (ed.), *A Mental Revolution: Scientific Management Since Taylor*, Columbus, OH: Ohio State University Press, 40–57.

Gomberg, L. (1903), *Handelsbetriebslehre und Einzelwirtschaftslehre*, Leipzig: B. G. Teubner.

Good, D. (1988), 'Individuals, Interpersonal Relations, and Trust', in D. Gambetta (ed.), *Trust: Making and Breaking Cooperative Relations,* Oxford: Blackwell, 31–48.

Goodin, R. E. (1996), 'Institutions and their Design', in R. E. Goodin (ed.), *The Theory of Institutional Design*, Cambridge: Cambridge University Press, 1–53.

Gordon, B. (1989), *The Economic Problem in Biblical and Patristic Thought*, Leiden and New York: E. J. Brill.

Gosling, J. (2002), 'Idealism in the Face of Tragic Realities', Conference Paper, Reason in Practice/Journal of Philosophy of Management Conference, 26–29 June 2002, Oxford: St. Anne's College.

Gosling, J. C. B. (1973), *Plato*, London: Routledge & Kegan Paul.

Granovetter, M. (1992), 'Problems of Explanation in Economic Sociology', in N. Nohria and R. G. Eccles (eds), *Newtworks and Organizations*, Boston, MA: Harvard Business School Press, 25–56.

Gray, J. (1992), *The Moral Foundations of Market Institutions*, London: IEA Health and Welfare Unit.

Greeley, A. M. (1993), 'Bricolage Amongst the Trash Cans', *Culture and Society* 30, 2, 70–75.

Green, D. P. and Shapiro, I. (1996), 'Pathologies Revisited: Reflections on our Critics', in J. Friedman (ed.), *The Rational Choice Controversy: Economic Models of Politics Reconsidered*, New Haven, CT: Yale University Press, 235–76.

Guillen, M. F. (1994), 'The Age of Eclecticism: Current Organizational Trends and the Evolution of Managerial Models', *Sloan Management Review* 36, 1, 75–86.

Guillen, M. F. (1997), 'Scientific Management's Lost Aesthetic: Architecture, Organization, and the Taylorized Beauty of the Mechanical', *Administrative Science Quarterly* 42, 682–715.

Gulick, L. and Urwick, L. (1937), *Papers on the Science of Administration*, New York: Institute of Public Administration.

Gutman, H. (1976), *Work, Culture, and Society in Industrializing America*, New York: Alfred A. Knopf.

Habakkuk, H. J. (1967), *American and British Technology in the Nineteenth Century*, Cambridge: Cambridge University Press.

Habakkuk, H. J. (1968), *Industrial Organization since the Industrial Revolution*, Southampton: University of Southampton Press.

Hahn, F. (1991), 'The Next Hundred Years', *Economic Journal* 101, 404, 47–50.

Hahn, F. and Hollis, M. (1979), 'Introduction', in F. Hahn and M. Hollis (eds), *Philosophy and Economic Theory*, Oxford: Oxford University Press, 1–17.

Hakansson, H. and Johanson, J. (1993), 'The Network as a Governance Structure: Interfirm Cooperation beyond Markets and Hierarchies', in G. Grabher (ed.), *The Embedded Firm: On the Socioeconomics of Industrial Networks*, London: Routledge, 35–51.

Hands, D. W. (1993), 'Popper and Lakatos in Economic Methodology', in U. Mäki, B. Gustafsson and C. Knudsen (eds), *Rationality, Institutions and Economic Methodology*, London: Routledge, 61–75.

Hardin, G. (1968), 'The Tragedy of the Commons', *Science* 162, 1243–8.

Hardin, G. (1993), *Living Within Limits: Ecology, Economics and Population Taboos*, Oxford: Oxford University Press.

Hardin, R. (1982), *Collective Action*, Baltimore: The Johns Hopkins University Press.

Hardin, R. (1996), 'Institutional Morality', in R. E. Goodin (ed.), *The Theory of Institutional Design*, Cambridge: Cambridge University Press, 126–53.

Hart, H. L. A. (1961), *The Concept of Law*, Oxford: Oxford University Press.

Hart, O. (1995), 'An Economist's Perspective on the Theory of the Firm', in O. E. Williamson (ed.), *Organization Theory: From Chester Barnard to the Present and Beyond*, New York: Oxford University Press, 154–71.

Hassard, J. (1993), 'Postmodernism and Organizational Analysis: An Overview', in J. Hassard and M. Parker (eds), *Postmodernism and Organizations*, London: Sage, 1–23.

Hatch, M. J. (1997), *Organization Theory: Modern, Symbolic, and Postmodern Perspectives*, Oxford: Oxford University Press.

Hausman, D. M. (1994), 'Kuhn, Lakatos and the Character of Economics', in R. E. Backhouse (ed.), *New Directions in Economic Methodology*, London: Routledge, 195–215.

Hayek, F. A. (1945), 'The Use of Knowledge in Society', *American Economic Review* 35, 4, 519–30.

Hayek, F. A. (1949), *Individualism and Economic Order*, London: Routledge & Kegan Paul.

Hayek, F. A. (1960), *The Constitution of Liberty*, London: Routledge & Kegan Paul.

Hayek, F. A. (1973), *Law, Legislation and Liberty: Rules and Order*, Vol. I, London: Routledge & Kegan Paul.

Hayek, F. A. (1976), *Law, Legislation and Liberty: The Mirage of Social Justice*, Vol. II, London: Routledge & Kegan Paul.

Hayek, F. A. (1979), *Law, Legislation and Liberty: The Political Order of a Free People,* Vol. III, London: Routledge & Kegan Paul.

Hayek, F. A. (1996), 'The Use of Knowledge in Society', in P. S. Myers (ed.), *Knowledge Management and Organizational Design*, Oxford: Butterworth-Heinemann, 7–15.

Hedström, P. and Swedberg, R. (1996), 'Rational Choice, Empirical Research, and the Sociological Tradition', *European Sociological Review* 12, 2, 127–46.

Heinen, E. (1976), *Grundfragen der entscheidungsorientierten Betriebswirtschaftslehre*, Munich: Goldmann.

Held, M. (1991), ' "Die Ökonomik hat kein Menschenbild" – Institutionen, Normen, Menschenbild', in B. Biervert and M. Held (eds), *Das Menschenbild in der ökonomischen Theorie*, Frankfurt: Campus, 10–41.

Hendry, C. and Pettigrew, A. (1990), 'Human Resource Management: An Agenda for the 1990s', *International Human Resource Management Journal* 1, 1, 17–43.

Herms, E. (1993), 'Mensch: Menschenbild', in G. Enderele (ed.), *Lexikon der Wirtschaftsethik*, Freiburg: Herder, 676–87.

Herzberg, F. (1966), *Work and the Nature of Man*, London: Staples Press.

Herzberg, F. (1982), 'Jumping for the Jelly Beans', *Management Classics*, London: BBC Training Videos.

Herzberg, F., Mausner, B. and Snyderman, B. (1959), *The Motivation to Work*, New York: John Wiley.

Hesterly, W. S., Lieberskind, J. and Zenger, T. R. (1990), 'Organizational Economics: An Impending Revolution in Organization Theory?', *Academy of Management Review* 15, 402–20.

Heyne, P. (1999), *The Economic Way of Thinking*, Upper Saddle River, NJ: Prentice-Hall.

Hickerson, S. E. (1987), 'The Normative Compass of Institutional Economics', *Journal of Economic Issues* 21, 1117–43.

Hicks, J. R. (1976), ' "Revolution' in Economics", in S. J. Latsis (ed.), *Method and Appraisal in Economics*, Cambridge: Cambridge University Press, 207–18.

Hikino, T. (1997), 'Managerial Control, Capital Markets, and the Wealth of Nations', in A. D. Chandler, F. Amatori and T. Hikino (eds), *Big Business and the Wealth of Nations*, Cambridge: Cambridge University Press, 480–96.

Hillard, M. (1991), 'Domination and Technological Change: A Review and Appraisal of Braverman, Marglin, and Noble', *Rethinking Marxism* 4, 61–78.

Hirschhorn, L. and Gilmore, T. (1992), 'The New Boundaries of the "Boundariless" Company', *Harvard Business Review* 70, 3, 104–15.

Hirschman, A. O. (1970), *Exit, Voice, and Loyalty*, Cambridge, MA: Harvard University Press.

Hodgson, G. M. (1988), *Economics and Institutions: A Manifesto for a Modern Institutional Economics*, Cambridge: Polity Press.

Hodgson, G. M. (1991), 'Socio-political Disruption and Economic Development', in G. M. Hodgson and E. Screpanti (eds), *Rethinking Economics: Markets, Technology and Economic Evolution*, Aldershot: Edward Elgar, 153–71.

Hodgson, G. M. (1993a), 'Evolution and Institutional Change: On the Nature of Selection in Biology and Economics', in U. Mäki, B. Gustafsson and

C. Knudsen (eds), *Rationality, Institutions and Economic Methodology*, London: Routledge, 222–41.

Hodgson, G. M. (1993b), 'Institutional Economics: Surveying the "Old" and the "New" ', *Metroeconomica*, 44, 1–28.

Hodgson, G. M. (1998), 'The Approach of Institutional Economics', *Journal of Economic Literature* 36, 1, 166–92.

Hoffmann, F. (1985), 'Umweltorientierte Strukturtypen – Eine theoretisch-empirische Analyse zur Umweltausrichtung durch organisatorische Maßnahmen', in H. Ulrich and G. J. Probst (eds), *Unternehmungsorganisation: Entwicklungen in Theorie und Praxis*, Bern: Paul Haupt, 19–32.

Hofstadter, D. R. (1979), *Gödel, Escher, Bach: An Eternal Golden Braid*, London: Penguin.

Hollis, M. (1977), *Models of Man: Philosophical Thoughts on Social Action*, Cambridge: Cambridge University Press.

Hollis, M. (1994), *The Philosophy of Social Science*, Cambridge: Cambridge University Press.

Hollis, M. and Nell, E. J. (1979), 'Two Economists', in F. Hahn and M. Hollis (eds), *Philosophy and Economic Theory*, Oxford: Oxford University Press, 47–56.

Homann, K. (1990), *Ökonomik und Ethik*, Conference Paper, 5th Symposium 'Kirche heute', 11–13 October 1990, Augsburg, Germany.

Homann, K. (1992), *Der homo oeconomicus – ein egositischer Nutzen- und Gewinnmaximierer?*, Conference Paper, Ringvorlesung University of Bayreuth, 7 December 1992, Bayreuth, Germany.

Homann, K. (1993), 'Wirtschaftsethik. Die Funktion der Moral in der modernen Wirtschaft', in J. Wieland (ed.), *Wirtschaftsethik und Theorie der Gesellschaft*, Frankfurt: Suhrkamp, 32–53.

Homann, K. (1994), 'Homo oeconomicus und Dilemmastrukturen', in H. Sautter (ed.), *Wirtschaftspolitik in offenen Volkswirtschaften*, Göttingen, Germany: Vandenhoeck & Ruprecht, 387–411.

Homann, K. (1997), 'Sinn und Grenze der ökonomischen Methode in der Wirtschaftsethik', *Volkswirtschaftliche Schriften* 478, 1–42.

Homann, K. (1997a), *Zur Grundlegung einer modernen Gesellschafts- und Sozialpolitik: Das Problem der 'sozialen Ordnung'*, extended version of a paper given at the 'Expertengespräch', 11/12 July 1997, Ludwigshafen.

Homann, K. (1997b), 'Normativität angesichts systemischer Sozial- und Denkstruturen', Working Paper, Catholic University of Eichstätt at Ingolstadt.

Homann, K. (1999a), 'Die Bedeuting von Dilemma Strukturen für die Ethik', Working Paper, Catholic University of Eichstätt at Ingolstadt.

Homann, K. (1999b), 'Zur Grundlegung einer modernen Gesellschafts- und Sozialpolitik: Das Problem der sozialen Ordnung', in U. Blum,

W. Esswein, E. Greipl, H. Hereth and S. Müller (eds), *Soziale Marktwirtschaft im nächsten Jahrtausend*, Stuttgart: Schäffer-Poeschel, 119–48.

Homann, K. and Pies, I. (1991), 'Gefangenendilemma und Wirtschaftsethik', *Wirtschaftswissenschaftliches Studium* 12, 608–14.

Homann, K. and Suchanek, A. (1989), 'Methodologische Überlegungen zum ökonomischen Imperialismus', *Analyse und Kritik: Zeitschrift für Sozialwissenschaften* 11, 70–93.

Homann, K. and Suchanek, A. (2000), *Ökonomik. Eine Einführung*, Tübingen: Mohr Siebeck.

Homans, G. C. (1976), 'What do we mean by Social 'Structure'?', in P. M. Blau (ed.), *Approaches to the Study of Social Structure*, London: Open Books, 53–65.

Hoover, K. D. (1994), 'Pragmatism, Pragmaticism and Economic Method', in R. E. Backhouse (ed.), *New Directions in Economic Methodology*, London: Routledge, 286–315.

Hottinger, O. (1998), *Eigeninteresse und individuelles Nutzenkalkül in der Theorie der Gesellschaft und Ökonomie von Adam Smith, Jeremy Bentham und John Stuart Mill*, Marburg: Metropolis.

Hoxie, R. (1915), *Scientific Management and Labor*, New York: Augustus Kelly.

Hunt, S. D. (2000), *A General Theory of Competition*, London: Sage.

Jacquemin, A. (1987), *The New Industrial Organization: Market Forces and Strategic Behavior*, Oxford: Clarendon.

Jarillo, J. C. (1988), 'On Strategic Networks', *Strategic Management Journal* 9, 31–41.

Jensen, H. E. (1987), 'The Theory of Human Nature', *Journal of Economic Issues* 21, 1039–74.

Jensen, M. C. and Meckling, W. H. (1976), 'Theory of the Firm: Managerial Behavior, Agency Costs and Ownership Structure', *Journal of Financial Economics* 3, 305–60.

Jensen, M. C. and Meckling, W. H. (1994), 'The Nature of Man', *Journal of Applied Corporate Finance* 7, 2, 4–19.

Jensen, M. C. and Meckling, W. H. (1996), 'Specific and General Knowledge, and Organizational Structure', in P. S. Myers (ed.), *Knowledge Management and Organizational Design*, Oxford: Butterworth-Heinemann, 17–38.

Jones, O. (2000), 'Scientific Management, Culture and Control: A First-hand Account of Taylorism in Practice', *Human Relations* 53, 631–53.

Jones, S. R. H. (1997), 'Transaction Costs and the Theory of the Firm: The Scope and Limitations of the New Institutional Approach', *Business History* 39, 4, 9–25.

Joskow, P. L. (1988), 'Asset Specificity and the Structure of Vertical Relationships: Empirical Evidence', *Journal of Law, Economics, and Organization* 4, 1, 95–117.

Kaldor, N. (1978), *Further Essays on Economic Theory*, London: Duckworth.

Kamoche, K. (2001), *Understanding Human Resource Management*, Buckingham: Open University Press.

Kanigel, R. (1997), *The One Best Way: Frederick Winslow Taylor and the Enigma of Efficiency,* New York: Viking.

Kanter, R. M. (1989), *When Giants Learn to Dance: Mastering the Challenge of Strategy, Management, and Careers in the 1990s*, London: Simon & Schuster.

Kappler, E. (1992), 'Menschenbilder', in E. Gaugler and W. Weber (eds), *Handwörterbuch des Personalwesens*, Stuttgart: Poeschel, 1323–42.

Kay, N. M. (1993), 'Markets, False Hierarchies and the Role of Asset Specificity', in C. Pitelis (ed.), *Transaction Costs, Markets and Hierarchies*, Oxford: Blackwell, 242–61.

Kelly, J. E. (1982), *Scientific Management, Job Redesign and Work Performance*, London: Academic Press.

Kieser, A. (1993), 'Human-relations Bewegung und Organisationspsychologie', in A. Kieser (ed.), *Organisationstheorien*, Stuttgart: Kohlhammer, 95–126.

Kieser, A. and Kubicek, H. (1983), *Organisation*, Berlin: de Gruyter.

Kirsch, W. (1979), 'Die verhaltenswissenschaftliche Fundierung der Betriebswirtschaftslehre', in H. Raffee and B. Abel (eds), *Wissenschaftstheoretische Grundfragen der Wirtschaftswissenschaften*, Munich: Vahlen, 105–20.

Kirsch, W. (1981) 'Funktionen der Führung', in M. N. Geist and R. Köhler (eds), *Die Führung des Betriebs*, Stuttgart: Poeschel, 27–42.

Kirsch, W. (1988), 'Zur Konzeption der Betriebswirtschaftslehre als Führungslehre', in R. Wunderer (ed.), *Betriebswirtschaftslehre als Management- und Führungslehre*, Stuttgart: C. E. Poeschel, 153–72.

Klein, P. A. (1994), 'An Assessment', in P. A. Klein (ed.), *The Role of Economic Theory*, Boston, MA: Kluwer, 229–48.

Klein, B., Crafword, R. G. and Alchian, A. A. (1978), 'Vertical Integration, Appropriable Rents and the Competitive Contracting Process', *Journal of Law and Economics* 21, 297–326.

Knight, F. H. (1948), *Risk, Uncertainty and Profit*, Boston, MA: Houghton.

Knowles, H. P. and Saxberg, B. O. (1967), 'Human Relations and the Nature of Man', *Harvard Business Review* 45, 2, 22–40 and 172–6.

Kreps, D. M., Milgrom, P., Roberts, J. and Wilson, R. (1982), 'Rational Cooperation in the Finitely Repeated Prisoners' Dilemma', *Journal of Economic Theory* 27, 245–52.

Kreps, D. M. (1990), 'Corporate Culture and Economic Theory', in J. E. Alt and K. A. Shepsle (eds), *Perspectives on Positive Political Economy*, Cambridge: Cambridge University Press, 90–143.

Kuhn, T. S. (1996), *The Structure of Scientific Revolutions*, Chicago, IL: University of Chicago Press.

Kukathas, C. (1992), 'Freedom versus Autonomy', in J. Gray (ed.), *The Moral Foundations of Market Institutions*, London: IEA Health and Welfare Unit, 101–14.

Küng, H. (1999), 'Leitplanken für die Moral', *Der Spiegel* 51, 20 December, 70–73.

Kymlicka, W. (2001), 'Multicultural Citizenship', in S. Seidman and J. C. Alexander (eds), *The New Social Theory Reader: Contemporary Debates*, London: Routledge, 212–22.

Lakatos, I. (1970), 'Falsification and the Methodology of Scientific Research Programmes', in I. Lakatos and A. Musgrave (eds), *Criticism and the Growth of Knowledge*, Cambridge: Cambridge University Press, 91–196.

Lakatos, I. (1976), *Proofs and Refutations*, Cambridge: Cambridge University Press.

Lakatos, I. (1978), *The Methodology of Scientific Research Programmes*, Cambridge: Cambridge University Press.

Lampman, R. J. (1966), 'Income Distribution of American Labor', in W. Haber (ed.), *Labor in a Changing America*, New York: Basic Books, 58–68.

Langlois, R. N. (1988), 'Economic Change and the Boundaries of the Firm', *Journal of Institutional and Theoretical Economics* 144, 4, 635–57.

Langlois, R. N. (1990), 'Bounded Rationality and Behaviouralism: A Classification and Critique', *Journal of Theoretical and Institutional Economics* 146, 691–5.

Langlois, R. N. and Csontos, L. (1993), 'Optimization, Rule-following, and the Methodology of Situational Analysis', in U. Mäki, B. Gustafsson and C. Knudsen (eds), *Rationality, Institutions and Economic Methodology*, London: Routledge, 113–32.

Latsis, S. J. (1976), 'A Research Programme in Economics', in S. J. Latsis (ed.), *Method and Appraisal in Economics*, Cambridge: Cambridge University Press, 1–42.

Lawrence, P. R. (1991), 'Socio-economics: A Grounded Perspective', in A. Etzioni and P. R. Lawrence (eds), *Socio-economics: Toward a New Synthesis*, Armonk, NY: M. E. Sharpe, 9–10.

Lawrence, P. R. and Lorsch, J. W. (1990), 'High-performing Organizations in Three Environments', in D. S. Pugh (ed.), *Organization Theory: Selected Readings*, London: Penguin, 76–94.

Lawson, G. (1995), 'An Examination of the Political Part of Mr. Hobbs His Leviathan' [spelling as in original], in G. A. Rogers (ed.), *Leviathan:*

Contemporary Responses to the Political Theory of Thomas Hobbes, Bristol: Thoemmes Press, 15–114.

Lawson, T. (1989), 'Abstraction, Tendencies and Stylised Facts: A Realist Approach to Economic Analysis', *Cambridge Journal of Economics* 13, 59–78.

Lawson, T. (1992), 'Realism, Closed Systems and Friedman', *Research in the History of Economic Thought and Methodology* 10, 236–58.

Lawson, T. (1994), 'A Realist Theory for Economics', in R. E. Backhouse (ed.), *New Directions in Economic Methodology*, London: Routledge, 257–85.

Lawson, T. (1997), *Economics and Reality*, London: Routledge.

Layder, D. (1994), *Understanding Social Theory*, London: Sage.

Lazonick, W. (1991), *Business Organization and the Myth of the Market Economy*, Cambridge: Cambridge University Press.

Lazonick, W. (1993), 'Industry Clusters versus Global Webs: Organizational Capabilities in the American Economy', *Industrial and Corporate Change* 2, 1, 1–24.

Lazonik, W. and O'Sullivan, M. (1997), 'Big Business and Skill Formation in the Wealthiest Nations: The Organizational Revolution in the Twentieth Century', in A. D. Chandler, F. Amatori and T. Hikino (eds), *Big Business and the Wealth of Nations*, Cambridge: Cambridge University Press, 497–521.

Lebergott, S. (1961), 'The Pattern of Employment Since 1800', in S. E. Harris (ed.), *American Economic History*, New York: McGraw-Hill, 281–310.

Lebergott, S. (1965), 'Labor Force Mobility and Unemployment, 1800–1960', in R. L. Adreano (ed.), *New Views on American Economic Development*, Cambridge, MA: Schenkman, 362–76.

Leibniz, G. W. (1969), *Philosophical Papers and Letters*, translated by L. E. Loemker, Dordrecht, Holland: D. Reidel.

Leijonhufvud, A. (1986), 'Capitalism and the Factory System', in R. N. Langlois (ed.), *Economics as a Process: Essays in the New Institutional Economics*, Cambridge: Cambridge University Press, 203–23.

Levasseur, E. (1897), 'The Concentration of Industry, and Machinery in the United States', *Annals of the American Academy of Political and Social Science* 9, 178–97.

Levi-Strauss, C. (1966), *The Savage Mind*, London: Weidenfeld & Nicolson.

Levitt, T. (1975), 'Marketing Myopia', *Harvard Business Review*, September–October, 26–44 and 173–81.

Libecap, G. D. (1989), 'Distributional Issues in Contracting for Property Rights', *Journal of Institutional and Theoretical Economics* 145, 6–24.

Likert, R. (1967), *The Human Organization: Its Management and Value*, New York: McGraw-Hill.

Likert, R. and Seashore, S. E. (1954), 'Increasing Utilization through Better Management of Human Resources', in W. Haber, F. H. Harbison, L. Klein and G. L. Palmer (eds), *Manpower in the United States: Problems and Policies*, New York: Harper & Brothers, 23–38.

Lindenberg, S. (1985), 'Rational Choice and Sociological Theory', *Journal of Institutional and Theoretical Economics* 141, 244–55.

Lindenberg, S. (1990), 'Homo Socio-oeconomicus: The Emergence of a General Model of Man in the Social Sciences', *Journal of Institutional and Theoretical Economics* 146, 727–48.

Lindenberg, S. (1996), 'Choice-centred versus Subject-centred Theories in the Social Sciences: The Influence of Simplification on Explananda', *European Sociological Review* 12, 2, 147–57.

Lindenberg, S. and Frey, B. S. (1993), 'Alternatives, Frames, and Relative Prices: A Broader View of Rational Choice Theory', *Acta Sociologica* 36, 191–205.

Lindsay, A. D. (1934), 'Introduction', in I. Kant (ed.), *The Critique of Pure Reason*, London: J. M. Dent and E. P. Dutton, vii–xx.

Lohmann, S. (1996), 'The Poverty of Green and Shapiro', in J. Friedman (ed.), *The Rational Choice Controversy: Economic Models of Politics Reconsidered*, New Haven, CT: Yale University Press, 127–54.

Lorsch, J. W. (1983), 'Organization Design: A Situational Perspective', in J. R. Hackman, E. E. Lawler III and L. W. Porter (eds), *Perspectives on Behavior in Organizations*, New York: McGraw-Hill, 439–47.

Luce, R. D. and Raiffa, H. (1957), *Games and Decisions: Introduction and Critical Survey*, New York: J. Wiley.

Luhmann, N. (1984), *Sozial Systeme: Grundriss einer allgemeinen Theorie*, Frankfurt: Suhrkamp.

Luhmann, N. (1988), 'Familiarity, Confidence, Trust: Problems and Alternatives', in D. Gambetta (ed.), *Trust: Making and Breaking Cooperative Relations*, Oxford: Blackwell, 94–107.

Lyotard, J.-F. (1984), *The Postmodern Condition: A Report on Knowledge*, Manchester: Manchester University Press.

MacIntyre, A. (1985), *After Virtue: A Study in Moral Theory*, London: Duckworth.

Machlup, F. (1967), 'Theories of the Firm: Marginalist, Behavioral, Managerial', *American Economic Review* 57, 1, 1–33.

Machlup, F. (1978), *Methodology of Economics and Other Social Sciences*, New York: Academic Press.

Madison, G. B. (1995), 'How Individualistic is Methodological Individualism', in D. L. Prychitko (ed.), *Individuals, Institutions, Interpretations*, Aldershot: Avebury, 36–56.

Mäki, U. (1992), 'Friedman and Realism', *Research in the History of Economic Thought and Methodology* 10, 1–36.

Mäki, U. (1994), 'Reorienting the Assumptions Issue', in R. E. Backhouse (ed.), *New Directions in Economic Methodology*, London: Routledge, 236–56.

Mannheim, K. (1944), *Man and Society in the Age of Reconstruction*, London: Routledge & Kegan Paul.

March, J. G. (1978), 'Bounded Rationality, Ambiguity, and the Engineering of Choice', *Bell Journal of Economics* 9, Autumn, 587–608.

March, J. G. and Simon, H. A. (1958), *Organizations*, New York: John Wiley & Sons.

Marginson, P. (1993), 'Power and Efficiency in the Firm: Understanding the Employment Relationship', in C. Pitelis (ed.), *Transaction Costs, Markets and Hierarchies*, Oxford: Blackwell, 133–65.

Margolis, H. (1982), *Selfishness, Altruism, and Rationality: A Theory of Social Choice*, Cambridge: Cambridge University Press.

Markoczy, L. and Goldberg, J. (1998), 'Management, Organization and Human Nature: An Introduction', *Managerial and Decision Economics* 19, 387–409.

Marshall, A. (1925), *Memorials of Alfred Marshall*, edited by A. C. Pigou, London: Macmillan.

Marsden, R. and Townley, B. (1996), 'The Owl of Minerva: Reflections on Theory in Practice', in S. R. Clegg, C. Hardy and W. R. Nord (eds), *Handbook of Organization Studies*, London: Sage, 659–675.

Marx, K. (1973), *Grundrisse: Foundations of the Critique of Political Economy*, Harmondsworth: Penguin.

Marx, K. (1974), *Capital: Volume 1*, London: Lawrence & Wishart.

Maskin, E. S. (1994), 'Conceptual Economic Theory', in P. A. Klein (ed.), *The Role of Economic Theory*, Boston, MA: Kluwer, 187–96.

Mayo, E. (1933), *The Human Problems of an Industrial Civilization*, New York: Macmillan.

Mayo, E. (1949), *The Social Problems of an Industrial Civilization*, London: Routledge & Kegan Paul.

Mayo, E. (1990), 'Hawthorne and the Western Electric Company', in D. S. Pugh (ed.), *Organization Theory: Selected Readings*, London: Penguin, 345–57.

McGregor, D. (1960), *The Human Side of Enterprise*, New York: McGraw-Hill.

McKenzie, R. B. and Lee, D. R. (1998), *Managing through Incentives*, Oxford: Oxford University Press.

Menell, O. S. (1992), 'Institutional Fantasylands: From Scientific Management to Free Market Environmentalism', *Harvard Journal of Law and Public Policy* 15, 2, 489–510.

Merkle, J. A. (1980), *Management and Ideology: The Legacy of the*

International Scientific Management Movement, Berkeley: University of California Press.

Merton, R. K. (1976), 'Structural Analysis in Sociology', in P. M. Blau (ed.), *Approaches to the Study of Social Structure*, London: Open Books, 21–52.

Meyer, J. W. and Rowan, B. (1991), 'Insitutionalized Organizations: Formal Structure as Myth and Ceremony', in W. W. Powell and P. J. DiMaggio (eds), *The New Institutionalism in Organizational Analysis*, Chicago, IL: University of Chicago Press, 41–62.

Meyer, M. (1995), *Of Problematology: Philosophy, Science, and Language*, Chicago, IL: The University of Chicago Press.

Miles, R. E. and Snow, C. C. (1981), 'Toward a Synthesis in Organization Theory', in M. Jelinek, J. A. Litterer and R. E. Miles (eds), *Organizations by Design: Theory and Practice*, Plano, Texas: Business Publications Inc., 548–62.

Miles, R. E. and Snow, C. C. (1986), 'Network Organizations: New Concepts for New Forms', *California Management Review* 28, Spring, 62–73.

Milgrom, P. and Roberts, J. (1988), 'An Economic Approach to Influence Activities in Organizations', in C. Winship and S. Rosen (eds), *Organizations and Institutions: Sociological and Economic Approaches to the Analysis of Social Structure*, supplement to the *American Journal of Sociology* 94, Chicago, IL: The University of Chicago Press, 154–79.

Milgrom, P. and Roberts, J. (1992), *Economics, Organization and Management*, Englewood Cliffs, NJ: Prentice-Hall.

Minford, P. (1992), 'Gray on the Market', in J. Gray (ed.), *The Moral Foundations of Market Institutions*, London: IEA Health and Welfare Unit, 115–18.

Mintz, S. I. (1962), *The Hunting of Leviathan*, Cambridge: Cambridge University Press.

Mischel, W. And Shoda, Y. (1995), 'A Cognitive-affective System Theory of Personality: Reconceptualizing Situations, Dispositions, Dynamics, and Invariance in Personality Structure', *Psychological Review* 102, 246–86.

Mitchell, Stewart, A. (1994), *Empowering People*, London: Institute of Management Foundation/Pitman.

Mohammadian, M. (2000), *Bioeconomics, Biological Economics. Interdisciplinary Study of Biology, Economics and Education*, Madrid: Edicion Personal.

Montemayor, E. F. (1976), 'Congruence between Pay Policy and Competitive Strategy in High Performing Firms', *Journal of Management* 22, November–December, 889–908.

Morgan, G. (1986), *Images of Organization*, Newbury Park, CA: Sage.

Morgan, G. (1989) *Creative Organization Theory: A Resourcebook*, London: Sage.

Morgan, M. S. (1997), 'The Character of "Rational Economic Man" ', *Dialektik* 1, 77–94.

Mortensen, D. T. (1978), 'Specific Capital and Labor Turnover', *Bell Journal of Economics* 9, Autumn, 572–86.

Moss, S. J. (1981), *An Economic Theory of Business Strategy*, Oxford: Martin Robertson.

Mount, M. K., Barrick, M. R. and Strauss, J. P. (1994), 'Validity of Observer Ratings of the Big Five Personality Factors', *Journal of Applied Psychology* 79, 272–80.

Mouzelis, N. (1995), *Sociological Theory: What Went Wrong? Diagnosis and Remedies*, London: Routledge.

Mueller, F. (1995), 'Organizational Governance and Employee Cooperation: Can We Learn from Economists?', *Human Relations* 48, 10: 1217–35.

Mueller, C. and Wallace, J. (1996), 'Justice and the Paradox of the Contented Female Worker', *Social Psychology Quarterly* 5, 338–49.

Muller, J. Z. (1993), *Adam Smith in His Time and Ours*, Princeton, NJ: Princeton University Press.

Mullins, L. J. (1999), *Management and Organisational Behaviour*, London: Pitman.

Mumby, D. K. and Putnam, L. L. (1992), 'A Feminist Reading of Bounded Rationality', *Academy of Management Review* 17, 3, 465–86.

Murphy, J. B. (1996), 'Rational Choice Theory as Social Physics', in J. Friedman (ed.), *The Rational Choice Controversy*, London: Yale University Press, 155–74.

Musgrave, A. (1981), 'Unreal Assumptions in Economic Theory: The F-twist Untwisted', *Kyklos* 34, 3, 377–87.

Myers, P. S. (1996), 'Knowledge Management and Organizational Design: An Introduction', in P. S. Myers (ed.), *Knowledge Management and Organizational Design*, Oxford: Butterworth-Heinemann, 1–6.

Nadworny, M. J. (1955), *Scientific Management and the Unions, 1900–1932: A Historical Analysis*, Cambridge, MA: Harvard University Press.

Nagel, E. (1963), 'Assumptions in Economic Theory', *American Economic Review* 53, Papers and Proceedings, 2, 211–19.

Nelson, D. (1980), *Frederick W. Taylor and the Rise of Scientific Management*, Madison, WI: University of Wisconsin Press.

Nelson, D. (1992a), 'Scientific Management in Retrospect', in D. Nelson (ed.), *A Mental Revolution: Scientific Management Since Taylor*, Columbus, OH: Ohio State University Press, 5–39.

Nelson, D. (1992b), 'Epilogue', in D. Nelson (ed.), *A Mental Revolution: Scientific Management since Taylor*, Columbus, OH: Ohio State University Press, 237–40.

Nelson, D. (1995), *Managers and Workers: Origins of the New Factory System in the United States 1880–1920*, 2nd edn, Madison, WI: University of Wisconsin Press.

Nelson, R. R. (1991), 'Why Do Firms Differ, and How Does it Matter', *Strategic Management Journal* 12, 61–74.

Nelson, R. R. and Winter, S. G. (1982), *An Evolutionary Theory of Economic Change*, Cambridge, MA: Belknap Press/Harvard University Press.

Neuberger, O. (1991), *Personalentwicklung*, Stuttgart: Enke.

Neumann, von, J. and Morgenstern, O. (1947), *Theory of Games and Economic Behavior*, Princeton, NJ: Princeton University Press.

Nichols, T. and Armstrong, P. (1976), *Workers Divided: A Study in Shop Floor Politics*, London: Fontana-Collins.

Nicholson, N. (1998), 'Seven Deadly Syndromes of Management and Organization: The View from Evolutionary Psychology', *Managerial and Decision Economics* 19, 411–26.

Nietzsche, F. (1903), *Nietzsches Werke*, Vol. XIII, Leipzig: Naumann.

Noon, M. (1992), 'HRM: A Map, Model or Theory?', in P. Blyton and P. Turnbull (eds), *Reassessing Human Resource Management*, London: Sage, 16–32.

Nord, W. R. and Fox, S. (1996), 'The Individual in Organizational Studies: The Great Disappearing Act', in S. R. Clegg, C. Hardy and W. R. Nord (eds), *Handbook of Organization Studies*, London: Sage, 148–74.

Nord, W. R. and Jermier, J. M. (1992, 'Critical Social Science for Managers? Promising and Perverse Possibilities', in M. Alvesson and H. Willmott (eds), *Critical Management Studies*, London: Sage, 202–22.

North, D. C. (1990), *Institutions, Institutional Change and Economic Performance*, Cambridge: Cambridge University Press.

North, D. C. (1993a), 'Institutions and Economic Performance', in U. Mäki, B. Gustafsson and C. Knudsen (eds), *Rationality, Institutions and Economic Methodology*, London: Routledge, 242–61.

North, D. C. (1993b), 'Institutions and Credible Commitment', *Journal of Institutional and Theoretical Economics* 149, 1, 11–23.

Novak, M. (1991), *The Spirit of Democratic Capitalism*, London: The IEA Health and Welfare Unit.

Nozick, R. (1993), *The Nature of Rationality*, Princeton, NJ: Princeton University Press.

Nussbaum, M. C. (1986), *The Fragility of Goodness: Luck and Ethics in Greek Tragedy and Philosophy*, Cambridge: Cambridge University Press.

Nyland, C. (1996), 'Taylorism, John R. Commons, and the Hoxie Report', *Journal of Economic Issues* 30, 985–1016.

Nyland, C. (1998), 'Taylorism and the Mututal-Gains Strategy', *Industrial Relations* 37, 519–42.

Ockenfels, A. (1999), *Fairneß, Reziprozität und Eigennutz*, Tübingen: Mohr Siebeck.
Olson, M. (1971), *The Logic of Collective Action*, London: Harvard University Press.
O'Neill, J. (1995), *The Poverty of Postmodernism*, London: Routledge.
Ordeshook, P. C. (1996), 'Engineering or Science: What is the Study of Politics?', in J. Friedman (ed.), *The Rational Choice Controversy: Economic Models of Politics Reconsidered*, New Haven, CT: Yale University Press, 175–88.
Oswick, C., Lowe, S. and Jones, P. (1996), 'Organisational Culture as Personality: Lessons from Psychology?', in C. Oswick and D. Grant (eds), *Organisation Development: Metaphorical Explorations*, London: Pitman, 106–20.
Outerbridge, A. E. (1895), 'The Prevailing Scarcity of Skilled Labor', *Engineering Magazine* 10, 227–35.
Palmer, D. A., Jennings, P. D. and Zhou, X. (1993), 'Late Adoption of the Multidivisional Form by Large U.S. Corporations: Institutional, Political, and Economic Accounts', *Administrative Science Quarterly* 38, 100–31.
Parker, B. (1996), 'Evolution and Revolution: From International Business to Globalization', in S. R. Clegg, C. Hardy and W. R. Nord (eds), *Handbook of Organization Studies*, London: Sage, 484–506.
Pearn, M., Roderick, C. and Mulrooney, C. (1995), *Learning Organizations in Practice*, London: McGraw-Hill.
Penrose, E. T. (1952), 'Biological Analogies in the Theory of the Firm', *American Economic Review* 62, 5, 804–19.
Penrose, R. (1989), *The Emperor's New Mind*, Oxford: Oxford University Press.
Penrose, R. (1994), *Shadows of the Mind*, Oxford: Oxford University Press.
Perrow, C. (1983), 'The Short and Glorious History of Organization Theory', in J. R. Hackman, E. E. Lawler III and L. W. Porter (eds), *Perspectives on Behavior in Organizations*, New York: McGraw-Hill, 90–96.
Persky, J. (1995), 'The Ethology of Homo Economicus', *Journal of Economic Perspectives* 9, 2, 221–31.
Person, H. S. (1964), 'Foreword', in F. W. Taylor (ed.), *Scientific Management*, New York: Harper & Row, v–xvi.
Pettit, P. (1996), 'Institutional Design and Rational Choice', in R. E. Goodin (ed.), *The Theory of Institutional Design*, Cambridge: Cambridge University Press, 54–89.
Pfeffer, J. (1995), 'Incentives in Organizations: The Importance of Social Relations', in O. E. Williamson (ed.), *Organization Theory: From Chester Barnard to the Present and Beyond*, New York: Oxford University Press, 72–97.

Phillips, U. B. (1929), *Life and Labor in the Old South*, Boston, MA: Little, Brown & Company.

Picot, A. (1991), 'Ökonomische Theorien der Organisation – Ein Überblick über neuere Ansätze und deren betriebswirtschaftliches Anwendungspotential', in D. Ordelheide, B. Rudolph and E. Büsselmann (eds), *Betriebswirtschaftslehre und ökonomische Theorie*, Stuttgart: C. E. Poeschel, 143–70.

Picot, A., Ripperger, T. and Wolff, B. (1996), 'The Fading Boundaries of the Firm: The Role of Information and Communication Technology', *Journal of Institutional and Theoretical Economics* 152, 1, 65–79.

Pies, I. (1993), *Normative Institutionenökonomik: Zur Rationalisierung des politischen Liberalismus*, Tübingen: J. C. B. Mohr/Paul Siebeck.

Plant, R. (1992), 'Autonomy, Social Rights and Distributive Justice', in J. Gray (ed.), *The Moral Foundations of Market Institutions*, London: IEA Health and Welfare Unit, 119–41.

Plato (1999), *The Essential Plato*, Introduction by A. Botton, translated by B. Jowett, Uxbridge: The Softback Preview.

Popper, K. R. (1957), *The Poverty of Historicism*, London: Routledge & Kegan Paul.

Popper, K. R. (1962), *The Open Society and its Enemies: The Spell of Plato*, Vol. I, London: Routledge & Kegan Paul.

Popper, K. R. (1972), *Objective Knowledge*, Oxford: Clarendon.

Popper, K. R. (1976), *Unended Quest*, La Salle, IL: Open Court.

Popper, K. R. (1977), *The Logic of Scientific Discovery*, London: Hutchinson.

Popper, K. R. (1978), *Conjectures and Refutations: The Growth of Scientific Knowledge*, London: Routledge & Kegan Paul.

Popper, K. R. (1992), *In Search of a Better World: Lectures and Essays from Thirty Years*, London: Routledge.

Popper, K. R. (1995), 'Das Rationalitätsprinzip', in K. Popper (ed.), *Lesebuch: Ausgewählte Texte zur Erkenntnistheorie, Philosophie der Naturwissenschaften, Metaphysik, Sozialphilosophie*, Tübingen: Mohr Siebeck, 350–59.

Porter, G. (1973), *The Rise of Big Business 1860–1910*, New York: Crowell.

Porter, L. W. and Lawler, E. E. (1968), *Managerial Attitudes and Performance*, Burr Ridge, IL: Irwin.

Porter, M. E. (1980), *Competitive Strategy*, New York: The Free Press.

Porter, M. E. (1985), *Competitive Advantage*, New York: The Free Press.

Poulson, B. W. (1981), *Economic History of the United States*, New York: Macmillan.

Prelec, D. (1991), 'Values and Principles: Some Limitations on Traditional Economic Analysis', in A. Etzioni and P. R. Lawrence (eds), *Socioeconomics: Toward a New Synthesis*, Armonk, NY: M. E. Sharpe, 131–45.

Preston, L. E., Sapienza, H. J. and Miller, R. D. (1991), 'Stakeholders, Shareholders, Managers: Who Gains What from Corporate Performance?', in A. Etzioni and P. R. Lawrence (eds), *Socio-economics: Toward a New Synthesis*, Armonk, NY: M. E. Sharpe, 149–65.

Pruijt, H. D. (1997), *Job Design and Technology: Taylorism vs. Anti-Taylorism*, London: Routledge.

Pugh, D. S. (1966), 'Modern Organization Theory', *Psychological Bulletin* 66, 4, 235–51.

Pugh, D. S. (1990), 'The Measurement of Organization Structures: Does Context Determine Form?', in D. S. Pugh (ed.), *Organization Theory: Selected Readings*, London: Penguin, 44–63.

Pugh, D. S. and Hickson, D. J. (1996), *Writers on Organizations*, London: Penguin.

Puth, R. C. (1982), *American Economic History*, Chicago, IL: Dryden.

Pyle, A. (1994), 'Introduction', in A. Pyle (ed.), *Liberty: Contemporary Responses to John Stuart Mill*, Bristol: Thoemmes Press, vii–xxi.

Quarstein, V. A., McAfee, R. B. and Glassman, M. (1992), 'The Situational Occurrences Theory of Job Satisfaction', *Human Relations* 45, 8, 859–73.

Rabin, M. (1998), 'Psychology and Economics', *Journal of Economic Literature* 36, 1, 11–46.

Rathenau, W. (1918), *Von kommenden Dingen*, Berlin: S. Fischer.

Rehberg, K. S. (1988), 'Arnold Gehlen's Elementary Anthropology – An Introduction', in A. Gehlen (ed.), *Man: His Nature and Place in the World*, New York: Columbia University Press, ix–xxxvi.

Reif, W. E. and Luthans, F. (1969), 'Does Job Enrichment Really Pay Off?', in M. Jelinek, J. A. Litterer and R. E. Miles (eds), *Organizations By Design: Theory and Practice*, Plano, TX: Business Publications Inc., 366–76.

Ridley, C. E. and Simon, H. A. (1943), *Measuring Municipal Activities*, Chicago, IL: International City Managers' Association.

Rippberger, T. (1998), *Ökonomik des Vertrauens*, Tübingen: Mohr Siebeck.

Robins, J. A. (1987), 'Organizational Economics: Notes on the Use of Transaction-cost Theory in the Study of Organizations', *Administrative Science Quarterly* 32, 68–86.

Roethlisberger, F. J. and Dickson, W. J. (1949), *Management and the Worker*, Cambridge, MA: Harvard University Press.

Rogers, G. A. (1995), 'Introduction', in G. A. Rogers (ed.), *Leviathan: Contemporary Responses to the Political Theory of Thomas Hobbes*, Bristol: Thoemmes Press, vii–xvii.

Roper, M. (1999), 'Killing Off the Father: Social Science and the Memory of Frederick Taylor in Management Studies, 1950–1975', *Contemporary British History* 13, 3, 39–58.

Rothbarth, E. (1946), 'Causes of Superior Efficiency of U.S.A. Industry as Compared with British Industry', *The Economic Journal* 56, 383–90.

Rothschild, J. (1979), 'The Collectivist Organization: An Alternative to Rational-bureaucratic Models', *American Sociological Review* 44, 509–27.

Rowlinson, M. (1988), 'The Early Application of Scientific Management by Cadbury', *Business History* 30, 4, 377–95.

Rowlinson, M. (1997), *Organisations and Institutions: Perspectives in Economics and Sociology*, Houndmills: Business Macmillan.

Rubery, J., Earnshaw, J., Marchington, M., Cooke, F. L. and Vincent, S. (2002), 'Changing Organizational Forms and the Employment Relationship', *Journal of Management Studies* 39, 645–72.

Rubinstein, A. (1998), *Modeling Bounded Rationality*, Cambridge, MA: The MIT Press.

Rumelt, R. P. (1974), *Strategy, Structure and Economic Performance*, Boston, MA: Harvard Business School Press.

Runge, J. F. (1984), 'Institutions and the Free Rider: The Assurance Problem and the Free Rider', *Journal of Politics* 46, 154–81.

Samuelson, P. A. (1963), 'Discussion', *The American Economic Review* 53, Papers and Proceedings 2, 231–6.

Sanchez, J. I. (1994), 'From Documentation to Innovation: Reshaping Job Analysis to Meet Emerging Business Needs', *Human Resource Management Review* 4, 1, 51–74.

Sarup, M. (1993), *An Introductory Guide to Post-structuralism and Postmodernism*, New York: Harvester/Wheatsheaf.

Saviotti, P. P. (1998), 'Product Differentiation', in R. Arena and C. Longhi (eds), *Markets and Organization*, Berlin: Springer, 487–505.

Schanz, G. (1977), *Grundlagen der verhaltensorientierten Betriebswirtschaftslehre*, Tübingen: J. C. B. Mohr/Paul Siebeck.

Schanz, G. (1982), *Organisationsgestaltung: Struktur und Verhalten*, Munich: Vahlen.

Schanz, G. (1988), *Methodologie für Betriebswirte*, Stuttgart: C. E. Poeschel.

Scheiber, H. N., Vatter, H. G. and Faulkner, H. U. (1976), *American Economic History*, New York: Harper & Row.

Schein, E. (1980), *Organizational Psychology*, Englewood Cliffs, NJ: Prentice-Hall.

Schlösser, H. J. (1992), *Das Menschenbild in der Ökonomie*, Cologne: Wirtschaftsverlag Bachem.

Schneider, B. (1987), 'The People Make the Place', *Personnel Psychology* 40, 437–53.

Schneider, D. (1978), 'Zur tautologischen Transformation empirischer Sätze in Handlunsgempfehlungen', in H. Steinmann (ed.), *Betriebswirtschaftslehre als normative Handlungswissenschaft: Zur Bedeutung der Konstruktiven Wissenschaftstheorie*, Wiesbaden: Gabler, 245–58.

Schofield, N. (1996), 'Rational Choice and Political Economy', in J. Friedman (eds), *The Rational Choice Controversy: Economic Models of Politics Reconsidered*, New Haven, CT: Yale University Press, 189–212.

Schotter, A. (1981), *The Economic Theory of Social Institutions*, Cambridge: Cambridge University Press.

Schotter, A. (1986), 'The Evolution of Rules', in R. N. Langlois (ed.), *Economics as a Process: Essays in the New Institutional Economics*, Cambridge: Cambridge University Press, 117–33.

Schramm, M. (1997), 'Spielregeln gestalten sich nicht von selbst: Institutionenethik und Individualethos in Wettbewerbssystemen', *Volkswirtschaftliche Schriften* 478, 147–76.

Schroeder, D. (2001), 'Homo Economics on Trial: Plato, Schopenhauer and the Virtual Jury', *Journal of Philosophy of Management* 1, 2, 65–74.

Schumpeter, J. A. (1947), 'The Creative Response in Economic History', *Journal of Economic History* 7, 2, 149–59.

Scott, A. (2000), 'Risk Society or Angst Society? Two Views of Risk, Consciousness and Community', in B. Adam, U. Beck and J. Van Loon (eds), *The Risk Society and Beyond: Critical Issues for Social Theory*, London: Sage, 33–46.

Scott, W. R. (1995a), *Institutions and Organizations*, London: Sage.

Scott, W. R. (1995b), 'Introduction: Institutional Theory and Organizations', in W. R. Scott and S. Christensen (eds), *The Institutional Construction of Organizations: International and Longitudinal Studies*, London: Sage, xi–xxiii.

Scott, W. R. and Christensen, S. (1995), 'Conclusion: Crafting a Wider Lense', in W. R. Scott and S. Christensen (eds), *The Institutional Construction of Organizations: International and Longitudinal Studies*, London: Sage, 302–13.

Scriven, M. (1959), 'Truisms as the Grounds for Historical Explanations', in P. L. Gardiner (ed.), *Theories of History*, New York: The Free Press, 443–75.

Sen, Amartya K. (1987), *On Ethics and Economics*, Oxford: Blackwell.

Sen, Amartya K. (1990), 'Rational Fools: A Critique of the Behavioral Foundations of Economic Theory', in J. J. Mansbridge (ed.), *Beyond Self-interest*, Chicago, IL: University of Chicago Press, 25–43.

Sen, Amartya K. (1999), *Reason Before Identity: The Romanes Lecture for 1998*, Oxford: Oxford University Press.

Sen, Anindya (1998), 'Introduction', in Anindya Sen (ed.), *Industrial Organization*, Dehli: Oxford University Press/Oxford India Paperbacks, 1–38.

Senge, P. M. (1993), *The Fifth Discipline*, London: Century Business.

Senior, B. (1997), *Organisational Change*, London: Pitman.

Shen, W. M. and Simon, H. A. (1993), 'Fitness Requirements for Scientific Theories Containing Recursive Theoretical Terms', *British Journal for the Philosophy of Science* 44, 641–52.

Shenhav, Y. (1995), 'From Chaos to Systems: The Engineering Foundations of Organization Theory, 1879–1932', *Administrative Science Quarterly* 40, 557–85.

Sievers, B. (1986), 'Beyond the Surrogate of Motivation', *Organization Studies* 7, 335–51.

Simon, H. A. (1945), *Administrative Behavior*, New York: The Free Press.

Simon, H. A. (1950), 'Modern Organization Theories', *Advanced Management* 15, October, 2–4.

Simon, H. A. (1952), 'Comments on the Theory of Organizations', *American Political Science Review* 46, 1130–39.

Simon, H. A. (1952–53), 'A Comparison of Organization Theories', *The Review of Economic Studies* 20, 40–8.

Simon, H. A. (1955), 'A Behavioral Model of Rational Choice', *Quarterly Journal of Economics* 69, 99–118.

Simon, H. A. (1956), 'Rational Choice and the Structure of the Environment', *Psychological Review* 63, 129–38.

Simon, H. A. (1957a), *Administrative Behavior*, 2nd edn, New York: The Free Press.

Simon, H. A. (1957b), *Models of Man: Social and Rational*, New York: John Wiley & Sons.

Simon, H. A. (1959), 'Theories of Decision-making in Economics and Behavioral Science', *The American Economic Review* 69, June, 253–83.

Simon, H. A. (1961), *Administrative Behavior*, 2nd edn, New York: Macmillan.

Simon, H. A. (1963), 'Discussion', *The American Economic Review* 53, Papers and Proceedings, 2, 229–31.

Simon, H. A. (1965), *The Shape of Automation for Men and Management*, New York: Harper & Row.

Simon, H. A. (1969), 'The Architecture of Complexity', in J. A. Litterer (ed.), *Organizations: Systems, Control and Adaptation, Vol. II*, New York: J. Wiley, 98–114.

Simon, H. A. (1976a), *Administrative Behavior*, 3rd edn, New York: The Free Press.

Simon, H. A. (1976b), 'From Substantive to Procedural Rationality', in S. J. Latsis (ed.), *Method and Appraisal in Economics*, Cambridge: Cambridge University Press, 129–48.

Simon, H. A. (1977), *Models of Discovery and Other Topics in the Methods of Science*, Dordrecht: D. Reidel.

Simon, H. A. (1985), 'Human Nature in Politics: The Dialogue of Psychology with Political Science', *American Political Science Review* 79, 293–304.

Simon, H. A. (1987), 'Rationality in Psychology and Economics', in R. M. Hogarth and M. W. Reder (eds), *Rational Choice: The Contrast Between Economics and Psychology*, Chicago, IL: University of Chicago Press, 25–40.

Simon, H. A. (1990), 'Invariants of Human Behaviour', in R. Rosenzweig and L. W. Porter (eds), *Annual Review of Psychology* 41, 1–19.

Simon, H. A. (1991), 'Organizations and Markets', *Journal of Economic Perspectives* 5, 2, 25–44.

Simon, H. A. (1992a), 'Book Review: "Organization Theory: From Chester Barnard to the Present and Beyond edited by O. W. Williamson" ', *Journal of Economic Literature* 30, 3, 1503–5.

Simon, H. A. (1992b), 'What is an "Explanation" of Behavior', *Psychological Science* 3, 3, 150–61.

Simon, H. A. (1993a), 'Decision Making: Rational, Nonrational, and Irrational', *Educational Administration Quarterly* 29, 3, 392–411.

Simon, H. A. (1993b), 'Altruism and Economics', *American Economic Review, Papers and Proceedings* 83, 2, 156–61.

Simon, H. A. (1993c), 'Strategy and Organizational Evolution', *Strategic Management Journal* 14, 131–42.

Simon, H. A. (1995), 'Rationality in Political Behavior', *Political Psychology* 16, 1, 45–61.

Simon, H. A. (1997), *An Empirically Based Microeconomics*, Cambridge: Cambridge University Press.

Simon, H. A., Divine, W. R., Copper, E. M. and Cherwin, M. (1941), *Determining Work Loads for Professional Staff in a Public Welfare Agency*, Berkeley, CA: University of California Press.

Simon, H. A. and Newell, A. (1956), 'Models: Their Uses and Limitations', in L. D. White (ed.), *The State of the Social Sciences*, Chicago, IL: University of Chicago Press, 66–83.

Sklar, M. J. (1988), *The Corporate Reconstruction of American Capitalism, 1890–1916*, Cambridge: Cambridge University Press.

Spulber, D. F. (1993), 'Economic Analysis and Management Strategy: A Survey', *Journal of Economics and Management Strategy* 1, 3, 535–74.

Stabile, D. R. (1987), 'The Du Pont Experiments in Scientific Management: Efficiency and Safety, 1911–1919', *Business History Review* 61, 3, 365–86.

Starr, M. (1946), 'Role of Union Organization', in W. F. Whyte (ed.), *Industry and Society*, New York: McGraw-Hill, 148–67.

Staudt, E. (1981), 'Betriebswirtschaftliche Theoriebildung zwischen Verhaltenswissenschaften und Technik', in G. Ropohl (ed.), *Interdisziplinäre Technikforschung: Beiträge zur Bewertung und Steuerung der technischen Entwicklung*, Berlin: Erich Schmidt, 111–21.

Steffy, B. D. and Grimes, A. J. (1992), 'Personnel/Organization Psychology: A Critique of the Discipline', in M. Alvesson and H. Willmott (eds), *Critical Management Studies*, London: Sage, 181–201.

Stigler, G. J. (1947), *Trends in Output and Employment*, New York: National Bureau of Economic Research.

Stigler, G. J. (1956), *Trends in Employment in the Service Industries*, Princeton, NJ: Princeton University Press.

Stigler, G. J. (1961), 'The Economics of Information', *Journal of Political Economy* 69, 213–25.

Stigler, G. J. (1982), *The Economist as Preacher*, Oxford: Blackwell.

Stigler, G. J. and Becker, G. S. (1977), 'De Gustibus Non Est Disputandum', *American Economic Review* 67, 2, 76–90.

Storing, H. J. (1962), 'The Science of Administration: Herbert A. Simon', in H. J. Storing (ed.), *Essays on the Scientific Study of Politics*, New York: Holt, Rhinehart & Winston, 63–150.

Suchanek, A. (1991), 'Der ökonomische Ansatz und das Verhältnis von Mensch, Institution und Erkenntnis', in B. Biervert and M. Held (eds), *Das Menschenbild in der ökonomischen Theorie*, Frankfurt: Campus, 76–93.

Suchanek, A. (1992), *Der ökonomische Ansatz und das Problem der theoretischen Integration*, Doctoral Dissertation, Univeristät Witten-Herdecke.

Suchanek, A. (1993), *Der Homo Oeconomicus als Heuristik*, Working Paper, Ingolstadt: Wirtschaftswissenschaftliche Fakultät der Universität Eichstätt.

Suchanek, A. (1999), 'Kritischer Rationalismus und die Methode der Sozialwissenschaften', in I. Pies and M. Leschke (eds), *Karl Poppers kritischer Rationalismus*, Tübingen: Mohr Siebeck, 85–104.

Sutton, J. (1998), *Technology and Market Structure: Theory and History*, Cambridge, MA: The MIT Press.

Swedberg, R. (1990) (ed.), *Economics and Sociology: Redefining their Boundaries: Conversations with Economists and Sociologists*, Princeton, NJ: Princeton University Press.

Swedberg, R. (1991a), 'Major Traditions of Economic Sociology', *Annual Review of Sociology* 17, 251–76.

Swedberg, R. (1991b), ' "The Battle of Methods": Toward a Paradigm Shift?', in A. Etzioni and P. R. Lawrence (eds), *Socio-economics: Toward a New Synthesis*, Armonk, NY: M. E. Sharpe, 13–33.

Taylor, F. W. (1895), 'A Piece Rate System', reprinted in F. W. Taylor (ed.) (1919), *Two Papers on Scientific Management*, London: Routledge & Sons, 33–125.

Taylor, F. W. (1903), *Shop Management*, reprinted in F. W. Taylor (ed.) (1964), *Scientific Management*, London: Harper & Row.

Taylor, F. W. (1909), 'Why Manufacturers Dislike College Students', *Society for the Promotion of Engineering Education: Proceedings*, Lancaster, 79–104.

Taylor, F. W. (1911), *The Principles of Scientific Mangement*, reprinted in F. W. Taylor (ed.) (1964), *Scientific Management*, London: Harper & Row.

Taylor, F. W. (1912), *Taylor's Testimony Before the Special House Committee*, reprinted in F. W. Taylor (ed.) (1964), *Scientific Management*, London: Harper & Row.

Temin, P. (1973a), 'Labor Scarcity and the Problem of American Industrial Efficiency in the 1850s', in P. Temin (ed.), *New Economic History*, Harmondsworth: Penguin, 113–36.

Temin, P. (1973b), 'Labor Scarcity in America', in P. Temin (ed.), *New Economic History*, Harmondsworth: Penguin, 165–80.

Thomason, G. (1991), 'The Management of Personnel', *Personnel Review* 20, 2, 3–10.

Thompson, P. (1993), 'Postmodernism: Fatal Distraction', in J. Hassard and M. Parker (eds), *Postmodernism and Organizations*, London: Sage, 183–233.

Tomer, J. F. (1999), *The Human Firm*, London: Routledge.

Tool, M. R. (1994), 'An Institutionalist Mode of Inquiry: Limitations of Orthodoxy', in P. A. Klein (ed.), *The Role of Economic Theory*, Boston, MA: Kluwer, 197–228.

Tullock, G. (1985), 'Adam Smith and the Prisoners' Dilemma', *Quarterly Journal of Economics* 100, 1073–81.

Turk, J. (1983), 'Conclusion. Power, Efficiency and Institutions: Some Implications of the Debate for the Scope of Economics, in A. Francis, J. Turk and P. Willman (eds), *Power, Efficiency and Institutions: A Critical Appraisal of the 'Markets and Hierarchies' Paradigm*, London: Heinemann, 189–204.

Ulman, L. (1961), 'The Development of Trades and Labor Unions', in S. E. Harris (ed.), *American Economic History*, New York: McGraw-Hill, 366–419.

Ulrich, H. (1988), 'Von der Betriebswirschaftslehre zur Managementlehre', in R. Wunderer (ed.), *Betriebswirstchaftslehre als Management- und Führungslehre*, Stuttgart: C. E. Poeschel, 173–90.

Urwick, L. F. (1945), *The Elements of Administration*, New York: Harper & Brothers.

Urwick, L. F. (1967), 'Organization and Theories about the Nature of Man', *Academy of Management Journal* 10, 9–15.

Uttal, B. (1983), 'The Cooperate Culture Vultures', *Fortune*, October 17, 66–72.

Vanberg, V. J. (1982), *Markt und Organisation – Individualistische Sozialtheorie und das Problem korporativen Handelns*, Tübingen: J. C. B. Mohr (Paul Siebeck).

Vanberg, V. J. (1986), 'Spontaneous Market Order and Social Rules: A Critical

Examination of F. Hayek's Theory of Cultural Evolution', *Economics and Philosophy* 2, 75–100.

Vanberg, V. J. (1993), 'Rational Choice, Rule-following and Institutions: An Evolutionary Perspective', in U. Mäki, B. Gustafsson and C. Knudsen (eds), *Rationality, Institutions and Economic Methodology*, London: Routledge, 171–200.

Vanberg, V. J. (1994), *Rules and Choice in Economics*, London: Routledge.

Vanberg, V. J. (2001), *The Constitution of Markets: Essays in Political Economy*, London: Routledge (Taylor & Francis).

Vargish, T. (1994), 'The Value of Humanities in Executive Development', in H. Tsoukas (ed.), *New Thinking in Organizational Behaviour*, Oxford: Butterworth-Heinemann, 221–34.

Veblen, T. (1898), 'Why is Economics Not an Evolutionary Science', *Quarterly Journal of Economics* 12, 373–97.

Vollmer, G. (1987), 'On Supposed Circularities in an Empirically Oriented Epistemology', in G. Radnitzky and W. W. Bartley (eds), *Evolutionary Epistemology, Rationality, and the Sociology of Knowledge*, La Salle, IL: Open Court, 163–200.

Vromen, J. J. (1995), *Economic Evolution: An Enquiry into the Foundations of New Institutional Economics*, London: Routledge.

Wagner, S. A. (1997), *Understanding Green Consumer Behaviour: A Qualitative Cognitive Approach*, London: Routledge.

Wagner, S. A. (2000a), 'The Exodus of the Wealth of Nations: "Rational Foolishness" and the Disequilibration of Interests in Social Interactions Between Egypt and Israel', Working Paper 2000/05, April 2000, Management Centre/Department of Economics, University of Leicester, UK.

Wagner, S. A. (2000b), 'The Image of Man in Organisation Theory: On the Institutional Problem and the Portrayal of Human Behaviour in the Social Sciences', unpublished *Doctoral Dissertation*, submitted July 2000, Department of Management and Economics, Catholic University of Eichstaett at Ingolstadt, Germany.

Wagner, S. A. (2000c), 'An Institutional Economic Reconstruction of Scientific Management: On the Lost Theoretical Logic of Taylorism', Working Paper 2000/14, December 2000, Management Centre/Department of Economics, University of Leicester, UK.

Wagner-Tsukamoto, S. A. (2001a), 'The Failure of the Quaker Experiments (1900–1940) in Corporate Social Responsibility: Implications for an Economic Approach to Business Ethics', Conference Paper, EBEN-Conference, 9–10 April, Nottingham.

Wagner-Tsukamoto, S. A. (2001b), 'Economics of Genesis: On the Institutional Economic Deciphering and Reconstruction of the Legends of the Bible', *Journal of Interdisciplinary Economics* 12, 3, 249–87, revised version of Working Paper 2000/01, January 2000, Management Centre/Department of Economics, University of Leicester, UK.

Wagner-Tsukamoto, S. A. (2002), 'Economics of Business Ethics: Systemizing Ethics, Ethical Capital and Stakeholder Management', Conference Paper, Reason in Practice/Journal of Philosophy of Management Conference, 26–29 June, Oxford: St. Anne's College; revised version of Working Paper 2002/02, March, Management Centre/ Department of Economics, University of Leicester, UK.

Wagner-Tsukamoto, S. A. (2003), 'A Holistic, Behavioural Economic Approach to Environmental and Biological Resource Problems?', *Journal of Interdisciplinary Economics* 14.

Wajcman, J. (2000), 'It's Hard to be Soft: Is Management Style Gendered?', in K. Grint (ed.), *Work and Society: A Reader*, Cambridge: Polity Press, 254–73.

Walker, G. and Weber, D. (1984), 'A Transaction Cost Approach to Make-or-buy Decisions', *Administrative Science Quarterly* 29, 373–91.

Walsh, J. P. and Seward, J. K. (1990), 'On the Efficiency of Internal and External Corporate Control Mechanisms', *Journal of Management Review* 15, 421–58.

Waring, S. P. (1991), *Taylorism Transformed: Scientific Management Theory Since 1945*, Chapel Hill, NC: The University of North Carolina Press.

Waring, S. P. (1992), 'Peter Drucker, MBO, and the Corporatist Critique of Scientific Management', in D. Nelson (ed.), *A Mental Revolution: Scientific Management Since Taylor*, Columbus, OH: Ohio State University Press, 205–36.

Warner, M. (1994), 'Organizational Behavior Revisited', *Human Relations* 47, 10, 1151–66.

Warner, W. L. (1962), *The Corporation in the Emergent American Society*, New York: Harper.

Warner, W. L. and Low, J. O. (1946), 'The Factory in the Community', in W. F. Whyte (ed.), *Industry and Society*, New York: McGraw-Hill, 21–45.

Weber, M. (1949), *The Methodology of the Social Sciences*, New York: The Free Press.

Weick, K. E. (1979), *The Social Psychology of Organizing*, Reading, MA: Addison-Wesley.

Weick, K. (1995), *Sensemaking in Organizations*, Thousand Oaks, CA: Sage.

Weinert, A. B.(1987), 'Menschenbilder und Führung', in A. Kieser, G. Reber and R. Wunderer (eds), *Handwörterbuch der Führung*, Stuttgart: C. E. Poeschel, 1427–42.

Wells, D. A. (1926), 'Scarcity of Skilled Labor in the United States', in E.

Abbott (ed.), *Historical Aspects of the Immigration Problem: Select Documents*, Chicago, IL: University of Chicago Press, 352–4.

West, E. G. (1976), *Adam Smith: The Man and His Works*, Indianapolis: Liberty Fund.

Wiggins, S. N. (1991), 'The Economics of the Firm and Contracts', *Journal of Institutional and Theoretical Economics* 147, 603–61.

Wilber, C. K. and Harrison, R. S. (1978), 'The Methodological Basis of Institutional Economics: Pattern Model, Storytelling, and Holism', *Journal of Economic Issues* 12, 1, 61–89.

Wild, J. (1988), 'Betriebswirschaftliche Führungslehre', in R. Wunderer (ed.), *Betriebswirstchaftslehre als Management- und Führungslehre*, Stuttgart: C. E. Poeschel, 265–90.

Williams, B. (1985), *Ethics and the Limits of Philosophy*, London: Fontana.

Williams, B. (1988), 'Formal Structures and Social Reality', in D. Gambetta (ed.), *Trust: Making and Breaking Cooperative Relations*, Oxford: Blackwell, 3–13.

Williamson, O. E. (1967), *The Economics of Discretionary Behavior: Managerial Objectives in a Theory of the Firm*, London: Kershaw.

Williamson, O. E. (1970), *Corporate Control and Business Behavior*, Englewood Cliffs, NJ: Prentice-Hall.

Williamson, O. E. (1975), *Markets and Hierarchies: Analysis and Antitrust Implications*, New York: The Free Press.

Williamson, O. E. (1981), 'The Modern Corporation: Origins, Evolution, Attributes', *Journal of Economic Literature* 19, December, 1537–68.

Williamson, O. E. (1983), 'Credible Commitments: Using Hostages to Support Exchange', *American Economic Review* 73, 4, 519–40.

Williamson, O. E. (1983a), *Markets and Hierarchies: Analysis and Antitrust Implications*, revised college edition, New York: The Free Press.

Williamson, O. E. (1985), *The Economic Institutions of Capitalism*, New York: The Free Press.

Williamson, O. E. (1988), 'Corporate Finance and Corporate Governance', *Journal of Finance* 43, 3, 567–91.

Williamson, O. E. (1990), 'The Firm as a Nexus of Treaties: An Introduction', in M. Aoki, B. Gustafsson and O. E. Williamson (eds), *The Firm as a Nexus of Treaties*, London: Sage, 1–25.

Williamson, O. E. (1991a), 'Introduction', in O. E. Williamson and S. G. Winter (eds), *The Nature of the Firm: Origins, Evolution, and Development*, New York: Oxford University Press, 3–17.

Williamson, O. E. (1991b), 'The Logic of Economic Organization', in O. E. Williamson and S. G. Winter (eds), *The Nature of the Firm: Origins, Evolution, and Development*, New York: Oxford University Press, 90–116.

Williamson, O. E. (1991c), 'Comparative Economic Organization: The

Analysis of Discrete Structural Alternatives', *Administrative Science Quarterly* 36, 269–96.

Williamson, O. E. (1991d), 'Strategizing, Economizing, and Economic Organization', *Strategic Management Journal* 12, 75–94.

Williamson, O. E. (1993a), 'Calculativeness, Trust, and Economic Organization', *Journal of Law and Economics* 36, 1/2, 453–86.

Williamson, O. E. (1993b), 'Calculated Trust: A Reply to Craswell's Comment on Williamson', *Journal of Law and Economics* 36, 1/2, 501–2.

Williamson, O. E. (1996a), 'Economics and Organization: A Primer', *California Management Review* 38, 2, 131–46.

Williamson, O. E. (1996b), 'Comment: "The Fading Boundaries of the Firm by A. Picot, T. Ripperger and B. Wolff"', *Journal of Institutional and Theoretical Economics* 152, 1, 85–8.

Williamson, O. E. (1996c), 'Prologue: The Mechanisms of Governance', in O. E. Williamson (ed.), *The Mechanisms of Governance*, Oxford: Oxford University Press, 3–20.

Williamson, O. E. (1996d) 'Transaction Cost Economics and the Evolving Science of Organization', in O. E. Williamson (ed.), *The Mechanisms of Governance*, Oxford: Oxford University Press, 349–75.

Williamson, O. E. (1998), 'Human Actors and Economic Organization', Conference Paper (revised version, September 1998), 7th Biannual Meeting of the International Joseph Schumpeter Society, June 1998, Vienna, Austria.

Wilson, J. O. (1991), 'Human Values and Economic Behavior: A Model of Moral Economy', in A. Etzioni and P. R. Lawrence (eds), *Socio-economics: Toward a New Synthesis*, Armonk, NY: M. E. Sharpe, 233–59.

Winship, C. and Rosen, S. (1988), 'Introduction: Sociological and Economic Approaches to the Analysis of Social Structure', in C. Winship and S. Rosen (eds), *Organizations and Institutions: Sociological and Economic Approaches to the Analysis of Social Structure,* Supplement to the *American Journal of Sociology* 94, Chicago, IL: University of Chicago Press, 1–16.

Wittgenstein, L. (1975), *Philosophical Remarks*, New York: Harper & Row.

Wolff, B. (1999), *Anreizkompatible Reorganisation von Unternehmen*, Stuttgart: Schäffer-Pöschel.

Wolin, S. (1960), *Politics and Vision*, Boston: Little & Brown.

Woodward, J. (1958), *Management and Technology*, London: HMSO.

Woolsey Biggart, N. and Hamilton, G. G. (1992), 'On the Limits of a Firm-based Theory to Explain Business Networks: The Western Bias of Neoclassical Economics', in N. Nohria and R. G. Eccles (eds), *Networks and Organizations*, Boston, MA: Harvard Business School Press, 471–90.

Wrege, C. D. and Greenwood, R. G. (1991), *Frederick W. Taylor: The Father of Scientific Management. Myth and Reality*, Burr Ridge, IL: Irwin.

Wunderer, R. (1988), 'Betriebswirtschaftliche Führungsforschung und Führungslehre', in R. Wunderer (ed.), *Betriebswirstchaftslehre als Management- und Führungslehre*, Stuttgart: C. E. Poeschel, 33–47.

Zey, M. (1998), *Rational Choice Theory and Organizational Theory*, London: Sage.

Zey-Ferrell, M. (1981), 'Criticisms of the Dominant Perspective on Organizations', *Sociological Quarterly* 22, 181–205.

Zintl, R. (1989), 'Der Homo Oeconomicus: Ausnahmeerscheinung in jeder Situation oder Jedermann in Ausnahmesituation?', *Analyse & Kritik* 11, 52–69.

Index